P9-CIW-408

Loathsome Jews and Engulfing Women

LITERATURE AND PSYCHOANALYSIS

General Editor: Jeffrey Berman

1. *The Beginning of Terror: A Psychological Study of Rainer Maria Rilke's Life and Work*
   by David Kleinbard

2. *Loathsome Jews and Engulfing Women: Metaphors of Projection in the Works of Wyndham Lewis, Charles Williams, and Graham Greene*
   by Andrea Freud Loewenstein

Loathsome Jews and Engulfing Women

Metaphors of Projection in the Works of Wyndham Lewis, Charles Williams, and Graham Greene

ANDREA FREUD LOEWENSTEIN

NEW YORK UNIVERSITY PRESS
New York and London

NEW YORK UNIVERSITY PRESS
New York and London

Library of Congress Cataloging-in-Publication Data
Loewenstein, Andrea Freud.
Loathsome Jews and engulfing women : metaphors of projection in the works of Wyndham Lewis, Charles Williams, and Graham Greene / Andrea Freud Loewenstein.
p. cm. — (Literature and psychoanalysis ; 2)
Revision of the author's thesis (doctoral—University of Sussex).
Includes bibliographical references and index.
ISBN 0-8147-5063-X (alk. paper)
1. English literature—20th century—History and criticism.
2. Jews in literature. 3. Lewis, Wyndham, 1881-1957—Characters—Jews. 4. Williams, Charles, 1886-1945—Characters—Jews.
5. Greene, Graham, 1904- —Characters—Jews. 6. Projection (Psychology) in literature. 7. Psychoanalysis and literature.
8. Women in literature. 9. Metaphor. I. Title. II. Series.
PR151.J5L64 1993
820.9'9287—dc20 93-16362
CIP

New York University Press books are printed on acid-free paper, and their binding materials are chosen for strength and durability.

Manufactured in the United States of America

10 9 8 7 6 5 4 3 2 1

For Joy Holland

Contents

Foreword

As New York University Press inaugurates a new series of books on literature and psychoanalysis, it seems appropriate to pause and reflect briefly upon the history of psychoanalytic literary criticism. For a century now it has struggled to define its relationship to its two contentious progenitors and come of age. After glancing at its origins, we may be in a better position to speculate on its future.

Psychoanalytic literary criticism was conceived at the precise moment in which Freud, reflecting upon his self-analysis, made a connection to two plays and thus gave us a radically new approach to reading literature. Writing to his friend Wilhelm Fliess in 1897, Freud breathlessly advanced the idea that "love of the mother and jealousy of the father" are universal phenomena of early childhood (*Origins*, 223–24). He referred immediately to the gripping power of *Oedipus Rex* and *Hamlet* for confirmation of and perhaps inspiration for his compelling perception of family drama, naming his theory the "Oedipus complex" after Sophocles' legendary fictional hero.

Freud acknowledged repeatedly his indebtedness to literature, mythology, and philosophy. There is no doubt that he was a great humanist, steeped in world literature, able to read several languages and range across disciplinary boundaries. He regarded creative writers as allies, investigating the same psychic terrain and intuiting similar human truths. "[P]sycho- analytic observation must concede priority to imaginative writers," he declared in 1901 in *The Psychopathology of Everyday Life* (*SE* 6: 213), a concession he was generally happy to make. The only exceptions were writers like Schopenhauer, Nietzsche, and Schnitzler, whom he avoided reading because of the anxiety of influence. He quoted effortlessly from Sophocles, Shakespeare, Goethe, and Dostoevsky, and was himself a master prose stylist, the recipient of the coveted Goethe Prize in 1930. When he was considered for the Nobel Prize, it was not for medicine but for literature. Upon being greeted as the discoverer of the unconscious, he disclaimed the title and instead paid generous tribute to the poets and philosophers who preceded him.

And yet Freud's forays into literary criticism have not been welcomed uniformly by creative writers, largely because of his allegiance to science rather than art. Despite his admiration for art, he viewed the artist as an introvert, not far removed from neurosis. The artist, he wrote in a well-known passage in the *Introductory Lectures on Psycho-Analysis* (1916–17), "is oppressed by excessively powerful instinctual needs. He desires to win honour, power, wealth, fame and the love of women; but he lacks the means for achieving these satisfactions" (*SE* 16: 376). Consequently, Freud argued, artists retreat from reality into the world of fantasy, where they attempt to make their dreams come true. While conceding that true artists manage to shape their daydreams in such a way as to find a path back to reality, thus fulfilling their wishes, Freud nevertheless theorized art as a substitute gratification. Little wonder, then, that few artists have been pleased with Freud's pronouncements.

Nor have many artists been sympathetic to Freud's preoccupation with sexuality and aggression; his deterministic vision of human life; his combative, polemical temperament; his self-fulfilling belief that psychoanalysis brings out the worst in people; and his imperialistic claim that psychoanalysis, which he regarded as his personal creation, would explore and conquer vast new territories. He chose as the epigraph for *The Interpretation of Dreams* (1900) a quotation from *The Aeneid*: "Flectere si nequeo superos, Acheronta movebo" ("If I cannot bend the Higher Powers, I will move the Infernal Regions"). Although he denied that there was anything Promethean about his work, he regarded himself as one of the disturbers of the world's sleep. The man who asserted that "psychoanalysis is in a position to speak the decisive word in all questions that touch upon the imaginative life of man" (*SE* 19: 208) could hardly expect to win many converts among creative writers, who were no less familiar with the imaginative life of humankind and who resented his intrusion into their domain.

Freud viewed psychoanalysts as scientists, committed to the reality principle and to heroic self-renunciation. He perceived artists, by contrast—and women—as neurotic and highly narcissistic, devoted to the pleasure principle, intuiting mysterious truths which they could not rationally understand. "Kindly nature has given the artist the ability to express his most secret mental impulses, which are hidden even from himself," he stated in 1910 in *Leonardo da Vinci and a Memory of His Childhood* (*SE* 11: 107). The artist, in Freud's judgment, creates beauty, but the psychoanalyst analyzes its meaning and "penetrates" it, with all the phallic implications thereof. As much as he admired artists, Freud did not want to give them credit for knowing what they are doing. Moreover, although he always referred to artists as male, he assumed that art itself was essentially female; and he was drawn to the "seductive" nature of art, even as he resisted its embrace lest he lose his masculine analytical power. He wanted to be called a scientist, not an artist.

From the beginning of his career, then, the marriage Freud envisioned between the artist and the analyst was distinctly unequal and patriarchal. For their part, most creative writers have remained wary of psychoanalysis. Franz Kafka, James Joyce, and D. H. Lawrence were fascinated by psychoanalytic theory and appropriated it, in varying degrees, in their stories, but they all remained skeptical of Freud's therapeutic claims and declined to be analyzed.

Most artists do not want to be "cured," because they fear that their creativity will be imperiled; and, agreeing with Wordsworth that to dissect is to murder, they do not want psychoanalysts to probe their work. Vladimir Nabokov's sardonic reference to Freud as the "Viennese witch doctor" and his contemptuous dismissal of psychoanalysis as black magic are extreme examples of creative writers' mistrust of psychoanalytic interpretations of literature. "[A]ll my books should be stamped Freudians Keep Out," Nabokov writes in *Bend Sinister* (xii). Humbert Humbert speaks for his creator when he observes in *Lolita* that the difference between the rapist and therapist is but a matter of spacing (147).

Freud never lost faith that psychoanalysis could cast light upon a wide variety of academic subjects. In the short essay "On the Teaching of Psycho-Analysis in Universities" (1919), he maintained that his new science has a role not only in medical schools but also in the "solutions of problems" in art, philosophy, religion, literature, mythology, and history. "The fertilizing effects of psycho-analytic thought on these other disciplines," Freud wrote enthusiastically, "would certainly contribute greatly towards forging a closer link, in the sense of a *universitas literarum*, between medical science and the branches of learning which lie within the sphere of philosophy and the arts" (*SE* 17: 173). Regrettably, he did not envision in the same essay a cross-fertilization, a desire, that is, for other disciplines to pollinate psychoanalysis.

Elsewhere, though, Freud was willing to acknowledge a more reciprocal relationship between the analyst and the creative writer. He opened his first published essay on literary criticism, "Delusions and Dreams in Jensen's *Gradiva*" (1907), with the egalitarian statement that "creative writers are valued allies and their evidence is to be highly prized, for they are apt to know a whole host of things between heaven and earth of which our philosophy has not yet let us dream" (*SE* 9: 8), an allusion to his beloved Hamlet's affirmation of the mystery of all things. Conceding that literary artists have been, from time immemorial, precursors to scientists, Freud concluded that the "creative writer cannot evade the psychiatrist nor the psychiatrist the creative writer, and the poetic treatment of a psychiatric theme can turn out to be correct without any sacrifice of its beauty" (*SE* 9: 44).

It is in the spirit of this equal partnership between literature and psychoanalysis that New York University Press launches the present series. We intend to publish books that are genuinely interdisciplinary, theoretically sophisticated, and clinically informed. The literary critic's insights into psychoanalysis are no less valuable than the psychoanalyst's insights into literature. Gone are the days when psychoanalytic critics assumed that Freud had a master key to unlock the secrets of literature. Instead of reading literature to confirm psychoanalytic theory, many critics are now reading Freud to discover how his understanding of literature shaped the evolution of his theory. In short, the master-slave relationship traditionally implicit in the marriage between the literary critic and psychoanalyst has given way to a healthier dialogic relationship, in which each learns from and contributes to the other's discipline.

Indeed, the prevailing ideas of the late twentieth century are strikingly different from those of the late nineteenth century, when literature and psychoanalysis were first allied. In contrast to Freud, who assumed he was discovering absolute truth, we now believe that knowledge, particularly in the humanities and social sciences, is relative and dependent upon cultural contexts. Freud's classical drive theory, with its mechanistic implications of cathectic energy, has given way to newer relational models such as object relations, self psychology, and interpersonal psychoanalysis, affirming the importance of human interaction. Many early psychoanalytic ideas, such as the death instinct and the phylogenetic transmission of memories, have fallen by the wayside, and Freud's theorizing on female psychology has been recognized as a reflection of his cultural bias.

Significant developments have also taken place in psychoanalytic literary theory. An extraordinary variety and synthesis of competing approaches have emerged, including post-Freudian, Jungian, Lacanian, Horneyan, feminist, deconstructive, psycholinguistic, and reader response. Interest in psychoanalytic literary criticism is at an all-time high, not just in the handful of journals devoted to psychological criticism, but in dozens of mainstream journals that have traditionally avoided psychological approaches to literature. Scholars are working on identity theory, narcissism, gender theory, mourning and loss, and creativity. Additionally, they are investigating new areas, such as composition theory and pedagogy, and exploring the roles of resistance, transference, and countertransference in the classroom.

"In the end we depend/On the creatures we made," Freud observed at the close of his life (*Letters*, 425), quoting from Goethe's *Faust*; and in the end psychoanalytic literary criticism depends on the scholars who continue to shape it. All serious scholarship is an act of love and devotion, and for many of the authors in this series, including myself, psychoanalytic literary criticism has become a consuming passion, in some cases a lifelong one. Like other passions, there is an element of idealization here. For despite our criticisms of Freud, we stand in awe of his achievements; and even as we recognize the limitations of any single approach to literature, we find that psychoanalysis has profoundly illuminated the human condition and inspired countless artists. In the words of the fictional "Freud" in D. M. Thomas's extraordinary novel *The White Hotel* (1981), "Long may poetry and psychoanalysis continue to highlight, from their different perspectives, the human face in all its nobility and sorrow" (143n.).

JEFFREY BERMAN
Professor of English
State University of New York at Albany

Works Cited

Freud, Sigmund. *The Letters of Sigmund Freud*. Ed. Ernst Freud. Trans. Tania and James Stern. New York: Basic Books, 1975.

———. *The Origins of Psychoanalysis*. Ed. Marie Bonaparte, Anna Freud, and Ernst Kris. Trans. Eric Mosbacher and James Strachey. New York: Basic Books, 1954; rpt. 1977.

———. *The Standard Edition of the Complete Psychological Works of Sigmund Freud*. 24 vols. Ed. James Strachey. London: Hogarth Press, 1953–74.

Nabokov, Vladimir. Introduction. *Bend Sinister*. New York: McGraw Hill, 1974.

———. *Lolita*. London: Weidenfeld and Nicolson, 1959.

Thomas, D. M. *The White Hotel*. New York: Viking, 1981.

Acknowledgments

This book originated as my doctoral dissertation at the University of Sussex. During the prolonged period of my work on it, my advisor, Sybil Oldfield, was a sustaining presence—helpful with ideas and advice, always patient and deeply supportive. The detailed suggestions of Geoffrey Hemstedt and Bryan Cheyette, both members of my committee, helped me revise the thesis for publication. Bryan Cheyette in particular saved me from what would have been an unforgivable error by informing me that Graham Greene had altered the anti-Semitic content of several of his works. Even after Professor Cheyette's official function was over he continued to offer useful advice and source references.

The administration of Goddard College, where I was a faculty member during the writing of this book, allowed me to take the time off necessary to complete it and supported my scholarship. I am particularly grateful to Deans Paul Garstki and Dean Elias and to colleagues Nicky Morris and Barbara Johnson. Friends and fellow writers Michael Bronski and Jan Clausen helped me with their ideas and support.

At New York University Press, Jeffrey Berman has been a true friend to me and to this book, from his enthusiastic initial reception of it, through his warm encouragement during the rewriting process, to his instant feedback on new drafts. Jason Renker has been a consistently interested and supportive editor. Vicki Wilson-Schwartz contributed intelligent and painstaking copy editing, which greatly improved the book's style.

My father, Paul Loewenstein, offered me ongoing support and love with this project and others. I wish he could have lived to see this book in print. My mother, Sophie Freud, spent two precious weeks making the index to this book. During its writing she offered valuable references and it was her guidance which helped me to form a psychoanalytic critical perspective. She was and is an intellectual companion and inspiration, whose heroic midnight trips to rescue an ailing computer will never be forgotten. Finally, my partner, Joy Holland, gave me whatever I needed most at each stage of the work. Her valuable input can be found in every aspect of the book's contents and ideas. Constant discussion with her helped me to clarify my thoughts, and during the final stages of the dissertation process she repeatedly abandoned her own work to aid in the seemingly insurmountable task of actually getting that enormous package finished and in the mail by deadline. I would never have been able to complete this book without her loving and continually sustaining presence.

I would like to thank the following:

The estate of the author and the Watkins/Loomis Agency for permission to reprint excerpts from the works of Charles Williams.

The Black Sparrow Press for permission to reprint excerpts from *The Apes of God* © 1930, 1981 by Wyndham Lewis, and from *The Art of Being Ruled* © 1926, 1989 by Wyndham Lewis.

Viking Penguin, a division of Penguin Books USA, Inc., for permission to reprint excerpts from *A Gun for Sale* by Graham Greene. © Graham Greene, renewed.

Introduction

Wyndham Lewis wrote:

> [A] man is made, not born: and he is made, of course, with very great difficulty. From the time he yells and kicks in his cradle, to the time he receives his last kick at school, he is recalcitrant.[1]

It requires only a slight textual alteration—the substitution of "book" for man and "it" for "he"—to make this statement applicable to the work in hand. In my introduction, I will attempt to give the reader a sense of the process of making this book—from the moment of its conception through its early yelling, the gentle kicks it received at school (it first saw the light as my doctoral thesis at the University of Sussex), and on to its final incarnation in this form. I will simultaneously attempt to guide you through the chapters, preparing you for what you may expect from each one, explaining the order in which I wrote them, and indicating where I see each one fitting into the larger picture of the book. For those ambitious readers who approach this book as a whole, the introduction will, I hope, serve as a general guide. For those who consult it in search of a specific reference or author, the introduction will advise you which chapters may be of use, and which may easily be skipped.

Before embarking upon this critical study, the only substantial pieces of writing I had completed were two novels. As a novelist, I begin with a plan, but soon leave it behind, as the process of writing teaches me more about my characters and plot, and each new piece of knowledge informs what I have already written and forces me back to the beginning again in a slow, circular process. I was surprised to find that I used very much the same process in researching and constructing a critical study. Each new insight, each new chapter, entailed rethinking and revising the previous ones. For the purpose of this introduction, I have attempted to recast this process in a linear way. In fact, it would be more accurate to describe my work as a series of interlocking circles.

My idea for this study began in the fall of 1985, when I was living in London. Charmed by the grace and culture of this cosmopolitan and ultimately civilized city, I was considering a permanent move. One of the factors which made me hesitate, however, was how much less comfortable I felt as a Jew in England than I had in the large Eastern and Midwestern American cities where I had lived most of my life. In England, a sort of mild, often quasi-humorous anti-Semitism seemed to me quite pervasive. As an open lesbian, I was not unfamiliar with prejudice. But what I was hearing people say about Jews in places as diverse as leftist political gatherings, my local East London caf, and comedy shows on the BBC, reminded me of the way many even quite liberal white people tended to talk about blacks where I was from. There was the same half-ashamed fascination, the same furtive glance to see if anyone was around to hear—then the defiant utterance.

All was not negative. Minority identity, I learned, has its secondary perks. On the affirmative action questionnaires handed out when I applied for teaching jobs with the now defunct Inner London Education Authority, I was no longer a mere "Caucasian"—for the first time I had a box of my own to check. In those progressive feminist circles where I was not suspect as an oppressor of the Palestinians, I was listened to with the respectful silence due a member of an out-group. I was surprised and rather pleased to find that women who knew of me by name only were prepared to find me exotic, unusually expressive, and innately sexual. But for the most part, I felt uncomfortable. I found myself restraining my love of bargaining at street markets, trying to speak more softly, waiting for a pause rather than breaking eagerly into conversations as was my habit at home. I would show the English, I vowed, that I was not the loud, pushy, and vulgar Jewish woman they seemed to expect. Such an effort soon made me angry, and pushed me to an occasional determination to act just as loud, pushy, and aggressive as I could.

All this was, admittedly, hard to sort out. Some of the characteristics which the English attributed to Jews were identical to the characteristics they attributed to Americans. While being stigmatized as a loud, pushy American had a sting, it was the sting of a mosquito bite, not the wasp sting I felt when I mentioned my Jewish last name and saw the exchange of looks. Still, neither of my coping mechanisms was satisfying. My newfound minority status had robbed me somehow of the personhood I was used to, which, while it certainly included something of the Jew, the lesbian, the feminist, the woman, and all of the various other identities which I, like everyone else, cart around—also seemed to leave some room for me as an individual.

At about that time I read an essay in Leslie Fiedler's *To the Gentiles* in which Fiedler tells a story about his experience teaching in an English university. "How does it happen . . . that there is no serious, no considerable Anglo-Jewish novel?" Fiedler asks his students, and is met with blank looks. "They're all so rich here," one of them answers finally, smiling benignly. "They don't have to write books, do they?"[2] In this essay, Fiedler decries the "mild-as-milk, matter-of-fact anti-Semitism" which he found everywhere in England. As opposed to American Jews, "The Jews in England," he notes, "are felt to be English only insofar as they seem to have ceased being Jewish" (157). My own experience in England, over a decade later, echoed Fiedler's. And because part of my particular inherited brand of Jewish identity is that of an intellectual—one who encounters discomfort by trying to understand how and why it arose, and who believes, against all odds, that understanding cannot only illuminate but palliate that discomfort—I began this study.

As a novelist, a student of literature, and a compulsive reader, it was natural for me to look for my answers in fiction. In doing so, I realized that my present inquiry was connected to a much older one. As an adolescent, I had encountered with a feeling of embarrassment and shame the villainous and grotesque Jews who peopled the Victorian novels which were my favorite reading matter. As the child of intellectual, assimilated refugees from Nazism, in a home where the Holocaust and the experience of anti-Semitism were present as a strong undercurrent but seldom discussed, I did not have the words to explain what was wrong, or even how I felt.[3] I simply read on, and tried to ignore the unpleasantness. As an adult with at least some of the words and concepts I needed to name those childhood feelings, I began my study by rereading the classics of Jewish villainy I had grown up with and been schooled in: *Oliver Twist*, *The Merchant of Venice*, Chaucer's "Prioress's Tale," Trollope's *Way We Live Now*, selected works of T. S. Eliot and D. H. Lawrence. In search of good Jews, I reread George Eliot's *Daniel Deronda* and Joyce's

Ulysses. At this stage I called my fledgling study "Representations of Jews in British Literature."

I soon realized that I was working in a vacuum. Surely the notes that I was so assiduously taking had been taken already, the conclusions gathered? I determined to find out what had been done in the field. Although I did not write it until much later, this research provided the basis for what is now chapter 2: "A Survey of the Surveys." As far as I know, there exists to date no organized comparison or discussion of the many books devoted to the representation of Jews in British fiction. I found that comparing the approaches taken by the critics in this chapter and attempting to codify these differences aided me in my own effort to define my theoretical approach. At the time I undertook the bulk of the research summarized in chapter 2, I had not yet made the connection between the authorial representation of Jews and women. This chapter accordingly confines itself to studies of the representation of Jews in British literature, with little examination of the issue of gender.

As I began to read more contemporary studies, I located critics such as Leslie Fiedler and Christopher Ricks who approached the authorial treatment of Jews in the context of the treatment of different groups of "Others" (women, blacks, Indians, members of colonized nations, gays).[4] I found such bridging intriguing and determined that I too would look at the Jew in literature not in isolation but rather in the context of authorial treatment of different "Others," that is, groups which are set aside in the cultural productions of white Western males as beings of an alien nature. I was already familiar with numerous critical works which examined the treatment of women and of gays and lesbians in literature, and I now read such works as Chinua Achebe's *Hopes and Impediments* and David Dabydeen's collection *The Black Presence in English Literature*, both revealing studies of the representation of black characters.[5]

Finally, I began to read contemporary, more theoretical studies in which critics, rather than concentrating on the representation of two or more particular groups of Others, studied the textual production of Otherness as a production or encoding of ideology.[6] While I gained tremendously from my introduction to "the rhetoric of power" and from my exposure to theorists who use Marxist, psychoanalytic, and poststructuralist outlooks to discuss the representation of the Jew, my own primary concentration in chapter 2 is on those critics who came before, establishing a ground for the rest of us to walk upon. I hope that the chapter will be useful to others seeking such a grounding, and that it may enable them to skip some of the painstaking steps I went through. Chapter 2 will also be useful to those readers who have not considered the representation of Jewish characters in English literature before. In comparing how Philipson, Modder, and Rosenberg regard Shylock and his relatives, I offer an introduction to the texts which critics in this area have traditionally examined, and to the persistent types and stereotypes who make their stubborn way through the years, refusing to be put to sleep. Chapter 2, then, provides a background to the body of my argument, which is to be found in chapters 4 through 6. It is not essential reading for a full understanding of those chapters.

Each critical book led me to new novels. By the end of my preliminary research, I had read virtually all the fiction that previous critics on the topic had included in their surveys, most of which ended around the year 1930. Accordingly, I decided to begin my own research with that date. At the time I assumed that I would produce another survey like those I had read, one which would update the available knowledge by covering a different period. I planned to read all the books published in Britain after 1930 which featured Jewish characters. Mine would be a survey with a purpose: to determine whether the Holocaust had significantly changed the representation of Jews in British fiction. I still believe that this is an important study, but it must be done by someone else.

I began my putative survey almost at random with what I thought would be a few pages on the work of Graham Greene, an author identified by Rosenberg and Fiedler, the two critics I had found most useful for my period, as a particular culprit in his use of Jewish stereotypes.[7] My preliminary method was a close examination of language and text, my focus the more unconscious subtexts revealed by Greene's treatment of Jewish characters. What I had assumed would be merely the first item in many, a matter of a few pages and a week's work, rapidly expanded. I soon had over sixty pages of notes on Greene's first novel.

I realized at this point that the survey approach was not for me. I abandoned my plan to cover a great deal of ground and decided to cover instead no more than five authors. I had already determined that I wanted to look at Gentile attitudes toward the Jewish Other rather than attitudes we as Jews take toward ourselves. In my preliminary work on Greene, I had been struck by the fact that all his Jews were male, and that his representation of them seemed to be closely tied to his struggle to defend his manhood. My desire to explore this lead caused me to eliminate female as well as Jewish authors from my list. Finally, I decided to concentrate on male authors whom the critics had identified as particularly offensive. It is important to stress here that this selection process was in no way random. At this point in my research, I was well acquainted with the wide range of positive and negative representations of Jews in books written from the late 1920s to the 1940s. If I had chosen E. M. Forster, Christopher Isherwood, or C. P. Snow, for example, three authors who took stands against anti-Semitism and created a range of positive or neutral Jewish characters, a totally different study would have resulted. I chose my authors precisely because of their documented anti-Semitism, which I had now decided to explore.

My subsequent close readings of the work of Wyndham Lewis, Charles Williams, George Orwell, Evelyn Waugh, Aldous Huxley, Hugh Massingham, and William Gerhardi confirmed the anomaly I had observed in Greene. In the works of all these authors, male Jews seemed to reproduce either by parthogenesis or by attaching themselves to Gentile women: there were no female Jews to be seen. In addition, each male Jewish character seemed to exist in close proximity to, in reference to, or in opposition to one or more Gentile female characters. I attempted to disentangle the Jews from the women with no success: it was impossible to ignore such striking systemic connections. To explore the connections between the representation of women and of Jews was thus not part of my initial plan, but was instead a focus which crept in, so to speak, by the back door. Although I subsequently sharpened and redefined my topic, and eliminated Orwell, Waugh, Huxley, Massingham and Gerhardi from the study, the close readings referred to above eventually led to chapters 4 through 6.

It was at this stage of the study that I became aware of some major theoretical and substantive holes in my knowledge. As I have mentioned, I originally chose the period from 1930 to 1950 because I wanted to find out how World War II and the Holocaust had influenced the representation of Jews in British fiction. While the very small sample of writers and texts I would be examining in my newly conceptualized study would prevent me from answering that question, I still badly needed a historical context for the material I was reading. My study of the surveys and of the fiction to which these surveys had directed me had given me a sense of where Graham Greene's Jews fitted into the larger picture of Jews in

British literature, but I lacked a sense of how his attitude compared to the norm of prewar and wartime English attitudes toward Jews, or indeed, of what the extraliterary fate of the Jews in England had been from medieval times on.

In addition, my reading of the new critical discourse had shaken the foundations of the few historical "facts" I had thought I knew. It is the frame which defines the picture, I reminded myself, and it is the owners of the frame who determine what will go inside it. As Edward Said points out in the introduction to *Orientalism*, the presentation of history is far from the innocent study it sometimes poses as: naming has a power and force of its own (27). My subsequent reading in Anglo-Jewish history served to reframe the prevailing version of that history which I had previously accepted, and to give me a more realistic context for the attitudes I was identifying in the literature.

What struck me most about my revised version of the history of the Jews in England and what seemed to remain consistent from the preexpulsion days through the present was the number of conflicting signals directed at British Jews and the hypocrisy behind governmental policies regarding them. From the beginning, British Jews were resented for their refusal to assimilate while being virtually prevented from doing so. The British liberal tradition, which I had previously seen as a force which served and protected the Jews of Britain, was instead consistently used as an enforcer of this hypocrisy. I had read about Mosley and the British Union of Fascists, but had assumed that, as my sources stated, they represented a tiny lunatic minority. I now concluded that the distinction between the fringe groups' ideology concerning Jews and the "parlor" anti-Semitism of the kind that I had experienced myself was a false one which obscured the larger continuum of British anti-Semitism.

Time constraints did not allow me to make the study of primary sources that I would ideally have liked to undertake in order to write chapter 1. My reading in history was that of a beginning student, certainly not that of a historian, and the resultant chapter reflects this. Still, I feel that the conclusions I present challenge the mainstream presentation of Anglo-Jewish history, and that the attitudes and discourse regarding Jews which I present in chapter 1 are recreated by all three authors and reproduced in all the texts I examine in chapters 4 through 6. Readers well grounded in Anglo-Jewish history may wish to skip chapter 1. Those, on the other hand, who think of Britain as an especially tolerant and liberal country which served as a haven to the persecuted Jews of Europe during the Second World War may find that this chapter challenges these preconceptions, and serves as a useful introduction to the body of material presented in chapters 4 through 6. Once again, I completed the research on what would become chapter 1 fairly early. By the time I had reframed my study, it was too late to make even a brief historical study of the role of women in Britain. I consoled myself by reasoning that many others had done this. Still, chapter 1, like chapter 2, ignores the dual approach of this book.

I now returned to Graham Greene, this time concentrating on autobiographical and biographical material. I spent some time questioning my own interest in these materials. Although I was writing my dissertation in the late 1980s and early 1990s, the last official classes in literature I had taken had been when I earned my M.A. in the early 1970s, a time when New Criticism reigned supreme in graduate English studies at the University of Wisconsin where I was a student. I had been briefly exposed to phenomenological and mythic criticism along the way, but both of these perspectives reinforced the New Critical admonition to focus solely on the text at hand, or at most on mythic meanings or associations to the texts, and to ignore even the most relevant biographical information.[8] Such a prohibition was difficult to disregard. In the end I decided to do so for several reasons. In the first place, much as I tried to exclude the author from his texts as I had been taught to do, he kept intruding. It was not only Lewis's authorial system that was paranoid; Lewis the man conducted his affairs and led his life within a paranoid framework which closely mirrored that system. Not only was Williams's authorial system a rigid, obsessive one; he himself lived his life within an obsessive framework which applied to his work habits as well as his sexual proclivities. Greene wrote about depressed, guilty, empty men. As his letters and autobiographical writing confirm, he was himself an empty and guilt-ridden man.

I searched for critical justification to do what felt right—to include autobiographical and biographical material on my authors in my discussion of their texts. The poststructuralist criticism I had begun to read tended to ignore the author, just as New Criticism had, and to focus on the text alone.[9] However, my exposure to this new theory gave me permission to "deconstruct" my received approaches and to meet texts in ways which broke the rules. If scholars are allowed to write articles on advertising copy, I reasoned, surely I am allowed to include an author's letters, journals, and autobiography as relevant texts? My exposure to poststructuralism also allowed me to reject my learned New Critical notion that texts exist in an artistic vacuum which must not be penetrated. I, like Terry Eagleton, decided that the idea that "any piece of language, 'literary' or not, can be adequately studied or even understood in isolation" must be illusory (Eagleton, *Literary Theory*, 44). I preferred to believe, with Eagleton, that literature is inextricably caught up in "material practices, social relations and ideological meanings" (*Literary Theory*, 21). It seems to me that biographical (and especially autobiographical) information reveals exactly how such factors have influenced an author's work. In a "Note on Method" in her book *Social Mobility in the English Bildungssroman*, Patricia Ann Alden, who connects biographical information about the authors in her study with the ideology reflected in their texts, asserts, "I see my work as part of the ongoing resistance to thinking about literature as a self-referential system instead of exploring its connections to all those social practices through which we constitute our world."[10] In the end, I saw my own decision to explore the lives of my authors as well as their texts as part of this ongoing resistance.

In making the decision to incorporate biographical information into a primarily textual study I knew that I was venturing into a field rife with pitfalls. I tried hard to avoid these, or at least to become aware of them. Always present was the danger of falling into the kind of solipsistic arguments employed by some of the earlier critics discussed in chapter 2, who maintained, for example, that Fagin could not possibly be a stereotyped portrait because Dickens claimed to be a friend of the Jews. As Wimsatt and Beardsley maintain in "The Intentional Fallacy" (1946), it is dangerous to confuse authorial intention with textual evidence.[11] This can lead in turn to the fallacy in which one attributes to the author an attitude properly belonging to his or her characters. (I found Wayne Booth's distinction between the implied author whom we construct for ourselves from the text, and the real author, whom we cannot know, to be especially useful in this context.) When I claim that Wyndham Lewis shows a loathing of women, I am not referring to a loathing held by one or more of Lewis's characters which may or may not reflect the attitude of the author, but rather to an attitude which seems to me pervasive, basic to the works in question, and clearly indicative of the author's own conscious or unconscious attitude or feelings. If I also see that loathing played out in Lewis's own life, for example, in his treatment of his wife, I have attempted clearly to indicate the distinction between the two realms, in order not to conflate literature with action. Unlike those feminists who view pornography as a form of violence against women, I see a distinction between the act of raping a woman and that of producing material which depicts rape in a positive light. Accordingly, while I was shocked by the similarities between the writing about Jews and women in the work of the Freikorpsmen who are the subject of Klaus Theweleit's study and in the three British writers in my own study, I urged myself to remember that the Freikorpsmen, unlike my three authors, were warriors who killed by day and wrote books by night.[12]

Linking an author's history and psychology to his texts is especially risky in this study, given that I limit my examination to those of each author's works in which there are Jewish characters. As I explain in chapter 1, as the war progressed, and especially after the news of the Holocaust became widespread, many authors chose to avoid writing about Jews, who had become a less convenient receptacle for stereotypical projection. While Williams remained fairly consistent in his treatment of Jews over time, Lewis made some attempt to modify his earlier views, and Graham Greene, who created a number of unsavory Jewish characters before the war, almost completely eliminated Jews from his postwar opus, except for an occasional reference to an almost stereotypically "good Jew." He also altered the text of three of his earlier books for a postwar edition, in one case turning an unsavory Jewish character into an Italian and in each case altering some of the language referring to Jews.[13] Accordingly, my discussion, which is limited to the original version of Greene's earliest novels, including one novel (*The Name of Action*, 1932) which he repudiated later, would be most unfair if my purpose, like that of the earlier critics in chapter 1, were to arrive at a moral (or clinical) evaluation of the author in question. As this is not my aim, I have attempted to concentrate my biographical inquiry on the periods in each author's life which precede the texts I examine, and not to make sweeping conclusions which preclude the possibility of later change.

Finally, my decision to look at the lives, especially the childhoods and schooling, of the authors I studied was not undertaken as a substitute for a close reading of the texts in question. Rather, it represents my effort to see those texts within a wider ideological and social context, as well as to explore some of the connections and disjunctions between art and life. I found that biographical information can expose not only logical connections but also seeming contradictions. In my examination of the lives of the writers, I attempted to keep this in mind and not to manipulate my "evidence" in order to bring life and literature into line with each other. It is important to remember that these seeming contradictions do not indicate that either action or text is "false" or "a lie," as was assumed by some of the earlier critics discussed in chapter 1. Human beings are notoriously ambivalent creatures, and writers are no exception. I asked what it means when an author works to rescue Jews in the real world, but caricatures them in his fiction, not as an effort to show that one or the other half of the equation is false, but merely in an attempt to look at the whole picture. What, if any, sex life did an author have whose texts show an obsession with sexual sin and purification? What kind of marriages did authors achieve whose texts showed a loathing and fear of women? My grappling with these questions led me to chicken-and-egg speculations on cause and effect, and to theories about why a particular author's life seemed more or less congruent with his fictional texts. I hope that I did not allow any of these speculations to keep me from a close and challenging investigation of the texts themselves.

With only a little more than a year left to complete my study, I changed its name to *Representations of Jews and Women in the Works of Graham Greene, Charles Williams, Wyndham Lewis, and George Orwell*, a vague title which included my new focus on women as well as Jews but reflected my lack of any true theoretical grounding. During the course of my research I had gradually evolved an approach which demanded close attention to the text and to the meaning under the surface of the text and allowed for psychological interpretations based on a combination of logic, some basic, rather outdated psychoanalytic theory, and the biographical information I had accumulated on each author. I now turned to various well-known sociological and psychological explanations of prejudice, including Jean-Paul Sartre's *Anti-Semite and Jew* (1946), T. W. Adorno's *Authoritarian Personality* (1958), Gordon Allport's *Nature of Prejudice* (1954), and Joel Kovel's *White Racism: A Psychohistory* (1970), in search of "a theory" which would work for me.[14] While all of these works contributed in different ways to my knowledge, none of them seemed to address the problem I faced in trying to find a theory to fit my close textual analysis, and none of them offered me a frame for what was now emerging in my study: a series of tightly woven individual authorial systems which applied to every text I studied by a particular author and which encompassed the treatment of both Jews and women.

The turning point came when my advisor, Sybil Oldfield, steered me to Klaus Theweleit's two-volume work *Male Fantasies* (1987, 1989), an examination of novels and autobiographies written by members of the German Freikorps, soldier males who, from 1918 to 1928, created the "White Terror" and from whose ranks and belief system came many Nazis and much of Nazi ideology. Theweleit allowed the literary productions of the men in the German Freikorps to speak for themselves—and these texts spoke very eloquently. At his best, Theweleit used psychoanalytic theory in the service of supporting and elucidating his texts rather than as a way to lock them into an esoteric and irrelevant system, as some of the more traditional psychoanalytic studies seemed to me to do. His books make exactly the kind of connection which I had noticed in my own research, between the Freikorpsmen's fascism and their misogyny.

Theweleit in many ways provided a theoretical model for me, but I felt critical of his brand of psychoanalytic theory. While object relations theory certainly seemed to offer a broader and more useful perspective for textual analysis than unreconstructed Freudian theory, I felt that Theweleit's use of that theory, and in particular his overly concrete reliance on the work of Melanie Klein and Margaret Mahler, was often narrow and limiting. But each individual theorist or "school" I identified in my own theoretical search seemed to be equally limiting. After weeks of trying to find one particular theory or "frame" which would perfectly fit and illuminate my conclusions, I turned in despair to my mother, Dr. Sophie Freud, a scholar of postpsychoanalytic theory. Through our exchanges and through reading and discussion of her paper "Social Constructivism and Research," she helped me to realize that psychoanalytic theory, like other bodies of theory, is only a system or series of systems conceptualized by human beings like myself in order to frame or better understand a particular set of behaviors.[15] My mother steered me in the direction of theorists she thought I would find useful, assuring me that it was perfectly valid to study various psychoanalytic theorists and select those which seemed relevant: in other words, to construct a theoretical "cluster" which I could use as a frame to clarify and push further my understanding of what I had already discovered.

It seems important therefore to reemphasize here that when I speak of my study's psychoanalytic grounding, I am not referring to any one theoretical school. Although for me, as for Theweleit, a broadly object relations framework proved in the end more useful than any other, I chose my theorists because they shed some light on the linking of woman hatred and Jew hatred and the way this twin preoccupation shaped literary texts, not because they belonged to the same school. Indeed, I begin chapter 3 with a brief discussion of Kate Millett and Virginia Woolf, two novelists and literary critics with no explicit psychological grounding. I next proceed to look at the work of three clinicians who (in those of their works I consult here) concentrate on diagnosis, classification, and treatment rather than on development and causality. I only then move to the work of five object relations theorists. I then survey four clinicians whose focus is on the effects of abuse on personality. Finally, I end this chapter with a look at the English public school system, an institution I identify as an inflictor of trauma, an enforcer of ideology, and a male rite of passage. As should be clear from the above, the theorists in this chapter do not share one theory, and would not be found in the same room or the same collection of essays. Nevertheless, instead of presenting me with contradictory and conflicting viewpoints, the more I read, the more similar their theories looked to me, until I began to see them as merely different systematic clothing for the same body.

This insight, which I am sure would not startle professionals in the field of psychology, was liberating for me. I found that Virginia Woolf, Kate Millett, Karen Horney, Melanie Klein, Dorothy Dinnerstein, Jessica Benjamin, Leon Salzman, David Shapiro, Otto Kernberg, Alice Miller, Ellen Bass and Laura Davis, Mike Lew, and Virginia Terr were telling me remarkably similar things about the authors I was studying, and that their insights illuminated my research on the public school experience. In chapters 1 and 2, my concentration was primarily on the representation of Jews, not women. In chapter 3, because object relations theory tends to concentrate on the early relationship of child and mother, my concentration was more on the representation of women, with the representation of Jews as a secondary concern. I hope I have achieved a balance in this respect in the three introductory chapters.

The theoretical background which I gained from this phase of my research had the effect of shifting and sharpening my perspective so that I was no longer satisfied with any part of my previous drafts of chapters 4 through 6 and was forced to rewrite each one. My thesis advisor had some doubts about the theoretical emphasis I had finally "found," worrying that my shift from an open perspective to a much more theoretically focused one might replace what had been an openly exploratory approach with a stale work in which my insights would be slotted into a preconceived "scheme of explanation that had been lying in wait for them." Perhaps because I am by nature a disorganized person who does best within a fairly firm structure, I found that the shift had the opposite effect. My sharpened perspective seemed to open up the texts to me, allowing me to make connections that had been invisible before. The broad authorial systems I had identified before now came into focus, on their own terms, in relation to one another and to the larger historical and social picture. The symbolic uses of the Jew and the woman now emerged, to use Sander Gilman's concept, as different branches of a larger structure or construct rather than as isolated, though connected, phenomena.[16] It was during these last five months of work that I came up with the present title. It was also during this final stage that I began to see my study not only as a close examination of the work of three rather unpleasant authors but also as a model which could be used to identify links between misogyny and anti-Semitism in other authors, and, more generally, to explore the authorial use of the "Other" in literature.

One criticism often used to discredit the psychoanalytic approach to literary criticism is that it is based on the individual in isolation from the larger community and society, concentrating on how his or her particular pathology or individual experience has influenced his or her textual representation. It is thus seen as a theory which avoids economic, historical, or social realities. I feel that this is in fact a false and unnecessary dichotomy. In my first two chapters and in my discussion of the institution of the English public school in chapter 3, I have attempted to establish both a historical and a literary context for the conscious and unconscious attitudes that my three writers held toward Jews and toward women. While I will suggest that some of these attitudes do fit into a psychologically "pathological" category, I at no time mean to imply that this pathology is unique to the writers in question, or that it is a product of purely personal experience. As history has made manifest again and again, pathology can be widespread and can encompass a whole gender, class, country, or group of countries—can reach to as large a group as is implied by the term "Western civilization." While it is true that one study cannot embody every approach, I do not see my psychoanalytic approach as one which negates broader, more societally based interpretations, but instead as one which opens the way to such interpretations. The rather striking pathology which is evident in these writers' symbolic use of women and Jews does not come as a surprise to us as readers, because similar images of both women and Jews are so deeply embedded in our own cultural context.

ONE

The Jews of Britain: A Historical Overview

As an American child in the late 1950s, I read in my history textbooks of the Spanish and Portuguese, hysterical Catholics who enjoyed burning people at the stake during the Inquisition and whose explorers gleefully destroyed entire Indian civilizations, complete with gold and plumbing. Quite different were the English explorers, gentlemen in boats with beautiful white sails, who, once they had sighted land, sailed straight home to make their report on bended knees to their lady queen. England, my textbooks told me, was a civilized country of religious tolerance and scientific inquiry. True, the English had once, briefly, fought against us, but this did not make them Evil. Instead, they had merely been foolish—vain men in red coats who suffered from the temporary illusion that a king was better than a president, and being ruled was better than Freedom and Democracy. It was a good war, the Revolution, a war between honorable men who knew the rules, stood up to die nobly on the battlefield, and never sneaked around and shot people from behind. The English were never Other. How could they be? They were Our Ancestors.

From my parents too, I learned that England was One of the Few Good Countries. Had the English people not fought Hitler from the very beginning, put up with the blitz and slept every night in the underground, all for the sake of the Jews? My Jewish refugee parents, who had escaped to America, often told me the story of how they referred to me as "Churchill" during the nine months before my birth in 1949. Had I been a boy, I would have been named after the Englishman they seemed to regard as the savior of the Jews. In addition, a famous relative of mine who had fled to Britain as a haven from the Nazis had been warmly received, a fact duly noted in the history books, which did not mention that this famous man's four sisters were somehow left in Austria, to perish at the hands of the Nazis.

Once established, myths die hard. I have already mentioned my mastery of the art of ignoring uglier passages about Jews in my favorite Victorian novels. In college, a "junior semester abroad" in London, designed to immerse me in modern British culture and history, firmly established my Anglophilia and left my illusions happily intact. England was, I knew, the seat of socialism and tolerance, its imperialist past long buried and forgotten—a civilized contrast to my own racist, warmongering country. It was only years later, as I began to explore the history of the Jews in England in an effort to place the literature I was reading for this study in a historical context, that I began to question my assumptions.[1]

Preexpulsion

"To speak of 'literature and ideology' as two separate phenomena which can be interrelated is . . . quite unnecessary. Literature . . . is ideology," writes Terry Eagleton (Eagleton, *Literary Theory*, 22). The key texts depicting Jews in British literature are indeed inseparably entangled with the ideology they embody. These texts are not only enshrined in the inner canon; they have been used as important pawns in the argument about the Jews' place (or lack of one) in British society. Judas, Shylock, and Fagin are still among the best-known Jews in our culture. Their names have passed into the common vocabulary and become metaphors for the alterity of the Jew. Even more central, the Old and New Testaments were used as the textual justification for the special status of the Jew in the preexpulsion years, and still provide a basis for the continued ambivalence shown to this group of Others. Any account of the Jewish presence in Great Britain must thus begin with these metatexts.

British Christians perceived the Jew at once as the patriarch and ancestor of the Old Testament and as the cursed member of a deicidal nation, with distinct links to the devil, of the New Testament. As Harold Fisch explains the dialectic: "He had to be kept outside the pale of society: but he also had to be preserved."[2] This textual ambiguity was reproduced in the royal strategies which governed the Jews' position in England before the expulsion of 1290. Small and vulnerable communities of Jews "enjoyed" a unique "royal protection," which placed them outside of the laws and expectations of the larger community, subject to the king alone.[3] The phrase "royal protection," with its encoded contradictions and broken promises, serves as a fit metaphor for the lives of these preexpulsion English Jews. The royal protection placed them at the mercy of each monarch's whim, making their status forever tenuous and uncertain. At the same time, its connotation of special privilege caused resentment in the Gentile community. The early English Jews, forbidden to enter guilds, to own or farm land, to own their own businesses, or to participate in government, quickly established themselves in the one trade familiar to them: banking. The Jews became an easily available source of revenue. Merciless taxation filled empty royal coffers and financed the Crusades. The church and throne combined forces to punish Jews by execution and torture for their insatiable need for the blood (or the phallus) of young Christian boys and gathered badly needed revenue through fining a miscreant's entire community and confiscating his property. In cases like that of "Little Hugh of Lincoln" in 1255, when Henry II himself supervised the hanging and torture of the accused Jew, the throne indirectly licensed such acts as the widespread sacking and burning of Jewish communities and the massacre of the Jews of York. Jews were persecuted for their refusal to assimilate, but forced by a decree of the Lateran Council in 1215 to wear distinguishing badges and a costume which virtually prevented assimilation.

In his "Statutum de Judaismo," imposed at a time when the Jewish community had been milked so dry that it was no longer financially useful to the crown, Edward I set up yet another double bind: Jews were forced by law to quit the practice of usury and to enter instead into small commerce, crafts, and farming; yet they were barred from the guilds through which commerce and crafts were carried out and could neither own nor rent land to farm. Damned if they did, damned if they didn't, the early Jews were finally expelled from England before their expulsion from any other country in Europe, an act which gained special praise from the Lateran Council for the English throne.

1290–1929

In *Difference and Pathology*, Sander Gilman notes that "stereotypes can . . . be perpetuated, resurrected, and shaped through texts containing the fantasy life of the culture, quite independent of the existence or absence of the group in a given society" (20). During their absence of 374 years, from 1290 through 1656, the only real Jews in evidence in England were occasional physicians, brought in to effect cures on royalty, and often persecuted as witches when they failed to do so. The same period witnessed the literary construction of the Jew: a figure whose dimensions quickly became so clearly delineated that he was awarded "mythic" and "archetypal" status by critics and commentators, and whom, like other mythic figures, we can easily recognize today in modern dress. Usually male, his devilish qualities could be largely comic or largely threatening. Miserly, gesticulating, hypervirile, or disturbingly female, he passed his generic youth in ballads and in miracle and mystery plays and came to maturity during the absence of his human "model," in the famous canonical Jews of Chaucer, Marlowe, and Shakespeare.

Between 1630 and 1664, Jews began gradually to enter England again, but every effort formally to legalize their presence was resoundingly rejected.[4] Charles II finally achieved their readmittance through a policy of quiet acceptance rather than a formal statute. The "Jew Bill" of 1735, which proposed that Jews resident in England for three years or more be naturalized and allowed to own land created an anti-Jewish furor which the gradually growing presence of the Jews had failed to do. The explosions of popular feeling taught an important lesson to the small and vulnerable established Jewish community. Jews, who might be tolerated if they contributed economically but otherwise remained invisible, would be subject to persecution if they spoke out, or in any other way called attention to themselves.

The Jewish Board of Deputies formed at this time bought the lesson wholesale. If, they reasoned, they could become assimilated enough not to stand out in a crowd, rich enough to provide the larger community with badly needed services, and quiet enough not to assert their rights, they might slip by. During the next period of Jewish visibility, the wave of immigration in the late nineteenth and early twentieth centuries, the Board of Deputies joined with the British authorities to keep the working-class newcomers out. A kind of conduit for the values of the Gentile ruling classes to the mass of the Jewish people, the Board espoused the idea that Jews brought anti-Semitism on themselves through their own behavior. Having internalized what W. Williams and Bryan Cheyette have termed the "antisemitism of tolerance," the Board of Deputies were indeed "Deputies"—enforcers of the standards which judged Jews "on the basis of their conformity to the values and manners of bourgeois English society."[5] In a logical correlate of this view, assimilation was seen as *the* way to eliminate anti-Semitism. Later, the Board of Deputies and the very small privileged and assimilated Jewish community it represented was the last Jewish group to call for a boycott of goods from Nazi Germany and initially even opposed urging the government to open its doors to refugees from Nazism.

Previous antagonism toward Jews had been voiced for the most part in terms of the difference in religion. A racially based anti-Semitism began to surface in the late nineteenth and early twentieth centuries with the flood of immigrants fleeing Russian pogroms. The "scientific" discourse of racial anti-Semitism stood in direct opposition to the emphasis on assimilation. As Ira B. Nadell puts it,

> Racial anti-Semitism precluded the salvation of the Jews by conversion or education since heredity and race were eternal laws; hence, the Jew was no longer "*Judaeus perversus*," a historical or dogmatic concept, but a physical entity whose attributes were quantifiable and established precise and continuous racial characteristics. The Jewish stereotype now had a scientific basis according to racial anti-Semitism and could easily be caricatured by representing his common features, and appearance.[6]

Much of this argument focused on the discourse surrounding the baptized Jew and prime minister Benjamin Disraeli. Through his person, Disraeli embodied the contradictory dialectic centered on the Jews. He was at once the ultimate achievement of Jewish assimilation—proof that a Jew could indeed become an English gentleman— and a personification of the stealthy Jew who, concealing his identity, inveigles his way into the Christian body, polluting the whole. It is not surprising that Disraeli, who was himself a believer in racial Semitism and who produced several important and influential philo-Semitic texts, also inspired a vast number of texts by others, including both racial attacks and a variety of positive and negative fictional portraits.[7]

Gilman points out that "[s]ince all of the images of the Other derive from the same deep structure, various signs of difference can be linked without any recognition of inappropriateness, contradictoriness, or even impossibility" (*Difference and Pathology*, 21). The new racial discourse comfortably housed the same contradictions as previous, religion-based anti-Semitism had contained. Jews who had previously been accused of being stubbornly unwilling to assimilate were now viewed as racially unable to do so. They were concomitantly cowardly and degenerate and fiendishly strong, powerful, and all-controlling, intent on their sexual and financial plots to invade and engulf the Christian community. In a kind of conflation which will be a key theme of this study, H. G. Wells, in *Marriage* (1912), compared Jews to female prostitutes and accused them of "prostituting" society for their own ends.[8]

Many of these themes were expressed in one of the most active and influential of the texts on Jews: *Protocols of the Elders of Zion*, a forgery by the tsarist secret police first published in Russia in 1903, which embodied the international conspiracy theory, attributing it to a sinister Jewish-Masonic collaboration. Although proven a forgery in 1920, the year after its publication in England, the *Protocols* could not be gotten rid of so easily. Perhaps because it accurately textualizes the discourse of Christian terror of and hostility toward Jews, it has had an amazingly long life, remaining a potent and frequently cited document to this day.[9]

While the lot of postexpulsion British Jews compared favorably to that of Jews in all other European countries, the fear and loathing expressed in the *Protocols* remained present in an undercurrent which tended to emerge in full force during periods of economic or social crisis, rapid change, or war. Thus Jews were widely believed to be the forces behind the Boer War of 1899–1902, the First World War, and even the Second World War. The newspaper magnate Lord Beaverbrook voiced a popular sentiment when he commented, in 1938, "[T]he Jews may drive us into war. . . . Their political influence is moving us in that direction."[10] Right-wing politicians and much of the general public blamed Jews for such instances of corruption in government as the Marconi Scandal of 1911–13, and Jews were blamed for the economic recession following World War I. The conservative press described the Russian Revolution of 1917 as the first step in a systematic takeover by the forces of world Jewry, while the very widespread attitude toward the founding of the League of Nations is revealed in the words of an editorial in the *Morning Post*: "We have always considered the League of Nations as a sort of Jewish pawnshop which holds the pledges of the British Government."[11]

It was during the wave of immigration in the early twentieth century that the idea of Palestine as a national home for the Jews was first framed by the British government. The government, daunted by the influx of Jews, was on the lookout for an alternative place, in Joseph Chamberlain's words, to "divert the flow of Jewish refugees away from Britain," and at this time North Africa as well as Palestine was considered for this purpose.[12]

The concept of a homeland, framed in this rhetorical context, neatly matched the ambivalence in the longstanding British discourse toward the Jews. It maintained the popular image of British friendliness to their Jews and provided for the preservation of the people of the Old Testament, while simultaneously offering a means of diverting the cursed and infectious New Testament Jews from Britain. When the Balfour Declaration of 1917 declared Palestine a national home for the Jewish people, the British reaction was highly positive. Representative in its sentiment if not in its vehemence of expression, was the delight of H. H. Beamish, founder of one of the right-wing patriotic groups of the day, The Britons. Beamish suggested that the Jews "should be forced to live in Palestine in the same way that snakes and other vermin should be forced to live in the jungle and not in people's houses."[13] H. G. Wells agreed that the idea of Palestine as a Jewish homeland was "altogether sane and practicable" (Cheyette, "Wells," 29).

The same forces could as easily be summoned a few years later against the Balfour Declaration at a time when the rhetoric surrounding the idea of a Jewish state had shifted. By the 1920s, Wells had become a prominent anti-Zionist, who saw the desire for a homeland as an an example of Jewish particularism and refusal to assimilate, which he held to be the cause of contemporary anti-Semitism (Cheyette, "Wells," 30–31). And a few years after the Balfour Declaration, not only the right-wing *Patriot* and somewhat more mainstream *Morning Post* but also the *Spectator*, the *Times*, the *Daily Mail*, and the *Daily Express* and *Sunday Express* combined in a heated attack on Zionism. Typical were the reports that Lord Northcliffe, owner of the *Times*, made from Palestine, in which he wrote that there had been peace and quiet "before the arrival of the undesirable Jewish element," who were "pushful, grasping and domineering."[14] W. E. B. Whittaker, the *Daily Express*'s special correspondent in Palestine, described the Jewish immigrants to that country as furtive ghetto waifs and gutter residents, and threats to white European womanhood: "They make way for none, and even European women must on occasions step into the gutters so that the serene progress of the disciples of Zion may be undisturbed."[15]

Such rhetoric, though by no means unique, was not typical of the mainstream of British society, which had a considerable investment in an image of racial tolerance. As Elaine Smith demonstrates, in the 1920s anti-Semitism often surfaced in the guise of the more acceptable antialienism.[16] During the decade after the First World War, a number of antialien measures which emanated from Parliament, the London County Council, and the borough councils chipped away at the rights of English Jews. The Aliens Act of 1919 made it possible to deport alien Jews at will. Housing, employment, and education discrimination affected British-born children of nonnaturalized Jews as well as their parents.

In this period, Jews in most other European countries suffered from pogroms and extremes of persecution. By contrast, in England from the turn of the century to the 1920s, except for some incidents of violence by the new and growing fascist groups in the East End of London, few Jews were physically harmed. Most historians credit England's tolerant liberal tradition for this difference. We have already discussed the pressure placed on the Jewish community to conform to bourgeois English standards imposed by the "antisemitism of tolerance." In his article "The British and the Shoah," Tony Kushner shares this view and explores the British liberal ideology which prohibits overt acts of violent persecution against minority groups but leaves members of these groups in a double bind, "urged to assimilate but at the same time denied free access to the resources of society through discrimination."[17]

The 1930s

The small, openly fascist and anti-Semitic groups who, in the years between the World Wars, met, held rallies and marches, and published widely are variously described by historians who have studied the phenomenon, including Gisela Lebzelter, Richard Griffiths, Colin Holmes, and Richard Thurlow, as "fringe," "marginal," "minority," or "extremist" groups, which never gained mass appeal and which were, to use Richard Griffiths's phrase, for the most part "detached" at the time of the war itself.[18]

Historians and other commentators often mention another strain of anti-Semitism, more often espoused by middle- and upper-class British in contrast to the not exclusively but predominantly working- class membership of the fringe groups (whose leadership, however, often came from the upper or middle classes.) These nonaffiliated anti-Semites are variously called "parlour anti-semites" (Griffiths), nonviolent anti-Semites (Lebzelter), "innocent anti-semites" (Orwell), and those who harbored "queasy, resentful feelings about Jews" (Lionel Trilling).[19] Similarly, the critic George Watson distinguishes between the more blameworthy racialists and those he calls "culturalists," who opposed Jews for "rational" or cultural reasons.[20]

Another kind of polarity often cited is between those who expounded their views before learning of the full extent of the persecutions and later of the Holocaust and those few, like Ezra Pound, who continued to do so even in the face of this knowledge. Gertrude Himmelfarb, in her defense of John Buchan, an adventure writer of the turn of the century, demonstrates a rather extreme version of such chronological polarization:

> [T]his kind of anti-Semitism, indulged in at that time and place, was both too common and too passive to be scandalous. Men were normally anti-Semitic, unless by some quirk of temperament or ideology they happened to be philo-Semitic. . . . It was only later, when social impediments became fatal disabilities, when anti-Semitism ceased to be the prerogative of English gentlemen and became the business of politicians or demagogues, that sensitive men were shamed into silence. It was Hitler . . . who put an end to the casual innocent anti-Semitism of the clubman.[21]

As T. S. Eliot is said to have put it, with some regret, the worst thing about Hitler was that "he made an intelligent anti-semitism impossible for a generation."[22] Once Hitler had given anti-Semitism a bad name, it became increasingly necessary for commentators and authors themselves to create a polarization between Us (the innocent non-anti-Semites) and Them (the guilty anti-Semites). Where and when this line was drawn, however, varied greatly. In 1948 George Orwell, himself no lover of the Jews in his early writing, labeled a letter accusing T. S. Eliot of anti-Semitism nonsense and distinguished between Eliot's (and incidentally his own) "innocent" prewar anti-Semitism, and the later virulent variety: "Of course you can find what would now be called antisemitic remarks in his early work but who didn't say such things at the time? One has to draw a distinction between what was said before and what after 1934."[23] Other authors and commentators, less percipient than Orwell, placed the dividing line at 1939, the date of Britain's entry into the war, while still others argued that such remarks must be judged "innocent" until their author could be shown to have indisputable knowledge of the existence of the concentration camps.

In fact, if one resists such binary divisions, the attitudes toward Jews held by the so-called fringe elements, the more mainstream "parlour anti-Semites," members of the government and its branches, and the greater public (as revealed by Mass Observation Polls during the period immediately before the war) reveal far more continuity than polarity. This view is shared by a group of historians and cultural critics including Bryan Cheyette, Bill Williams, David Cesarini, and Tony Kushner, each of whom has questioned the division between margin and center. As Kushner puts it, such a division "served to emphasize the decency and tolerance of the rest of British society" ("Shoah," 5). Cheyette agrees and argues that the polarization allowed for a dismissal of the centrality of British anti-Semitism:

> Part of the problem for students of British antisemitism is that it has been deemed political only in so far as it resembles the genocidal model of German national socialism. By comparison with the German experience, Jewish stereotyping in Britain has been depoliticized and labelled as a private or "social" phenomenon which is characterized above all as an "unsystematic, non-theoretical, and casual" prejudice. ("Jewish Stereotyping," 12)

It is essential to refuse such a polarization while examining the various so-called fringe groups, which included, in the early and late 1930s, Arnold Lees's Imperial Fascist League, the British Fascists, the Imperial Fascist League, the Nordic League, the Right Club, the Military Christian Patriots, the Link, the January Club, and the best-known of them, Mosley's British Union of Fascists or BUF. The "fringe" groups themselves differed in that some identified themselves with Mussolini's fascism, others with Hitler's, and still others claimed to have discovered a unique English variety of fascism; but all were anti-Semitic to some degree. Most of the earlier groups shared a hatred for Germans and Jews alike. The right-wing paper, *The Patriot*, for example, was both strongly anti-German and anti-Jewish until 1936. At that point, as Lebzelter puts it, "When anti-Semitism superseded anti-German agitation after the war, it was simply argued that Germany, too, was Jew-ridden, and both England and Germany victims of the Jewish yoke" (16).

After World War I and the Russian Revolution, the belief in an international Jewish Marxist conspiracy (often also linked, as in the *Protocols*, to the Masons) was central. Typically, Nesta Webster, an upper-class right-winger and one of the few women whose wealth gave her the power to publicize her views, referred to Jewish agitators as "the tsetse fly carrying the poison germ of Bolshevism from the breeding ground of Germany."[24] John Wolf's popular *Nazi Germany* linked the Jew with Marxism, the destruction of German society, and sexual offenses.

> [F]ollowing a sinister impulse of the blood, he strives after world domination and the means of achieving this is the destruction of the so-called Christian European culture.... A time will come when the world will express its gratitude to Hitler for having checked the downfall of the Western lands.[25]

The only group which attracted a mass following, Oswald Mosley's British Union of Fascists, orchestrated physical attacks on Jews in East London and violence on a grander scale at such famous events as the Olympia Rally of June 1934. While the BUF originally declared itself free of anti-Semitism, Jew-hatred became an important principle of the organization as it increasingly modeled itself on its German prototype.

As Kushner notes, the BUF contributed in an extreme form to the already central discourse which maintained that the Second World War, like all other wars, was a plan by and for the benefit of world Jewry: "The Jews' War," as it was called in BUF propaganda.[26] Such opinions were not limited to extreme fascists like Webster and Wolf. The right-wing but respectable Hilaire Belloc, with G. K. Chesterton and later the far more virulent anti-Semite A. K. Chesterton, spoke for the so-called Chester-Belloc group of the Edwardian years, a well-regarded circle of nostalgic Catholics who looked back to a preindustrial, medieval world as yet unspoiled by the scheming Jewish financiers, the "hidden hand" behind the corruption of the day. Belloc wrote in *G. K's Weekly* in August 1936:

> Moscow is only a symbolic word for a group of men which is cosmopolitan and largely Jewish, with the Jewish intensity of purpose... the Jewish ability to act in secret, the Jewish indifference to property and national ideals, the fierce Jewish sense of Justice, and above all the Jewish tenacity.[27]

In every realm, "fringe" and mainstream formed a continuity rather than a division. Right-wing authors, including Alexander Ratcliffe, John Hooper Harvey, and Douglass Reed, moved easily between "dogmatic" anti-Semitic propaganda and best-selling popular writing.

It is also important to remember that these attitudes were not limited to the right. Kushner's analysis of Mass Observation material reveals that the fear of international Jewish finance, which persisted, against all logic, even after news of the Holocaust was made public, was particularly strong among respondents on the left.

As we will see, members of the Chamberlain and Churchill governments were in no way immune from these central beliefs. Winston Churchill, who stood out during the war for his unwavering and often lonely defense of the Jewish cause, had written in 1918 to Lloyd George, "There is a point about Jews—you must not have too many of them,"[28] and had joined wholeheartedly in the attack against Jewish-Bolshevism after 1918. Lord Londonderry, secretary of state for air from 1931–35, sounded a familiar note in his letter to the German ambassador to England, Joachim von Ribbentrop, in 1936: "I have no great affection for the Jews. It is possible to trace their participation in most of those international disturbances which have created so much havoc in different countries."[29]

Members of the government and of the public who shared these attitudes always shared a common perception of their own lack of anti-Semitism. In a recapitulation of Cheyette's "antisemitism of tolerance," typical Mass Observation respondents differentiated between assimilated British Jews, to whom they did not object, and those Jews they identified as foreign, or "foreign acting," whom they blamed for all the "trouble." Such distinctions were elucidated in attempts to prove the respondents' lack of anti-Semitism. As the war continued and the news of the fate of the Jews became public, most people felt that Hitler had gone too far. However, they continued to believe that Jews caused anti-Semitism themselves through their own behavior and that ultimately it lay with them to end it.[30] Kushner concludes his survey of the Mass Observation polls by noting "an unshakeable conviction that antisemitism had been well-earned by the Jews" through their exclusiveness and refusal to assimilate, their greed, and their need to take control of culture, institutions, and finance ("Shoah," 12). There may be a difference of degree between this belief and the "fringe" belief in an international conspiracy, but the line of demarcation is a wavering one indeed.

Despite the centrality of anti-Semitism on the left and right, it is also important to remember that, throughout this period, a strong leftist coalition of workers and intellectuals, including many Jews, maintained an antiracist stance. When the Kristallnacht Pogrom of 1938 was reported in the media, there were widespread denunciations from the British press and public, though these were relatively short-lived. United Front actions against fascism drew consistently large audiences, and the strength of the anitfascist movement was evident in the Battle of Cable Street in October 1936, when a coalition of Jewish, leftist, and labor forces collected seventy-seven thousand signatures against fascism and anti-Semitism and blocked Mosley's demonstration. The East-End–based Jewish People's Council against Anti-Semitism and Fascism (the JPC) was the strongest of a number of Jewish organizations which linked protection of the local Jewish community with the international fight against fascism. The JPC, which had a working-class, leftist base, organized mass meetings, agitated aggressively against racial incitement, and countered Blackshirt political organizing. It cooperated with non-Jewish antifascist bodies and organized a joint conference against fascism with the National Council for Civil Liberties in 1937. The JPC and its principles were denounced by the Board of Deputies, who, through their paper, the Jewish Chronicle, urged Jews to stay home and refrain from such antifascist action as the Battle of Cable Street.[31] To give credit where it is due, the Board of Deputies, along with other representatives from the wealthy, established Anglo-Jewish community, did make a pledge to bear the total financial burden for Jewish immigrants from Germany. "This essential foundation for the Government's willingness to permit substantial immigration from Germany until outbreak of the war"[32] allowed the government to maintain its image as a body friendly to the Jews. A Cabinet meeting's minutes record a discussion of the benefit of securing for Britain "prominent Jews who were being expelled from Germany." Not only would these Jews have something to contribute, but the action "would also create a very favourable impression in the world, particularly if our hospitality were offered with some warmth" (Wasserstein, "The British Government," 68).

In fact, the favorable impression would be gained on borrowed credit. Apart from not restricting Jewish immigration before 1939, the government did not implement any kind of rescue effort and made no financial contribution to immigrant needs. Private individuals and organizations were responsible for rescuing the large number of Jews who managed to escape to England before the war, and the Jewish organizations covered the expense. While some organizations like the British Medical Association opposed the entry of more than a small number of refugee doctors, others, like the Academic Assistance Council, welcomed many Jewish scholars into England. Other private citizens and charitable organizations like *Care For Children*, which took ten thousand children in 1938, contributed to the rescue of great numbers.

While, as I have demonstrated above, anti-Semitism was much more pervasive than is usually assumed, what Wyndham Lewis contemptuously referred to as the "Left Wing Orthodoxy" of writers and intellectuals certainly existed at least to some extent at this period, and, especially before the war, was responsible for the sparing of considerable numbers of Jewish lives.

Writers and Jews in the 1930s

Chroniclers of the literary thirties have offered a number of reasons to explain the relative uninvolvement of the writers and intellectuals of the 1930s when it came to the fate of the Jews of Europe. All seem to agree that the Spanish Civil War had a key impact on the emotional and political lives of young intellectuals and that it also played a central role in their subsequent disillusionment and withdrawal from political involvement.[33] The participation of many writers and intellectuals in antifascist organization around the Spanish Civil War may have led to what most commentators feel is a somewhat erroneous definition of the thirties as a "red" era for writers. The *Left Review*'s survey of 1936, later made into a pamphlet, "Authors Take Sides on the Spanish War," came out with an outstanding majority on the side of the republicans. In fact, as Valentine Cunningham points out, many of the "for" answers were in fact equivocations which were interpreted by the leftist authors, Stephen Spender and W. H. Auden, as being "against Franco and Fascism" (Cunningham, 438–39). Cunningham writes: "[T]he journey to Spain, which was supposed to accelerate the doubting leftist author into commitment and action, to seal him into the public mode, the public arena, ended by returning him sooner . . . or later . . . to the personal, the inactive, the uncommitted or differently committed" (460). Many, like Virginia Woolf's nephew, Julian Bell, were killed in Spain. George Orwell was forced to question his conviction of the possibility of a clear- cut struggle of good against evil, a movement of the people's socialism against a fascist dictatorship. His disillusionment with the Left caused an aversion to communism which almost equaled his aversion to fascism. Others reacted in the manner of French writer Simone Weil, whose experience of the dehumanization of war convinced her anew that there could be no such thing as a just war.

The horror and disgust against war, established by the devastating experience of the First World War and reinforced by the experience of Spain, moved intellectuals such as Weil to embrace pacifism and to pledge to avoid war at all costs. Thus the same writers and intellectuals who were the most profoundly antifascist and who might have been counted on to mount an early protest against government indifference to the fate of the Jews were also those who advocated an appeasement policy with Germany. Although this was not its aim, the policy they advocated of nonintervention in "domestic" affairs included perforce Germany's right to dispose of its Jews as it saw fit. It is, however, important to make the distinction between government appeasers and pacifists such as Weil, Maude Royden, Mary Sheepshanks, Shera Simon, Dr. Hilda Clark, and Virginia Woolf, whose philosophies were grounded in deep opposition to the Nazis' racist and dehumanizing values and whose mission was to stop Hitler through peaceful strategies rather than to accommodate to him. Most of these renounced their pacifism and entered into the war effort around 1938. They were also instrumental in private efforts to denounce Nazism and to rescue European Jews—attempts which had no influence on government policy. When Maude Royden renounced her world-famous pacifism in 1939, for example, it was because "she could not bear what Hitler was doing to the Jews." As she put it, "there had come into the world something worse than war."[34] Like Royden's, Orwell's and Weil's convictions that war must be prevented at all costs were relatively short-lived. Both eventually took a strong stand against Hitler, and Weil publicly stated that she had been tardy in abandoning her pacifism (Oldfield, 82).

Perhaps even more than the Spanish Civil War, the Nazi-Soviet Pact of August 1939 led to a widespread withdrawal from politics and a feeling of personal impotence, a "movement from active anti-fascism" at a time when active vigilance and a determination to put one's body on the line might have made a difference (Watson, 60). In the words of Cecil Day Lewis, "Spain was a death to us, Munich a mourning."[35] For many, the fight against anti-Semitism had become identified with the Communist party which, especially in London, had effectively organized against the BUF and on behalf of British Jews. After the Nazi-Soviet pact, when communism had lost its appeal, this association too worked against the Jews.

David Daiches maintains that the progressive earlier thirties, dominated by a group of young, largely gay, male writers, including W. H. Auden, Christopher Isherwood, Stephen Spender, Louis MacNeice, and Cecil Day Lewis, deteriorated into the increasingly conservative decade of the forties. He asks, rhetorically, "Who . . . foresaw that an avant-garde that was agnostic and left wing would soon give way to one that was right wing and religious?" (12). Stephen Spender points out in retrospect that these young men remained under the shadow of the older generation, whose most revered spokesperson was T. S. Eliot. We have already noted Eliot's regret at the impossibility of intelligent anti-Semitism after the war, and his distaste for Jews is well documented. Eliot, who flirted with the fascistic and anti-Semitic French movement Action Française, advocated a rural, Christian society, run by an elite of theological intellectuals like himself—this "roughly at the time when Hitler's troops were marching into Poland" (Eagleton, *Literary Theory*, 40).

Other literary forefathers included the Chester-Belloc group of writers and the more extreme Ezra Pound, whose anti-Semitism was linked to his misogyny and was shared by those in his imagist movement.[36] Pound believed that "[p]oetry had . . . become a mawkish, womanly affair . . . language had gone soft and lost its virility," thus rendering it unequal to the task of fighting the Jewish conspiracy. Eagleton recounts Pound's hope and belief that "middle class liberalism was finished and would be ousted by some version of that tougher masculine discipline which Pound was to discover in fascism" (Eagleton, *Literary Theory*, 41, 42). As Eagleton and Judith Ruderman also point out, D. H. Lawrence, regarded by many of the writers of the thirties as an inspirational representative of freedom and working-class progressiveness, shared Pound's sexism, racism, and anti-Semitism.[37] The centrality of this anti-Semitic discourse among "the older generation" of literary forefathers becomes clear when one notes that Yeats, Shaw, Wells, Arnold Bennett, and Rudyard Kipling each at one time recorded their own less virulent beliefs in the international Jewish conspiracy.

Forefathers and foremothers were of course not all right-wing anti-Semites. Younger leftist writers could look to the Woolfs; to E. M. Forster, who, while no longer writing fiction, was still active against fascism and spoke out strongly against anti-Semitism; and to James Joyce, whose portrait of Leopold Bloom in *Ulysses* is generally regarded as a milestone in the representation of Jewish characters. Spender, Graham Greene, Harold Nicolson, and George Orwell consistently fought fascism and anti-Semitism. The Left Book Club, started in 1936, took a consistent stand against fascism and anti-Semitism in its publications, and its outreach was seen by many within and without literary circles as the center of Britain's attempts at a united front against fascism.

But as we have already noted, a position on the left of the political line did not always serve as an indicator of authorial attitudes toward Jews. Aldous Huxley, a leftist member of the Peace Pledge Union, gave a surprisingly equivocal answer when asked by Jacob Zeitlin to make a public statement about Nazi atrocities in 1938:

> It is better not to do these things. . . . Expressions of generalized opinions, outbursts of indignation and the like don't seem to me to fulfill any very useful purpose . . . one is merely indulging in and permitting others to indulge in the pleasures . . . of using intemperate language. . . . The persecution of the Jews in Germany is horrible in the extreme; but it is not by proclaiming the fact in a loud voice that this particular persecution will be stopped . . . [it] is immensely old . . . and bound up with habit of thought, feeling, action, and belief[.][38]

Some writers, from both left and right, including Isherwood, Auden, Huxley, and Wyndham Lewis, emigrated to the United States or Canada when war was declared. The majority of those who remained, like the majority of the British people, actively supported the war against Hitler and vocally condemned his treatment of the Jews. However, like the rest of the population, they were either unaware of, or did not consider questioning, the government's immigration policy.

Once the war began, overt anti-Semitism became unacceptable among almost all writers. Wyndham Lewis and Ezra Pound, who transgressed this code, were at least temporarily ostracized. George Orwell, who made a conscious though not always successful effort during the war to rid himself of his own anti-Semitism, comments in his essay "Notes on Nationalism" in 1945:

> There is little evidence about this at present, because the Nazi persecutions have made it necessary for any thinking person to side with the Jews against their oppressors. Anyone educated enough to have heard the word "anti-semitism" claims as a matter of course to be free of it, and anti-Jewish remarks are carefully eliminated from all classes of literature. Actually, anti-semitism appears to be widespread, even among intellectuals, and the general conspiracy of silence probably helps to exacerbate it.[39]

Orwell notes that if conservatives, neo-Tories, and political Catholics are the worst offenders, "people of Left opinion are not immune to it" either ("Nationalism," 92). Nor, it seems, were writers. No caucus of writers organized to push the government to bomb Auschwitz; no petitions by writers were got up to challenge the immigration laws; and war writers who worked for the Ministry of Information accepted the news blackout and refusal to name the Jews. The conspiracy of silence seems to have embraced politicians and writers alike.

Sander Gilman urges us "to look for links which illuminate the interdependence of systems of stereotypical representation." I have mentioned the link between anti-Semitism and misogyny in the work of Pound and Lawrence, and we will meet it again in the work of the three writers featured in this study. Here it is enough to note, as does Valentine Cunningham: "Misogyny was rife in the writing of this period . . . even the determinedly womanizing and married found it hard to steer their texts clear of the prevailing hostility to women and marriage" (152–53). With the exception of Virginia Woolf and (in an occasional passing reference) Katherine Mansfield, the various surveys of writers of the thirties are conspicuously silent about women writers. Cunningham, who is as guilty as any of them of this omission, notes: "As for women, they frequently count for little in the Old Boy world of the all-male school and college . . . when in 1939, Auden and Isherwood drew up . . . a list of the ten most promising British writers of the day, they included no women at all" (151).

1939–1945: Response to the Nazi Atrocities— Disbelief and Denial

The prominent English historian A. J. P. Taylor records an event of 1938:

> After the incorporation of Austria into Germany, Sigmund Freud, founder of psychoanalysis, was admitted into England with none of the usual formalities, and, against all the rules, was made a British citizen the next day.[40]

In the same paragraph, Taylor tells us definitively, "Nazi treatment of the Jews did more than anything else to turn English moral feeling against Germany, and this moral feeling in turn made English people less reluctant to go to war" (20).

Taylor's phrase "the usual formalities" indicates that the welcome was less warm for less illustrious refugees, but nowhere in his book on this period does he mention that in 1939, when England entered the war, these "usual formalities" became a solid wall. Regardless of the English "moral feeling" about Hitler's treatment of the Jews, they were left to perish rather than gain entry to Britain or any of its territories. The picture Taylor and other mainstream historians of the period paint corresponds to the child's version of history with which I started this chapter. In this reading, the British people's brave battle against Nazism was a battle for the survival of the Jews. In biographies and reminiscences, others recall the period and the British attitude toward the Jews through the same rose-colored spectacles. For instance, in his book *The Thirties and After*, Stephen Spender explains how the leftist resistance to authority during the late twenties and early thirties yielded, during the war, to a state of unified grace: "a sense of belonging to a community where all classes were drawn together in sympathy. England was holy, so was France, so were the Jewish people in concentration camps."[41]

As we have noted, the BUF used the term "The Jews' War" to signal that the war had been designed as a money-making prospect by the Jews themselves. A corollary construction was the denial that Jews suffered at German hands in any special way. Early revisionists dismissed all reports of Jewish oppression as "sob stuff" and expended considerable energy in disseminating the denial. The familiar image of the evil and grotesquely comic Jew, gesticulating and complaining in a hysterical "female" manner rather than taking his knocks with a stiff upper lip like a proper British male, was manipulated in texts such as George Bolitho's *The Other Germany* (1943) to deny the reality of Jewish slaughter: "The Jews are brilliant propagandists. . . . The Jews wail more loudly than any other oppressed people. So we hear their voices first."[42]

Bolitho's book is a product of the far right, but his construction and even his vocabulary was shared by Prime Minister Chamberlain and by high officials in the Foreign and Colonial Offices and in the Ministry of Information. A typical Foreign Office minute by A. R. Dews, head of the Southern Department of the Foreign Office, noted, in 1944: "In my opinion a disproportionate amount of the time of this office is wasted in dealing with these wailing Jews."[43]

As Bernard Wasserstein, Walter Lacqueur, and Monty Noam Penkower all prove indisputably in their books, the government received clear, well-documented reports of Hitler's intentions toward, discrimination against, and finally wholesale extermination of the Jews of Europe beginning with his ascent to power in 1933.[44] These reports came from countless eyewitness accounts, from the reports of neutral diplomats and governments, from mail sent from occupied territories, from innumerable British intelligence agents, and from the British ambassadors to Berlin. As Walter Lacqueur stresses, "Nazi Germany was not a hermetically closed society . . . despite secrecy and disinformation the 'final solution' was an open secret almost right from the beginning" (3). The British (and the American) governments steadfastly chose not to believe this evidence and ignored and suppressed it.

One example of this pattern occurred in August of 1942, when Dr. Gerhart Riegner of the World Jewish Congress gave what was by then a familiar report. He had proof that the recent murder by the German government of more than 700,000 Polish Jews was part of a larger plan; all the remaining Jews in Nazi Europe were to be deported and exterminated. Frank Roberts of the Foreign Office, who had heard from a colleague months earlier of the disappearance of one and a half million Jews, reacted to this report by claiming "naturally we have no information bearing on this story" (Lacqueur, 79). Ever mindful of the Office's image, he added, "I don't see how we can hold up this message much longer, although I fear it may provoke embarrassing repercussions."[45]

One reason for the widespread disbelief of those in Chamberlain's conservative government was that many of these reports came from Jews. Attempting to suppress a rather innocuous white paper, Under Secretary of State Alexander Cadogan pointed out that the British consuls in Germany had derived most of their information from "persecuted Jews, who are not, perhaps, entirely reliable witnesses."[46] Reginald Leeper of the Foreign Office agreed. "As a general rule, Jews are inclined to magnify their persecutions."[47] Even as late as 1945, an official of the Refugee Department of the Foreign Office could write: "Sources of information are nearly always Jewish whose accounts are only sometimes reliable and not seldom highly coloured. One notable tendency in Jewish reports on this problem is to exaggerate the number of deportations and deaths."[48]

This denial pervaded the government and civil service. It was also valorized by the media and incorporated into public opinion. Leading journalists of the day, including Beverly Nicols, Douglass Reed, and George Price-Ward, all expressed doubt and disbelief about the accuracy of the atrocity stories. Even the *Manchester Guardian*, the newspaper which consistently showed the most sympathy for the Jews, in August 1941 denied reports of mass extermination in Europe, claiming that "the deportation of Jews to Poland means that Jewish muscles are needed for the German war effort" (Lacqueur, 75). Socialists on *Peace News* and even members of the Council of Christians and Jews, a group formed in March 1942 specifically in sympathy with the Jewish plight, all concurred in this disbelief. The conservative Catholic press was especially dubious, with the *Catholic Herald* warning its readers "to avoid swallowing wholesale the current reports of anti-Jewish persecutions."[49] Kushner demonstrates the widespread public denial, typified by one Mass Observation respondent who wrote, when reminded in 1940 of the plight of the Jews, "Must you? . . . One had almost forgotten them" ("Shoah," 9).

On the part of the government, denial was accompanied by a virtual black-out of any reference to Jews in war propaganda. The term "German nationals" or some other euphemism was always used instead of "Jews." "Jewish persecution" and "atrocity stories" were both on a Ministry of Information list of undesirable themes for British propaganda purposes. A Ministry of Information memorandum in July 1941 stated that atrocity propaganda "must deal with undisputably innocent people. Not with violent political opponents. And not with Jews."[50] Among the various explanations for this policy were that to acknowledge the Jews as a separate group would be to "give in to" German racialism; that "awarding protective status to all endangered Jews would overlook very extensive Third Reich brutality above all in Poland, against non-Jews," and that any mention of atrocities inflicted on Jews would be counterproductive (that is, would reverberate with the British people's own anti-Semitism, stirring up public sympathy for the Germans, rather than disapproval).[51] Lacqueur notes, "Anti-semitism figured throughout 1940 and 1941 in almost every issue of the 'Home Intelligence Weekly Report' " (92).

While public anti-Semitism certainly existed, it seemed to be much less virulent than that of the government officials themselves. The rabid anti-Semitism which was believed to lie just below the surface, and which was probably a projection of their own feelings, was used to justify the total closed-door policy of the government toward Jews. Kushner explains:

> Herbert Morrison, the Home Secretary, was particularly anxious not to make manifest what he regarded as dangerous latent antisemitism in Britain.

> This philosophy, which indirectly blamed Jews for the creation of antisemitism, was also used as a reason for refusing asylum to Jews escaping from Nazi Europe . . . by putting the state on the defensive so that its priority was to appease antisemitic sentiment, British fascists partially achieved their anti-Jewish objectives. ("Paradox," 86)

The government policy of refusing to "name" the Jews as special targets of the Nazis also served such objectives. As long as Jews were not specifically named, the British government could pursue its closed-door policy, refusing all plans for rescuing the Jews by removing them to Palestine or other British territories—this while retaining its good name as a friend and rescuer of the Jews.

The image of a line separating "parlour" and "fringe" anti-Semites is especially deceptive when considering governmental policies. The conservative upper- and upper–middle-class English clubmen who tended to be "parlour anti-Semites" were also heads of government and of the Civil Service, including the Foreign and Colonial Offices and the Ministry of Information, three offices which were among the most culpable in the governmental collusion in the extermination of the Jews of Europe. Harold Nicolson's often-quoted quip of 1930, "Although I loathe antisemitism, I do dislike Jews," is unpleasant but not exactly frightening in the mouth of one who wielded relatively little power, and who, in any case, became one of the most active supporters of the Jews by 1939.[52] The attitude of the prime minister, Neville Chamberlain, in power during the years in which Britain was offered and rejected the chance to rescue the Jews of Europe, is more disturbing. Chamberlain, who was known for his dislike of the Jews, is quoted as saying, "No doubt Jews aren't a lovable people; I don't care about them myself" (Kushner, "Shoah," 7). According to a political reporter of the time, "Any questions put across the table about, say, reports of the persecution of the Jews, Hitler's broken pledges, or Mussolini's ambitions, would receive a response on well-established lines: he [Chamberlain] was surprised that such an experienced journalist was susceptible to Jewish Communist propaganda."[53]

Chamberlain's hostility toward the Jews was thus concretized in his policies. Denial and inaction characterized the policies of his appeasement government when it came to these unlovable people. Governmental spokespeople simultaneously denied the reports of atrocities and discrimination and indicated that these reports were indeed true but were none of Britain's business. A typical reaction was that of the Prince of Wales, who, in 1933, maintained that "It was no business of ours to interfere in German internal affairs whether re Jews or anything else."[54]

It is one thing to sit back passively and watch a people be exterminated and another to take active steps to insure that the atrocity be inevitable. Immediately after war was declared, despite the new prime minister's friendliness toward the Jews, such active steps were taken. As Wasserstein succinctly puts it:

> The British Government . . . found itself superseded by the Germans from 1941 onwards as the major agency preventing Jewish escape from Europe to Palestine. During the early part of the war, when the German Government openly tried to dispatch large numbers of Jews beyond the borders of the Reich, every practicable tactic was employed by the British Government to prevent significant numbers of Jews reaching Palestine (or indeed anywhere else in the Empire, including . . . Britain itself). . . . As the escape routes were sealed so too was the fate of the majority of the Jews imprisoned in Nazi Europe. (*Britain and the Jews*, 80)

Britain's relatively generous immigration policy before the war changed abruptly in 1939, when "the not inconsiderable expanse of the British Empire was found . . . to have an absorptive capacity of nil" when it came to the admission of Jewish refugees.[55] Between 1939 and mid-1941, expulsion of the Jews was one of Germany's central goals, changing to a policy of extermination only in October of 1941, when, for the first time, Jews were forbidden to leave the country. During this time, contrary to recent accusations that Zionists rejected other proffered havens in order to flood Palestine with Jews, Zionist and other Jewish groups sought refuge in Ethiopia, North Africa, or any country at all which might provide asylum. As new possibilities were suggested, the British government rejected each one remotely under its jurisdiction, citing the same vague fears of embarrassment and anti-Semitic uprisings among the local population. This policy was in striking contrast to Britain's immigration policy toward Yugoslavian, Greek, Dutch, and Belgian non-Jewish refugees, all of whom were welcomed into Britain without restriction.

The policy was actively, even vindictively, enforced. The British repeatedly fired on ships with refugees bound for Palestine, or sent them back to sure death. With the excuse that such action might hamper "security," they even sought to prevent an American charity from sending food to dying families marooned on one such ship. Conferences on "the refugee question" in 1938 at Evian and in Bermuda in 1943 provided "an agreeable setting for a lamentable succession of speeches in which delegate after delegate expressed sympathy for the plight of the refugees from the Reich and then proceeded to explain why it was impossible for his government to offer anything other than a token contribution" (Wasserstein, "British Government," 74).

When the Salvador, a refugee ship full of Bulgarian Jewish refugees was sunk with two hundred deaths, including seventy children, the head of the Foreign Office refugee section, T. M. Snow, commented: "There could have been no more opportune disaster from the point of view of stopping this traffic."[56] A memorandum from the Foreign Office in June 1940 stated: "Illegal immigration is not primarily a refugee movement. . . . The problem is an organized invasion of Palestine for political motives, which exploits the facts of the refugee problem and unscrupulously uses the humanitarian appeal of the latter to justify itself."[57] Another minute agreed: "[W]e simply cannot have any more people let into the United Kingdom on merely humanitarian grounds. . . . Furthermore, these particular refugees . . . are hardly war-refugees in the sense that they are in danger because they have fought against the Germans, but simply racial refugees."[58]

Notable in almost all these minutes is a reversal in which the victims become the oppressors and the officials themselves the victimized: a tendency we will encounter repeatedly in the literary texts addressed in chapters 4 through 6 of this study. These officials, in a bizarre and egocentric reading of the situation, seemed not to grasp that the refugees were people intent on saving their lives. Instead, subscribing to a personalized version of the Jewish conspiracy theory, they reasoned that the refugees acted as they did as part of a plot to humiliate or "embarrass" them (or their larger "body"— the British government). J. S. Bennet, one of the Colonial Office's Middle East experts, recapitulates the "sobbing and wailing" metaphor as well as his perception of himself and his colleagues as the real victims in his complaint in 1941 about the United States' censorious attitude toward the British treatment of the Jews: "The Jews have done nothing but add to our difficulties by propaganda and deeds since the war began . . . when coupled with unscrupulous Zionist 'sob-stuff' and misrepresentations, it is very hard to bear."[59]

Sir John Shuckburgh, the deputy under secretary at the Colonial Office, struck the same note of victimization in his remarks on the Jews of Palestine in 1940:

> I am convinced that in their hearts they hate us and have always hated us; they hate all Gentiles. . . . So little do they care for Great Britain as compared with Zionism that they cannot even keep their hands off illegal immigration, which they must realize is a very serious embarrassment to us at a time when we are fighting for our very existence.[60]

Officials in the Foreign Office, the Colonial Office, and the Ministry of Information took passive but lethal action congruent with their perceived role of oppressed victims. They regularly used delays, lies, and inaction to counter schemes by the new prime minister, Churchill, and others to provide aid to the Jews of Europe. The Foreign Office "lost" or withheld topographical material which Jewish organizations had donated to the Air Ministry for the bombing of Auschwitz and Treblinka, then ignored an instruction from the prime minister and the foreign secretary to plan and carry out the bombing of Auschwitz. While industrial plants and oil refineries as near as five miles from Auschwitz and the railway lines connecting these plants were repeatedly bombed in 1944, neither the railway lines to the camps nor the camps themselves were ever bombed, despite pleading from Jewish representatives. The deportations and gassings thus continued until the very end of the war (Penkower, 218).

Even after the war, with newsreels of Buchenwald and Belsen on every screen, the government maintained that Jews must be treated as nationals of existing states rather than as a separate group. Clement Atlee's Labour government continued the closed-door policy until British withdrawal from Palestine, continuing to intercept boatloads of refugees and return them to the same concentration camps they had come from and attempting to force the remnants of European Jewry to "return home" to Germany and Austria. An official film on the camps, produced in 1945, achieved the amazing feat of removing all references to Jews and to the Nazi extermination program (Kushner, "Shoah," 11).

It is difficult to judge just how aware the majority of the British people were of their government's closed-door immigration policy toward the Jews after 1939. What is clear is that the British public, while coping courageously with a war against both civilians and enlisted men and women, reacted in a far more generous and varied way to the fate of the

Jews than did their government. One Gallup poll taken in February 1943 on the question of admitting Jews threatened with death to Britain found 78 percent in favor—this in striking contrast with the government policy of total nonadmittance, which was not influenced by this poll. A public memo of 1943, which explained the closed-door policy in terms of embarrassment to the government in the case of "flooding" by alien Jews and a possible outbreak of British anti-Semitism, was greeted by considerable public outcry and demands to cut the red tape and allow the refugees in, demands which were again ignored. After a series of London *Daily Telegraph* stories in June 1942 revealed the slaughter of more than 100,000 Polish Jews, the use of gas vans, and the horrors of the Chelmno camp, and stated that it was the aim of the Nazis "to wipe the race from the European continent," the National Executive Committee of the Labour Party and the trade unions made resolutions condemning the Nazis, and a Labour delegation went to see Anthony Eden, the foreign secretary, in an attempt to get him to take a more active role in rescue efforts. Szmul Zygielbojm, the Jewish representative of the Polish National Council who had been the source of the *Telegraph* stories and who later committed suicide in despair at Allied refusal to help the Jews, and Jan Masaryk, another eyewitness, spoke at one of many big rallies at Caxton Hall, in London, where Zygielbojm reiterated that "[i]n Poland, a whole people is being exterminated in cold blood" (Lacqueur, 76). In 1943 the National Committee for Rescue from Nazi Terror was set up to publicize the fate of the Jews, and throughout the war many individuals, including Harold Nicolson, James Parkes, and Eleanor Rathbone, devoted themselves to the cause. While anti-Semitic incidents in London's East End rose during the war, so did the frequency with which people opened homes and purses to the refugees.

On the other hand, as we have noted, a considerable percentage of the population continued to blame the Jews for the Holocaust. H. G. Wells, one of the more influential holders of this opinion, when given an eyewitness account of the gas chambers, could only comment, "[T]here is room for very serious research into the question why antisemitism emerges in every country the Jews reside in."[61] The majority of Mass Observation respondents polled just after the Kristallnacht pogrom, throughout the war, and immediately after it agreed with Wells; while they found Hitler extreme, they felt, in the words of one respondent, that "the Jewish problem is created by the Jews themselves. . . . Nobody would interfere with Jews, not even Nazis, if they had not made themselves so conspicuous and hateful" (Kushner, "Shoah," 12).

Even this very guarded sympathy seemed to have been short-lived. Polls indicated sympathy for the Jews for about two years following the war, but when Zionists in Palestine killed two sergeants in 1947, there were widespread anti-Jewish riots in all major cities in England, and Mass Observation polls indicated that "people are no longer moved by the thought of Jewish suffering in concentration camps" (Kushner, "Shoah," 7, 12–13).

Cheyette suggests that the widely held liberal ideal of an English melting pot in which Jews must lose their particularity and become indistinguishable had as its most extreme consequence the fact that "during their darkest hour, Jews could be tragically regarded by Britain as either a non-distinct entity—merely nationals of existing states—or as adherents of Nazi racial categories ("Wells," 33). A Holocaust survivor who settled in England states the same theme more simply: "We. . . . were not supposed to embarrass people by saying a word" (Kushner, "Shoah," 13).

Conclusion

The nomenclature which defined the British as a tolerant society, placed the burden of assimilation on the Jews, and blamed any deviation from that tolerance on their own failure to carry out that task has indeed been sustaining. It has created a cover from under which the reality of the British collusion in the extermination of the Jews has only recently emerged.

Between 1939 and 1941, Hitler was willing and eager to expel the Jews from the Third Reich. The governments of Great Britain and the United States, while all the time professing their deep commitment to and sympathy for the refugees, shunned all offers from the Nazi government as efforts to "embarrass" them by unloading masses of unwanted alien Jews on them.[62] They shut their doors, and the Jews were killed. The level of denial, double-talk, and hypocrisy is remarkable. Just as Edward I expelled the early British Jews using the rhetoric of crusading Christian doctrine, the British government couched its actions against more modern Jews in virtuous conferences and rhetoric which condemned anti-Semitism. In both cases, the Jews were kept out of England, and England's collective hands remained clean. The English liberal ideology prevented overt violence against Jews in England but encouraged less open, more passive forms of prejudice which were in the end equally lethal. This liberal ideology also encourages a kind of historical complacency and an unwillingness to look beneath the surface. Accordingly, though the evidence of collaboration is there, neither England nor the United States ever bore the burden of blame or guilt that France and other collaborating countries assumed.

I have already mentioned the forces of projection which were at work in the Foreign Office's insistence that Jewish immigration to any country would cause a wave of violent anti-Semitism. This form of projection will appear again and again in the texts of the three authors I shall examine in this book. In evidence too will be the mythical Jew who appears so often in the memoranda and minutes of the Foreign Office—that Jew whose aim, more even than to preserve his own life, seems to be to "embarrass" and humiliate the victimized British official.

TWO

A Survey of the Surveys

In my introduction, I spoke of the experience I had as a young and naive Jewish reader of encountering with a feeling of internalized shame the Jews who peopled my favorite books. Ever since David Philipson's pioneering work *The Jew in English Fiction* (1901), critics have been doing what would have been so helpful to me at that time: taking that shame out of the closet and naming it. The work has been done inclusively and well, with each new critic building on the scholarship of the last. What has, to my knowledge, never been done and what I will make an attempt to do in this chapter, is to compare the major past studies of the representation of Jews in English literature and to address some of the questions they raise as critical works. Time and space limitations force me to limit my discussion to the books and articles I judged to be most central to the formation of the ongoing critical discourse. I have included other books, articles, and dissertations in my footnotes to this chapter.

Current literary theorists tend to assign all criticism published before the "New" Criticism of the late 1960s to some murky hinterland in which "general readers" or, at best, interpretive critics muddled along with nothing but an unreasoned and unreliable common sense to guide them on their way. As Raman Seldon, author of an especially knowledgeable and clear guide to contemporary literary theory, put it in 1985: "Critics talked comfortable good sense about the writer's personal experience, the social and historical background of the work . . . criticism spoke about literature without disturbing our picture of the world or of ourselves as readers."[1]

Such a dismissal rather condescendingly lumps together unlike critical texts, some of which may in fact, depending on who we are and what our assumptive picture of the world is, challenge us as readers and disturb our picture of the world. While the critical works I will discuss in the first part of this chapter examine virtually the same body of texts and tacitly accept many of the same theoretical assumptions, they do present different views of the relationship of text, writer, and reader and of the causes of anti-Semitism and the appropriate methods of fighting it. These differences lead in turn to strikingly different readings of the same texts.

In *The Company We Keep: An Ethics of Fiction*, Wayne Booth writes that until quite recently " '[e]veryone' assumed that such practice [the reading of fiction] had an effect on conduct . . . on the more enduring *habits of conduct* to which the word 'character' applies."[2]

Booth comments that "the great eighteenth century English novelists took for granted a close connection between reading and conduct" (233). The critics I will discuss in the main body of this chapter all shared that assumption and most built their critical arguments around it. However, some of them saw authors primarily as *agents*, whose role was directly or indirectly to influence the society around them, while others saw authors primarily as *reflectors*, whose role was to mirror the attitudes they found in that society.

Critics also interpreted texts differently according to their goals in undertaking the study, usually stated in the introduction to each book. While I noted these overt goals, I also tried to look for other, unstated, and often unconscious, underlying goals or purposes which seemed to me to be the alternative driving force behind each book. These critics, who are predominantly Jewish and who include several Jewish scholars and rabbis, share an overtly ethical goal: to protect and defend the reputation of their own, much maligned people.[3] Such a goal could be achieved by attempting to disprove (and sometimes to justify or excuse) the "arguments" or unjust stereotypes presented in the texts; or by directing the unsuspecting reader toward examples of anti-Semitism in the texts, thus performing the "naming" function I mentioned earlier and exposing the author in question. Through the latter operation, the "good" or philo-Semitic authors could be separated out from the "bad" or anti-Semitic ones, presumably allowing the reader to preselect his or her reading material accordingly.

The discourse and assumptions of each critic also differed according to whether the implied reader was a Jew or a Gentile. Presumably (though not necessarily) Jews were less in need of an argument refuting Jewish miserliness than Gentiles, but more in need of a naming and classification operation. In 1947, Milton Hindus identified this opposition in his discussion of the commonly experienced problem of how to deal with a much-admired or canonized author whose texts malign Jews:

> Since the liberation from the ghetto . . . anti-Semitism has been as omnipresent as germs in the air about us. . . . When it appears as an element, even a minor one, in the work of a writer whom we are bound to admire by all the canons of art, it has several possible effects. In the case of the Gentile reader, it either escapes his notice, or it confirms a notion he has already had of the Jews, or it may be noticed by him and rejected, or it may plant the seeds of a new suspicion within him. As for the Jewish reader, he either ignores it as unimportant in the sum of the entire work, or else his aesthetic enjoyment even of a master like Shakespeare is soured by this drop of vitriol.[4]

Another difference lay in the critics' models of historical progression. Some saw anti-Semitism in literature as an ongoing and unchanging motif; others saw it as one which was gradually disappearing. Still others saw it as one which was growing increasingly deadly with time. The particular texts each critic chose as well as the judgments he or she made of these texts were often determined by this difference.

The goal of understanding anti-Semitism and its causes through an examination of literature was also important to several of these critics, who hoped that such understanding would contribute to the eventual extinction of anti-Semitism. To this end some turned for their answers to biographical information about the authors and to other fields of inquiry such as sociology, psychology, economics, or history; while others stayed firmly with the text itself. An important activity among the latter group was that of classification. Avoiding the duality of positive and negative portraits, these critics grouped types of Jewish stereotypes or traits, in their effort to learn more about the dynamics at work.

In order to pinpoint some of these differences, I looked, whenever applicable, at how each critic approached two key figures in the debate: Shylock and Fagin. While several of the critics examined Jewish as well as Gentile authors, in keeping with the aim of my own study, I restricted my discussion to their reading of Gentile authors. I discuss these critics in a roughly chronological sequence but abandon that chronology in the case of critics whose work seems to me to be more closely related to that of critics of an earlier or later period.

The Surveys

In 1901, David Philipson's book *The Jew in English Fiction* appeared, the first published study of the representation of Jews in English fiction. Philipson's stated, rather surprising goal is to determine "whether or not it is legitimate to introduce Jews into works of fiction."[5] In response to his own question, Philipson reasons that as English Jews, "having stepped out of the ghetto into the free light and air" have lost their "peculiar customs" and become in their patriotism and habits, indeed in everything but their religion, exactly like their neighbors, it is *not* legitimate to introduce the Jewish character into fiction unless in the role of "follower and confessor of his religion, and this only by such as have made a long and exhaustive study of the same" (12, 17). The only author to have achieved this goal, according to Philipson, is George Eliot, in *Daniel Deronda*. All the others who wrote from 1590 to 1900, the period comprising Philipson's study, created in their Jewish characters "coarse loud individuals" who "speak a frightful jargon." As for these authors, "no worse enemy of the Jews exist[s]" (13–14). Philipson's underlying goal is to convince his assumed (presumably Gentile) readership that Jews are actually capable of behaving like normal people: that is, like any bourgeois English gentleman.[6]

Philipson's theory of agency, while not as central to his argument, is equally clear: it is bad books which incite crowds to bad action. The books he condemns "contain the insidious seed which sinks deeply and produces poisonous and noxious weeds" (14). Complaining of Barabas's description of himself and his people in Marlowe's *The Jew of Malta* (1592), he comments, "No wonder that a populace . . . should be goaded on to all excesses imaginable when they hear such words as these" (29).

In his discussion of texts, Philipson attempts to determine whether each presentation of a Jew is accurate (true) or not, using 'true' in the factual or literal sense. He explains that the tradition of Jewish usurers is a false one, as Christians were usurers too, and often more cruel than the Jewish ones. Christopher Marlowe's portrait of Barabas in *The Jew of Malta* (1592) is also a false one, because "no Jew ever employed his child for the purpose that Barabas is made to employ Abigail" (25). Philipson feels less comfortable rebutting some of the other charges levied against the Jews by the authors in his study. Perhaps, he admits, the newer immigrants *are* in fact loud, coarse, vulgar, uncultured, and generally objectionable, but then, so are the Irish, the French, and indeed, all those who had not had the civilizing advantage of long exposure to English culture or the great privilege of being born English. "Culture takes time," Philipson reminds us. "The children of the upstart will be more cultured and refined than he; his grandchildren still more so" (15–16). He urges us to generalize, if generalize we must, on the basis of the great old families of British Jewry, rather than from the uncouth newcomers. Philipson's goal of representing the Jew as cultured, patriotic, and exactly like his Gentile compatriots leads him into trouble with Shakespeare, "the myriad-minded dramatist, England's first genius" (7). As an Englishman, Philipson loves the bard, and yet he is troubled by *The Merchant of Venice*. After an uneasy defense of Shylock, he finally concludes that "the feelings of the poet . . . are with him [Shylock]" and adds wistfully, "It had all been well done had not this element of the pound of flesh been introduced; anything less atrocious (if the Jew, in deference to popular opinion, had to be defeated in the end) had served the purpose better, especially as it is so peculiarly un-Jewish" (47).

Fagin, on the other hand, is "a blot on the otherwise fair fame of the great fictionist" (95). However, Philipson asserts, Dickens *meant* no harm, and in *Our Mutual Friend* he balanced the score with Riah, "the most beautiful character of the whole novel" (97–98).

Philipson's theory of historical progression is closely connected to his underlying goal of convincing his readership of the Jews' rapid progress toward assimilation. English Jews, he complains, are rapidly advancing to the goal of becoming ordinary Englishmen. Why have Gentile authors failed to remark this advance? *The Jew in English Fiction*, pioneering when published, is now of interest largely in terms of the light it sheds on the strong pressure placed on the Jewish community to assimilate—or else. In it, Philipson, an Anglo-Jewish scholar and rabbi, textualized the enforcement of this dominant discourse on the larger Jewish community by its more assimilated leaders.

Rabbi Edward Calisch's *The Jew in English Literature as Author and Subject* (1909) offers a more spirited and less apologetic defense of the Jew, whom Calisch assured the reader "the world utterly misjudged and mistook."[7] More positive in his outlook than Philipson, who approves only of George Eliot, Calisch presents a nonetheless unevenly loaded scale. On one side are noble Jews such as Richard Cumberland's Sheva

(*The Jew*, 1794), Scott's Rebecca (*Ivanhoe*, 1819), and George Eliot's Mordecai and Daniel (*Daniel Deronda*, 1876). On the other side, Christopher Marlowe's Barabas (*The Jew of Malta*, 1592), William Shakespeare's Shylock (*The Merchant of Venice*, 1594), and Dickens's Fagin (*Oliver Twist*, 1838) join a host of lesser-known candidates. Calisch's stated goal is a defense of the Jew in the face of "a torrent of abuse and misrepresentation" (23). He sees the condition of English Jews in his own time as "among the happiest" and assures us that at last "the wonderful devotion of the Jews to their religion and their unflinching loyalty in the face of centuries of fearful persecution are being recognized" (23).

Calisch's study begins with early medieval ballads and plays, and he is the first to identify the New Testament as one of the earliest and by far the most influential piece of literature which attacked the Jews. He traces the early stories of ritual killings directly to their biblical source and to the influence of the church and the clergy.

Calisch includes histories in his survey and berates early historians Mathew Paris, John Speed, and Ralph Holinshed, who "narrate the unhappy tragedies that befell the Jews, without one trace of feeling for them" (20). Unlike Philipson, he objects strongly to Shylock, and in his discussion of *The Merchant of Venice* he attempts to prove that Shakespeare could have known no Jews personally and so must have based Shylock on a stereotype rather than on "reality." He especially objects to the revenge motif in the play, as "vengefulness and thirst for blood are not characteristic qualities of the Jews" (76). In a more contemporary argument, he demonstrates that Shylock functions not only as an individual but also as a representative Jew, and as such is associated with usury, cruelty, vindictiveness, and revenge. Shakespeare, he points out, painted many other Christian villains, "yet no reproach has ever come through them upon the Christian religions or Christian peoples" (76).

Despite this reservation, Calisch does not renounce Shakespeare entirely. In an early effort to grapple with the perennial question of whether or not a writer can escape the mores of his times, he suggests that Shakespeare's genius enabled him "to create a character nobler than he intended" (74).

Like Philipson, Calisch reproaches Dickens for creating Fagin, an act he calls a "monstrous wrong to the Jews." Unlike his predecessor he is not mollified by Riah, whom he calls "an unconvincing spineless saint [who]... does not offset Fagin in the least" (128). It is only by introducing Jewish authors into the debate that Calisch manages to balance the scales enough to retain his theory of rapid progress toward more positive representation.

A book by another member of the Anglo-Jewish intelligentsia, M. J. Landa's *The Jew in Drama* (1926), continues along much the same lines, although his pessimistic theory of progression and his tone of outrage represent a departure. To the modern reader, Landa's book is useful as an inclusive catalogue of every British play produced up to its date of publication that includes Jewish characters. Even more than his predecessors, Landa holds literature directly responsible for behavior. Shakespeare, in creating Shylock, "spread the plague of prejudice in all lands and climes," crystallizing medieval hatred of the Jews and giving "to the masses a weapon of easy persecution that will exist for all time."[8] In Fagin, "Charles Dickens . . . through sheer ignorance and thoughtlessness . . . saddled the stage with a wretched character whose evil influence appears to have been instantaneous" (166). According to Landa: "The cause of emancipation seemed to be proceeding normally, step by step. Then came check—with the appearance of Fagin—and it was not until 1858 . . . that a Jew was admitted into Parliament" (166).

Montagu Modder's *The Jew in the Literature of England: To the End of the 19th Century* (1939) is the most inclusive and ambitious study to date, but one of the most contradictory. Modder presents a conflicted text in which several of his arguments subvert one another. His aim, a somewhat startling one in view of the date of his writing, is to show that things are improving for the Jews. As he puts it in his introduction, "As a chapter in Jewish history this book inspires optimism."[9] He concludes the book on the same hopeful note, without mentioning current events: "No base tyranny can be perpetrated on the Jews with the old impunity. The pen is the sword of modern warfare, and it is the friend and champion of the Jew" (364).

Unlike the other critics we have discussed so far, Modder states his belief that the writer does not create reality but instead reflects it in a mirror image. Faced by unsavory images of Jews that are clearly *not* mirrors of reality, he solves the dilemma by suggesting that some writers may be liars, who purposefully distort rather than reflecting faithfully. Modder reasons that a "true" portrait, that is, one based on actual Jews, would be positive; therefore, negative, stereotypical portraits must be false. Like the other critics I have discussed so far, Modder does not consider the possibility of positive stereotypes: instead, all negative portraits are bad (lies) while positive ones are good (truth).

Modder agrees with Calisch that Shakespeare must have been "lying" when he created Shylock. He is not as willing, however, to renounce Dickens, who, he explains, *was* familiar with Jews, but, unfortunately, only with the wrong kind. This eagerness to recruit Dickens for the side of the angels leads Modder to cast aspersions on those critics who place him on the other side, classing them with his contemporary, the noted anti-Semite, Hilaire Belloc: "It is absurd . . . for critics like Hilaire Belloc . . . to say that Dickens dislikes Jews . . . and that, in creating Fagin he shows a prejudice unworthy of a humanitarian novelist. Dickens has no intention of maligning the Jewish people. He is merely describing a reprobate in the dens of London . . . who, it so happens, is of Jewish origin" (218).

As a way of exonerating him, Modder paraphrases without acknowledgment Dickens's famous defense of Fagin in answer to Mrs. Eliza Davis's complaint. Dickens himself wrote, "[I]t was unfortunately true of the time to which the story refers, that that class of criminal almost invariably *was* a Jew."[10] In Modder's version: "Unfortunately at the time to which the story refers, the class of criminals operating in the manner of Fagin was frequently composed of persons commonly designated as Jews" (217). Modder here lightens the effect of Dickens's "almost invariably" by changing it to "frequently" and softens the impact of "Jews" with the euphemistic "persons commonly designated as Jews," but otherwise repeats Dickens's own defense, which he quotes a few pages later, as a final proof of the author's innocence. Disregarding Dickens's rather confusing defense that Fagin "is called 'the Jew' not because of his religion but because of his race," Modder insists that the real proof that Dickens did not dislike Jews is that he claimed that he did not. Such a denial of the possibility of unconscious motivation, typical of Modder's literal approach to literature, was also a defense used by a far more sophisticated author and critic, T. S. Eliot, who, disregarding the evidence of his own texts, claimed that the proof of his lack of prejudice lay in his own assertion of it.[11]

In his discussion of Trollope's *Way We Live Now* (1875), Modder once more falls into the trap of distinguishing better from worse classes of

Jews. Melmotte, the evil financier, declares Modder, is not a stereotype after all but instead a "personification of the commercial corruption of the seventies," based on an actual financier of the times who just happened to be "the wrong kind of Jew" (276). In the previous chapter, I discussed the argument made by those, who, in an effort to defend themselves against the charge of anti-Semitism, distinguished between the "good" English Jews and the "bad" foreign ones, who provoked anti-Semitism by their behavior. It is disturbing to see these Jewish critics making the same distinction.[12]

To his credit, Modder was the first to move from simple naming or identification of prejudiced attitudes toward a system of classification of Jewish types or stereotypes. His list of types include the Wandering Jew, the Shylock type, the Jewess as Comely Daughter and Heroine, and the type of the Jewish Hero, exemplified by Disraeli's character Coningsby in his novel of the same name. Modder's effort to trace these types, however, is once more undermined by his concreteness and his need to demonstrate an upward progress "under the inspiration of the new humanitarian and evangelical movements" (353).

Hermann Sinsheimer's *Shylock: The History of a Character* was first published in England in 1947 but was originally written and suppressed in Hitler's Germany of 1936 and 1937. Sinsheimer traces Shylock through his historical incarnations of Wandering Jew, Judas, and usurer, but his study is mainly a close and careful examination of the text. The book is a passionate effort, by "a Jew who, having been born and brought up as a German and a Jew (not as a Jew and a German) but [who] was no longer . . . a German at heart" to cleave to the playwright he loves, and to acquit him of the charge of anti-Semitism.[13] Denigrating contemporary Nazi productions of the play in which Shylock was presented as a repulsive and bloodthirsty laughing-stock, Sinsheimer maintains that "Shakespeare must have realized that something was wrong with the treatment of the Jews. And . . . he took sides unequivocally with the oppressed and injured" (110).

Sinsheimer's arguments, like Modder's, occasionally oppose one another, as when he claims that the famous lawsuit actually should have been resolved in Shylock's favor, because "the warping of what is just and logical can never serve as a means of developmental progress in law"; or when he names Shylock "the spokesman of the bondsmen of medieval

Christianity" (100, 146). Sinsheimer's goal, an understandable one in the circumstances, is clear: "the anti-Semites must not be allowed to call Shakespeare as a witness for their side" (144).

While Sinsheimer's evidence, however shaky, is based on a close examination of the text, another book on Shylock, Bernard Grebanier's *Truth about Shylock* (1962), is not. Grebanier also defends Shakespeare, but on quite different grounds. Shylock's Jewishness is a coincidence, Grebanier explains, and those who see him as representative are merely indulging in typical Jewish oversensitivity. This is self-defeating and "too indulgent of the shortcomings of those who are Jewish . . . [O]ne could wish that everyone would be a little more objective." There are bad and good in all people, Grebanier continues; after all, "it has been said" that there were influential Jewish bankers who poured money into Hitler's coffers. Grebanier recommends avoiding the morass of Shakespearian commentary and "walking surefootedly among the lines Shakespeare has written," a task he seems convinced that he alone has achieved (18). Grebanier's arguments are invariably ill-founded and depend on sources outside the text, while his complaints about typical Jewish oversensitivity and self-indulgence sound the note we have heard in chapter 1 from the victimized "parlor" anti-Semites in England's wartime government. In one of his more unfortunate arguments, he explains that Shakespeare could not have been anti-Semitic; had he been, the Nazis would certainly have made more use of *The Merchant of Venice* for their propaganda, but "the Germans knew their Shakespeare too well to admit of such a use" (92).[14]

Rabbi Joshua Trachtenberg defines his book *The Devil and the Jews: The Medieval Conception of Jews and Its Relation to Modern Anti-semitism* (1943) as a broad cultural study rather than as literary criticism.[15] Trachtenberg does not divorce his present inquiry from the then ongoing extermination of the Jews of Europe, although he never directly names his concern, speaking instead in euphemistic terms of a time when "our culture and perhaps civilization itself are in jeopardy."[16] He admits to feeling guilty "to be caught rummaging in musty medieval texts" at such a time, especially as he is "under no illusion as to the immediate practical utility" of his investigation, but he justifies his study for its truth-telling qualities, and for its indirect relevance to contemporary concerns: "If the Jew is today despised and feared it is because we are heirs of the Middle

Ages . . . because the figure of the Demonic Jew, less than human, indeed antihuman, the creation of the medieval mind, still dominates the folk imagination" (viii).

Trachtenberg is more interested than his predecessors in exploring the causes of anti-Semitism. He identifies various theories of causation: xenophobia, social and economic frictions, the propaganda techniques of demagogues, and the human need for a scapegoat. In the end, however, he rejects these as "merely immediate stimuli of active Jew hatred," and identifies, not the literature itself, but the myth beneath the literature, as the key factor: "the powder keg of emotional predisposition" (3).

The concept of myth, as Trachtenberg uses it, is a new one among these critics and obviates the necessity for the kind of debate that all the critics I have examined so far engaged in: whether or not Shakespeare knew any Jews, whether or not the need for revenge was a Jewish trait, and whether Jews are family men who love their daughters or fiends who are likely to sell them off.

Trachtenberg, the first to argue that "hatred of the Jew is not the result of a rational process," was also the first to locate the source of literary representation in the unconscious as well as the conscious process of the writer. He locates the myth of the Jew in Jung's archetypal or "mass subconscious":

> the source of many a weird notion—of the horned Jew, of the Jewish thirst for Christian blood, of the Jew who scatters poison and disease broadcast, of the secret parliament of world Jewry, meeting periodically to scheme and plot, of a distinctive Jewish odor, of Jews practicing black magic and blighting their surroundings with the evil eye—notions that still prevail among the people and that have been advanced by official Nazi publications, for all the "scientific" verbiage of current antisemitism. (6)

We have already encountered some of these "notions" in chapter 1, advanced not by Nazis or British fascists but by the British government, the press, and members of the British public.

In his exploration of myth and his demonstration of the close link between the Jew and the devil in medieval poetry, plays, and drama, Trachtenberg convincingly demonstrates his theory that the Jew is a stand-in for "the mysterious, fearsome evil forces which. . . . have menaced the peace and security of mankind . . . his inherited dread" (47). Although he does not explore this subject at length, he also mentions sexual dread as part of the greater picture, as in texts and drawings in which the Jew was pictured with the horns and beard of the goat, a symbol of Satanic lechery.

Trachtenberg's decision in 1943 never to refer directly to the concentration camps or to mention the Jews as the target of Hitler's "bloodshed and tyranny," instead referring vaguely to a "world in turmoil" and to "modern, scientific anti-semitism," is reminiscent of the British government's refusal to name the Jews in its propaganda. Whether this avoidance was a misguided attempt to avoid German racialism, the result of a publisher's suggestion, or merely a personal and less conscious evasion is, as in the case of Modder's silence, unclear.

Edgar Rosenberg's *From Shylock to Svengali* (1960) is the most inclusive study to date on the subject of Jews in English literature. Rosenberg's close attention to texts, his intellectual scope, and his exhaustive research made his book one of the most useful that I consulted for this study. In addition, my reading of all the fictional texts to which he referred enabled me to establish the solid background I needed for my own research.

In his introduction, Rosenberg criticizes previous studies for a parochialism which related the portrayal of Jews in literature "either to a particular climate of opinion or to the private prejudice of the author."[17] Such direct correlations, in his opinion, are "apt to slight the massive durability of a stereotype, which is almost by definition the least pliable of literary sorts, the one least sensitive to social vibrations" (14).

Rosenberg's model of the relationship among author, text, and reader approaches Roman Jacobson's model, in which the author and reader of any text are related to one another as the sender and the receiver of a message that in turn depends on a shared code of communication.[18] As Rosenberg puts it, novelists do not necessarily reflect the attitude of contemporary society: "at most, they reflect the taste of the reading public, which is not quite the same thing" (14). He rejects the simple equation of a positive presentation of Jewish characters as desirable and a negative one as undesirable and explores the idea of a positive stereotype: "the depressingly uniform presentation of the Jewish paragon as a moralizing apologist, a tolerant and educated bore" (14).

Although he does not explicitly refer to the unconscious, Rosenberg dissociates himself from the long debate about whether or not a particular author was personally anti-Semitic and focuses on the text and what lies beneath its surface rather than on authorial statements of belief. He writes with admirable distinctness of the conflict about Dickens:

> I suspect that the gulf which separates Fagin from Dickens's public professions of tolerance defines the difference between metaphor and statement, creation and criticism, and that one of the defects endemic to earlier studies . . . lies in the general failure to distinguish the two. (17)

Finally, he frees himself from the exercise taken on so whole-heartedly by the other critics, both those who "would be happiest if all distinctions between Jews and other folk could be obscured or suppressed altogether" and those who attempted to right each wrong through rational argument: "In the long run the argument that 'Jews are not like that' confuses life and art, experience and literature; it ignores the possibility that a fiction may be all the more convincing and durable for being a basic distortion" (19).

Rosenberg's method, like Modder's earlier attempt, is primarily one of classification of types. In his model, these types do not fall into any kind of chronological progression, but rather come out of a kind of archetypal vein into which each succeeding generation taps. He chooses the types for "their recurrence from one writer to the next, their inexplicable resemblance, their sovereign position in literature and their final imperturbability and resistance to fashionable winds of doctrine and changes in weather" (11). He traces these types through a large number of works of fiction, as well as through a close analysis of six novels written between 1795 and 1895, examining each one first within a historical context and then in an in-depth focus on the particular treatment of Jewish characters.

For Rosenberg, Shylock and Fagin are relatives, two versions of a stable myth which "different generations do not so much reinterpret for themselves as they rehabilitate it" (187). He, like Calisch and Trachtenberg, points out that "the Jewish criminal in a variety of masks—as Christ-killer, traitor, financial hog . . . had Scriptural sanction from the first" (22). Chaucer's use of blood sacrifice and knife mutilation in "The Prioress's Tale" is thus not new, but rather a recapitulation of themes "current for some two and a half centuries before Chaucer fictionalized them" (25). This Jew-Villain type can be found in Herod, in Judas ("the original businessman with the contract in the pocket"), and in the anonymous Jew who forced a reed filled with vinegar between Christ's lips in answer to his "eli, eli." By the time Shakespeare got to it, "the type was fully constituted as he found it, and it had been for centuries" (33). Shakespeare's only addition to the myth is his combination of the two roles of mutilator and usurer: "The Jew's knife was now poised for purposes of extortion" (25).

Rosenberg's description of the characteristic Jew-Villain as he existed at the time of Scott is worth repeating here, as we will meet it again and again in my subsequent chapters:

> He was a fairly thoroughgoing materialist, a physical coward, an opportunist in money matters, a bit of a wizard in peddling his pharmaceutica; queer in his religious observances in so far as he still paid attention to them, clannish in his loyalties, secretive in his living habits, servile in his relations with Christians, whom he abominated; for physical signposts he had an outlandish nose, an unpleasant odor, and frequently a speech impediment also. . . . Though a widower, he had the comfort of an attractive daughter . . . he was bound to be defeated in all fundamental contests by the other party. His conversation was attended by much frenzied gesticulating, and when he did not have his way he resorted to a disgusting display of self-indulgence. His affections were unevenly divided between his ducats and his daughter. . . . He himself sat, spider-like, in the center of an impressive commercial network. Other animal metaphors which described him were the hog, the dog, the rat, the vulture, the weasel, the fox, the toad, the serpent, and the wasp. As a creature less sinned against than sinning, he hardly qualified for tragedy; on the other hand, his repulsive physiognomy, his eccentric habits, and his hostile motives conspired to suit him ideally for purposes of the comic and the horrific. (35–36)

For Rosenberg, Fagin, even more than Shylock, embodies the archetypal Jew-Villain type. Existing outside of society, outside even of Judaism itself, he murders indirectly, out of diabolical cupidity rather than revenge. His knife is raised against the innocent young boy, the mythological victim and the persona from whose traumatized and terrified eyes we see him. While he views Fagin as existing in opposition to society, he sees Melmotte, the upstart Jewish swindler of Trollope's *Way We Live Now* (1875), as an insider—a symbol of that society and its depravity.[19]

Rosenberg's chapter on George Du Maurier's *Trilby* (1894), "The Jew as Degenerate and Artist," is of special interest here because, as he points out, *Trilby* is one of the first books in English in which a Jewish male character is allowed sexuality. Svengali, a bestial and repulsive figure, seduces and virtually inhabits a pure English girl. "[T]he crime at the heart of the novel is not really one of occult sorcery but the specifically 'Jewish' crime to which the Germans have since given the name Rassenschande, the (legally punishable) mating of the inferior racial type with the higher" (256).

The book's final chapter, "What News on the Rialto," briefly brings the work up to date, pointing the way to more current authors whose Jews are drawn from the same vein of stereotype, and naming two authors, James Joyce and C. P. Snow, whom Rosenberg identifies as the only ones to have successfully escaped stereotyping in their representation of Jews. The appendices to *From Shylock to Svengali*, which include an excellent bibliography and several key historical letters and texts, are almost as invaluable as the book itself.

Harold Fisch, whose short book *The Dual Image* appeared in 1971, further explores the concept of the Jew as a dual image of good and evil, a projection of the basic and lasting Christian ambivalence toward the Jew as expressed in the Old and New Testaments. While Fisch covers no real new ground in his description of texts and spends some time at the old exercise of determining which representations are realistic or "true" Jews and which are not, he does make an effort to explore some of the psychology behind the myth of the Jew, an area which Rosenberg "prefers to leave to the psychiatrists." For Fisch, as for Trachtenberg, the Jewish character in recent literature is a "Jungian archetype issuing from the collective unconscious of modern man."[20] He also offers a new and intriguing explanation of one of the myths: the charge of blood guilt which appears over and over in the literature. Fisch points out that while Gentiles murdered hundreds of thousands of Jews because of their faith, there is no example on record of non-Jews being murdered by Jews for this reason.[21] In a significant passage, he explains the charge as "a simple example of guilt transference or substitution":

> The guilt one feels in one's own conscience . . . is transferred imaginatively to the victim who is made guilty of precisely the same crime. In this way the burden of guilt is diverted, while at the same time the crime is obscurely justified by being visualized as a punishment for a previous crime committed by the victim! . . . It is no accident that the revival of the blood libel charge has always been associated with actual outbreaks of violence against Jews: the myth is clearly produced to justify by anticipation the crime already meditated by the unconscious. (22–23)

Interestingly, the same process is described by objects relations theorists such as psychoanalyst Otto Kernberg. In his discussion of defense mechanisms as they function in the narcissistic personality, Kernberg describes the process of projective identification, in which the patient attributes to the other an impulse he has repressed in himself and then, "under the influence of that projected impulse," experiences fear and loathing toward that Other, as well as the need to control him or her.

> These shadowy external objects sometimes suddenly seem to be invested with high and dangerous powers, as the patient projects onto others the primitive characteristics of his own superego and of his own exploitative nature. His attitude towards others is either deprecatory— he has extracted all he needs and tosses them aside—or fearful— others may attack, exploit, and force him to submit to them.[22]

Fisch's speculations about the role of projective identification in anti-Semitism and its literary representations are new, and will be an important keystone of my own study.[23]

Charlotte Lea Klein was born Jewish, converted to Catholicism, and founded an order devoted to Catholic-Jewish understanding. Her contributions to the subject include her doctoral thesis of 1967, "The Portrait of the Jew in English and German Fiction and Drama, 1830–1933" and two significant articles in the magazine *Patterns of Prejudice*. Klein's work, which is not new in its theoretical approach, is of special interest here because her comparison of English and German literature of the same period makes her the first among the critics we have considered who does not treat British literature in isolation and because her examination of lesser-known and more popular works brings a new body of texts into the debate.

While Klein uses Rosenberg's research as a base, she disagrees with both Rosenberg's and Fisch's models of the dual image. She finds that the type of the saintly Jew is so rare as to be scarcely a type, and that Gentile authors, whether German or English, express little ambivalence in their long-established pattern of Jew-hating. She also quarrels with Rosenberg's nonhistorical approach, claiming that there *are* in fact some important ways in which literature reflects the times, and that his approach neglects the real function of Jews in literature: to mirror "the problems and anxieties of society at large."[24]

In German literature Klein finds an unbroken line of preoccupation with and fear of the Jew (she is referring here specifically to the male Jew) as a powerful sexual and economic threat. This preoccupation intensifies in the late part of the nineteenth century but does not materially change. In English literature before 1880, on the other hand, she finds that Jews were viewed as a negligible, asexual, and nonthreatening quantity. Klein correlates this with their general nonthreatening social position in England and the fact that Jews made up such a small percentage of the population in comparison to their representation in Germany.

In the previous chapter, I discussed the shift to a racial anti-Semitism in the late nineteenth century, coinciding with the influx of Jewish immigrants between 1881 and 1905. Klein, with Ann Arresty Naiman (see n. 14), points out this shift, locating it first in Trollope's *Prime Minister* (1876), in which the "Jew-Gentile competition is shown . . . as political, social, and for the first time, racial and sexual" ("Image," 23). She points out the growing racial threat felt by British men as reflected in the new portrait of the male Jew, who "is . . . often no longer an old man but combines the two vices, luxuria and avaritia in himself." An example is Daphne Du Maurier's Julius Levy in *The Progress of Julius*, a character his creator introduces with the words "He was oriental, he was a sadist, he was a pervert."[25]

Klein's discussion of several novels about intermarriage in which the Jewish strain is portrayed as malign, and inevitably more powerful than the Gentile or "English" strain, is especially germane to this study. Her chapters on the representation of Jewish women are particularly strong. She corrects the dichotomy other critics have noticed between the beautiful and good Jewess and the evil Jew, pointing out that "while there is a constant tradition of very appetizing young Jewesses, the old Jewess . . . is particularly ugly and repellent" ("Portrait," 138).

In her excellent discussion of both George Eliot's *Daniel Deronda* (1876) and Henry James's *Tragic Muse* (1890), Klein escapes from the dualistic frame which classifies each author as either a friend or an enemy of the Jews. She shows how these authors, while able to break free from the hold of the stereotype when consciously creating a major character, succumbed to stereotypical portraits in the less conscious construction of more minor characters ("Portrait," 132).

I found Klein least convincing in her discussion of the evils of Zionism.[26] Here, for the first time, she reproduces the "anti-semitism of tolerance" in her conviction that portrayals of Jews in fiction (and, by inference, their treatment in British society) would have been different if only Gentile British authors had known the right type of Jews. Citing the opposition to Zionism of "established and official Anglo-Jewry" (the Board of Deputies, the Chief Rabbi, and their newspaper, the *Jewish Chronicle*), she blames early Zionists for emphasizing their Jewish rather than their British identity, feels that "Zionism helped to propagate the legend of an organized Jewish threat to the Gentile world," and can hardly blame the English for doubting the British Zionists' loyalty to "their host nation" ("Portrait," 70). This last phrase is especially insidious as it buys into the commonly voiced and still-extant view that British Jews are in some sense guests who owed special loyalty and gratitude to their kind "hosts."

While she, like most other critics in this study, identifies Joyce's *Ulysses* (1922) as a shining exception, Klein concludes that the line from Trollope to writers of the 1930s is unbroken. She describes her surprise and dismay when she found that the representation of the Jew in the literature of England was remarkably similar to their representation in German literature in the period between 1890 and 1933, a reaction which mirrored my own feelings when I identified the remarkable similarities between the texts of the British authors in my study and those of the German Freikorpsmen in Klaus Theweleit's study.

Klein's work first appeared in the monthly magazine *Patterns of Prejudice*, the source of many significant articles on this subject. The American magazine *Commentary* supplied several others. It is not possible to list all of these articles here, but I will briefly mention several which, because they made new connections rather than merely cataloguing and identifying anti-Semitism, I found particularly pertinent.

Bryan Cheyette's article, "H. G. Wells and the Jews: Antisemitism, Socialism, and English Culture" (1988), to which I also refer in chapter 1, was especially useful because Cheyette traces the progress of Wells's anti-Semitism rather than treating it as a static fact. In *Tono-Bungay* of 1909, Wells saw the Jew somewhat as Trollope did, as "a cultural symbol for a corrupt, decaying capitalist society" (Cheyette, "Wells," 25). Later, in *Marriage* (1912), he focused on the sexual fears prevalent in British anti-Semitism at that time, using the prevailing image of the Jew as society's prostitute. Between 1920 and 1940, Wells's anti-Jewish venom was turned against Zionism, which he felt to be an expression of Jewish particularity and refusal to assimilate, or "disappear." Finally, during the Second World War, Wells's anti-Semitism found expression in his often-expressed theory that the Jews had provoked (and, one can infer, deserved) their punishment. In a later article, Cheyette emphasizes the ambivalence of Shaw's portrait of Jews, situating him in a British cultural context in which "the master text . . . is Matthew Arnold's *Culture and Anarchy* (1869) [with its] distinction between 'Hebraism' and 'Hellenism.' "[27] Cheyette, who is the author of the forthcoming book *Jewish Representation in English Fiction and Society, 1875–1925: A Study in Semitism*, was an important resource for the present study.

Gina Mitchell's article on the adventure writers "Sapper" (Herman Cyril McNeile) and John Buchan, "Caricature of the Bulldog Spirit: When Peace Seems Dull" (1974), is of interest here because of the connections Mitchell makes between specifically male militarism, with its exaltation of war and murder and its equation of virility and killing, and the need to identify a racially inferior "other" who can be dehumanized: "labeled to the level of a pest who should be exterminated."[28] Mitchell points out that this verbal dehumanization is typical of the language of right-wing extremists, including the Nazis, who referred to the Jews they were murdering as "cargo," among other terms.

Two articles on the representation of Jews in other than British literature were also especially helpful. In "F. Scott Fitzgerald and Literary Anti-Semitism" (1947), Milton Hindus describes Fitzgerald as a representative of the "decorative, fashionable, literary anti-Semitism" common in the literary worlds of England and the United States in the 1920s. I was interested in the continuity Hindus finds between this kind of "parlour" anti-Semitism and the less fashionable, more overt variety, as I came to a similar conclusion in chapter 1.

I found Vera Ebels Dolanova's "On 'the Rich Jew' of Fassbinder: An Essay on Literary Antisemitism" (1989) an interesting and provocative argument which extends the dialogue into the present. In her discussion of the controversy over the leftist writer Rainer Werner Fassbinder's play "The Garbage, the City, and Death" (1975), Dolanova makes the point that modern stereotypical depictions of Jews, regardless of authorial intention, are inextricably linked with ancient images and ancient and recent history, and authors must be conscious of this—as, in Dolanova's opinion, Fassbinder failed to be.[29]

Leslie Fiedler wrote the first of the works I will discuss here in 1949, a rather large chronological step backward. However, Fiedler's theoretical approach to the ongoing discussion is so far ahead of his time that I decided to place him toward the end rather than at the beginning of this discussion. Fiedler wrote "What Can We Do about Fagin?" (1949), "Negro and Jew, Encounter in America" (1960), and *The Stranger in Shakespeare* (1972) during a twenty-three-year period in which his increasing growth of consciousness concerning issues of race and gender is evident. Nevertheless, because of Fiedler's psychoanalytic orientation, and because in all three works Fiedler examines literary representation of Jews as part of a broader study of the representation of the "Other" in literature, the three works form a cohesive whole and stand apart from the other works I have discussed so far in this chapter. I will accordingly group them together, treating them as a whole.

Taking his theory from the fields of Freudian psychoanalysis, mythology, and sociology, Fiedler attempts to answer one of the questions many of the critics in this chapter have posed: how are we (and for Fiedler the "we" has, refreshingly, a Jewish referent) to deal with an admired and canonized author whose texts treat Jews in a stereotypical way? How, Fiedler asks more specifically, are we to deal with Fagin—that demonic image of ourselves that has been preserved in literature throughout history?

Fiedler frames and answers this question in several ways. First, he insists, it is essential that we locate the myth not in ourselves, as many of the critics we have examined so far have done, but rather "in the barbarous depth of the white Gentile heart."[30] Though theatrical, the phrase is significant. It indicates Fiedler's determination to firmly close the door on the discourse, promulgated by Jew and Gentile alike, which views anti-Semitism as the Jews' own problem: one we created through our own behavior and our very being and one which only we can solve.[31] According to Fiedler, for the white Gentile, the task is one of acknowledgment:

> The Gentile must learn for himself that Shylock is the creature of *his* fantasy and fear, *his* stratagem to transfer the evil that haunts us all on to an alien, an Other.[32]

For the Jew, on the other hand, the task is one of transcendence:

> We must translate for ourselves, as we read, passionate avarice, nihilism, and the desire to mutilate, into terms more universal than the mythic, bestial Jews; the archetypal image that realizes these black qualities is, in one sense, no lie; we know such impulses exist, even in us, though not of course as we are Jews, but as we are men. ("Fagin," 418)

While Fiedler's use of language in this essay ("men" for "humans," "black" for "evil") is dated, his solutions are not. He first clearly identifies two groups of "implied readers," with differing needs and tasks. He then focuses on the Jewish "we" as implied reader, discussing the different options available to us. These include avoiding the problem and withdrawing into "some spiritual ghetto," disassociating ourselves from the myth, kidnapping or appropriating it for ourselves, and censoring the myth and the literature which contains it. His solution is a variety of the option of appropriation: we must retain the literature and look within ourselves for the uneasiness we feel before "those terrible others." Such a self-examination may reveal internalized self-hatred or our own propensity to in turn project the myth onto different groups of Others, such as blacks ("Fagin," 100). He recapitulates this theme in *The Stranger in Shakespeare*:

> What is demanded of us . . . is not so much that we go back into the historical past in order to reconstruct what men once thought of Jews and witches, but rather that we descend to the level of what is the most archaic in our own living selves and then confront the living Shylock and Joan.[33]

In his examination of *The Merchant of Venice* in "What Can We Do about Fagin?" and, at greater length, in *The Stranger in Shakespeare*, Fiedler traces Shylock back to the archetypal myth of the evil father, "the male equivalent of the witch mother [and] like her associated with the killing and eating of children" (*Stranger*, 109). Fiedler finds an early reincarnation of Shylock, the knife-wielding, devouring, and castrating father, in the Old Testament story of Abraham and Isaac and a later one in the castrating Jew of early ballads and morality plays. He convincingly employs the theory of castration anxiety to trace this myth backward to biblical and medieval sources and forward to the work of T. S. Eliot, Ezra Pound, and two of the authors I will be focusing on here, Charles Williams and Graham Greene.

> The sense of a threat greater than that explicitly stated, a threat to sexuality, is really there in [*The Merchant of Venice*] and it seems to me, even the

> standard atrocity attributed to the Jew, the ritual murder of a child, is a rationalization of that original nightmare of the circumcisor, ritual blade in hand. ("Fagin," 414)

In "Negro and Jew: Encounter in America," Fiedler describes some of the ways in which African and Jewish Americans are bound together and kept apart. In literature as in life, he argues, the Negro has traditionally embodied the "primitive and instinctive" "id" wishes and fears of white Gentiles, while the Jew has embodied "the uses and abuses of intelligence," or the "ego" wishes and fears. Both archetypes, however, are defined by "the primitive fear of the contamination of blood" ("Negro," 239).

In *The Stranger in Shakespeare*, Fiedler effectively applies his model to Shakespeare's representations of women, blacks, and Jews. To him, the effort to rehabilitate Shylock through sympathetic direction of the play seems an exercise in bad faith—an unsuccessful and naive effort to appropriate and kidnap the myth. *The Merchant of Venice*, he says, "celebrates, certainly releases ritually, the full horror of anti-Semitism. A Jewish child, even now, reading the play in a class of Gentiles, feels this in shame and fear" (*Stranger*, 98).[34]

In his examination of the woman as Other in Shakespeare, Fiedler explicitly connects the Jew and the woman as Other, the central paradigm of my own study. Using the theory of projection which I mentioned in my discussion of Fisch, he identifies the male fear of castration as the source of male prejudice and violence against the object of their projective identification: "Both female witchcraft and Jewish usury . . . reflect the male Gentile's fear of loss of potency" (*Stranger*, 125).

Fiedler's work is not without its faults. His theory of how "id" qualities are attributed to blacks and "ego" qualities to Jews, one common to psychiatrists and sociologists who have studied prejudice, such as Joel Kovel, is of only limited value.[35] In fact, both "id" attributions, such as filth and sexual promiscuity, and "ego" attributions, such as avarice and scheming, are often embedded within the same Jewish character, or appear in different Jewish characters within one book, as chapters 3 through 5 will demonstrate. Studies such as John Garrard's "Now and Seventy Years Ago," a comparison of complaints against Jews between 1870 and 1914 and against Afro-Carribeans and Asians living in the same East End neighborhood in the early 1960s, show that the stereotypes attributed to new immigrants to Britain, whether black or Jewish, are strikingly similar, involving filth, the spreading of disease, sexual promiscuity, and "savage" or barbaric social customs.[36] Sander Gilman also demonstrates quite definitively how the "id" qualities at first attributed to black characters were shifted onto Jewish characters when, in late nineteenth-century Europe, Jews were seen as increasingly threatening and blacks as less so. "[T]he very concept of color is a quality of Otherness, not reality. For not only are blacks black in this amorphous world of projection, so too are Jews" (*Difference*, 30).

Fiedler, who wrote before the widespread challenges to orthodox Freudian psychoanalytic theory, is also less than convincing in the application of the Oedipal theory, which he sees everywhere and in pursuit of which he sometimes seems to leap away from the text in question. The language of the earlier essays also consistently reflects his white male assumptions, as in the paragraph cited earlier from "What Can We Do about Fagin?" in which he urges the Jewish reader to acknowledge his own "black" feelings not as a Jew but as a "man" (418). In the same essay, his references to "the Gentile" and "The Jew" actually refer to white male Gentiles and white male Jews, again reflecting his white male assumption. Thus, his important thesis that the fear of the Jew by the Gentile is based on a fear of literal or symbolic castration or loss of manhood is marred by his failure to realize that such a theory has no relevance to female Jews or to black female Gentiles, to name only two examples.

By 1960, Fiedler's awareness of the racial Other has somewhat increased, but he is still blind to the female Other. His faulty belief that the "Negro" has always represented the id while the Jew has represented the ego or superego is also marred by his lack of awareness of gender issues, as the Negro man and woman clearly represent different things to the white Gentile man and woman, as do the Jewish man and woman. By 1972, Fiedler has realized that women, like Jews and blacks, represent a significant important Other in the writing of men, and he acknowledges that a "Gentile" can be female, but he is still making the assumption that his readers share whiteness and maleness with him, speaking repeatedly about how "we" are threatened by the otherness of the female and the black.

These are significant lapses, but we notice them because of, not in spite of, Fiedler's awareness of sexual and racial bias as a factor in textual representation. His consciousness in this respect is so far ahead of that of his contemporaries in this study that we expect more of him, and subject him to the kind of feminist criticism we would not attempt in the case of the other, more entrenched white male critics. Fiedler is an ethical critic in Wayne Booth's best sense of the word: one who consistently confronts moral issues and owns up to his personal baggage rather than pretending to be dispassionate or objective. The questions he asks and the kinds of connections he makes were essential for me as I looked for a theoretical model for my own study. Just as Rosenberg's book provided me with a solid base to work from, Fiedler's work provided a kind of springboard.

"What Can We Do about Fagin?" provoked so much comment that it led to a symposium in 1949 in *Commentary* in which various prominent Jewish English and American authors (*all* male) were asked to respond to some of the questions Fiedler had posed. In a response which shocks in 1992, these Jewish authors, with a few notable exceptions, angrily disowned the topic, claiming, as Harry Levin did, "There is . . . no reason why writers of Jewish ancestry should not feel at home within the broad perspective of Anglo-American literary tradition."[37] Harold Rosenberg accuses Fiedler of Jewish paranoia, claiming that Shylock is no different from any other Shakespearian villain, and is no brother of his, and that anyway such stereotypes have never interfered with *his* reading pleasure. He concludes, rather surprisingly, "[A]rt does no harm."[38] Stephen Spender, after assuring the reader that he is, being only a quarter Jewish, "not a Jew," identifies the real problem not as anti-Semitism, which has "ennobled, purified and made whole the Jews in our epoch," but as the Jewish problem of self-consciousness, and goes on to berate Jewish writers for dwelling on their miseries and to invite them instead to enter into the new, lively tradition, "where corpses and ideologies and racial grievances are not admitted."[39] With the exception of three American writers, Irving Howe, Karl Schapiro, and Alfred Kazin, these writers seem offended and even furious at this reminder of their Jewish identity. "We are Americans or English," they respond, or "As creative artists we exist outside tradition. Why bother us with the painful and bloody past?"

Fiedler, who asks, "[I]n the light of Dachau . . . what response can we make to a culture in which so terrible and perilous a myth of ourselves is inextricably involved?" ("Fagin," 416) seems, sadly, to be in the minority here.

Christopher Ricks's *T. S. Eliot and Prejudice* (1988) is of interest here in terms of both its subject and its theory. Eliot, a key figure in current examination of literary anti-Semitism, was a tremendous influence and an important symbolic figure for Wyndham Lewis, Charles Williams, and Graham Greene, all three of the writers I concentrate on here. The dialogue which took place on both sides of the Atlantic on the occasion of Eliot's commemoration in 1989 has been well publicized, with one side maintaining that an anti-Semite like Eliot deserves no commemoration and the other side arguing either that Eliot was not in fact an anti-Semite or that his work deserves attention regardless of his personal peccadillos.[40]

Of the critics we have examined so far who discuss Eliot, Rosenberg's and Klein's moral condemnation and rejection is unambiguous. However, while he agrees that to Eliot the Jew is "an object of horror, a symbol of illegitimate dispossession, of bestiality" ("Fagin," 415), Fiedler is nevertheless eloquent about his own need to hold on to this literary forefather.

> The more philistine among us are driven to cry hysterically, "Boycott the anti-Semite! Don't read the reactionary swine!" But the Jewish intellectual of my generation cannot disown him without disowning an integral part of himself.... We are not yet willing to resign from Western culture; and speaking English, we cannot afford to abjure... the voice which has made in our own rhythm and idiom elegant patterns of our arid despair and quiet oases of hope. ("Fagin," 412)

Christopher Ricks's book covers not not only Eliot's representation of Jews but also his representation of women and suburbanites and his textual discussions of issues of difference and prejudice. Ricks also uses Eliot as a model for a larger discussion of the nature of literary prejudice itself. Like Fiedler, who urges us to look at the darkness within, and like Virginia Woolf, who in 1940 urged her readers to find the "subconscious Hitlerism" in themselves,[41] Ricks objects to the tradition among literary critics, sociologists, and social historians, including Gordon Allport and Sander Gilman, of the making of the prejudiced into a class apart, a pathological "them." On this point Ricks quotes Eliot himself: "How easy it is to see the servitude of others, their obedience to prejudice, to the group among which they live... and how difficult to recognize and face our own."[42]

Speaking directly to some of the questions I posed at the beginning of this chapter, Ricks posits four different ways to consider the question of Eliot's anti-Semitism: the bibliographic, the historical, the disassociated, and the continuous. Predictably, he rejects the first two methods, which are used to the exclusion of all others by the earlier critics in this survey. He also rejects the disassociative method espoused by most of the writers who responded to the *Commentary* symposium. Just as Fiedler maintained that to deny the dark myth in Shylock is to sanitize or dishonor the complexity of Shakespeare's play, Ricks feels that "to maintain that Eliot's relation to anti- Semitism is one thing, his poems are another" is to ignore Eliot's complexity as a poet (71). The anti-Semitism "is not easily or neatly to be severed from things for which the poetry is not to be deplored or forgiven but actively praised" (72). Ricks's choice is what he calls the continuous method, "which believes that the matter of anti-Semitism has a particular importance because it cannot be isolated from the larger issues of categorizing and prejudice in Eliot's poetry" (61).

This method implies a close, even microscopic examination of the texts involving Eliot's use of Jews and of women. It also involves the making of distinctions between the degrees and kinds of prejudice involved. Ricks discusses the same objectionable passages pinpointed by other critics in the poems "Gerontion," "Burbank with a Baedeker: Bleistein with a Cigar," "Sweeney Among the Nightingales," and "Dirge" and in the essay "After Strange Gods." What is new is his identification of the method of "profound insinuation" by which Eliot uses his lines to trigger the reader's own prejudice, a "precipitate collusion" which Ricks claims is an intrinsic part of Eliot's purpose rather than a demonstration of the poet's own prejudice.[43]

Another device which Ricks points out is the technique of giving such offensive lines as these in "Gerontion," "My house is a decayed house,/ And the Jew squats on the windowsill, the owner," to an unreliable narrator. As Ricks asks in this case, "Who would wish to be he, and what endorsement then is being asked for thoughts of his dry brain in its dry season?" (29). While the degree to which the poet does in fact inhabit this particular narrator is debatable, the point is an important one and one often neglected by less sophisticated critics. In making these distinctions, as Ricks points out, he is countering the school of thought espoused by Bruno Bettelheim, among others, which maintains "that any discriminations within anti-Semitism . . . are gratuitous and indulgent" and which holds that any attempts at "rational" discussion of such an irrational phenomenon as anti-Semitism or racism, apart from a blanket condemnation, is itself a collusion and a blaming of the victim (29).

Ricks enters much shakier ground when he calls for an examination of the causes of prejudice within the object of the prejudice: "The fact that there could, appallingly, be no doubt in the case of Hitler and the Jews should not be allowed to petrify or putrefy our entire world into one in which all prejudice is indubitable in being entirely dissociated from any antecedent causes, provocation, or evidence" (76).

The words "evidence" and "provocation" imply a kind of rational connection in which one thing causes another; prejudice in its very definition does not work this way. I find Fiedler's insistence on locating the prejudice within the prejudiced, not within his victim, far preferable as well as more logical. Nevertheless, Ricks's effort to combat the pressure against rational discussion of anti-Semitism and other forms of prejudice is an important one. The refusal to look closely is a kind of throwing up of the hands in despair—a withdrawal which, I believe, is not useful to anyone in the end. The T. S. Eliot Ricks shows us is a complex and contradictory man, and Ricks does not attempt to defend or condemn him. Neither does he attempt to guess at the influence Eliot's anti-Semitism has had, or to explain the social or personal pathology which could lead Eliot to write such disparate lines about Jews within the same time period. What he does instead is to subject Eliot's references to Jews and to prejudice and anti-Semitism, in both his poems and his critical writing, to such a close scrutiny that he splits the texts open, allowing them to reveal more than we would have thought possible.

Postscript: The Discourse of Power

Most of the critics I have discussed so far looked only at the treatment of Jews in the various works they scrutinize. Ricks and Fiedler, who alone among the critics in this chapter examine the representation of Jews in the larger context of the textual representation of the Other, make a bridge to those current poststructuralist critics whose focus is the representation of the Other. This focus, which has variously been called "the rhetoric of power" and "discourse and power" is usually associated with Michel Foucault and Edward Said.[44] While critics who might be placed in this group differ widely and include those who define their approaches primarily as psychoanalytic, Marxist, deconstructionist, or feminist, it is safe to conclude that most of them reject the New Critical concept of the text as an isolated object for study and stress that all cultural discourse is a production of social and economic forces and thus reflects the dominant ideology of the existing power structure. For example, in *Orientalism*, Said demonstrates how the Western myth of the "Orient" and the "Oriental" has been constructed through generations of Western ethnocentric discourse.[45] As we have already seen, Terry Eagleton, whose orientation is primarily Marxist, also stresses the complete indivisibility of the two concepts of literature and ideology. In his model, one which would have been endorsed by the earliest critics in this chapter, Philipson, Calisch, and Modder, literature is a powerful force which is itself a form of "social control and social cement" (*Literary Theory*, 23–24). An earlier theorist, Louis Althusser, expresses a similar sense of the interrelatedness of literature and ideology: "art makes us *see* . . . the ideology from which it is born in which it bathes, from which it detaches itself as art, and to which it alludes."[46]

Just as ideology determines what is written and published, so does it determine what is excluded. As Michel Foucault emphasizes: "Individuals working within certain discursive practices cannot think or speak without obeying the unspoken 'archive' of rules and constraints; otherwise they risk being condemned to madness or silence."[47]

Even the most effective "strategies of containment" are not entirely successful, and even the most inclusive ideologies contain ambivalence. As the theories of both Roland Barthes and Jacques Derrida stress, it is important to look not only at what a text sets out to do but at what happens when it transgresses its own laws and definitions or undermines itself. In chapters 4 through 6, while I have not attempted to adopt the dominant poststructuralist vocabulary, I have tried to be aware of underlying ideology as well as societal constraints and containment.

I will end my survey with a discussion of two recent poststructuralist texts which, while they do not confine themselves to the representation of Jews, raise some important issues about that representation.

Henry Louis Gates, Jr. is the editor of the anthology *"Race," Writing, and Difference*. This collection, which originally appeared in two issues of *Critical Inquiry* in 1985 and 1986, is the work of many hands; it contains essays by twenty-two theorists as well as several "responses" to these essays. Because they seemed particularly germane to my own study, I was especially interested in those essays which concern writing by whites about blacks. Most of these essays demonstrate how, as Gates writes, "In much of the thinking about the proper study of literature in this century, [race] has been an invisible quantity, a persistent yet implicit presence."[48] The constructed paradigm of "race" consistently objectifies people of color, who are textualized as invisible and/or subhuman projections on the part of white authors. Most of these essays are daunting in their vocabulary, seeming to visualize as their implied reader other contemporary literary theorists. Despite this difficulty, several of them served as models of intellectual brilliance for me, expanding my critical vocabulary and in many cases the bounds of my own vision. However, *"Race," Writing, and Difference* also contains a disturbing subtext.

Edward W. Said's essay "An Ideology of Difference" attacks Israeli imperialism, which, he argues, is a dominant ideology which has produced harmful and deeply racist textual representations of Palestinians. In this essay, Said refers repeatedly to "Israel's more muscular supporters . . . the largest, wealthiest and most organized Jewish community in the world—the one in the United States," which he claims has moved on several fronts since the Israeli invasion in 1982 to censor, punish, and attack all critics of Israel.[49] In particular, Said labels two books which he considers anti-Palestinian as "instruments" of this conspiracy. While Said's arguments are convincing, and his anger powerful, it is ironic that the author of an article about "the ideology of difference fueling Zionism" should slip so easily into the Jewish conspiracy myth we encountered in chapter 1. By ignoring the Jewish forces for peace and settlement in both the United States and in Israel and lumping all Jews together as one wealthy, organized community intent on destruction, he reproduces a familiar text, privileged by centuries of repetition.

In a "reaction" to this essay, Houston A. Baker writes:

> It is difficult to hear a Palestinian voice separate from the world of Jewish discourse. (Of course, Jews are not likely to feel this way, and will probably call for Said's head on a platter. But that is the necessary reaction of well-financed client states.)[50]

Baker's first sentence refers in the singular to "a Palestinian voice." He opposes this lone individual voice to "the world of Jewish discourse"—again making Jews into an organized and oppressive group: a whole "world." He then makes a quick biblical reference to "Said's head on a platter," a biblical association to either the Jewish woman Salome, who demanded and got the head of the (pre-Christian) John the Baptist on a platter, or to the Old Testament Judith, another Jewish woman who stealthily slew the Assyrian general Holofernes while he was asleep and showed his head to her countrymen, who then rushed in to defeat his army.[51] In both references, "Jews" are pictured as a stealthy female intent on the decapitation (or symbolic castration) and murder of Said—the lone, non-Jewish male who is the representative of his vulnerable people. This image too, is a familiar one, which will appear over and over again in the misogynist and anti-Semitic texts in this study. Finally, in a quick jump, Baker transforms "Jews" into "well-financed client states," presumably a reference to the dependence of Israel on the United States. Once again, he is back on familiar ground with this image of all Jews as rich and greedy warmongers. Such labeling undermines the purpose of a book presumably devoted to the debunking of the harmful construction of race.

In his "reaction" to the book, Tzvetan Todorov wonders whether the authors in the anthology chose to "actively ignore" anti-Semitism[52] (Gates, 377). While I have no quarrel with Gates's definition of "race," it does seem to me that the inclusion of the material I have described does more than to ignore: it actively embeds the familiar discourse of anti-Semitism into a vehicle whose purpose is, as Gates puts it, to challenge the concept of race as "a trope of ultimate, irreducible difference" (5). At issue here is the need for critics who are studying the representation of the "Other" to, as Fiedler put it, look within ourselves for "that terrible other" rather than to complacently assume that we ourselves exist outside of the ideology of power.

In his book *Difference and Pathology*, an examination of the tropes of sexuality, race, and madness, Sander Gilman makes no such assumption. Gilman reasons that humans form stereotypes in order to try to gain control over an uncontrollable universe. Textual stereotypes are "a rich web of signs and references for the idea of difference [which] arise out of a society's communal sense of control over its world" (20). Gilman uses the psychoanalytic concept of splitting to explain how each individual strives to achieve such control. In this model, a child splits the world and himself into good and bad. The bad self is then distanced and placed at a remove, and the world can be safely divided into the good self (us) and the bad Other (them). Stereotypes are:

> [a] crude set of mental representations of the world . . . palimpsests on which the initial bipolar representations are still vaguely legible. They perpetuate a needed sense of difference between the "self" and the "object" which becomes the "Other." (*Difference*, 18)

Stereotypes are particularly needed when an individual experiences anxiety due to an alteration of the sense of order (real or imagined) between himself and the Other (*Difference*, 20). The pathological personality, whose boundaries are more than ordinarily shaky, consequently has an exaggerated need to stereotype. Such an individual "sees the entire world in terms of the rigid line of difference" (*Difference*, 18).

Gilman sees the making of stereotypical images as a combined product of the universal need to split and dichotomize and of historical and cultural circumstances. He explains the fluid, shifting, and often contradictory locus of the stereotypes in terms of shifting historical and cultural images of the Other. Although a particular stereotype may be activated by a real experience with a person or group, stereotypes can, as we saw in chapter 1, also exist in the absence of the group in question (*Difference*, 20).

Gilman suggests that stereotypes do not exist as isolated phenomena, but instead function like metaphors, which in turn cluster other associative assumptions around them. Gilman uses Stephen Pepper's term "root metaphor" to describe the original stereotype or metaphor which becomes a clustering base around which one's assumptive reality can be framed. Because stereotypes are not isolated images but rather associative clusters, their branches become connected and interrelated. Gilman comments that otherwise insightful studies of textual stereotypes often lose sight of these interrelationships (*Difference*, 26). In his discussion of the stereotypes of sexuality, he writes: "What is fascinating to me about the set of images in the texts I have chosen is that they link certain focal points of anxiety. The black, the proletarian, the child, the woman, and the avant-garde are all associated in a web of analogies" (*Difference*, 37).

Just as Gilman's other conclusions parallel many of my own, his "focal points" are similar to those I locate in the three authors in this study. As we will see in chapter 4, Wyndham Lewis, the first author I will discuss, devotes entire books to each of these shifting focal points for his dread and anxiety.

I discovered Gilman's book only after completing the first draft of my own, and was interested to see the different ways in which his findings, based on an entirely different group of texts, paralleled my own.

Conclusion

In the introduction to this book, I looked back and identified the reader I was at fifteen as naive. Similarly, the critics who first studied the representation of Jews in British literature may appear naive to those of us who swim in a critical pond which includes the ultrasophisticated criticism of such masters of the subtle as Lacan and Derrida. Most, though not all, of the critics in the first part of this chapter defined the contours of their task in a fairly limited way: as the identification, the condemnation, and sometimes the classification of stereotypes of Jews.

Nevertheless, we must not be too quick to dismiss these initial and key acts of naming, nor the tone of moral urgency which fueled them. These predominantly Jewish scholars wrote in the absence of any contemporary examination of anti-Semitism or of the representation of Jews in literature. Wayne Booth, discussing the need of modern critics to separate doctrine from aesthetics, cites the problem faced by the judges who had to decide whether to award the Bollingen Prize to Ezra Pound's *Cantos* in 1948. These " 'good poems' expressing abhorrent doctrines" were awarded the prize in the end, the committee of writers explaining that the contest had to do with the use of language rather than with doctrine. None of the earlier critics in this survey would have been troubled by such a problem, and none of them would have let Ezra Pound anywhere near the prize. In fact, of all the critics in this survey, only Christopher Ricks absolves himself from the task of "guessing at the influence Eliot's anti-Semitism has had, either on the world of literature or outside that world" or from any explanation of the social background or personal pathology which could lead to Eliot's disparate textual statements about Jews (Ricks, 101). Interestingly, the contemporary critics in the postscript to this chapter, writing from a methodology very different from and far more consciously elucidated than that of the earlier critics, share with them a definition of literature as a powerful force of "social control and social cement" and a sense that the critic's task is a moral as well as an aesthetic one (Eagleton, *Literary Theory*, 23–24).

Rosenberg, Trachtenberg, Fisch, Klein, and Fiedler, who envisioned a less direct connection among author, text, and society, did not withdraw from the ethical criticism which was the earlier critics' focus but were increasingly aware of the duality and ambivalence in the Gentile representation of Jews. They studied both positive and negative stereotypes and approached each of an author's works separately, rather than treating them as a monolithic whole. The earlier critics all felt that an author's personal behavior and his or her own self-definition as a tolerant or prejudiced person were relevant information for their task of judgment. Critics who wrote within the joint contexts of psychoanalysis and the New Critical discourse, including Fisch, Rosenberg, and Fiedler, tended to exclude such biographical information about the author, focusing instead on the unconscious revelations of the text. For the most recent critics, a strong focus on the text and a disregard of authorial intention and presence is coupled, not always consistently, with a focus on social and historical context.

For the most part, the earliest critics, including Philipson, Calisch, and Modder, viewed anti-Semitism in literature as a phenomenon which was gradually but steadily disappearing, making way for more positive and realistic portraits of Jews. Surprisingly, chronology was not the only determining factor here: M. J. Landa, in 1926, was as pessimistic in his historical outlook as the post-Holocaust critics, and Montagu Modder, in 1939, offered the most optimistic forecast of all. In the years immediately following the Second World War such optimism was no longer possible, and gave way to a view of the Jewish stereotype as either an unchanging given or as a phenomenon which had worsened with time. However, with the passage of time, anti-Semitism began to be seen as a less pressing societal issue, leading to a book like Gates's anthology, which incorporated an anti-Semitic subtext into a discussion of textual racism.

Finally, the critics I have discussed in this chapter concerned themselves in varying degrees with the origins of the anti-Semitism they identified. The earlier critics, for the most part avoided this question, relying on ethics, relatively close reading, and common sense to form their judgments. Later critics, more concerned with the origins of anti-Semitism, have found such belief systems as Marxism and psychoanalysis increasingly useful. For Fiedler, the psychoanalytic approach meant an orthodox Freudianism, with its focus on the Oedipal challenge and castration anxiety. For Gilman, it meant an objects relations theory close to the one which I will employ in this study. For the most current critics, including Gates and Said, current critical theory, a professional discourse with its own methods and vocabulary, has increasingly taken center stage.

In undertaking my own study, I found the identification and grounding supplied by the earlier critics, especially Rosenberg, invaluable. As a model for my own work, however, I turned to those critics, beginning with Fiedler, who viewed the representation of Jews within the larger context of the treatment of various groups of Others.

THREE

In Search of a Psychoanalytic Theory

A Composite Profile

The more closely I approached the work of the three authors in this study, the clearer it became to me that for each of them the representation of Jews was integrally tied up with the representation of women, and both were part of an intricate associative cluster or defensive system; as Gilman puts it, "heuristic structures that the self uses to integrate the various stereotypes associated by analogy" (Gilman, *Difference and Pathology*, 22). As I studied these structures, each one seemed to take on a life and shape of its own, and I saw each system's capacity to take in new material to incorporate or transform into its own image. In the course of my research, I began to refer to these systems privately as "extrusion presses," an image I later applied to the work of Charles Williams in particular. This image originated in a memory of a set of variously sized and shaped machines I saw as a child when my metallurgist father took me to work with him. Men fed raw molten metal into the complicated coils of these machines, each of which produced or extruded a variety of molded metallic sausages at the other end. Similarly, each of the three authorial systems looked different and utilized different mechanisms, but each one produced surprisingly similar interlocking stereotypical and symbolic representations of Jews and women.

To turn to a different metaphor, I began to see that while each writer/director staged his own play, in which women and Jews played idiosyncratic and different parts, crossing and meeting in different ways, each one worked from the same basic plot. Before moving to a consideration of the theorists whose work helped me to construct my own psychoanalytic theory, I will accordingly describe a larger authorial system: the common "press" or plot which emerged from this study and which I here ascribe to a composite implied authorial profile. I will use this profile in the ensuing pages to concretize a discussion of theory which could otherwise become too abstract and ungrounded. During the course of this discussion I will allow myself to shift at times from an analysis of this implied profile to an analysis of a particular author himself, but I will attempt to signal clearly when I am shifting ground in this way.

In the work of Wyndham Lewis, Graham Greene, and Charles Williams, the woman is seen as distinctly "Other." As such she is sometimes idealized, more often denigrated, but never regarded as a fellow human being. She is the object sometimes of attraction, most often of disgust and contempt, emotions which are directed at her mind or inner being and at her body, and are specifically fixed upon her breasts, mouth, and genitals; that is, upon her sexual (or childbearing) self. For these authors, the sexual and reproductive aspect of the woman takes on a larger-than-life quality. It makes her both dangerous and powerful; through it she can engulf the helpless male in a kind of swallowing up or subsuming. This terror can be expressed in literal, physical terms: the male characters in Williams's "ghost stories" repeatedly lose their physical shapes, and Lewis's male characters fear being transformed into women. Or it can be expressed in more psychological terms, as when Greene's male characters desperately fear that their true evil and cowardly inner selves will be exposed by virtuous and engulfing women.

All three writers perceive their own boundaries as especially vulnerable, easily entered into or destroyed by the invasive female. Sometimes, in contrast to the evil, usually whorish woman, there exists a good one—a young, powerless virgin who nonetheless embodies the female threat of engulfment as much or more than her counterpart, and must be destroyed or dominated. Whether the woman in question is defined as good or evil, violent aggression against her is textualized as a necessary defensive measure against her female force. Sometimes this aggression appears as a direct countermeasure against female attack, while at other times the attack is a preemptive move—a safety measure undertaken to prevent the woman from doing her worst. Despite these attacks, the woman is most often the victor, while the man, ostensibly the aggressor, is almost invariably seen as the victim.

While positive relationships in these writers' books are few, those that do occur are largely between two men, and homoerotic elements abound, although all three of the writers are aggressively heterosexual. Lewis, whose work is the most profoundly homoerotic of the three, demonstrates a fear and loathing of effeminate men which is almost as strong and obsessive as his fear and loathing of women. Greene's characters struggle desperately and usually unsuccessfully to maintain their shaky manhood, while Williams's characters, less overtly virile in presentation, share a propensity toward a form of sexual sadism in which women are punished "for their own good."

The role played by the Jewish character is somewhat more varied, though equally bound by available historical and mythic possibilities. He is almost inevitably male, with Jewish women appearing only twice in all of the books in question, and then only in walk-on roles. In the work of all three authors he is at times seen as an effeminate man—a horrifyingly hermaphroditic link to the loathsome female. As such, he exhibits the "female" traits of physical weakness, cringing cowardice, greed, pettiness, and corruptibility. He can alternatively embody a rapacious male sexuality which is both perverse and powerful. In this guise, he corrupts the virginal females, stealing them from the victimized Gentile male. At his most dangerous, he is the Gentile male's castrator or murderer, usually acting in league with the woman. Another role, often assumed simultaneously with the last, is that of the all-powerful mastermind who runs, or schemes to run, the world, and who, in league with women and/or homosexuals and often with other members of a designated "Other" (children, blacks, communists, members of the working class, and foreigners are all prime candidates), victimizes, enslaves, or castrates the helpless and powerless male. In this chapter, I will briefly discuss the different theorists whose work formed my theoretical framework, attempting to show how each one sheds light on the profile above.

The Theorists

The Monstrous Male: Virginia Woolf, Kate Millett, and Klaus Theweleit. Among the many important feminist theorists who find an explanation for personal and social pathology in the social conditioning of men, Virginia Woolf and Kate Millett, each a pioneer in her time, consistently linked the misogyny which was the main subject of their theories with racism.

Virginia Woolf was born in 1882, the same year as Wyndham Lewis, the earliest of the three authors I will discuss. An influential novelist, critic, and feminist theorist, Woolf was a contemporary of all three of the authors in this study, who refer to her with attitudes ranging from fury (Williams) to a guarded respect (Greene). In *Three Guineas* (1938) Woolf reflects on what she called the psychopathology of masculinism: the traits in men which seemed to cause them to love to fight, divide, and dominate.[1] Woolf felt that man's primary domination of women was the root of his need to dominate other groups.

> There [in the domination of women] we have in embryo the creature, Dictator as we call him when he is Italian or German, who believes that he has the right, whether given by God, Nature, sex, or race is immaterial, to dictate to other human beings how they shall live; what they shall do.[2]

Unlike later feminist theorists, including Mary Daly, Susan Griffin, and Luce Irigaray, whose writing reflects their belief in innate feminine superiority, Woolf reasons that men are born whole but are quickly programmed through the conspiracy of societies that "sink the private brother . . . and inflate in his stead a monstrous male, loud of voice, hard of fist," who, unlike his sister, is consumed with the principles of division, separation, power, and dominion (*Three Guineas*, 105).

Woolf never underestimates the power of that conditioning, which she feels has become part of men's bodies and brains, just as the wild rabbit differs in its brain and body from the rabbit in the hutch (*Three Guineas*, 140).[3] Dominance, she reasons, has become so much a part of the male role that unteaching it will take "millennia, not decades" (*Three Guineas*, 142). In England she locates that conditioning for domination specifically in university education, which was restricted to men and taught them "the arts of dominating other people . . . of ruling, of killing, of acquiring land and capital" (*Three Guineas*, 34). In Germany this programming produced a Hitler: "the quintessence of virility, the perfect type of which all the others are imperfect adumbrations" (*Three Guineas*, 187).

In the first chapter of her book, *Women Against the Iron Fist*, Sybil Oldfield demonstrates that the link which Woolf points out between the male need to dominate women and his need to dominate other groups is far from new. She shows how, in the late 1800s, Bismarck and his disciple, Heinrich von Treitschke, persistently grouped war, manliness, and the "Aryan" race together, similarly conflating peace with femininity and the lesser races.[4] Marinetti's *Futurist Manifesto* of 1909, which Oldfield calls "an extraordinary premonition of the woman-despising necrophilia of fascism," similarly declares:

> We want to glorify war—the world's only hygiene—militarism, deed, destructor of anarchisms, the beautiful ideas that are death- bringing, and the contempt of women. (Oldfield, 12)

Woolf's description of "monstrous men," preoccupied with division, separation, power, and dominion, is congruent with our authorial profile, which reflects hierarchal dichotomies, assumptions of domination, and contempt and fear of women and Jews. Her comments on the role of education for domination are also applicable to our profile, although she concentrates on the university rather than, as I shall do at the end of this chapter, on earlier boarding school education.

In her ground-breaking book, *Sexual Politics* (1969), Kate Millett takes up the argument where Virginia Woolf left off, and extends it to textual representation. Millett's focus is on "patriarchal government . . . the institution whereby that half of the populace which is female is controlled by that half which is male."[5] Millett, like Woolf, locates male pathology not in biology but in social conditioning, which is enforced by patriarchy's chief institution, the nuclear family, and which "runs in a circle of self-perpetuation and self-fulfilling prophecy" (53). In our patriarchal society, according to Millett, gender is endowed with the pervasive and determining force which Marxist theorists have traditionally reserved for class. "Because of our social circumstances," she writes, "male and female are really two cultures and their life experiences are utterly different" (53). In such a culture, relations between men and women fall into a dichotomous pattern of dominance and victimization: a pattern which we will find repeated again and again in works by Lewis, Williams, and Greene. Our three authors would agree that male and female are two cultures with different life experiences, but see the male culture as the only true one—a beleaguered and precious entity which women are attempting to infiltrate and infect. The sadism and dominance Millett cites become in this frame a necessary defense against the process of infiltration. In Millett's words: "Patriarchal societies typically link feelings of cruelty with sexuality, the latter often equated both with evil and with power . . . the rule here associates sadism with the male . . . and victimization with the female" (70).

Millett, like Woolf, consistently links misogyny with racism. Gilman noted the textual similarities between the Victorian representation of Jews and blacks, both groups being inscribed with the same traits and even the same appearance. Millett notes that studies of commonly held attitudes toward blacks and women reveal that these two groups also are inscribed with the same traits, including "inferior intelligence, an instinctual or sensual gratification, an emotional nature both primitive and childlike, an imagined prowess in or affinity for sexuality . . . a wily habit of deceit, and concealment of feeling . . . an ingratiating or supplicatory manner invented to please" (86).

With the exception of inferior intelligence, one of the few qualities rarely ascribed to the stereotypical Jew, all of these attributes can be found in Rosenberg's and Fiedler's descriptions of the Jew-Villain in my chapter 2.

Millett's exploration of the relationship between anti-Semitism and misogyny in the Third Reich is especially relevant here. She demonstrates that the Nazi regime attempted "probably the most deliberate attempt ever made to revive and solidify extreme patriarchal conditions" (217). The Nazi "Gleichshaltung" or "bringing-in-line" of the feminist organizations which had been so prominent in pre-Nazi Germany and the policies of banning women from higher education and the professions, excluding them from legal or political office, and prohibiting female contraception and abortion were all part of a profoundly misogynist system which underpinned "the male supremacist temperament of the Nazi state" (223). Gottfried Feder, a prominent Nazi ideologist, verbalized this system when he linked feminists and Jews in an unholy alliance:

> The Jew has stolen woman from us through the forms of sex democracy. We, the youth, must march out to kill the dragon so that we may again attain the most holy thing in the world, the woman as maid and servant.[6]

The unholy alliance of Jew and female against victimized Aryan appears repeatedly in the work of all three authors in this study. Millett quotes Hitler himself on this subject: "The message of woman's emancipation is a message discovered solely by the Jewish intellect and its content is stamped with the same spirit."[7]

Millett's analysis of texts convinced her, as my own research convinced me, that racism and anti-Semitism are components of the same system as misogyny and cannot be neatly separated:

> [O]ne is forced to conclude that sexual politics, while connected to economics and other tangibles of social organization, is, like racism, or certain aspects of caste, primarily an ideology, a way of life, with influence over every other psychological and emotional facet of existence. It has created, therefore, a psychic structure, deeply embedded in our past [.] (229)

While Millett finds Freud's identification of female dissatisfaction and longing accurate, she firmly disagrees with his location of that dissatisfaction in female anatomy (the penis envy theory). She attributes this mistake to Freud's phallic assumptions and points out Freud's intellectual debt to Otto Weininger, a contemporary Viennese author whom she calls "a misogynist thinker" (22).

Weininger was not only a misogynist but also a tormented and self-hating Jewish anti-Semite. A Protestant convert and the son of an anti-Semitic Jew, he was the author of the acclaimed best-seller *Sex and Character* (1903). In *Freud and Vienna 1900* (1991), Hannah Decker describes the linkage between Weininger's self-hatred as a Jew and his misogyny:

> Weininger argued that a woman is pure sexuality, contaminating a man "in the paroxysm of orgasm" . . . [E]ven the most superior woman was immeasurably below the most debased man, just as Judaism at its highest was immeasurably below even degraded Christianity. Judaism was so despicable because it was shot through with femininity. As women lacked souls, so too did Jews. Both were pimps, amoral and lascivious. Both sought to make other human beings suffer guilt. Women and Jews did not think logically, but rather intuitively, by association. . . . Jews were even worse than women; Jews were degenerate women. Weininger killed himself because he felt he could not overcome the woman and the Jew in him.[8]

Weininger was a self-hating Jew, but in the texts we will examine here we will witness three Gentile authors almost equally intent on overcoming and weeding out the loathsome woman and Jew inside themselves.

Millett views misogynist literature as one of the primary vehicles of what Woolf called male socialization in pathology (Millett, 71). In *Sexual Politics* she brilliantly analyzes these vehicles: selected texts by male authors.

In his two-volume work *Male Fantasies* (first published in German in 1977 as *Männerphantasien*) Klaus Theweleit concentrates on a particularly pathological group of men, the German Freikorpsmen. Also known as the White Terror, these German soldiers refused to lay down their arms after the end of the First World War and instead carried out their own fight against forces of the German revolutionary working class during the "warless" years between 1923 and 1933. Many of them went on to become the core of Hitler's SA and key functionaries in the Third Reich. In addition to murdering countless men and women, the Freikorpsmen wrote copious volumes of autobiography, novels, and eye-witness accounts. "We ourselves are the War," wrote one. "Its flame burns strongly in us. It envelops our whole being and fascinates us with the enticing urge to destroy."[9] As their productions make clear, the Freikorpsmen's fear and loathing of women are intimately linked to their hatred and fear of communists and the working class, and are intrinsic to their violence. Theweleit makes these connections explicit. As Jessica Benjamin and Anson Rabinach put it in the foreword to volume 2 of *Male Fantasies, Male Bodies: Psychoanalyzing the White Terror*, "it is Theweleit's insistence on the primacy of violence—originating in the fear and hatred of the feminine—that distinguishes his approach from the older social-psychological models."[10]

Perhaps because these are texts which are not "literary" in the ordinary sense, the soldier males, as Theweleit presents them to us, seem to speak openly for themselves and to need little interpretation. Their desire to kill and maim women, for instance, is by no means unconscious. It is openly felt and expressed and regularly carried out. In Theweleit's words:

> Concealing the kinds of thoughts we've been discussing, the ones traditional psychoanalysis would call "unconscious," is the last thing on earth these men would want to do. . . . The "fear of castration" is a consciously held fear, just as the equation of communism and rifle-woman is consciously made. (1: 89)

Theweleit's Freikorpsmen, like Lewis, Williams, and Greene, demonstrate in their writing their desperate need to defend themselves against female power. Like my authors, they divide women into two groups. On one side are the white virgins; on the other, the "female communists," "proletarian women," "rifle-women," or "seductive Jewesses," all profoundly dangerous to men. "The sexuality of the proletarian woman/gun slinging whore/communist is out to castrate and shred men to pieces" (1: 76).

Like my three authors, the Freikorpsmen "lack any secure sense of external boundaries" (2: 213). Their fear of women is not only a fear of murder and castration at their hands, but also of "total annihilation and dismemberment" (1: 205). When they shoot and smash women's bodies, as they do again and again in these texts and in their lives, they feel that they are acting in self-defense, imposing the annihilation they fear on their would-be destroyers:

> Once she . . . is reduced to a pulp, a shapeless, bloody mass, the man can breathe a sigh of relief. The wound in question here goes beyond castration, in which one can at least still identify the body to which the wound belongs. What we are dealing with . . . is the *dissolution* of the body itself. (1: 196)

In addition to their horses and their rifles, the Freikorpsmen loved only each other. But for them, as for Lewis, Williams, and Greene, actual acts of homosexuality were deeply taboo. Theweleit explains:

> It seems increasingly doubtful that terms such as hetero or homosexuality can usefully be applied to the men we are studying. The actual sexual act is described in these writings as a trancelike act of violence . . . they have little to do with a sexuality understood as the desire for physical love with another person (female or male). These men seem less to possess a sexuality than to persecute sexuality itself—one way or another. (2: 61)

Like my profiled author, these men were cut off and isolated. To them, the desire for pleasure was "a contagious disease." To open the gate to pleasure, and indeed to feeling, means to open oneself to lust, to engulfment, and finally to annihilation. As Theweleit puts it: "Inside this man is a concentration camp, the concentration camp of his desires" (2: 6).

I was especially interested in Theweleit's explanation of how the Freikorpsmen's several hatreds—of women, of the working class, and of communists—were subsequently combined in the Nazi hatred of Jews. Just as women, communists, and the working classes embodied the liberation of dangerous desires for the Freikorpsmen, so Jews played the same role for the Nazis, who used the concept of an alien race to embody this fear in one entity: "the alien race is predominantly encoded with the inexorably murderous forces of the man's own interior; it must therefore be exterminated" (2: 76).

The Jewish riflewoman who, through an appeal to their desire, lures men to a bloody death provides another example of the barriers of race, class, and gender embodied in one image. This prominent figure in the Freikorpsmen writings, carries "the Jewish pox," syphilis, of which Theweleit writes:

> "[S]yphilis" is one name only for the dissolution to which a man falls prey if he comes into contact with the external incarnation of his devouring, dead unconscious. But it is a particularly apposite name, a rich code, containing, as it does, the corrosions of femininity, Jewishness, epidemic disease, criminality (the contagion is international) and emasculating death. (2: 16)

In a passage from a novel of 1930 by the Nazi writer Ernst Salomon, Jews and females are embodied in one alien, sexual enemy: "During coitus the male semen is fully or partly absorbed into the lining of the female uterus, where it enters the bloodstream. A single act of intercourse between a Jew and an Aryan woman is enough to poison her blood forever."[11]

Theweleit's sense of the pitfalls of his method does not always prevent him from falling into them. On his use of psychoanalytic theory, he writes: "I have attempted to avoid supporting my own prejudices with quotations from psychoanalytic writers and have tried instead to present typical specimens of the writing of soldier males, sticking closely to the text in every case" (1: 57). *Male Fantasies* succeeds brilliantly when its author does allow the texts to speak for themselves. His overliteral use of object relations theory, in particular of Margaret Mahler's, is much less successful and leads him to several interpretations which seem to me incongruent with the Freikorps texts.

In one such reading, he suggests that the real trouble with the Freikorpsmen is arrested development: they got stuck in "the pre-Oedipal struggle of the fledgling self before there is even an ego to sort out the objects of desire and the odds of getting them."[12] This theory is only valid if one accepts the idea of unique developmental stages in which one can "get stuck," rather than reasoning, as do more recent object relations theorists like Hans Loewald, Jessica Benjamin, and Nancy Chodorow that " 'Oedipal' projects of individuation and morality and 'pre-oedipal' concerns with boundaries, separation, connection, and the transitional space continue through life."[13] Theweleit's belief that the Freikorpsmen have been emotionally trapped in pre-Oedipal infanthood assumes that infants are in fact bundles of rage and desire with no ability for mutuality: a belief which most recent theorists, including Jessica Benjamin, Beatrice Beebe, Nancy Chodorow, and Daniel Stern, have disputed.[14] Theweleit's use of Melanie Klein's theory of how infants perceive parts of the mother rather than the whole to explain the Freikorpsmen's tendency to attack women's breasts relies once again, on an overly literal interpretation of Klein's theory, and an outdated perception of infantile development. The fragmented objectification of the female body which the Freikorpsmen exhibit seems to be quite different from that of a normally developing infant, who perceives its mother as a whole rather than in pieces. Furthermore, it seems more logical that the Freikorpsmen should attack women's breasts because they are the symbolic location both of dependence on the mother and of female sexuality than because they were stuck in an infantile stage and were only able to focus on one part of a woman at a time.

Theweleit's equation, without any textual evidence, of the Freikorpsmen's pathology with that of autistic children is also unconvincing. After a long tradition of blaming mothers for their children's autism, experts now believe the condition to be a result of brain damage at birth, rather than faulty parenting. While autistic children do in fact have faulty boundaries, so do sufferers from many other forms of organic brain damage and from schizophrenia. Finally, Theweleit's idea that in their drive for cleaner rivers environmentalists are really expressing a drive for purer, cleaner women is simply silly. In all these cases, Theweleit compares two like things and then uses an overly concrete interpretation of early objects relations theory to suggest causal relationships which are in fact highly dubious.

While Theweleit does include a short and very interesting chapter on the German military academy, he minimizes the effect of such schooling, even though many of the Freikorpsmen attended military boarding school from a young age. Theweleit also minimizes the effect of childhood trauma, but it is probable that most of them, as middle-class German children, were brought up according to the methods of "poisonous pedagogy" which Alice Miller describes in her chapter on Adolf Hitler's childhood in *For Your Own Good* (1983), which I will discuss later in this chapter.[15] In his re-vision of Freud's Schreber case, William Niederland describes chillingly and convincingly how such pedagogy resulted in one father's barbaric but widely accepted child-rearing practices undergoing metaphoric reconstruction in the son's psychosis.[16] David Shapiro also uses Niederland's work to explain how childhood experience can lead to rigid personality. I believe that Miller's, Niederland's, and Shapiro's theories, which all focus on paternal abuse coupled with denial and which I will discuss later in this chapter, are a more useful tool for understanding the pathology of the Freikorpsmen and the authors in my study than Theweleit's use of object relations theory.

My final criticism of Theweleit's study is a stylistic one. While his nonconventional discursive style is part of Theweleit's brilliance and part of what gives his books their impact, he is often excessively rambling, repetitive, and disconnected. I believe that with proper editing this very uneven two-volume book could have made one superb volume.

Despite these criticisms, Theweleit's books were tremendously useful to me. Theweleit, like Millett, insists on the interconnection of misogyny and racism. He explains that his own understanding "evolved step-by-step as I read the books, rather than from any preconceived theory," a permission which enabled me to allow myself the same unfolding (1: 57). I learned from both his use of and his (in my opinion) abuse of psychoanalytic theory. Finally, the fact that the Freikorpsmen's systems strongly resembled the systems of the authors in my study pushed me toward the historical research which resulted in chapter 1 of this book.

The Rigid Personality, Diagnosis and Description: Leon Salzman, David Shapiro, and Otto Kernberg. In my attempt to place my authorial systems somewhere within the discourse of normalcy and pathology, I turned to the diagnostic categories of three clinicians: Leon Salzman, David Shapiro, and Otto Kernberg. My aim was not to find an appropriate diagnostic label for each one of the authors but rather to examine the authorial profile in the context of clinical diagnostic systems—to see how the two categories would cathect. A more playful image for this process would envision the reader/critic as diagnostician and the composite implied author (Greene/Williams/Lewis) as the patient who has come in for a diagnostic interview.

Sander Gilman explains the need to stereotype as a (fruitless) attempt to gain control. The authorial systems of Greene, Williams, and Lewis are each characterized by rigidity and a preoccupation with control, boundaries, and power. In *The Obsessive Personality* (1968), Leon Salzman describes his work with individuals who suffer from a need for control and an overestimation of their power to control themselves and the universe. In such people, who are usually men, "all emotional responses must be either dampened, restrained, or completely denied."[17] However, "the enormous ground swell of feelings" must go somewhere and is often split off from the self and attached to another person, idea, or group of people. Salzman's typical obsessive client was a man who showed an alternation of grandiosity with a nagging feeling of doubt and inferiority. His need to maintain control caused his relationships with others to be dominated by manipulation, distortions, and double binds. While he was prey to intrusive homosexual thoughts, these thoughts were "symbolic or metaphorical statements about his weakness and inadequacy" rather than real homosexual desires (29). When such a man married and became dependent on his spouse, awareness of his dependency needs was experienced as a great threat.

In *Autonomy and Rigid Character* (1981) David Shapiro also emphasizes the suppression of feelings as a component of the rigid personality. According to Shapiro, such rigidity results from a failure in the course of development to internalize autonomy. A child who is allowed gradually to become an independent agent in his world will be able to internalize the principles of adult authority. The rigid person who has been unable to internalize this authority must, on the other hand, constantly and forcibly impose it on himself, often through the idealization of some outward authority figure or institution.[18] The rigid person is able to visualize or experience only relationships "between superior and inferior—the degradation or humiliation of one by another, the imposing of will by one, the surrender of the other" (*Autonomy*, 101–2). When he feels inferior, ashamed, or humiliated, his rigidity hardens, as does his attitude toward those he regards as inferior:

> Such persons—who, for certain rigid men, may include women in general, and even more, "effeminate" men—embody what the rigid individual is ashamed of, defensively repudiates, and therefore hates. He regards them as unworthy of respect. He is disgusted by them, sometimes outraged by them, even obsessively so; and if he is also in a position of actual power or authority, he may be driven to punish them. This contemptuous punishment of weakness or inferiority . . . is what we call sadism. (*Autonomy*, 107)

In a statement that echoes Theweleit, Shapiro reasons that for such men the erotic is located not in one's own feelings (these are inaccessible) nor in mutual engagement but rather in the degradation of the other.

Shapiro's discussion of the sadism associated with rigidity is not confined to pathological individuals but applies to pathological institutions and societies (like that of the Freikorpsmen) as well. He mentions in particular military organizations, giving as an example the sadistic practices of Marine boot camp: "sadism is regularly associated with and justified by pedagogical, moral, disciplinary, or corrective purposes . . . sadistic behavior is often supposed to teach the child, the prisoner, the subordinate, the recruit, respect for authority and 'right' values and standards" (*Autonomy*, 107).

In *Autonomy and Rigid Character*, Shapiro discusses obsessive-compulsives and paranoids as two types of rigid personalities. In an earlier book, *Neurotic Styles* (1965), he distinguishes between the two types. The obsessive-compulsive typically operates out of "a compelling objective necessity, some imperative or higher authority than his personal choice or wish, which he is obliged to serve."[19] Obsessive-compulsives are "intensely and more or less continuously active at some kind of work" and are "most comfortable feeling they have their own little niche or bailiwick in which they devote themselves to carrying out their established duties ordained by higher authorities" (*Neurotic Styles*, 41). As we will see, such a description fits Charles Williams the man and is reflected in his authorial system.

The paranoid person, also most likely to be male, is hypersensitive, suspicious, and hyperalert, with a rigid and biased directiveness of attention. He is constantly in a state of tense mobilization, sometimes careful and controlled, sometimes ready for defensive counterattack. Paranoid types experience disdain for humanness; especially for softness and femininity: "one may easily get the impression that they would prefer a world that was completely mechanized" (Shapiro, *Neurotic Styles*, 79). Nevertheless, "a major category of paranoid delusions has to do with being directly controlled or immobilized by special or supernatural devices, machines, or powers possessed by enemies" (*Neurotic Styles*, 84). Paranoid people, like obsessive-compulsives, are in general extremely aware of power and rank. Shapiro agrees with Salzman that while paranoid men are especially prone to obsessive worry about homosexuality, they are usually not homosexual. It is the longing to assume what he thinks of as the woman's will-less eroticism and sexual surrender, as well as the desire to "become the instrument of a strong and authoritative figure," which Shapiro gives as the reason why men with paranoid features so often worry obsessively about their own homosexuality and project this worry outward into a hatred of homosexuals and effeminate men (*Neurotic Styles*, 155).

Wyndham Lewis was a rigid paranoid personality, and his authorial structure reflects such a paranoid system.

Otto Kernberg's description of the narcissistic personality overlaps in many ways with Shapiro's and Salzman's descriptions of the rigid personality. Kernberg's narcissistic patients are marked by a shallow emotional life and the inability to believe in the reality of others genuinely to care about them. They consequently suffer from a constant and torturous internal experience of emptiness and boredom.[20] They alternate between self-devaluation and a pathological grandiosity:

> The interpsychic world of these patients is populated only by their own grandiose self, by devaluated, shadowy images of self and others, and by potential persecutors representing the non-integrated sadistic superego . . . as well as primitive, distorted object images onto whom intense oral sadism has been projected. . . . The grandiose self permits the denial of dependency on others, protects the individual against narcissistic rage and envy, creates the precondition for ongoing depreciation . . . (282)

Because they are unable to integrate or synthesize "the good and bad introjections and identifications" (34) they must constantly split off and project the "bad self" onto others, whom they they then despise and fear. "Good" others, those from whom they expect narcissistic supplies, are idealized, but are depreciated and treated with contempt the moment they fail to deliver (228). Kernberg notes that such patients often admire some public figure whom they see as an extension of themselves. When the admired individual rejects them or otherwise fails to satisfy, "they experience immediate hatred and fear, and react by devaluing the former idol" (236). Kernberg's patients feel they had the right to control, possess, and exploit others. In love relationships they idealize and long for the love object, but this longing, which is a defense against primitive rage, is liable to rapid breakdown, and then turns to rage or withdrawal. In such personalities "the projection of primitive conflicts around aggression onto sexual relations between the parents increases distorting and frightening versions of the primal scene, which may be extended into hatred of all mutual love offered by others."[21]

Kernberg's typical patient presents "a hungry enraged, empty self, full of impotent anger at being frustrated, and fearful of a world which seems as hateful and revengeful as the patient himself" (233).

It is easy to recognize the Freikorpsmen in this description, but it is also easy to recognize our composite profile. Once again Wyndham Lewis appears to be a classic narcissistic personality, but Greene's agonizing emptiness and boredom and Williams's sadistic religious mentorship also fit the pattern. In all the texts we will examine, male characters repeatedly express their horror and disgust at the primal scene. In addition, the picture of an empty, self-absorbed narcissist, with his alternation of grandiosity and self-hatred and his need to split off and project his unacceptable "female" self, is deeply congruent with our authorial profile.

Modified Objects Relations Theory: Melanie Klein, Karen Horney, Dorothy Dinnerstein, Jessica Benjamin, and Nancy Chodorow. If we turn to Woolf, Millett, and Theweleit, to help us understand our profiled author, we may see him as a "normal" recipient of phallocentric values. If we turn to Salzman, Shapiro, and Kernberg, on the other hand, we might classify him as a sufferer from a clinically diagnosable condition. In the next two sections of this chapter, I will abandon classification and turn to theories of development in order to understand why our profiled author turned out the way he did.

In my discussion of Kate Millett, I mentioned Sigmund Freud's phallocentric viewpoint. Freud saw the root of the male's aggression in his final identification with his father and adoption of his authority and located the formation of that aggression in the Oedipal stage. While this theory offers some explanation for male repudiation of females and femininity, it does not really explain the terror of women felt by the men in our study. In its focus on the father it also fails to acknowledge that in our society most children are parented by and identify with their mothers during the important early years. Jean Stockard and Miriam Johnson write:

> Gynocentric theories suggest a psychological explanation of male dominance that rests on the universal social assignment of mothering to women. To escape from the power of the mother and the intensity of their first feminine identification, males create ways of coping that deny this identity in themselves and establish their own independent power.[22]

Melanie Klein and Karen Horney, two female psychoanalysts who wrote in the 1930s and 1940s, were early gynocentric theorists who challenged phallocentric Freudian theory. Melanie Klein, arguably the first object relations theorist, posits a model of development which speaks in terms of disembodied parts, with a baby relating not to its mother in her entirety but rather to "the good or bad breast" or "the good vagina." This tendency, Klein's disconcerting way of attributing incredibly sophisticated powers of self-analysis to infants, and her inference that mothers are to blame for adult pathology has led to Klein's dismissal by many contemporary theorists. However, if one interprets Klein's language symbolically rather than literally, her theories can be extremely useful as an approach to the authors in this study. As Nancy Chodorow notes: "Klein turned psychoanalysis from a psychology of the boys' relation to the father to a psychology of the relation of the mother in children (people) of both sexes. For Klein, children's intense reactions to and infantile fear of their mother, her breast, her insides, and her powers, shape consequent emotional life" (3).

Klein was also the originator of two concepts which I use repeatedly in this book: splitting and projective identification. In Klein's concept of splitting, the infant splits off a hated or resented aspect of a needed object (the "bad breast") in order to retain it for himself or herself. Through projective identification, that badness is then projected onto something or someone else, or onto a group which is identified as "Other." In "Notes on some Schizoid Mechanisms," Klein writes:

> In psychotic disorders this identification of an object with the hated parts of the self contributes to the intensity of the hatred directed against other people. As far as the ego is concerned the excessive splitting off and expelling into the outer world of parts of oneself considerably weaken it.[23]

As we have already seen, the authors in this study frequently use projective identification to split off the despised "female" part of themselves and project it onto the woman and the Jew.

Karen Horney, another neglected female analyst who challenged the dominant discourse of Freudian theory, agrees with Klein on the primacy of the early mothering experience. In a pioneering paper, "The Dread of Women" (1932), Horney demonstrates how the young boy's longing to be a woman, originating in his primary identification with his mother, is challenged in a way which creates a terrible "menace to his self respect."[24] She notes: "[A]ccording to my experience the dread of being rejected and derided is a typical ingredient in the analysis of every man"

(357). The boy reacts with a dread of the female and moves "in the direction of a heightened phallic narcissism." His task at puberty is "not merely to free himself from his incestuous attachment to his mother, but more generally, to master his dread of the whole female sex" (355).

Horney very accurately describes the deep ambivalence shown by our profiled author, who felt torn by his conflicting needs regarding women, experiencing on the one hand "the violent force by which the man feels himself drawn to the woman" and on the other "his longing, lest through her he might die and be undone" (349).

While she reasons that this struggle "leaves more or less distinct traces in every man, and give to his general attitude toward women a more particular stamp," a man who cannot resolve the conflict "is invariably a man whose whole attitude toward women has a marked neurotic twist" (356–57). His attempt to cope with his dread and to regain self-respect may result in a disparagement of women or an objectifying glorification of them. His relations with women may "take on a sadistic tinge" (356). Of such men Horney writes:

> The simple craving of love . . . is very often overshadowed by their overwhelming compulsion to prove their manhood again and again to themselves and others. A man of this type . . . has therefore one interest only: to conquer. . . . We find a remarkable mixture of this narcissistic overcompensation and of surviving anxiety in those men who, while wanting to make conquests, are very indignant with a woman who takes their intentions too seriously, or who cherish a lifelong gratitude to her if she spares them any further proof of their manhood. (359)

A man can also "avoid the soreness of the narcissistic scar" through an inability to desire any woman who is his equal. Horney comments: "From the prostitute or the woman of easy virtue one need fear no rejection and no demands in the sexual, ethical, or intellectual sphere: one can feel oneself the superior" (359).

For a reader familiar with the work and lives of Lewis, Williams, and Greene, these descriptions, based on the analytic encounter, are almost uncanny—it is as if the authors in this study had themselves spent time on Horney's analytic couch.

Finally, Horney makes the connection between this male struggle and male creativity. She wonders whether the need for mastery of his dread of females may be "one of the principal roots of the whole masculine impulse to create work—the never ending conflict between the man's longing for the woman and his dread of her?" (349). Like Millett and like me, when Horney began to look at actual texts (her examples are poetry by Heine and Schiller), she found the underlying theme of the dread of women in male texts rather overwhelming. "Is it not really remarkable (we ask ourselves in amazement) when one considers the overwhelming mass of this transparent material, that so little recognition and attention are paid to the fact of men's secret dread of women?" (350).

A later gynocentric theorist, Dorothy Dinnerstein, in *The Mermaid and the Minotaur*, believes that it is female-dominated child-care which "guarantees certain forms of antagonism against women." Her elucidation of this antagonism reads like a description of both the Freikorpsmen's and my authors' attitudes toward women:

> fury at the sheer existence of her autonomous subjectivity; loathing of her fleshly mortality; a deeply ingrained conviction that she is intellectually and spiritually defective; fear that she is untrustworthy and malevolent. . . . an assumption that she exists as a natural resource, as an asset to be owned and harnessed, harvested and mined . . . [25]

Dinnerstein also stresses the man's need to keep a rigid boundary between himself and women; if he relaxes that boundary, "she can shatter his adult sense of power and control; she can bring out the soft, wild, naked baby in him" (66). The fear of women is thus closely linked to the fear of being infantilized, of "sinking back wholly into the helplessness of infancy" (164). Such frightened men feel a "deep-rooted tendency to renounce the sensuous-emotional world of early childhood, to seal off the layer of personality in which the primitive erotic flow between the self and the surround has its source" (32).

The image of being captured by a malevolent female and transformed into an infant is a recurring one for Lewis, and, in a more symbolic sense, for the other authors as well. The rigidity, the effort to seal oneself off, and the terror of what might happen should the vulnerable boundaries of the self be penetrated have been noted by Theweleit as basic to his subjects' systems. It is also key to the systems of all three of my authors.

In *The Bonds of Love: Psychoanalysis, Feminism, and the Problem of Domination* (1988), Jessica Benjamin uses what she calls her intersubjective theory to explore the genesis of domination. Recognition of the other is one of the most important concepts in her theory, and is a necessary ingredient for healthy development. She demonstrates how Freudian psychoanalytic theory itself, like other male productions, embodies male fear of the female and the need to dichotomize and split off men's "female" libidinal impulses.

Benjamin is more critical than Theweleit of Margaret Mahler's theory of individuation. In the late 1960s, Mahler described the child's gradual separation and individuation from a symbiotic unity with the mother and his or her movement toward the ideal of autonomy. Benjamin sees this image of a ladder, with symbiosis with the mother on the lowest rung and successful separation or autonomy on the highest, as a model which is still dichotomous and hierarchical. Instead, she offers the image of an interactive system, with mutual recognition of the other as the ideal end goal. This is an especially difficult goal for the boy to achieve:

> The boy does not merely disidentify with the mother, he repudiates her and all feminine attributes. The incipient split between mother as source of goodness and father as principle of individuation is hardened into a polarity in which her goodness is redefined as a seductive threat to autonomy. (136)

When such mutual recognition is not achieved, there is "the absence of a differentiated sense of self and other," and the boy is unable to establish any relationships other than those involving dominance and victimization (73). In a passage that brings to mind E. M. Forster's famous phrase "only connect," Benjamin describes the "desperate anguish of those who feel dead and empty, unable to connect to themselves or to others" as the result of a failure of mutual recognition (19). This resonates most deeply with Greene, but applies in varying degrees to all three of the authors under discussion here.

Benjamin agrees with Dinnerstein, Klein, and Woolf that when a boy splits off the "female" part of himself, the result is a hardening and rigidity which she calls the loss of "inner space." When such a boy becomes a man, he lacks a sense of having the source of goodness inside, and can neither soothe himself nor find a way to communicate his needs to someone who can help (Benjamin, 173). Outwardly strong and individuated, he is inwardly empty, inhabited only by "a new kind of helplessness, one which has to be countered by a still greater idealization of control and self-sufficiency" (174).

Nancy Chodorow's book *Feminism and Psychoanalytic Theory* was especially helpful to me in providing a framework for object relations theory, which she defines as "a set of accounts about the constitution of self in the context of primary emotional relationships" (7). Although Chodorow has moved to a more decentered and multiple stance than that held by earlier object relationists Klein and Mahler, she writes: "I have yet to find a convincing explanation for the virulence of masculine anger, fear and resentment of women, or of aggression toward them, that bypasses, even if it does not rest with—the psychoanalytic account, first suggested by Horney, that men resent and fear women because they experience them as powerful mothers" (6).

Like Benjamin, Chodorow views life not as a series of stages to be transcended but rather as "a course of transactions between self and other[s] that. . . . throughout life are renegotiated to recreate the sense of self and others in terms of connection, separation, and in between" (10).

In her discussion of theorist Hans Loewald, Chodorow praises his refusal to privilege either conscious or unconscious processes, instead capturing "the way that unconscious processes resonate with conscious and thus give conscious life depth and richness (12–13). It is easy to fall into separating these two realms into binary oppositions, but Chodorow's theory is far more congruent with my own experience of the creative process—as well as with the way I observed it in operation in the writers in this study.

Chodorow expands on Horney's basic scenario for the male internalization of the dread of women, concentrating on the boy's initial identification with his mother and desire to be a woman. She explains that for both girls and boys a core gender identity is established in the first two years of life concomitantly with the development of a sense of self.

> Underlying . . . core male gender identity is an early, non-verbal, unconscious, almost somatic sense of oneness with the mother, an underlying sense of femaleness that continually, usually unnoticeably, but sometimes insistingly, challenges and undermines the sense of maleness. Thus, because of a primary oneness and identification with his mother . . . the seemingly unproblematic sense of being male is an issue. A boy must learn his gender

> identity as being not-female or not-mother. . . . developmentally, the maternal identification represents and is experienced as generically human for children of both genders. (109, 111)

In a society where males have power and cultural hegemony, but begin life with a primary female identity, the problem of achieving adequate masculinity is a crucial life task. Chodorow quotes Margaret Mead: "[M]aleness in America [and I would suggest elsewhere] is not absolutely defined, it has to be kept and re-earned every day" (Chodorow's interpolation).[26] Societal norms enforce gender roles more fiercely for boys and punish them more for transgressing them. Chodorow points out the existence, especially in cultures where boys spend most of their early life with women, of male initiation ceremonies whose purpose is to exorcise the female role, or to "brainwash the primary feminine identity and to establish firmly the secondary male identity."[27] In such societies indications of the compulsive assertion of masculinity, including violent behavior toward women, male narcissism, and phobia toward mature women, are especially prevalent.

Once again, this theory resonates deeply with our authorial profile and helped me to understand the incredible amount of energy which these authors seem to devote to the Sisyphian task of earning and retaining their manhood. We will end this chapter with a discussion of the male initiation ceremony of boarding school, a rite which is certainly designed to accomplish the brainwashing I described above.

Finally, Chodorow makes the point that the "dread of women" is aroused by internal as well as external stimuli. As Benjamin and Theweleit also stress, "it is the fear of that womanly power which has remained within men—the bisexual components of any man's personality" which poses the primary threat (Chodorow, 40).

The Role of Trauma; or, Surviving Childhood: Alice Miller, Ellen Bass and Laura Davis, Mike Lew, and Lenore Terr. Objects relations theory can encompass pathological development but is more properly concerned with the underlying whys and hows of normal experience rather than attempting to explain why some men are more and some less whole than others. Theweleit mentions several ex-soldiers with backgrounds similar to those of the Freikorpsmen who became pacifists instead of killers, but he does not explain why each group of men made the choices they did.

To address this question it will be useful to turn to theoreticians who have concentrated on the influential role of trauma in pathological adult development.

In *For Your Own Good* (1980), Alice Miller identifies hidden cruelty and abuse of children as the cause of dominance and aggression in the adult personality. An abused child reasons, according to Miller, "[As] what was done to me was done for my own good . . . I am expected to accept this treatment as an essential part of life and not question it" (115). Such a child is not free to hate or condemn his or her persecutors, but must instead deny his or her own feelings "at the high price of surrender of self" (121). He or she is forced into the familiar inner rigidity described by all our theorists, and is forced to project his or her anger and hatred either inward, onto the self, or outward. Through the mechanism of repetition compulsion, the child compulsively repeats some form of what he or she has experienced. Like the idea of a floating fear and loathing which, when it cannot be felt or expressed at the source, must be projected either onto the self or onto other people or groups, the concept of repetition compulsion will be extremely helpful in understanding the fiction in this study, in which the same scenarios, involving similar stereotypes, are evoked over and over again.

Miller illustrates her theory through a discussion of the childhood of Adolf Hitler. She describes the way in which Hitler's family structure was the prototype of a totalitarian regime, with the father as brutal ruler and the mother as oppressed victim, who in turn acts as overseer of the children. Adolf in particular was the father's scapegoat. Without recourse or any chance to express his suffering, he was forced to deny it, splitting it off and storing it up. Later, "through the agency of his unconscious repetition compulsion [he] . . . succeeded in transferring the trauma of his family life onto the entire German nation" (161). While some brutalized children are able to turn to the other parent, if not for protection, then at least for a witness who can provide validation, Hitler's mother, depressed and subjugated herself, was unable to protect her child. After his father's death, Hitler's teachers were "only too happy to take over for the father when it [came] to disciplining the pupil" (168). They were no longer really needed, however; the brutal father had already been internalized.

Miller cites the famous passage in *Mein Kampf* in which Hitler declares, "Wherever I went, I began to see Jews." He quite graphically describes the way in which he redirected his bottled up hatred toward the Jews, and the relief it afforded him to do so. For Hitler, as for other anti-Semites before him, Jews had become

> the bearer of all the evil and despicable traits the child had ever observed in his father . . . a specific mixture of Lucifer- like grandeur and superiority (world Jewry and its readiness to destroy the entire world) on the one hand and ugliness and ludicrous weakness and infirmity on the other. (Miller, 178)

Hitler obviously could not have carried out his Final Solution without enthusiastic cooperation, and Miller reasons that his experiences were shared by millions of other children with similar upbringings. For them, "the Jews could now be blamed for everything, and the actual erstwhile persecutors—one's own, often truly tyrannical parents—could be honored and idealized" (187). Jews, according to Miller, provided the perfect scapegoat because of the well-established history of anti-Semitism which made it "the only permissible discharge" of "the right to hate" (166). Like Shapiro's example of military boot camp or the Freikorps organization, Nazism provided a societally sanctioned and institutionalized context for action: a group pathology which fit the individual's needs.

Miller's belief that the secrecy and denial accompanying abuse are even more damaging than the abuse itself is a new and most important insight to us here. Theorists like Gregory Bateson and R. D. Laing have argued, along similar lines, that it is not abusive parents or traumatic childhood experiences per se that are crazy- making, but instead such experiences when accompanied by inconsistency and denial.

In *The Courage to Heal: A Guide for Women Survivors of Sexual Abuse* (1988), Ellen Bass and Laura Davis share many of Miller's conclusions. Speaking to the survivors, the authors write: "If you told someone about what was happening to you they probably ignored you, said you made it up or told you to forget it. They may have blamed you."[28]

Survivors of sexual abuse, which is rarely acknowledged by its adult perpetrators and may not be consciously remembered by its victims, experience mental and physical numbing, a feeling of leaving one's own body, the sense of being divided into more than one person, a desperate need for control, and the need to split, which Davis and Bass define in a different way than the previous theorists as:

> a way of coping that allows a person to hold opposite, unintegrated views. . . . The child separates the father whom she depends on for love from the father who abuses her. This allows her to preserve an image of the "Good" father but at great cost. Your reality was denied or twisted. . . . Rather than see the abuse or your parents as bad, you came to believe that you did not deserve to be taken care of, that you in fact deserved abuse. (42)

Survivors of such abuse are usually subject to depression and anxiety and are sometimes self-destructive and suicidal. For them, "memories are vague and dreamlike, as if they're being seen from far away" (72).

In *Victims No Longer: Men Recovering from Incest and Other Sexual Child Abuse* (1988), Mike Lew confirms Bass and Davis's findings of the effects of abuse on male survivors, and adds that the victim role is especially difficult for men in our society who fear emasculation or transformation into something "less than" male: "the victimized man wonders and worries about what the abuse has turned him into . . . he may see himself as a child, a woman, gay, or less than human—an irreparably damaged freak."[29] Some survivors resort to broad parodies of "acceptably masculine" behavior in order to counteract this self-perception, spending their lives in a tireless exertion to prove themselves "real" men. Like the abused female, the abused male learns to "hide, deny, and control his emotions" (73). He is subject to anxiety and to sometimes suicidal depression. Like the rigid men Shapiro studied, "his perception of the world is that there are only two kinds of people, abusers and victims" (73).

Lenore Terr, who studied the effects on children of one terrifying event, such as a kidnaping, a survived plane crash, or a traumatic molestation, also observed psychic numbing, depression, and repetition compulsion in her subjects. She quotes Selma Fraiberg as saying, "Trauma demands repetition."[30] Through an examination of the textual productions of Alfred Hitchcock, Edgar Allan Poe, and Stephen King, she demonstrated how each one of these authors experienced a traumatic experience of terror which he reenacted over and over again in his works. I was especially interested in Terr's reports of childrens' repetitious dreams and play, which might be exact repetitions of the traumatic event, modified repetitions, deeply disguised dreams, or terror dreams forgotten upon awakening. Keeping in mind Chodorow's injunction not to separate conscious and unconscious material, one could view the reproduction of traumatic events in dreams, in play, and in textual productions as all part of the same process of reenactment.

In her study of the children who survived a traumatic event in 1976 in Chowchilla, California, in which a busload of children were kidnapped, terrorized, and buried in a hole before being restored to their families physically unharmed, Terr also witnessed the phenomenon of displacement of anger onto groups which are perceived as more vulnerable than the actual objects of the anger. Several white Chowchilla children, who never spoke of their anger at their (white) kidnappers, whom they still feared and experienced as powerful and dangerous, developed a hatred and fear of blacks or Hispanics after the event.

While none of the authors in this study suffered the kind of continual abuse that Hitler underwent as a child, and none seemed to have suffered the one overwhelmingly traumatizing event which scarred Terr's subjects, each of them emerged into adulthood bearing some of the scars of abused children whose experience was denied or hidden. I will trace Graham Greene's history of abuse in chapter 6 and link it to the numbed, alienated and despairing men who people his fiction. The theory of abuse coupled with denial held by Miller, Bass and Davis, and Lew is also most helpful in understanding the English public school experience.

The Public School Experience: Group Trauma and the Enforcement of Ideology. In what he calls his "Theory of Permanent Adolescence," Cyril Connolly claims that "the experiences undergone by boys at the great public schools, their glories and disappointments, are so intense as to dominate their lives and to arrest their development."[31] Graham Greene and George Orwell both go so far as to explain their entire opus as a way to compensate for the trauma of public school, while Christopher Isherwood, only half-humorously, attests to the lasting effect of the authority figures in his public schooling: "If the Nazis got over here, I should be terrified of them, of course; but I could never, at the deepest level of my consciousness take them quite seriously. Not as seriously as I took my first headmaster."[32] And in his famous discussion of the dangerous influence of the public school, W. H. Auden concludes: "[T]he best reason I have for opposing Fascism is that at school I lived in a Fascist state."[33]

It is impossible to read fiction by British male writers of the 1930s and the 1940s without acknowledging the tremendous influence of the public school experience. This influence appears even in the works of those writers like Charles Williams who did not attend public school. The public school "system" embodied, encoded, and enforced the linked attitudes toward women and Jews investigated in this study. At the risk of separating the inseparable, I will examine this experience first in terms of its traumatic impact and then in terms of the ideology it valorized and promulgated.

For the men who, in the 1930s and 1940s, described their experience of being sent away to school, preparatory and public schooling was almost inevitably a traumatic experience which left permanent emotional scarring.[34] Its survivors resort to terms such as torture, slavery, concentration camps, and Gestapo, more usually associated with dictatorships than schooling, to describe their experience. And yet public schooling is now and has been for the most part reserved for the members of the dominant class and is considered a badge of privilege. To go through what feels like torture and be told you are privileged to do so is an example of Alice Miller's poisonous pedagogy—a widely unacknowledged and thus doubly harmful instance of the societally accepted abuse of children.

Being sent away to school was a particularly brutal example of the severing of the tie to the mother and things female described by Jessica Benjamin and an example of the male initiation rites Chodorow cites as particularly prevalent in societies in which the father is largely absent and parenting is carried out by the mother and/or other females.

To judge from autobiographical evidence, most middle- and upper-class English boys who came to adulthood in the thirties and forties had distant and remote fathers, themselves emotionally scarred products of the public school system. The boys were brought up in early childhood largely by their mothers and by female servants: nurses or "nannies" whose job was to look after their needs. Their early schooling was inevitably by women teachers, and in some cases the first part of their lives was spent in a wholly female society. Boarding school meant an abrupt and total severance from this female nurturing; a sudden immersion in a world which was often physically without women and totally without warmth or nurturance. In addition, the new male world quite consciously set itself up as an exorcism of femininity. Orwell is particularly poignant in his description of this sudden severance from home:

> Your home might be far from perfect . . . but at least it was a place ruled by love rather than by fear, where you did not have to be perpetually on your guard against the people surrounding you. At eight years old you were suddenly taken out of this warm nest and flung into a world of force and fraud and secrecy.[35]

Greene and Lewis both wrote of the shock and anger they felt when their formerly all-powerful and protective mothers could or would not protect them from this brutal new world.

Going away to school, the initiation rite used to transfer middle- and upper-class boys from the "soft" female world to the "hard" masculine world to which they would henceforth belong, differed from initiation rites in other tribes, studied by Mead, Chodorow, and others, in that this one lasted, not for a few hours or days, but (except for the weeks of holiday) for eight or nine years. It is not surprising that boys in this situation felt the need to do more than disidentify with their mothers: they needed to repudiate them and all their feminine attributes (Benjamin, 136). The hatred and loathing of the woman and things female which we find in all the works of fiction in this thesis may well have its roots at least in part in this repudiation.

Most male initiation rites in other societies, while separating boys from the nurturing female world, provide alternative pleasures in the form of warm male bonding and the mastery of new adult tasks, as well as sexual and material privileges. Again in contrast, young boys sent to boarding school received no benefits except the greatly delayed gratification of enforcing the same pattern of abuse on younger boys at a future date. In exchange for female nurturance, they were given into the care of a hierarchic, repressive, and dominating authority which placed them under the arbitrary rule of older boys, prefects, staff, and headmaster. This system, reproduced in some way in most of the works of fiction in this thesis, did its best to prevent the child's own internal development of a sense of himself as an independent agent in his world (Shapiro, *Autonomy*, 73). As Hugh Walpole put it in the introduction to his schoolboy novel, *Jeremy at Crale* (1927), the public school, "catches personality by the throat and chokes it."[36]

E. M. Forster, Graham Greene, George Orwell, Hugh Walpole, Evelyn Waugh, Stephen Spender, Aldous Huxley, Somerset Maugham, and Cyril Connolly are only a few of the legion of men who wrote eloquently of the persecution and suffering they underwent at school.[37] Common elements in their descriptions are systematic and accepted bullying and beating, very often with a sexual element, by both older boys and staff; a rigid and feudal system of hierarchy in which older boys used younger ones as slaves; a denial of physical and mental privacy which attacked the root of a boy's autonomy and sense of himself as an individual; isolation and loneliness; a lack of physical nurturance; and the daily experience of hunger, cold, and filth. These unacknowledged abuses certainly constitute the kind of traumatizing mistreatment identified by the theorists in the previous section.

Graham Greene describes the school where his father was headmaster and from which he tried to escape through suicide attempts as "a savage country of strange customs and inexplicable cruelties: a country in which I was a foreigner and a suspect, quite literally a hunted creature."[38] This country, which his critics named "Greeneland," would appear in all his fiction.

In *Enemies of Promise* (1938), Cyril Connolly, who calls the preparatory school system an "incubation of persecution mania," describes a feudal system which permanently ruined his nerves and which turned him, at least temporarily, into a sadist. In that school, young boys, systematically tortured and beaten with rubber tubing, developed "such a feeling of persecution that we bullied each other to forget it."[39] After being "broken under the strain of beatings at night and bullying by day," Connolly in turn became a bully. The language he uses to describe this is significant:

> We now became the rulers of Chamber, in which Godfrey Meynell was the Hitler, Highworth the Goering, and I the Goebbels, forming a Gestapo who bullied everyone we could and confiscated their private property. (183)

As with other torture, the effects were long-lasting. Ten years after leaving school, Connolly wrote, "[T]o this day I cannot bear to be sent for or hear of anyone's wanting to see me about something without acute nervous dread" (183). His classmate Orwell wrote to Connolly upon reading the essay: "I wonder how you can write abt. St. Cyprian's. It's all like an awful nightmare to me."[40] Nine years later, in 1947, Orwell did allow himself to remember St. Cyprian's and what he had learned there:

> a deeper grief which is peculiar to childhood and not easy to convey: a sense of desolate loneliness and helplessness, of being locked up not only

> in a hostile world but in a world of good and evil where the rules were such that it was actually not possible for me to keep them.[41]

The descriptions of beatings and other sadistic activity nearly always contain elements of sexual abuse by those in power, similar to the kind described by Lew and Davis and Bass. Stephen Spender described the effects of one of the two preparatory schools to which he was first sent at the age of nine:

> I was like all the other boys from the preparatory school, sadistic. . . . We had . . . deeply and instinctively realized that the head master was sadistic. It would have surprised my parents to have known that they might just as well have had me educated at a brothel for flagellants as at the school referred to.[42]

The abused child Miller describes is told and believes that his beatings are for his own good. Similarly, the English public school boy, sometimes sent off to school as young as five years old, had no way of trusting his own perceptions or receiving validation of them from others. He arrived at school excited to enter this new adventure and full of its romantic myth as conveyed by his father, who had disowned or split off his own painful memories, and by popular boys' books such as Thomas Hughes's *Tom Brown's School Days* (1857) and Kipling's *Stalky and Co.* (1897). The new world's strictly enforced taboo against complaining to adults prevented him from expressing his own misery.

In *Abinger Harvest*, E. M. Forster describes this bottling up of the emotions which creates men with "undeveloped hearts": "[I]t is not that the Englishman can't feel—it is that he is afraid to feel. He has been taught at public school that feeling is bad form."[43]

Like Miller's future mass criminals and Shapiro's future rigid men, unhappy boys reasoned that since school was a good thing, they themselves must be bad. It is no wonder that the key words, often repeated in all the descriptions of school life, are betrayal, shame, and humiliation.

Besides developing self-loathing, boys at public school were forced to deny their own feelings and individuality "at the high price of surrender of self" (Miller, 121). The surrender of self is emphasized over and over again in accounts of school life, which stress the malleability of the new boy at school and the nonexistence or looseness of his boundaries: an issue for each of the three authors in this study. In John Reed's words: "Moral sleight of hand left the unprepared boys in a formless condition upon which the authorities could impress at will their pet beliefs like seals on warm wax" (71). And as George Orwell puts it, "the weakness of the child is that it starts with a blank sheet" (*Such*, 241). Later, Orwell describes a young boy of seven or eight being sent off to prep school as "jelly-like"—a striking image for the lack of autonomous boundaries which we observe in each of our authors.

As all the theorists emphasize, "the enormous ground swell of feelings" which are a residue of unacknowledged abuse do not simply disappear (Salzman, 30). Through the mechanism of repetition compulsion, the adult must somehow express and repeat the abuse he or she has experienced and denied as a child. Especially when acknowledgment of the abuse is never fully achieved, the anger, hatred, and fear are projected onto the self or the outer world. Given all this, it is perhaps not surprising that ex–public school boys made so much use of clearly designated "Others" in their writing, whether these others were Jews, women, gays, members of the working class, people of color, or foreigners. The surprise, in fact, may be that, unlike the Freikorpsmen, they were able to use such a benign activity as fiction writing to express their projections.

While it is not always separable from the psychological imprinting which it accompanies, the importance of the ideological system which is reproduced and enforced on both the overt and covert level through public schooling cannot be underestimated. Virginia Woolf identified Cambridge and Oxford as the seats of male training in dominance, but boys who attended these universities as the culmination of a public school career had long since integrated such teaching into their value systems. Boys who had been transferred from their home environments to school, deprived of their sense of autonomy and individuality, in a state like "jelly" or "a blank page," were in a particularly vulnerable condition, ideal for ideological programming. It will be worthwhile to end, then, with a closer examination of the values transmitted at preparatory and public schools, as reflected in several novels about school life.

Rudyard Kipling's *Stalky and Co.* (1897) takes place in a school which prepared boys for the military rather than in an ordinary public school, but it is mentioned over and over again by the authors in this study and their peers as perhaps the most influential of the schoolboy novels. Read by almost all schoolboys of this era before they went away to school, it served, in Eagleton's terms, both as social cement and as an instrument of ideological control. *Stalky and Co.* features three fun-loving, brave, virile, and sexually innocent friends who never express their feelings, the most profound of which is a deep love for their country. They exemplify the values of Thomas Arnold's "Muscular Christianity," a system designed to form a schoolboy into "an English gentleman . . . of moral strength."[44]

On a more covert level, however, the boys inhabit a world governed by a homoerotic and sadomasochistic code in which beatings play an important role. The head, a much-loved authority figure who has proven himself through outstanding bravery in the war and through saving the life of one of "his" boys, regularly beats his students, who enjoy this activity tremendously, lining up for punishment. In another situation the roles are reversed, with our heroes, who have been asked by the friendly school "padre" to intervene in the bullying of some smaller boys, gleefully assuming the positions of sadistic torturers:

> The method and silence of the attacks was breaking their nerves. Between each new torture came the pitiless, dazing rain of questions, and when they did not answer to the point, Isabella-coloured handkerchiefs were thrust into their mouths.[45]

At the end of this highly erotic effort, the torturing heroes "were all dripping with excitement and exertion" (177).

In contrast to boys and men, women in *Stalky and Co.* are seen as either untouchable virgins of the boys' own class, or working-class, grotesquely voluptuous figures, intent on sexually entrapping the boys. The virgins (sisters of other boys and the daughter of the head) are too noble even to think about, let alone to touch, while kissing the other kind of girl is both immoral and disgusting, as becomes evident in a scene where the gang of three sets up a bookish young prefect to be kissed by a vulgar local girl in a pub in order to shame, frighten, and humiliate him.

Despite the revulsion against women, and the profoundly homoerotic content which has made this book a favorite with gay men ever since its publication, the boys are established as particularly heterosexual ("virile" and "red-blooded"), and Kipling informs us several times that later in life they will marry.[46] Homosexuality, on the other hand, (referred to obliquely in *Stalky* and other school books as "beastliness") is the cardinal sin—one of the two misdeeds that the beloved headmaster punishes with automatic expulsion. (One assumes that the other sin is masturbation, although Kipling, who was writing for a young audience, never refers to it, even obliquely.) Embedded in this system, with its homoerotic and sadomasochistic subtext, its aggressive heterosexuality, and its overt disapproval of homosexuality, is a subtext of the loathing of women, who are separated into untouchable goddesses and whores. It is a subtext we will meet again and again in the novels of Lewis, Williams, and Greene.

In addition to an ideology of sexuality and gender roles, *Stalky and Co.* enforces and valorizes secrecy and hypocrisy. Orwell, whose novel *1984* I believe refers more directly to his schooling than is generally acknowledged, named this kind of hypocrisy, when internalized and adopted on a national level, "double-think." As we have seen, Alice Miller is eloquent on the poisonous effects of such double-think on mental health, and in chapter 1 we saw numerous examples of it in the public school boys who grew up to hold governmental and civil service posts.

Stalky and Co. also delivers messages about blood, which, whether good or bad, will inevitably out. The three boys range from solidly middle to upper class, but all are from "old" families, and Kipling treats foreigners, the working class, and "social climbers" with contempt. This ideology, in which anyone different (women, Jews, the working classes, the non-English) is considered alien and not fully human, is evident in two parallel "humorous" incidents in which the boys shoot a drunken working-class man and a cat. The cat dies, the man does not—and the two shootings are both regarded as harmless pranks which give boys who must learn to carry guns later on some useful experience.

There are no Jewish boys at Kipling's prototypical school, and the only mention of Jews comes when the boys successfully start a row by posing to a naive and upstart master as moneylenders, calling each other "cold blooded Jew" and "filthy Shylock" (126–29). The joke is on the master, whose bad breeding prevents him from recognizing true English gentlemen, for whom such alien behavior as moneylending would be impossible. The mythic connotations of the Jew are used in this case to sort out true from false English gentlemen.

Another characteristic of the group of three is their ability to repress their feelings. In an interesting encoding which opposes the alien race and alien femininity with the male code of the suppression of feelings, the boys are horrified at a sentimental speech by an M.P. "born in a gutter and bred in a board school" in which he voices their unspoken but holy feelings about patriotism. The boys have learned: "the lesson of their race, which is to put away all emotion and trap the alien at the proper time. . . . The reserve of a boy is tenfold deeper than the reserve of a maid, she being made for one end only by blind nature, but man for several" (242–43).

Virginia Woolf noted how such values lead to the enthronement of war, and in an Afterword describing a school reunion that takes place years later, Kipling assures us that the boys in question have gone on to lead lives as courageous Empire builders. Stalky, the particular hero of the book, has become a fearless wiper out of those "Fuzzies" (or blacks) who do not uphold the proper English values and a protector of those who do.

Lest we dismiss the ideology in *Stalky and Co.* as peculiar to Kipling's nationalistic and militaristic world of 1897 and to the military school he attended as a boy, it must be noted that the values I have identified above can be found in any writing about the public school experience from the nineteenth century to the present. In Graham Greene's autobiographical *A Sort of Life*, for instance, he recalls his sadomasochistic relationship with a boy called Carter: "I admired his ruthlessness, and in an odd way he admired what he wounded in me. Between the torturer and the tortured arises a kind of relationship" (82).

In Hugh Walpole's *Jeremy at Crale* (1927), the young hero's boyish inarticulateness and disgust at expressed emotion are much like the qualities of the gang of three in *Stalky*. Walpole's hero, like the gang of three, remains "pure": he is allowed a platonic worship of a slightly older boy, but when a much older one touches him and shows inclinations to be "soppy" he rejects him firmly. *Jeremy at Crale* boasts one Jewish character, a boy named Scholdz, who, Walpole tells us, is ostracized or "barred," "not so much because he was a Jew as that he was a worm, a sneak, a dirty skunk, a 'scat.' "[47] Unlike another blond and blue-eyed victim of bullying in the book, who refuses to tell on anyone, Scholdz has complained to the adults. He is a stereotypical Jew, whose experience at school "had reduced his soul to a fine state of crawling and subsequent sycophancy" (148). A similar Jewish boy appears in Simon Raven's memoir, *The Old School* (1986), and in this case too Raven carefully explains that he was ostracized not because of his Jewishness but because of the other boys' natural reaction to "extreme ugliness of a kind unfamiliar to Anglo-Saxons":

> the trouble was that a combination of the most distressing features of underfed and overgrown pubescence with such Levantine characteristics as blubber lips, bulbous nostrils and greasy black hair was so appalling that all instincts of decency in the beholder were from time to time wiped out.[48]

As in *Stalky and Co.*, the value being taught is not only contempt for the alien but hypocrisy. While the schoolboy worlds of Kipling, Walpole, and Raven are obviously highly anti-Semitic, that anti-Semitism, like the loathing of women, must never be openly acknowledged. It is not difficult to make the leap from this attitude to that of the British government during World War II, which, while proclaiming their sympathy for the Jewish plight, sealed the escape routes for these same Jews.

Unlike *Stalky and Co.*, Alec Waugh's *The Loom of Youth* (1917), written when he was seventeen and had just been expelled from Sherborne School for "unnatural practices," was designed to expose rather than to glorify the values taught at public schools. *The Loom of Youth* was violently condemned and banned, supposedly because of its homosexual theme. In fact, the homosexuality is so carefully handled that I had to read the book several times to find the scene in question, and the book itself is far less homoerotic in its content than *Stalky and Co.* It was assuredly not the book's innocuous gay scene but the positive acceptance of homosexuality, along with the young author's effort to expose his school's hypocrisy, which caused the uproar. Significantly, men who had attended Waugh's own school, Sherborne, were most invested in banning *The Loom of Youth*.

As a new boy at "Fernhurst," Gordon, the hero of *The Loom of Youth*, is exposed to and reflects on the values around him. These include the usual hierarchical and sadistic prefect system, a one-sided and doltish worship of games and athletic prowess, and a prevalent, but taboo, homosexuality. Gordon's happiest hours at Fernhurst are those spent with a loved younger boy, and he realizes that the danger lies not in the sexual act but in discovery: "That was the one unforgiveable sin—to be found out."[49] Although Gordon himself is not found out, another boy, Jeffries, is. "Fernhurst taught me everything," Jeffries complains. "And now Fernhurst, that made me what I am, turns around and says, you are not fit to be a member of this great school! And I have to go" (60).

Waugh's acceptance of his youthful homosexuality was the exception to the rule, and part of what his contemporaries found so shocking in his book. It comes as no surprise that many of the men who passed through this system of double messages and hypocrisy grew up with some degree of confusion, repression, shame, and fear about their sexuality, whichever direction it took. Many who later became homosexual, like E. M. Forster, who remained a virgin until he was over forty, repressed their sexuality for years out of learned fear and shame, while others, like the authors in our study who successfully achieved the heterosexual ideal, never learned to regard women as human beings. Some, both gay and straight, became secretly attached to the ritualistic, fetishistic sexual practices which were so great a part of public school life.

George Orwell's essay "Such, Such Were the Joys," first published posthumously in 1954 and probably written around May 1947, is especially interesting to us here because of Orwell's later linking of his own early anti-Semitism (traceable in the fiction he wrote during the 1930s) to the trauma he received and the values he learned in preparatory and public school. Orwell felt that he had managed to retain some measure of autonomy, "an incorruptible inner self," throughout his experience at St. Cyprian's preparatory school (*Such*, 39). In his effort to recover psychically and morally, from St. Cyprian's, from Eton, and finally from his five years in the Burmese Civil Police, which he experienced as an extension of public school, Orwell waged a desperate inner struggle to hold on to this incorruptible inner self, with its hatred for the hierarchical and oppressive values he had been taught. At the same time, and less successfully, he struggled with the need to escape the self-hatred, humiliation, and self-disgust he had learned as a victimized small boy.

"Such, Such Were the Joys," its title taken from Blake's poem "The Echoing Green," paints a devastating picture of St. Cyprian's, which both Orwell and Cyril Connolly attended from the age of eight, and which Orwell calls "Crossroads" in the essay. I have already described Orwell's misery at school. When the the homesick eight-year-old began wetting the bed, he was publicly shamed by the sadistic headmaster's wife and beaten by the headmaster. His asthma too was diagnosed as "a moral disorder, caused by overeating" (*Such*, 32). Other memories of the "squalor and neglect" include constant hunger and inedible food, a human turd floating in the bath, the "filthy, dilapidated lavatories, which had no fastenings of any kind on the doors . . . a sort of compound of sweaty stockings, dirty towels, faecal smells" (*Such*, 35).

Much of the essay is written in a tone of outrage. Orwell angrily questions the assumption: "that a little boy of eight or ten should be a miserable, snotty-nosed creature, his face almost permanently dirty, his hands chapped, his nails bitten, his handkerchief a sodden horror, his bottom frequently blue with bruises" (*Such*, 32).

However, like the abused children described by Lew and by Bass and Davis, Orwell also internalized his abuse. Long after leaving school he continued to believe that he smelled and was "preternaturally ugly" (*Such*, 52). "I was an unattractive boy," he assures his reader. Even more poignant is this indirect portrait of himself as a child: "Even a creature that is weak, ugly, cowardly, smelly, and in no way justifiable still wants to stay alive and be happy after its own fashion" (*Such*, 52). In their studies, Bass and Davis, Lew, and Terr all cite suicidal depression as one of the symptoms of the victims of abuse. The self-hatred and despair Orwell internalized at preparatory school were so profound as to make him doubt his very ability or right to survive: "Until I was about thirty I always planned my life on the assumption not only that any major undertaking was bound to fail, but that I could only expect to live a few years longer" (*Such*, 52).

In addition to self-hatred, Orwell learned that, as Lew puts it, life consisted of abusers and victims:

> Virtue consisted in winning: it consisted in being bigger, stronger, handsomer, richer . . . than other people. . . . Life was hierarchical and whatever happened was right. There was [*sic*] the strong, who deserved to win and always did win, and there were the weak, who deserved to lose and always did lose, everlastingly. (*Such*, 50)

In "Such, Such Were the Joys" and many other works, Orwell recognizes and attempts to unlearn the contempt he was taught for foreigners, Jews, and members of the working class. He never recognizes that his contempt for homosexuals and, greatest of all, his contempt for women, stemmed from the same source.[50]

Alice Miller discusses the adult need to deny a child's experience of abuse, explaining it as a way adults manage to split off the pain of their own childhood abuse. She notes that many biographers who "have difficulty identifying with the child . . . quite unconsciously minimize mistreatment by the parents" (153). Miller's theory is helpful in trying to understand the widespread dismissal of the many exposés of the public school system. Valentine Cunningham, for example, who also mocks gay writers for their arrested development, scoffs at the "inflated idea . . . that life at your prep school and public school was . . . seriously endangering and traumatic and testing." In his otherwise fascinating and informative book on the literary scene of the thirties, Cunningham dismisses the link among public schools, concentration camps, and fascism, calling it a "conventional piece of schoolboy and youthy exaggeration" (119). Similar denial and silencing greeted the publication of "Such, Such Were the Joys," which Orwell dared not publish during his lifetime but which was found among his papers after his death and published in 1952.

Orwell's biographer, Bernard Crick, devotes an entire chapter to very dubious proof that Orwell was fabricating in what he calls the "virulent" essay. He questions every detail, down to the famous "turd" in the baths, using as evidence Orwell's (censored and corrected) letters home from school and letters by, and interviews with, the many people who objected to the essay's publication. Among these are Orwell's first literary executor, Sir Richard Rees, who advised Sonya Orwell not to publish the essay, claiming, "[I]t is such a bad piece of writing, far below G's standard . . . he was already past his best when he wrote it"; and Andrew Gow, Orwell's tutor at Eton, who wrote to Sonya advising that the essay be suppressed, calling it shocking and monstrously unfair.[51] Orwell's childhood friend, Jacintha Buddicom, objected not only to the besmirching of the school's image but to that of the man: "The picture painted of a wretched little neurotic, sniveling miserably before a swarm of swanking bullies, suspecting that he 'smelt' just was not Eric at all" (Crick, 42). Crick also quotes at length one Colin Kirkpatrick, of Salisbury, Rhodesia, "a very eminent Old Cyprianite whose memory seems excellent," who wrote, "NOT TRUE! YOU SOD! LIBEL!" in the margins of Orwell's essay (23). Crick introduces a rebuttal by Mrs. Wilkes (the headmaster's wife) and finally questions Orwell's evidence on the grounds that, after all, he was not liked at school, and an unpopular boy might be prone to lying. He concludes: "The English upper class tend to exaggerate the effect of their school days, whether for better or worse. . . . [B]oys of his class expected to go away to school and can have been under no illusions" (20, 33).

Crick's attempt to discredit "Such, Such Were the Joys" is apparently an effort to rescue *1984* by showing that the totalitarian world Orwell created in that book was not a reproduction of his school experience, as so many critics have maintained. He evidently feels that no book which arose from "childhood trauma at St. Cyprian's" could be a "rational work of political reflection" (365). In fact, it is just such efforts as Crick's at separation and silencing which Orwell is attacking in "Such, Such Were the Joys," as well as in such essays as "Shooting an Elephant" (1936), "Notes on Nationalism" (1945), and "Anti-Semitism in Britain" (1945). In these essays he asserts again and again that the ideology taught in public school leads directly to totalitarian regimes, imperialism, racism, and anti-Semitism. Orwell's exposé of the public school system is an effort to break that very British "conspiracy of silence" which he felt characterized both the public attitude toward the Holocaust and the attitude of the British left toward Stalin's labor camps and his policy of mass murder. Orwell might well have connected the British officials who complained of too much time spent on "wailing Jews" and censored the news of their fate and the critics who attempted to censor the sniveling of the "wretched little neurotic" who was trying to tell the truth about what happened to him at school.

While Orwell's analysis stops short of sexual and gender dynamics, Christopher Isherwood describes the way in which the sexual and gender imprinting he received at public school was directly connected to a system of values he calls fascistic and led to the worship of war. His analysis illustrates, in a way Millett and Woolf would approve, that values involving war and dominance cannot finally be isolated from those involving sexual and gender programming. Isherwood's analysis of his own unconscious and fantasy process allows us valuable insight into the unconscious processes and productions of the writers in my study. In *Lions and Shadows* (1938) he describes his schoolboy preoccupation with "the complex of terrors and longings connected with the idea 'War.' " For him, "War" was associated with a test—"of your courage, of your maturity, of your sexual prowess"—which ended with the question, compulsively posed to himself, "Are you really a man?"[52] He managed to convert this obsession, which he found too anxiety-provoking, into one which was set in his school rather than on the battlefield. Slowly, he began to evolve "a cult of the public school system"—a comforting and romantic dream very similar to the vision in *Stalky and Co.*, which had in part inspired it:

> In this daydream, the central figure, the dream I, was an austere young prefect called upon unexpectedly to captain a "bad" house, surrounded by sneering critics and open enemies, fighting slackness, moral rottenness, grimly repressing his own romantic feelings toward a younger boy, and finally triumphing over all obstacles, passing the tests, emerging,—a Man. (*Lions*, 77)

In describing his daydream, Isherwood muses that a clever English fascist might have converted him "inside half an hour" at that time in his life: "the rulers of Fascist states do not sneer—they profoundly understand and make use of just these phantasies and longings" (*Lions*, 78–79).

E. M. Forster, too, understood that the racism, anti-Semitism, and woman-hating which were all parts of the public school ideology were inseparable: all part of one dehumanizing package. In his essay denouncing anti-Semitism, "Jew Consciousness" (1939), he remarks on how well his preparatory school, with its cult of sister- and mother-hating, prepared him for "anti-Semitism. . . . now the most shocking of all things . . . assailing the human mind at its source."[53]

Of the three authors in this study, Wyndham Lewis was expelled from Rugby after two years, and Charles Williams's parents could not afford to send him to public school. Only Graham Greene attended public school from the age of ten on, and even he had a year off, thanks to the nervous collapse brought on by the school experience. Nevertheless, the public school system of values extended to each of the authors. Lewis's label as a Rugby man was an extremely important part of his identity and one he constantly referred to. Charles Williams bitterly regretted his lower–middle-class origins, and became, as Valentine Cunningham points out, "more devoted an honorary Oxonian" than many who actually attended public school and Oxford (137). And Graham Greene continued to write almost compulsively about his public school in novel after novel. The public school system did not, of course create its own values anew, but instead reproduced and conducted the values of the dominant class to its young males. It would accordingly be overly simplistic to place all of the pathology we find in the work of our three authors at the polished and ornamented doors of Britain's public and preparatory schools. But the public school system of values did extend far beyond its obvious boundaries. The inner rigidity and inability to feel, the attachment to hierarchic systems of dominance and subjection, the inability to regard either the opposite sex or those who are different from oneself in terms of nationality, class, race, sexual preference, or religion as fully human—all these are qualities inherent in the public school ideology, and all are evident in the work of Lewis, Williams, and Greene.

FOUR

The Molten Column Within: Wyndham Lewis

Introduction: Why Study Wyndham Lewis

One could argue that to begin the main body of this book with an in-depth examination of the life and work of self-proclaimed "Enemy" Wyndham Lewis hardly promises a balanced approach. As Fredric Jameson puts it in his *Fables of Aggression*:

> The polemic hostility to feminism, the uglier misogynist fantasies embedded in his narratives, the obsessive phobia against homosexuals, the most extreme restatements of grotesque traditional myths and attitudes—such features, released by Lewis's particular sexual politics . . . are not likely to endear him to the contemporary reader.[1]

Were this an attempt at a balanced survey of authorial attitudes during this time period, I would certainly begin with another author. As it is, the extreme nature of Lewis's system makes him an ideal first author for this study. His attitudes, while more intense in their expression, and often closer to the surface, are not, in fact, different in essence from those I will go on to explore much more briefly in the ensuing chapters, when I turn to Charles Williams and Graham Greene.

Wyndham Lewis, as even his most sympathetic critics are forced to admit, was a rigid, narcissistic man whose life and work both exhibit a marked tendency toward paranoia. While his biographer, Jeffrey Meyers, insists that he could not have "led such a carefully organized and intensely productive existence if he were paranoid or suffered from persecution mania,"[2] sufferers from a paranoid personality disorder are in fact very often driven and ambitious people who accomplish a great deal in an outward sense, and whose main difficulties occur in their relations with others and their feelings of chronic unhappiness and discontent.[3] While Lewis's personality disorder never prevented him from writing and painting, it did stop him from ever concentrating fully on one project at a time and from living in any kind of comfort, ease, or happiness. Of the many people who had known Lewis whom Meyers interviewed while researching his biography, every one except his wife mentioned his "persecution complex." Julian Symons, a close friend and admirer, is typical in his memory of his friend's "inner rage, at the conditions of life, the nature of society, the dullness of other people."[4] Another friend, John Rothenstein, commented: "As a talker he was largely defensive, expressing his suspicions that this person or that had plotted or was plotting to do him an injury" (Meyers, 201). Wyndham Lewis habitually sat with his back to the wall to watch for enemies. He constructed secret doors and keyholes in his homes, and even when in direst poverty, always maintained several different homes and concealed his various addresses. Lewis fought compulsively with everyone—especially with those who attempted to help him or to become close to him. Like Kernberg's narcissistic borderline patients, Lewis was unable to perceive of others as real. His shadowy world was populated largely by his "own grandiose self, by devaluated shadowy images of self and others, and by potential persecutors representing the non-integrated sadistic superego" (Kernberg, 282).

Lewis's work reveals a similarly narcissistic paranoid system. At its base is a conspiracy spearheaded by women—in league with (depending upon the occasion) feminine homosexual men, Jews, children, nonwhites, members of the working class, communists, and various other groups. The white male, especially the white male artist and genius (of whom Lewis himself may be the only example of his time), is the victim and designated prey of this conspiracy. Unless he keeps up a constant vigilance and maintains a tireless and aggressive self-defense, he will soon find himself turned into a helpless infant at the mercy of a woman who will swallow him up, engulf and obliterate him, or transform him into one of her own kind.

In those of Lewis's books upon which I will concentrate here, written between 1926 and 1939, the alliances involved in the conspiracy constantly shift and regroup, with one group of "Other" taking center stage only to be replaced by another, but the basic plot remains the same. Wyndham Lewis often called himself the "Enemy." In fact, his stance, reflected both in his life script and in every one of his published works, is that of a victim, desperately defending himself against the enemy world which surrounds and besieges him. When his friends begged him to stop biting the hands that fed him, his inevitable explanation was that he had no choice but to make the first move in order to defend himself against the attack that he knew was coming.

Lewis is a prime example of the male socialization in violence described by Millett and Woolf and discussed in chapter 2. Like one of his temporary mentors, Marinetti, Lewis linked war with art and beauty. Valentine Cunningham describes him as the writer

> who did more than any other . . . to carry over a war-time violence into art and criticism, and to make that toughness fashionable, who thought of his typewriter as a machine-gun, who declared that art was "like" war, who sought by his published preachments to "leave upon your retina a stain of blood[.]" (64)

Lewis's particular *process* as a writer also makes his work especially accessible for the purposes of this study. The image he uses most often to describe that process is that of a volcano, either immediately before or in the act of eruption. Whether he produced fictional texts or didactic books of criticism or political theory, his writing was an expression of the "molten column within."[5] Though many critics feel that Lewis's real ability was as a painter rather than as a writer, the manic force of his need to name his obsessions could not be harnessed to painting alone, but needed the release of words. Lewis's autobiographical persona, Tarr, the eponymous hero, gives his friend a lecture on the "daily ooze" of sex:

> [Y]ou must listen. I cannot let you off before you have heard, and shown that you understand. If you do not sit and listen, I will write it all to you in a letter. YOU WILL BE MADE TO HEAR IT![6]

This urgency allowed Lewis little time for deliberation or revision, and material which other authors might have removed in the process of revision, or censored in the first place, is all here, available for our scrutiny.

Lewis was also his own most frantic critic. He regularly organized friends to review his books and often reviewed them himself in other books or in special pamphlets and magazines he printed for that purpose. Each negative review was a personal insult which must be countered in print. When public opinion went against his published views, or when those views began to change, he wrote new books and articles in which he justified and explained himself. In some of these revisionist texts, including *The Jews, Are They Human* (1939), *The Hitler Cult* (1939), and *Rude Assignment: An Intellectual Biography* (1950), Lewis attempts a kind of self-study, reinterpreting his earlier books on the same subject. Neither of the other authors in this study felt the pressure to undertake this kind of revisionist self-analysis. Wyndham Lewis, in many ways a most unappealing author, is thus the perfect subject for this book.

A Man Only His Biographer Could Love: Wyndham Lewis and Jeffrey Meyers

Wyndham Lewis expounded upon his political beliefs very freely, writing books and pamphlets even when he had scanty information on the subject or when he knew that revealing his views would harm him personally. He had a different attitude when it came to revealing details of his personal life, especially those involving his relations with women or anything to do with his childhood and youth. His two openly autobiographical works, *Blasting and Bombardiering* (1937), an account of his World War I experience, and *Rude Assignment* (1950), each sheds some significant light on his life and thinking, as do his collected letters, which also reveal significant patterns in his ideas and relationships. But on the whole Lewis carefully avoided what he called "the very dark cavern" of his early life (*Rude Assignment*, 126). Fortunately, Jeffrey Meyers's well-researched biography, *The Enemy* (1980), illuminates this darkness.

Meyers regards his subject as "a genius," "the most important painter of the twentieth century," and "one of the most lively and stimulating forces in modern English literature."[7] He finds Lewis "more sympathetic than menacing" and identifies with him, finding that "Lewis and I had . . . a similar physique, quarrelsome temperament, hatred of publishers, capacity for work and commitment to intellectual life." One of Meyers's acknowledged aims in his biography is to "restore Lewis's reputation."[8]

It may be that the development of a certain degree of sympathy and even identification is necessary in order to write an excellent biography. Nevertheless, I found Meyers disturbingly eager to justify Lewis's stances in everything from his support of Hitler to his conviction that "Bloomsbury" was a group of puerile cowards whose main aim was to destroy the career of one Wyndham Lewis. Meyers tends to take Lewis at his own word, justifying his subject's more dubious attitudes by citing Lewis's idealism or his philosophy of artistic creation. One example out of many is his acceptance of Lewis's post facto explanation that his support of Hitler was in fact a pacifist effort which came out of his desire to avoid another war. These rationalizations distort our picture of Lewis and are reminiscent of the earlier critics' efforts to justify Dickens by quoting his own philo-Semitic statements. They also allow Meyers to avoid any psychological interpretation or explanations and to remain for the most part on the surface of his complicated and deeply troubled subject's psyche. Lewis, who advocated a concentration on the surface rather than the "intestines" of his subjects and who wrote "Give me the outside of all things, I am a fanatic for the externality of things," would doubtless have appreciated his biographer's approach.[9] However, it is an approach which I find limiting, and which I have attempted to challenge here.

Despite his own admiration for Lewis, Meyers never hesitates to share other, less glowing opinions held by his contemporaries, and a disturbing portrait of the artist seems at times to emerge in spite of the valiant rescue efforts of his biographer. While my own evaluation of Lewis is obviously quite different from Meyers's, I have great admiration for his research, and I am in debt to him for much of the information (though not its interpretation) in this chapter. Meyers's chronology of Lewis's life, his careful and painstaking footnotes, and his references to other sources such as reviews of Lewis's work were also invaluable to me. My own discussion will, of necessity, be limited to those parts of Lewis's life which seem most relevant to the issues at hand. For a more comprehensive discussion of Lewis's life, including his career as a visual artist, a thorough study of the evolution of all his published work, and an account of his illness and later years, I recommend the reader to Meyers.

The Vortex of Betrayal: Wyndham Lewis's Life

Psychoanalytic theory, which purports to explain all of human behavior in terms of childhood experience, has always been (and is still) especially susceptible to projective interpretations. For example, Virginia Woolf, whose girlhood incest experiences had been so traumatic and whose own father so invasive, interpreted psychoanalytic concepts such as infantile fixation and the Oedipal complex to refer to the incestuous desires of "fathers" for their daughters.[10] Similarly, psychoanalysis was invariably associated in Wyndham Lewis's mind with the idea of mother-son incest. He applied his own brand of obsessive and angry rumination to this theme, often suggesting, with some confusion, that Freud himself was responsible for unhealthy mother-son relationships. In the light of his childhood experience, it is not surprising that Lewis's concern about "the incest theme" led him to project it onto Freud—as well as onto assorted Others.

Percy Wyndham Lewis was born on a yacht in Canada in 1882, the same year as James Joyce and Virginia Woolf, three years before Ezra Pound and six years before T. S. Eliot. Lewis's American father, Charles, married his English mother, Anne, when she was sixteen and he was thirty-three. Charles, who never worked after he left the American army, was an erratic and distant man whose main activity was sailing, perhaps because it took him away from his family for prolonged periods. The marriage was stormy, and Charles's reputation for lechery, which his son would inherit and surpass, was soon established. Charles eloped with a housemaid in 1893, when Percy was eleven and the family was living on the Isle of Wight. For Anne Lewis, this was the last straw. Although Charles soon abandoned his mistress and appealed for a reconciliation, she refused all his attempts. Apparently glad to be rid of her husband, she accepted a small stipend from him and established a home for her adored son with a loyal female relative. The entire household functioned around the needs of young Percy, as he was then called. As his letters to her make clear, Percy and his mother had a strong and exclusive attachment which allowed for no other men in the mother's life, and no women in the son's during his mother's lifetime, except for a series of despised and objectified sexual partners.

Before finding a new family, Charles repeatedly wrote abject letters to both his wife and his son. One such letter to the twelve-year-old Percy begs him to intercede with his mother, blames himself, bemoans his lonely fate, and accuses Anne of cruelty and of excessive attachment to her mother (Meyers, 5). It is normal for any child to blame himself or herself in the event of a parental separation, and an appeal of this kind laid an especially strong burden of responsibility on young Percy, who must have felt that he had quite literally won his mother and destroyed his father. At the same time, he must have experienced his mother, who had demonstrated her power to expel his father and now required her son to take his place with her, as both omnipotent and dangerously engulfing.

It is not surprising that Lewis was preoccupied with the theme of incestuous relationships between mother and son, or that he split off or projected the very concept of such relationships onto any "Other" available—Freud himself, "non-europeans," or women.

In his right-wing political tract, *The Art of Being Ruled* (1926), Lewis speaks of the husband and wife as natural enemies and of the son and mother as natural allies and friends. He reasons, "It is perhaps as well to add that all the freudian oeudipus-complex propaganda has greatly assisted this situation."[11] In his defense of the beleaguered white race, *Paleface* (1929), he again blames Freud for creating the "incest-theme" and goes on to assure us that this theme does not apply to him, as it is "inappropriate to the european communities, on whom no severe religious restrictions of race or of caste have been imposed."[12] Over and over again, Lewis paints a picture of a powerless male child, the victim of the two forces of Jewish Freudianism and feminism, which, in league together, intend to force him to fulfill the Oedipal script:

> [T]his same figure—the highly educable sensitive child—has already been stirred up against papa by his feminist mama, and is pondering already, if he is a reader of Freud, if he shall slay and eat him. (*Art*, 287)

Lewis's close tie with his mother and what he must have experienced as her expulsion of his father made the need to "escape from the power of the mother and the intensity of the first feminine identification" an even more pressing task (Johnson and Stockard, 222). The longing to return to the feminine world in which he had been a pampered and worshiped young prince was also a powerful force and one which would have to be forcibly destroyed if it were not to overwhelm him. Horney describes the longing of the young boy, whose primary identification is with his mother, to be a woman, or as Chodorow puts it, his "underlying sense of femaleness" (9). In the appropriately named *Doom of Youth* (1932), in *The Apes of God* (1930), and indeed in all of his other works, Lewis argues that most men, given half a chance, will attempt to return to the womb—that is, to a primitive female (and female-dominated) infancy. In *Rude Assignment*, Lewis describes this powerful longing, once again projecting it onto Freud: "The great influence of the psychoanalytic doctrines of the Unconscious (the desire to return back into the womb type of suggestion) has had the effect of leading an entire generation back to the frontiers of primitive existence" (194).

For Lewis, both childhood and femininity would become objects of the most rigid splitting off. Dinnerstein mentions men's terror "of sinking back wholly into the helplessness of infancy" (164), and this was a particularly potent fear for Lewis all of his life. Like the Freikorpsmen, who saw the desire for human pleasure as a contagious disease, Lewis needed to "renounce the sensuous emotional world of early childhood" in order to "seal off the layer of personality in which the primitive erotic flow between the self and the surround has its source" (Dinnerstein, 32). Indeed, Lewis, like Shapiro's paranoid patients, aspired to become a machine and proclaimed his goal of writing in a way which transcended all human emotion.

Lewis hardly saw his father after 1900, the year Charles paid his son's fees at Rugby school. In letters to his mother, Lewis refers to him facetiously as the "Parent Over the Water" and "Old Rip" and discusses possible ways the two of them might "extract" money from him.[13] After his father's death, Lewis wrote about him more sympathetically and began to identify with him, calling him "that odd-man-out in a society of go-getters."[14]

After being educated at home and at a series of prep schools, at none of which he remained more than a few months, the thirteen-year-old Lewis was sent to Rugby. While the story of the many prep schools remains untold, it is probable that neither mother nor son could endure prolonged separations, and that Lewis's mother withdrew him from school when he was unhappy. Lewis has also always kept silent on his Rugby experience, but clues are available. The intelligent boy came at the bottom of his class of twenty-six. His school reports describe him as lazy, lethargic, sluggish, and thoroughly idle (Meyers, 8). Meyers points out that "his lethargic school report was a striking contrast to the demonic energy of his maturity," but fails to note that the report reads like a description of clinical depression (Meyers, 8). After two years, Lewis was expelled from Rugby for failing to work, a rare occurrence there. In an early draft of a chapter in *Rude Assignment*, which he later deleted from the final copy, Lewis describes Rugby in terms of beatings: "I . . . was frequently beaten by my house master, both for idleness and breaches of the rules. He used to rush up and down his dark study, lashing at me with his whistling cane."[15] He concludes, "I left Rugby after about two years of kicking balls and being beaten for lack of work" (*Rude*, Appendix, 250). Beating takes a prominent role in all his school memories. Much later, Lewis "proudly" told Marshall McLuhan that he was the first Rugby man to receive six beatings in one day (Meyers, 7). Also, in an unpublished "vitae" he wrote when applying to teach in an American university in 1949, he writes: "Scarcely did I learn to spell, certainly. Masters noticing this, and pretending it was my fault, took advantage of the fact to beat me unmercifully. They gave me a note to hand to my Housemaster. When he read it he beat me too. But I understood it was their fun, and being quite healthy, didn't mind" (Meyers, 8).

Behind the casual dismissal, one can perceive the misery of a boy brought up in an adoring, exclusively female household as his mother's beloved companion, thrust into an atmosphere where his homesickness and depression made him seem stupid, and where he was constantly, sometimes ritualistically beaten. While Lewis shies away from direct statement, the implication is that the masters in question got sexual enjoyment—"their fun"— from beating young boys. Aware of the prominence and sexual connotation of beatings in such "homosexual" boarding school novels as Alec Waugh's *The Loom of Youth* (which he attacked savagely in his own *Doom of Youth* and elsewhere), Lewis describes his own beatings in a flat, neutral tone, stressing his immunity from such forms of sexuality. Like the abused children Alice Miller describes, whose denial festers and is reborn in their later sadism, Lewis needed to deny his own pain and abuse (and certainly any sexual feelings related to it) at all costs. Yet the boarding school experience undoubtedly left its mark.

Lewis regarded women as a species apart. Heterosexual activity, was a compulsive and addictive need for him and for the male characters in his fiction, and his relationships with his many sexual partners was one "between superior and inferior—the degradation or humiliation of one by another, the imposing of will by one, the surrender of the other" (Shapiro, *Autonomy*, 102). Homosexuality, on the other hand, was a despised and abhorred taboo for which Lewis felt obsessive rage and horror. At the same time, as we shall see, homosexual fantasies which featured Lewis in a submissive role in relation to a masculine hero played a prominent role in his work.

In the final version of *Rude Assignment*, Lewis eliminates the beating episode, substituting a sentence more characteristic of his archenemy, George Orwell. Public school, Lewis says, "caused a boy to be content for the rest of his days, to feel that he is 'playing the game,' oblivious to what the particular game happens to be" (119).

While early experiences can help explain our adult attitudes, they cannot, of course, ultimately determine them. In both Orwell and Lewis, the experience of public school led to a lifelong resolve never to "play the game," and an obsession with the roles of victim and oppressor, dominant and dominated. However, Orwell's resolution involved a system in which he defended or rescued an identified oppressed Other against the oppressor, while, as we have seen, Lewis's more narcissistic system featured himself as the overt aggressor but actual victim.[16]

After his expulsion from Rugby, Lewis's mother, who had noticed his talent for drawing, sent him to the Slade School of Art. Here he met Augustus John, one of the first of a series of father figures whom he would worship, then cruelly reject. At the Slade, Lewis's talent was appreciated, but, in a pattern which would be repeated with later authority figures, he had repeated conflicts with the school's administration and left after two years, without completing the course. He then embarked on an extended trip to Europe, where "gradually the devastating effect of English school life wore off."[17] In a rare stab at self-analysis in *Rude Assignment*, Lewis describes a "psychological factor" which he feels may have contributed to his strong reaction against "civilization." He mentions that, having left school early, he was younger than his contemporaries. He describes himself as having

> remained, beyond the usual period, congealed in a kind of cryptic immaturity. In my social relations the contacts remained for long, primitive. I recognized dimly this obstruction; was conscious of gaucherie, of wooden responses—all fairly common symptoms of course. It resulted in experience with no natural outlet in conversation collecting in a molten column within. This *trop-plein* would erupt; that was my way of expressing myself. (126)

As we have seen, these "wooden responses" and primitive social relations are typical of men who have never known mutual recognition and who consequently feel "dead and empty, unable to connect to themselves or to others" (Benjamin, 136).

Lewis's letters to his mother from abroad are, as Robert Chapman writes admiringly, "remarkable in their candour."[18] They shed light both on Lewis's relationship with his mother and on what would be an enduring pattern of relationships with women.[19] From Holland, along with detailed reports on his bowels and packets of dirty laundry for her to wash, he sends his mother the story of the landlord's daughter, whose bosom he has stroked. Shortly afterward, in a letter with marked paranoid content, he reports that her parents, whom he has heard quarreling, are plotting to marry him to their daughter:

> I think that I am often the subject of these disputes—also, which is very unpleasant, the people here talk about me in a disagreeable way in the next room. . . . I really have a most absurd dread of the very thought of marriage; I feel like packing up and flying to the British Consul for protection. (*Letters*, 14)

As Chapman acutely notes: "This incident . . . presents the lodger as victim, an unwitting catalyst in a situation which almost engulfs him" (17).

Lewis's next relationship, with a German woman named Ida, lasted longer but followed the same pattern. In 1905, he writes to his mother of a German lady who

> came round to see me one day and to my unquenchable amazement asked me to kiss her, and threw herself into my arms and kissed me with unabated vigour for three hours; well I'm very glad . . . it saves me a lot of trouble and expense to have a very beautiful and nicely bred mistress. (*Letters*, 18)

During the course of this relationship, which began with Lewis as the childlike, passive recipient of female passion, he appears to grow smaller and smaller as Ida grows larger. Unable to disentangle himself from this engulfing female, he writes to his mother of his inability to leave or forget Ida, despite "a hopeless feeling" in her presence. Caught, as Horney says, between "the violent force by which the man feels himself drawn to the woman" and "the dread lest through her he might die and be undone" (349), he writes: "I suffer very much about all of this, and spend many hours of great despondence; I don't see any prospect of this feeling passing" (*Letters*, 27). Months later, he writes: "I don't like her at all and avoid her as much as possible: it naturally is a cause of great annoyance, her presence, but then if I hadn't that I should have another" (*Letters*, 33). Like the paranoid men described by Salzman and the narcissistic borderline men described by Kernberg, Lewis's awareness of his own dependency on Ida fills him with anger and despair. Nevertheless, he is unable to conceive of life without a woman to provide sustenance.

In a later letter, he identifies with his father as a man persecuted by women: "I think I may go a step farther than my august father, and say there are 'too many bitches in this *world*'; I've had a lesson in the matter of women, such as I shan't forget in a hurry" (*Letters*, 35). Anne Lewis, presumably one of the "bitches" his father had complained about, apparently did not object to her son's statement. In his next letter to her on the subject, Lewis wishes Ida at the bottom of the sea and explains: "[H]appily I have a tender feeling in another direction, which may ripen into covetousness: then farewell... german" (*Letters*, 36). In the end, Lewis childishly pleaded with his mother to visit Ida and end the affair for him, which she proceeded to do. Meyers writes, rather nonchalantly:

> In November 1908 Lewis' mother sent five guineas to Ida, who was expecting Lewis' baby the following month. When the infant was born, Lewis disowned it, left Ida and returned to England, establishing a pattern he would repeat with his later illegitimate children. He once told Kate Lechmere that he had accidentally dropped and killed Ida's baby... though this was probably not true... (Meyers 22)

"I am yours ever," Lewis signed his letters to his mother during this period, reassuring her of his continuing allegiance.

Meyers quotes Lewis as complaining about "his abnormal addiction to sex" (Meyers, 89). Sexuality for him, as for his fictional heroes, was a compulsive need which had little to do with attraction or choice. Lewis's character Tarr is certainly speaking for his maker when he explains that artists "discharge themselves" by satisfying their bodily appetites and when he calls sex with his German mistress, Bertha, a "milking process" (*Tarr*, 219). This metaphor, in which Lewis pictures himself as a female domestic animal, dependent on his "milker" to relieve him, appears throughout his work and reveals his self-disgust at his own dependency, as well as the resentment he felt for the women whom he needed.

In his sexual addiction and his close, though ambivalent, relationships with women, Lewis differs from the Freikorpsmen, who found sexual release in killing, not in intercourse, who tended to be celibate, and who found their primary relationships and their proof of masculinity within a male group. For Lewis, who would have found participation in such a group intolerable, unremitting sexual activity served as a continuous proof of his masculinity. He often boasted about his many attacks of gonorrhea, which caused year-long periods of illness and indirectly led to his death, and which, as he was seldom completely free from it, one imagines he may have transmitted to some of his sexual partners. In his letters, he refers to his friends' wives and mistresses as "cunts" and "sickening bitches." Hugh Porteus noted Lewis's combination of lechery and hostility to Porteus's Jewish girlfriends and affectionately remembers a painting at the doorway of one of Lewis's residences, showing "a shrewish female face, the lips neatly sewn together with jagged stitches of black cobbler's thread. This I learned to read as a reminder that no women were allowed to enter here" (Meyers, 203).

Like his paranoia, Lewis's misogyny was one of the characteristics noted by every contemporary Meyers interviewed, male or female, approving or disapproving—with the one outstanding exception of his wife. Jameson comments on the "obsessive sexism and misogyny which can go unnoticed by no reader of Lewis's work . . . so extreme as to be virtually beyond sexism," and this quality was as evident in his life as in his work (Jameson, 30).

If Lewis had ambivalent and contradictory feelings about sex and women, he felt no ambivalence for what he called "breeding" and for children themselves. Like the men in Kernberg's study, Lewis felt disgust at "the primal scene," which he evoked time and again in his fiction. In a rather strange grouping, Meyers comments on his "almost Swiftian disgust about bodily functions and newborn infants," a disgust which he explains in terms of Lewis's ideology: "sex and birth emphasized the horrifying dichotomy of mind and body" (Meyers, 89). A more satisfying explanation can be found in Lewis's often reiterated fear of regression into infancy, coupled with his need to be supreme in his mother's and in his other women's affections. In a striking instance of Miller's repetition compulsion, Lewis abandoned his five illegitimate children in a manner even more total than that in which his father had abandoned him, leaving each woman before she gave birth and never seeing or contacting any of them.

In 1908, Lewis returned to England, where he entered into a period of energy and fame and became a star of the avant-garde. He created numerous murals and stage sets, founded a group, which his friend and mentor Ezra Pound named "The Vortex," that produced two issues of a magazine, *Blast* (1914 and 1915), and wrote his first novel, *Tarr* (1918). During this time he fell under the influence of F. T. Marinetti, whom he had first heard lecture in London in 1910 and whose futurist movement, "an extraordinary premonition of the woman-despising necrophilia of fascism" (Oldfield, 12), I discussed briefly in chapter 2. In *Blasting and Bombardiering* (1937), in an early effort to erase his own fascist connections, Lewis denied any connection with Marinetti, but in fact the futurist movement, with its glorification of violence as necessary "hygiene" and its contempt for femaleness, provided the philosophical underpinnings for Vorticism and for *Blast*, as well as for Lewis's political writing of the 1920s and 1930s. Lewis's public break with Marinetti in 1914 was similar to his break with other mentors: Augustus John, Walter Sickert, Roger Fry, Sturgis Moore, Ezra Pound, and T. S. Eliot, to name only a few.

The list of mentors whom Lewis managed to attract and then viciously turned on is at least as numerous and as renowned as his list of mistresses. He was particularly vicious to anyone who helped him financially. In the collected letters one sees a pattern of initial warmth and gratitude, followed quickly by feelings of mistrust and suggestions that the friend or benefactor might be about to betray him; and then by a venomous attack, repeated until the friend finally withdraws, at which point Lewis accuses him of betrayal, disloyalty, venality, and other sins, and instructs him to stay away from then on. In a pattern typical of the narcissistic borderline personality as described by Kernberg, over and over again Lewis ejected the father who had abandoned him to the clutches of his mother.[20] Only those with the remarkable ability to ignore his insults were able to continue to support his work, although most of these discontinued any personal relationship.[21] Lewis longed for a strong and caring father and found plenty of men who were eager to play that role for the tough genius, as he was known. However, he was too terrified of his own homosexual leanings to tolerate such patronage for long, and the idealization of these father figures soon gave way to rage. We have seen how his dependence on women caused him to experience them as threatening and consequently to defend himself against them with great hostility. The same pattern existed with those men who attempted to help him financially or in other ways.

Meyers, eager to prove that Lewis was not in fact paranoid, explains that "the severe and degrading poverty he suffered during his entire adult life accounts in large measure for Lewis' suspicious character and hostile behaviour" (Meyers, 87). He also mentions Lewis's "fierce and ultimately self-destructive need to sacrifice people for ideas" and praises the way he "successfully separated the degrading poverty and squalor of his daily existence from his exalted intellectual and artistic life" (Meyers, 120). Again, he explains that Lewis's bizarre behavior toward the end of his life, including his chronic secretiveness about his address and telephone number, was merely an attempt to avoid creditors (Meyers, 11). While it is true that Lewis experienced chronic poverty, I would suggest that it was not poverty which created his behavior, but rather that his paranoid behavior created and sustained his poverty. While Lewis's books consistently lost money for his publishers and never supported him financially, he was an extraordinary portrait painter who was widely admired and could have made a good living painting portraits of those in the artistic and literary world. Instead, just as he insulted the patrons who attempted to help him financially, he insulted and degraded his subjects during their sittings. As if this were not enough to alienate them, he consistently set one price and afterward demanded more money than had originally been agreed upon.[22] The same was true for his literary career, in which he consistently alienated admirers and reviewers. Most of his contemporaries, even those who disliked him, agreed that Lewis was a man of great energy and talent. It took what amounted to a concerted campaign on his part to achieve his state of chronic need.

Typical of this campaign was his battle with "Bloomsbury," a group whose "members" embodied his obsessions with effeminate men, engulfing women, Jews, and leftists. Engaged as an artist for the Omega workshop, Lewis accused Clive Bell of stealing a commission for the Ideal Home exhibition which Lewis claimed was meant for him. In the round-robin that he circulated after the event, Lewis accuses the workshop members of being feminine and having to call him in "to do the rough and masculine work" (*Letters*, 49). The Bloomsbury group continued to be a focus for his rage throughout his life. He projected his personal failures onto them, believing that it was their scheming which prevented him from ever attaining critical or financial success in England, and constantly attacking the group's financial privilege, their homosexuality, their feminism, and their pacifism. In *Blasting and Bombardiering* he speaks venomously of "the Bloomsburies," who spent the war years

> under the wings of powerful pacifist friends . . . haymaking . . . in large sun-bonnets . . . disgustingly robust . . . all . . . of military age. . . . Yet they had money and we hadn't; ultimately it was to keep them fat and prosperous—or thin and prosperous, which is even worse—that other people were to risk their skins. (184–85)

Lewis himself joined the army in 1916 and, between repeated bouts in hospital due to his venereal diseases, spent most of the war in the north of England attempting to become an officer. He was sent to France in May of 1917 and stayed on the front until October 1917, when he gained a post as a war artist.

Unlike the Freikorpsmen, whose need for war was so extreme that they created their own war when none was available, Lewis found neither fulfillment nor release in battle. He did not, however, seem to feel the horror and despair some of his contemporaries did. In *Blasting and Bombardiering*, Lewis confesses that it was hard for him to feel the reality of war. Speaking through his fictional "mask," Cantleman, he notes: "[T]he news [of war] brought into relief a novel system of things. Everything was going to be delightfully *different*" (67). Referring to his "disinvoluture" (*sic*) in both art and war, Lewis explains: "My attitude to the war was unsatisfactory . . . I experienced none of the conscience-prickings and soul-searchings, none of the subtle anguish, of so many gentlemen whose . . . books poured out simultaneously upon the market about ten years ago" (*Blasting*, 7).

While much of this is a pose (readers are expected to conclude that Lewis, with his stiff upper lip, actually felt more than the wordy gentlemen), it does speak to the emptiness, numbing, or inner rigidity identified by every one of our theorists: the same "wooden responses" Lewis referred to in *Rude Assignment*. Lewis explains his own "disinvoluture" or inability to feel the reality of human death in war by confessing that "people seem to me to be rather walking notions than real entities" (*Blasting*, 8). This inability to conceive of others as real, a mark of the narcissistic personality, is a persistent theme for the male characters in Lewis's novels and other prose, where the idea of human beings as either machines or puppets, incapable of real feeling, occurs again and again. This characteristic metaphor was clearly based on Lewis's own cut-off and mechanized experience of self. All his fictional characters are marked by a strangely wooden, rather surreal quality, a trait which may be less a conscious stylistic choice than an inevitability, given Lewis's manner and limits of perception. As Julian Symons puts it, "He saw men and women as machines walking, their appendages of ears, nose, hands, stuck oddly on, their activities, from speech and eating to excretion and copulation, stutteringly awkward and comic" (2).

If war was not as devastating for Lewis as for others, it was not without its ill effects. The strongest emotion which comes through in his description of his wartime experiences, as in most of his writing, is personal betrayal. For Lewis, the war was the instrument which "robbed me of four years, at the moment when, almost overnight, I had achieved the necessary notoriety to establish myself in London as a painter" (*Blasting*,

13). In a characteristic metaphor, he describes the war—and life—as a male friend who has mortally betrayed him:

> Life was good and easy, and I called Life "friend." I'd never hidden anything from him, and he'd never hidden anything from me. Or so I thought. I knew everything. He was an awfully intelligent companion, we had the same tastes (apparently) and he was awfully fond of me. And all the time he was plotting up a mass-murder. . . . It took me some time to realize this *fully*. But from the very beginning of the War I got wise to it, in fits and starts. (*Blasting*, 64)

Lewis's father died ten days after the Armistice, leaving him nothing. About this event he writes bitterly: "how he got there [Philadelphia, where he died] is unimportant—except in so far as I was cheated of my patrimony" (*Blasting*, 211). Lewis did feel cheated of his patrimony, not only financially but in a much larger sense. Meyers suggests that this monetary deprivation was the cause of his subsequent poverty and consequently of his increasingly paranoid behavior after the war (Meyers, 87). But Lewis would probably have squandered any inherited wealth as he did all other possibilities of financial gain. The feeling of having been cheated and betrayed was not only a concrete reality but a life stance. Wyndham Lewis suffered from a far deeper wound than could have been repaired, as Meyers suggests, by the inheritance of a house in America.

Far more devastating was the death of his mother in 1920, the only event of which Lewis speaks with real emotion in his autobiographical books. A few months before his mother's death, Lewis met Gladys Anne Hoskins (always called "Froanna" by Lewis), an eighteen-year-old working-class woman, who modeled for him and became his mistress. Soon after his mother died, he moved in with this second Anne, and she became his life partner, although he always maintained other residences and relationships with other, more powerful and intellectual women. Lewis married Anne Lewis ten years later, to facilitate a passport to Germany for her. She was twenty years younger than he, as Lewis's mother had been twenty years younger than his father, but unlike Lewis's mother, who did not tolerate her husband's promiscuity, "Froanna" accepted his other relationships and even the fact that he continued to father children with other women during their marriage, though he denied children to her and threatened to leave her should she have any. She also accepted Lewis's need to own her as his exclusive property and lived with him in purdah, apparently not allowed to leave the house without him. Lewis never mentions the existence of a wife in his autobiographical writing. In discussing a move they made together, he invariably uses "I" and not "we." Most of Lewis's close friends and his mistresses, including those who often visited his flat, never knew of his wife's existence. Even some of those who had known him for thirty years were surprised to learn that he had been married when Meyers revealed the fact during his interviews with them. Hugh Porteus, one of Lewis's closest friends, "saw Froanna's disembodied hands appear through the serving hatch for many years before he actually met her" (Meyers, 100). Others heard her "scuttling into the next room of their tiny flat when a visitor approached" (Meyers, 100).

While Hugh Porteus calls Anne Lewis "a masochistic doll," Meyers praises her as "a placid woman who prided herself on her ability to endure adversity" (Meyers, 100). She certainly needed this ability. In 1939, "Froanna" accompanied Lewis on his self-imposed removal to Canada, where they lived together in grim exile for six years. After his return to England, his blindness forced him to bring her more into the open to assist and nurse him, and many people learned of her existence for the first time. Anne remained devoted to Lewis, was heartbroken when he died, and never complained about him before or after his death. She was the one respondent to deny his misogyny. Meyers reports that she "expressed surprise when someone suggested that Lewis seemed hostile to women and replied: 'Was Lewis anti-women? Some cheek, a womanizer like that!' " (Meyers, 100).

In his marriage, Lewis was able to replicate his relationship with his mother, with himself as the adored center of a female universe. He was also able to handle his fear of dependency on his wife by maintaining a nonreciprocal, dominating relationship with her—one which few other women would have tolerated. As Meyers claims, Anne Lewis was indeed his ideal companion.

Just as Lewis's misogyny was much more consistent and basic to his work than was his anti-Semitism, so the quality of his real-life relations with Jews was much less definitive than were those he had with women. Some of his friends, several of the women he had affairs with, and many of his patrons were Jews. While he turned on each one of them, accusing them of betrayal and venality, he acted in the same way with all of his friends and patrons, and their Jewishness does not appear to have been a focus of his recriminations.[23] Lewis makes occasional derogatory references to Jews in his letters, though these are not much worse than Virginia Woolf's scornful references to her Jewish relations in her letters and do not approach the venom in Evelyn Waugh's.[24] From 1926 through 1938, the period in which he expressed the most anti-Semitism in his writing, he retained Jewish friends and correspondents. However, both Lewis's writing during the 1930s, which often amounted to Nazi propaganda, and some of his political activities place him squarely in the virulently fascist and anti-Semitic camp of his friend Ezra Pound.

In 1916 Lewis had volunteered as a gunner in the Royal Artillery in order "to defend civilization against German barbarism," but his wartime experience taught him that the German soldier, "like myself was an instrument" (*Blasting*, 187). After the war, he identified with the Germans and increasingly saw Germany as a male "enemy" or "outsider" like himself. In a conciliatory letter of 1925, T. S. Eliot urged him, "[I]t would be in your own interest to concentrate on one book at a time and not plan eight or ten books at once" (Lewis, *Letters*, 151). But during the ten years which followed, Lewis seemed less able to follow this advice than ever before.

While working on *The Art of Being Ruled*, he became particularly interested in Adolf Hitler, and in 1930 *Time and Tide*, a woman-owned and edited feminist weekly, whose editors may not have known what they were getting into, commissioned Lewis to do a series of articles on Hitler and financed the first of many trips he would make to Germany in the next seven years. In Berlin he became enamored of Hitler and the Nazi movement. *Hitler*, the book which resulted from these articles, was a panegyric to Lewis's new hero, whose *Mein Kampf*, easily available at that time in English as well as German, Lewis had neglected to read. *Hitler* was published in England in 1930 and translated and published in Berlin in 1932. It was the book which most damaged Lewis's reputation and the one which has been most responsible for his label as a fascist and an anti-Semite. The anti-Semitism in *Hitler* did not, however, come out of nowhere. It had appeared in his attacks on Jewish writers like Gertrude Stein and Marcel Proust in *The Art of Being Ruled* (1926) and in his defense of the white race, *Paleface* (1929). Cunningham points out that even before the publication of *Hitler* Lewis habitually labeled his enemies "Untermenschen," and that he admired pilots, a "new race of men" whom he habitually contrasted with those "gutter-people," the Jews

(Cunningham, 88, 190). In a letter he wrote to *Time and Tide* in 1931, Lewis compares Berlin after dark to Golders Green, a predominantly Jewish area of London, and mocks the *Time and Tide* correspondent, who had written about Nazi persecution, as a "keen hearer" who selectively hears "the groans of those struck by truncheons and so on . . . but always a Communist groans, never a Nazi groans" (*Letters*, 199).

Hitler was not Lewis's first political idol. Like other narcissistic men, he idealized a series of prominent figures, whom he saw as extensions of himself, then devalued. We have noted his embrace of Marinetti and his movement. Visiting Italy in 1922, as the guest of his then lover, Nancy Cunard, he had greatly admired Mussolini's march on Rome, and had followed his progress enthusiastically thereafter. Meyers explains that Lewis was "fascinated by the arm of authority" and that he saw first Mussolini and then Hitler as possible saviors of art and of artists like him, who were at present being trampled by the "masses" (Meyers, 85). Shapiro describes how the longing to "become the instrument of a strong but authoritative figure" is often coupled with phobic hatred of homosexuals in rigid men, and indeed it was during this same period that Lewis's hatred of homosexuals took on a phobic quality.

Lewis's earlier anti-Semitism is matched and even surpassed in the other political books which he wrote between 1930 and 1938: *Doom of Youth* (1932), *Left Wings over Europe* (1936), and *Count Your Dead: They Are Alive!* (1937), as well as in his novel *The Apes of God* (1930). The same period saw Lewis's close association with Oswald Mosley's British Union of Fascists, an association which would last until 1938. In a German essay of 1937, one of six he wrote for Nazi journals between 1937 and 1939, he praised Mosley's "great political insight and qualities as a leader" (Meyers, 191); and *Count Your Dead: They Are Alive!* is full of references to England's wrongful persecution of the heroic Mosley and angry mockery of the Public Order Act of 1937, a governmental measure intended to curb BUF violence. Also in 1937, six months after the start of the Spanish Civil War, Lewis's profascist article " 'Left Wings' and the C_3 Mind," which echoed Ezra Pound's theory of the international Jewish control of banks and finance, appeared, with an article by Pound, in the first issue of Mosley's *British Union Quarterly*.

Unlike the Freikorpsmen, Lewis was no joiner. He never actually became a member of Mosley's party, and while he was enthralled in turn by Marinetti, Mussolini, Mosley, and Hitler, each of these violent enthusiasms was followed by a later strong rejection. As in the case of his literary patrons, his intense need for a male authority or father figure was countered by an equally intense homophobic reaction and the need to reject and repudiate each one of his idols. In 1937, Lewis and his wife went to Berlin, his seventh trip to Germany, and two years later he somewhat ambivalently recanted his support of Hitler. The publication of the ambiguous *The Jews, Are They Human?* in March 1939 signaled this change.

Meyers seems unsure whether Lewis's shift was a matter of conviction or convenience. He credits Lewis's visit to Germany with opening his eyes to the reality of Nazism and asserts that Lewis "felt a personal revulsion for the Right-wing people who tried to take him up after the Hitler book, and regretted his hasty conclusions and political errors as much as the harm he had suffered for espousing them" (Meyers, 245). Meyers also acknowledges, however, that "critics and friends who noticed the change in Lewis's political views in 1938–39 inevitably wondered about the sincerity of his clumsily expressed recantation" (Meyers, 245). Perhaps, Meyers admits, there was indeed a "pragmatic side to his recantation, an ineffectual attempt to rehabilitate himself and achieve popularity" (Meyers, 246).

Meyers is only one of many modern critics who suggest that Lewis's "superficial formulations" in *Hitler* and his other openly fascist books were merely a natural mistake which grew out of his hatred of war, and that he supported fascism out of "ignorance of its true character and true danger." He points out that Isherwood, Sartre, and Churchill, among countless others, also praised Hitler at one time and argues that the poor judgment and stubborn individuality which caused Lewis to hold on to his beliefs a little longer than they did caused him to be unfairly and permanently "tainted and condemned" (Meyers, 192). In a review in the 1969 issue of *Agenda* devoted to Lewis, C. H. Sisson claimed that the real fault in *Hitler* "lay in the stupidity of his readers," who should have read it "with less hostility and more understanding."[25] In the same issue, Martin Seymour-Smith claims that Lewis saw Hitler as "a comic figure" and that his "unfortunate" book was consistently misunderstood by critics who missed his "supreme subtlety."[26] While Fredric Jameson, unlike Seymour-Smith, disapproves of Lewis's books of the thirties, he feels that Lewis's support of fascism is understandable in that it stems from his primary attitude toward "the more central position of Communism" (184).

I would disagree with both these views. Lewis's fascist opinions, including his anti-Semitism of the 1930s, cannot be explained away as a side effect of a more central hatred of communism or as an unfortunate and foolish mistake that anyone might have made. My own view is closer to that of William Chace, who reasons that Lewis's political attitudes were the natural outcome of his indifference to others: those "messy complexities of human beings (humans who ruinously resolve themselves into entities Lewis found deplorable, such as 'women,' 'negroes,' 'jews,' 'pacifists,' 'feminists,' and lovers of 'jazz')."[27] Chace cites Lewis's overwhelming narcissism, reproduced by the character Argo in his play "Enemy of the Stars," who declares, "Anything but yourself is dirt. Anybody that is" (Chace, "On Lewis's Politics," 151). Lewis's extreme attitudes of the 1930s cannot be separated from the rest of his thinking and development. His fear and hatred of women, as well as his sense of himself as a beleaguered and victimized male fighting to defend himself, made Lewis a natural candidate for Marinetti's, Mussolini's, Mosley's, and finally Hitler's woman-hating and life-destroying philosophies. For the Freikorpsmen in Theweleit's study, the fear of engulfing women was inextricably linked to fear of the masses and of socialism. For Wyndham Lewis, who fought with words rather than with guns, the links are equally inextricable. The narcissist Lewis saw his idols as extensions of himself. When British public opinion turned against Hitler, wiser British supporters of Hitler switched their allegiance. Lewis, the victimized male, felt personally attacked. His unpopular defense of Hitler was a movement of self-defense.

Perhaps because the members of the literary establishment, many of whom had shared Lewis's enthusiasm for Hitler a few years earlier, were now eager to disown their own former opinions and to banish those who served as uncomfortable reminders of these mistakes, Lewis's books virtually stopped selling in England after the publication of *Hitler*. His commissions for portraits also finally petered out. For perhaps the first time, the "enemy" had a reason beyond his own alienating behavior to feel himself persecuted. In 1939 Lewis formally denounced the Nazis in the revisionist *The Hitler Cult*, but this book, like the revisionist *The Jews, Are They Human?*, contains so much undermining of its own overt message that one can safely conclude that Lewis's sympathies had not entirely changed. For reasons which were, then, both political and financial, he and his wife left England for Canada, on 2 September 1939, one day before England declared war on Germany. The six years in

Canada, described in *Self Condemned* (1954), were the lowest point in Lewis's life. Although he made the decision to leave, he regarded himself as unfairly and cruelly banished and felt that England had betrayed him.

Lewis never regarded himself as an anti-Semite and resented the implication that he was one. In *The Jews, Are They Human?* he presents himself as one of the few objective voices on the subject of anti-Semitism and as a longtime friend of the Jews. In contrast, he would never have publicly presented himself as a friend of homosexuals, socialists, children, feminists, or even women. Such a stance would have placed him in closer proximity than he could have tolerated to the rejected and split-off parts of himself. Lewis's hatred of Jews thus never had the phobic, obsessional quality we find in his misogyny or his homophobia. It was only when Jews were identified as a fit object of hatred by his current male authority figure that they took on the prominent position they held in Lewis's obsessional structure during the 1930s. When he rejected Hitler, anti-Semitism was put on a back burner, and unlike the objects of his other obsessions, Jews were not prominent in any of the books he wrote after his return from the United States and Canada in 1945.

Lewis returned to England an ill and broken man, his health destroyed by the brain tumor which pressed on his optic nerve and caused complete blindness by 1956. His illness did not prevent him from continuing to write—during this period he produced seven more books—or from continuing to do battle. He died in 1957, not of the brain tumor but of chronic kidney failure caused by his gonorrhea-related urinary disease (Meyers, 371). He was survived by the faithful Anne Lewis, who nursed him until the end.

To Swallow or Be Swallowed: The Didactic Books, 1926–1937

The Structure Revealed: The Art of Being Ruled *(1926) and* Paleface *(1929).* "YOU WILL BE MADE TO HEAR IT," Lewis wrote to his friend. Perhaps more than the two other writers in this study, his writing was the result of a conscious need for expression so pressing that he used the metaphor of a volcano threatening to erupt to describe it. Just as volcanic flow respects no boundaries, the force of Lewis's preoccupations flowed over and broke the boundaries between genres. Lewis's "didactic" writing, poorly researched, full of personal and familial scenarios and seemingly unmotivated eruptions of rage, often reads more like fiction;

while his modernist, nonrealist "fiction," with its one-dimensional, surreal characters, its lack of linear plan, and its frequent pauses for didactic explosions of exposition, crosses the border into didactic prose. For this reason, I have chosen to discuss Lewis's nonfiction and fiction texts together in this chapter.

Like many people who see themselves surrounded by conspiratorial forces, Wyndham Lewis felt a pressing need to make others see the connections which were so blindingly clear to him. In *Paleface*, the book he wrote to protect and rescue the white race, he explains this mission:

> The majority of people are deeply unconscious of the affiliations of the various phenomenons of our time, which on the surface look so very autonomous and even hostile, yet . . . they are often closely and organically related to one another. If you test this you will be surprised to find how many things do belong together . . . it is our business, especially, it appears, mine, to establish these essential liaisons, and to lay bare the widely flung system of cables connecting up this maze-like and destructive system in the midst of which we live—destructive, that is, of course to something essential that we should clutch and be careful not to lose[.] (142)

The didactic books which Lewis wrote between 1926 and 1937 represent his effort to publicize and expose this web of connections or "liaisons."

While Jews do not figure explicitly in *The Art of Being Ruled* (1926) (except, as in the attacks on Gertrude Stein, Marcel Proust, and Karl Marx, as representatives of the types Lewis hated most), the book contains the first complete version of the system we will trace in all of his books of the 1920s and 1930s. It is accordingly worth considering here at some length. *The Art of Being Ruled* was published to critical acclaim in 1926. In his discussion of the book, Julian Symons attempts to explain why Lewis was "not merely neglected but positively ostracized . . . the most hated writer in England" (9): "To place such a low value on human life as such, and to make the assumption that some lives are important, most of no interest or value, outraged the conventional beliefs of Lewis's own time, and even more the pieties of ours" (7).

Although Symons's summary of the beliefs Lewis expounded in *The Art of Being Ruled* is accurate, his memory of the book's reception seems faulty. *The Art of Being Ruled* may have been received with private outrage, but publicly Lewis was neither silenced nor condemned. Judging from its highly positive reception, Lewis's book was an accurate production of at least one dominant discourse. W. A. Thorpe, in *Criterion* (edited by T. S. Eliot), called the book a plea for "the political sovereignty of the intellect," praised Lewis's "penetration," and compared him with Aristotle in his belief that "some should rule and others be ruled."[28] In *Calendar*, Edgell Rickword praises Lewis's goal of "arresting the degradation of the values on which our civilization seems to depend . . . and of re-asserting the terms on which the life of the intellect may regain its proper ascendancy over emotional and economic existence."[29]

In *The Art of Being Ruled*, Lewis outlines his theory of the rule of the few great men over the mediocre mass. He praises Mussolini's Italy, where, as he supposes, "all the humbug of a democratic suffrage, all the imbecility that is wastefully manufactured, will henceforth be spared these happy people . . . all the clumsy and gigantic characteristic shams of anglo-saxon life will have no parallel in such a regime" (370).

But the political theme which is the overt purpose of this book is surprisingly hard to locate. To read *The Art of Being Ruled* is a bewildering activity until one gives up on the overt message and concentrates instead on the subtext, which explodes from every chapter in a kind of furious, free-associative process. Thorpe, whose *Criterion* review demonstrates that Lewis's preoccupations, rather than being a bizarre product of individual pathology, were openly shared by at least one contemporary reviewer, addresses this subtext openly: "Mr. Lewis examines with great skill this fungus of delusion—feminism, inversion, the aping of the child, the masculisation [*sic*] of women and the effemisation [*sic*] of men" (63). While Fredric Jameson considers both *The Art of Being Ruled* and *Paleface* highly unfortunate and Julian Symons admires them, these two modern critics agree as to the real import of the two books—and agree that it has little do to with either fascism or democracy. Jameson sees them as: "a variety of registers in which a single theme, the loss of reality in modern life, or if you prefer a somewhat franker version, the systematic undermining of the European White Male Will is implacably pursued" (123).

In Julian Symons's view, the books describe the insidious process in which: "the advance of feminism, closely linked with the development of homosexuality, is eroding and will finally destroy the family as a factor of social importance" (7).

Once identified as the book's real theme, this subtext is presented as a sequence or process which is recapitulated again and again in, to use one of Lewis's chapter titles, "a vicious circle," which begins before the birth of the male child and continues throughout his lifetime. Lewis, like Kate Millett, views the nuclear family as "a circle of self-perpetuation and self-fulfilling prophecy" (Millett, 53), but while Millett sees this circle systematically dominating and crushing the female, Lewis identifies the male as its victim. The parents, who may have begun with an illusion of romantic love, quickly find that they are natural adversaries:

> The step from a beneficent activity to a malevolent one is imperceptible. All love . . . could be said to turn to hate . . . this *romance* can become a *rage* . . . this *romance of destruction* can easily pass over into sadism and homicide[.] (*Art*, 256)

Once the romance is gone, it is a only question of who will engulf or devour whom:

> [L]ove can only exist on the surface. An inch beneath, and it is no longer love but the abstract rage of hunger and reproduction, of which the swallowing of the oyster, or the swallowing of the male by the female epira, is an illustration. (260)

Lewis then free-associates for some pages on the repulsiveness of the oyster, which he clearly associates with the female genitalia. He quotes Samuel Butler, "[W]ho would kiss an oyster?" (253), and reflects, "Men dislike the appearance of an oyster, as they dislike the appearance of the underneath of their tongue . . . but they find it lovely to *eat*" (254). Men, reasons Lewis, are repulsed by females (and their genitalia) but drawn compulsively to them. Repulsed or not, they must consume the female or be consumed by that larger and more powerful entity:

> "I could eat you!" one lover says to another at the paroxysm of their lubricity. And indeed, if one were considerably smaller than the other, as in the case of the male of the epira, that no doubt would happen very often. (254)

In the next chapter, Lewis turns to the masses: that *howling foaming mob*, which desires the *real and living blood* of the lone artist. This thought, like most others, brings him back to the oyster and the epira, and that "abstract rage of hunger and reproduction" (260). Without specifying who the pronoun "they" refers to, he quotes Julien Benda's *Belgaphor*:

> Let us learn to recognize also, in their will to install themselves inside things, a kind of thirst to sexually invade everything—to violate any intimacy, and mix themselves in the most intimate recesses of the being of everything met. (260)

What Lewis is telling us urgently and repeatedly in this book, just as he did in his own life script, is that while he depends on women and on sexual union with them for his survival, that connection is also, and literally, life-threatening to him. To feel so dependent on a being determined to engulf or swallow one up is indeed a no-win situation, especially for a narcissist like Lewis, whose greatest fear is dependency (Kernberg, 235). No wonder he concludes this chapter with the statement that religion and science, the ostensible "topics" of the chapter, both prophesy "the suicide of our race" (*Art*, 261).

After the male child's birth his mother immediately chooses him as "her friend, for whom she keeps her best affection," and with the aid of "freudian oedipus-complex propaganda" she attempts to turn him against his father (*Art*, 285). In a passage which strikingly recapitulates his own perceived history, Lewis explains:

> The child as a symbol and object of worship, with exclusive claims, is a woman-value, then. That it should at once develop an antagonism for the adult or "the man" is natural enough, seeing that at the time of its birth, the woman was engaged in a "war" of freedom with "the man." (286)

The male child is now subjected to a barrage of persuasion and propaganda intended to force him to give up his role. Lewis, who, like the Freikorpsmen, repeatedly conflates class and gender in this book, envisioning women and the masses joined together against the lone, intellectual male, tells us of the "insidious and disgraceful proposal made to man when in the war of the sexes, turned into a class war, he has been defeated" (272). He even presents us with the gist of the proposal itself:

> *I will show you how you can just step aside* and avoid all further labour or anxiety. You will neither be rich nor "great" nor beautiful, nor anything troublesome of that sort. Who wants all that? You can, if you want to, be eternally in the position of a little silent, giggling, crafty child; or of an imbecile that no one takes seriously, and of whom *nothing is expected*, and in whom there is no ambitious vanity that can be wounded, of whom no martial virtue is expected, nor lover's absurd devotion—with the extravagant claims of the over-indulged woman, overestimating her sex-leverage. Nothing of all that! Would you like to be *a woman*? It sounds a come-

> down but why? She has the best of it! There is always some fool to look after her. She is outside the life of bustle, boring business, mechanical work done to get *money* (to keep her)—war, politics and all the rest of the solemn rigmarole—almost as much as the child is. (272)

Lewis is describing the phenomenon which Chodorow identified as "the male longing to return to the original sense of oneness with the mother . . . an underlying sense of femaleness . . . that continually . . . undermines the sense of maleness" (9). For Lewis such undermining is constant and pervasive, and to give in to it is a fate worse than death. A man, Lewis tells us emphatically, "*does not want, if he can possibly help it, to be a man*, not at least if it is so *difficult*." Margaret Mead wrote that the masculine role must "be kept and re-earned every day" (Chodorow, 40). In a similar statement, Lewis asserts that a man: "is made, not born: and he is made, of course, with very great difficulty. From the time he yells and kicks in his cradle, to the time he receives his last kick at school, he is recalcitrant" (280).

Men are a species at risk. Of those who manage to survive the kicks of public school, most are, like the epira Lewis dwells on, "willingly eaten . . . devoured by its mate in the midst of its tumescence" (282). It is no wonder that they are recalcitrant and long to return to the safety of female-dominated infancy or to choose the easy, passive life of women. But the weak man who gives in to the "insidious proposal," unlike the victimized but still "erect" hero, will be sorry. Lewis's portrait is devastating:

> At thirty-five, forty-five, fifty-five, *und so weiter*, you find them still luxuriously and rebelliously prostrate; still lisping, and sobbing, spread-eagled on their backs, helpless and inviting caresses, like a bald-stomached dog. (280)

To avoid this fate, a male must assume the paranoid stance described by Shapiro and the other theorists in chapter 2. He must be eternally vigilant, trust no one, constantly fight his longing for softness and tenderness, eradicate vulnerability in himself, and despise it in women and other suspects. In fact he must act just as Lewis himself did all his life.

Foremost of the enemies he must face is, of course, the woman who is so eager to devour him. She lies in wait for her foe:

> By turns maudlin and vicious, cruel like a child, inconsiderate, with no disciplined sense of "fairness," living on her mimetic sense solely . . . [with

her] narrow specialist intelligence, the sterility of her mind, like the potential fecundity of her body. (276–77)

In league with her is the male's other most bitter enemy, "the turncoat, or 'turn-sex' male feminizing invert" (275). In the same way as he threatened Shapiro and Salzman's rigid patients, this enemy presents a major threat to Lewis, who devotes more than half his book to maligning him. For Lewis, the connection is obvious. "The homo," he states, "is the legitimate child of the suffragette" (244). Invert and woman unite in their common goal of destruction of the man.

> The male-invert . . . is hostile to many things to which the average woman is hostile . . . the stupider, more excitable and aggressive kind of woman will revenge herself on those things towards which she has always been in a position of veiled hostility. It is often said that the male invert shelters himself behind—uses and acts through—women. But it would be equally true to put it the other way around. (245)

Lewis takes care here to except the "male-pole type of invert," whom he describes sympathetically in what sounds like something of a self-portrait. As opposed to the "feminizing" invert, the "male-pole" type has "pride . . . often enormous in his maleness. If perhaps over-fine and even mad, he can meet on equal terms the male of any other species" (238). Lewis's hatred is reserved for those members of "the ruling male sex" who, in an "instinctive capitulation of the will," have renounced their identity (269).

In Lewis's nightmare world, the carefully imposed distinctions between men and women, children and adults, which "substitute for and make unnecessary an objective relationship with the external world," have disappeared, and emotion, once safely sealed off as female baggage, has infected the whole (Shapiro, *Autonomy*, 76). Everything exists within a giant, swallowing female mouth:

> The "passions," "intuitions," all the features of the emotive life—with which women were formerly exclusively accommodated—are enthroned on all hands, in any place reached by social life; which is increasingly (in the decay of visible public life) everywhere. . . . First the salon . . . will be pitched next door to the nursery; then gradually the connecting door will become a large folding-door; and then at length all septum of any sort will disappear. The *précieuses ridicules*, dressed in baby frocks, will be on the floor with their dolls[.] (242–43)

The paranoid framework of *The Art of Being Ruled* closely recapitulates the themes of Lewis's own early history as he experienced it. His parents were indeed antagonists who seemed to be engaged in a war of power which resulted in the father "spread eagled . . . inviting caresses"—as much at his mother's mercy as a "bald-stomached dog." Although Lewis's early role as his mother's partner was deeply threatening to his own sense of autonomy, once at school, where he was beaten and despised, that safe woman-dominated life must have indeed beckoned sweetly, offering an insidious proposal to return to the helpless engulfment of female-dominated childhood. As Shapiro and our other theorists have emphasized, the longing to assume what they envision as the woman's passivity and sexual surrender and the desire to become the instrument of a strong and authoritative figure are among the reasons that heterosexual men with paranoid features are drawn to homosexuality, worry obsessively about their own homosexuality, and often project that worry outward onto a hatred of homosexuals, especially effeminate ones, who most accurately embody their own desire. *The Art of Being Ruled* is the first book in which Lewis demonstrates his fascination for the object who seems always to be waiting in the wings of his nightmare: the loathsome feminine invert it is his lifework not to become.

It is easy to see how women and children took on their threatening role within Lewis's symbolic framework and how the connection with feminine homosexuals was forged. It is perhaps more difficult to understand the connection between this framework and Lewis's choice of Mussolini and fascism. In this context it is helpful to remember the Freikorpsman with his terror of female engulfment, the "concentration camp of his desires," and his encoding of the dangerous crowd or mass with equally dangerous women (Theweleit, 2: 6). For Lewis too, women and inverts were in collusion with the "howling foaming mob"— still a vague and nonpolitical entity in *The Art of Being Ruled* but clearly associated in Lewis's later books with socialists and communists. Faced with such a dangerous array of enemies, the lone man craves a strong father or hero, who, by providing protection, might allow at least a temporary respite from persecution. Unlike most men, whose natural position is prone, there stands "the abnormal or exceptional man, whom we worship as a 'hero' and whose unnatural erectness arouses almost more hatred than surprise" (*Art*, 281). While, as the last part of this sentence reveals, Lewis views *himself* as such a persecuted hero, he also longs for one to rescue him so that he can "get some sort of peace to enable us to work" (369). Such a hero will create a world safe from the invasive threat of women, in which the amount of fraternization with them is strictly limited to physical necessity, and in which "the nightmare 'sex' will not force people into each other's society for life, when half an hour would answer the purpose" (217).

> Eventually, I believe, a considerable segregation of women and men must occur, just as segregation of those who decide for the active, the intelligent life, and those who decide . . . for the lower or animal life, is likely to happen, and is very much to be desired. (199)

Without fascism, "the most powerful and stable authority that can be devised" and the only system which promises such a separation, the result will be "the extermination of the white race" (370, 275).

In *Paleface* (1929) Lewis expands on this threatened extermination of "the white race"—clearly, a term for white *men* only. The book contains a lengthy attack on D. H. Lawrence, a writer who shares many of Lewis's obsessions about women but whom Lewis viewed as a race-traitor because of his glorification of sensuality and the emotions and his worship of Mexican Indians. The attack on Lawrence is a revealing projection of Lewis's own sense of "the essential liaisons . . . connecting up this maze-like . . . system" (*Paleface*, 142).

> (1) The Unconscious; (2) the Feminine; (3) The Communist; those are the main principles of action in the mind of Mr. Lawrence, linked in a hot and piping trinity of rough-stuff primitivism, and freudian hot-sex stuff. (180)

In *Paleface*, Lewis identifies the nonwhite's "primitive" universe with its "*consciousness in the abdomen*" with the similarly mindless, emotional, universe of the woman. As he puts it:

> I would rather have the least man that *thinks* than the average man that squats and drums and drums. . . . I would rather have an ounce of human "consciousness" than a universe full of "abdominal" afflatus and hot unconscious "soulless," mystical throbbing. (196)

In a theory which demonstrates the centrality of Lewis's affection for Nazi doctrines, he explains that the dark races, like the invert, share with women the desire to engulf and destroy the white man. Intermarriage, or miscegenation, in which the white man links with a being who encompasses both darkness and femininity, is a particularly lethal danger. In expounding upon this idea, Lewis implies, though he never directly alludes to, the existence of black females. As a rule, blacks, like Jews, seem to exist for Lewis only in the male gender. As an alternative to miscegenation, Lewis urges a purely European melting pot, as "practically all european intermarriage presents no problem at all" (278). Just as, in *The Art of Being Ruled*, Lewis's nightmare consisted of a terrible merging of men, women, inverts, and children, and his ideal world was one in which women would be segregated from men, here in *Paleface* he advocates a splitting-off from his new Other, the object of his projective identification: "We should . . . see less and less of such other kinds of men, between whom and ourselves there is no practical reason for physical merging, nor for spiritual merging, or even many reasons against both" (258).

The alternative is, once more, a terrible collusion—this time between blacks, women, and Russian Communists. In a particularly vivid paranoid image, Lewis repetitively ruminates about "Black and Red Laughter in Russia" and visualizes blacks, Russians, and women meeting to laugh at and plot against white men (286). He warns: "Let the usual Black Laughter, or Red Laughter, directed at us go on: but let it become a thing of the past for us to remain as its amiable, accommodating and self-abasing butts" (271).

Inverts are, of course, in on the plot as well. The man who, like Lawrence, worships the primitive dark races rather than guarding his own white male identity "has grown to desire to be a woman and has taken obvious steps to effect this transformation." The actual physical transformation into a female is already far gone in Lewis's fantasy world:

> [T]he widespread phenomenon of male inversion [is] . . . an example of the form that this collapse was taking. As the starch went out of them, the males relapsed into what in Sodom are technically called "bitches" in a process of almost physiological transformation. (156)

Paleface presents us with essentially the same obsessional framework we find in *The Art of Being Ruled*, with the "mazelike network" or paranoid system which in that book included women, children, homosexuals, and the masses, now expanded to include, and indeed focus upon, blacks. The two books illustrate Gilman's model of the "mutable and constantly shifting" stereotypical flux (*Difference and Pathology*, 23).

Read together, they provide a frightening and illuminating illustration of the psychological process through which racial prejudice can be constructed—and reconstructed.

The book's critics, however, were neither frightened nor illuminated. Just as Lewis's later anti- Semitism would be ignored by contemporary and even modern critics, the blatant and virulent racism in *Paleface* went unmentioned in both positive and negative contemporary reviews of the book. The reviewer from the *Times Literary Supplement* praised the book, commenting blandly, "It seems to him [Lewis] vital to combat the idea that the white races are done and the coloured in the ascendant."[30] Other reviewers and commentators concentrated on the attack on D. H. Lawrence, approving or not depending on their views of that author.[31] Rebecca West, who criticizes the book for its "exaggeration and distortion," is the only one to hint at its racism, though she claims, "[T]here is no one who can more deeply thrill one by a vivid and novel vision."[32] Once more, Lewis's obsessional system set him at one rather than at odds with the dominant discourse of his society.

Meyers, in one of his more farfetched rescue efforts, describes *Paleface* in terms of Lewis's opposition to "the spurious and sentimental expropriation of African culture" and his rejection of "the fashionable, arty assumption that the emotional and sensuous life of the black race was superior to the white" (Meyers, 143). He, however, does admit that "*Paleface seemed* racist" (Meyers, 150; my italics). *Paleface*, in which Lewis's focus shifted from women and homosexuals to blacks as the feared and hated Other, paved the way for Lewis's next shift—to a racist anti-Semitism in *Hitler*.

Jews Join the Plot: Hitler *(1930),* Doom of Youth *(1932),* Left Wings over Europe *(1936), and* Count Your Dead: They Are Alive! *(1937).* To today's reader, *Hitler* (1931) reads like a piece of Nazi propaganda, loaded with a kind of sneering, particularly offensive anti-Semitism. Upon its publication, however, the *Times Literary Supplement* not only described the book as brilliant and persuasive, but also praised Lewis's treatment of and attitude toward Jews in it—an attitude that the reviewer clearly shared.

> Mr. Lewis gets on to firmer ground . . . when he expounds upon the real character of Hitlerite anti-Semitism. He reminds the British public that

"the vulgar Jew of the British caricaturist is largely a reality in Central Europe . . . Jews dominate German life . . . he [Hitler] logically wants to eliminate them."[33]

None of the other reviews mentioned his attitude toward Jews. Just as Hitler's own openly proclaimed anti-Semitism had not made him unpopular with the English people in 1930, Lewis's support of that stance was not even considered worth mentioning by his reviewers in that year. Instead, it fit neatly into the prevailing discourse: the "anti-Semitism of tolerance" described in chapter 1, which blamed Jews (in particular foreign or unassimilated Jews) for anti-Semitism while congratulating its adherent on his or her lack of anti-Semitism. However, other aspects of Lewis's support of Hitler were less acceptable to his English reviewers. His perceived lack of patriotism and his support for a leader who was gradually being acknowledged as the enemy earned him the disapprobation which his anti-Semitic stance did not, and several reviewers labeled him gullible and even narcissistic.[34] However, the strong disapproval which Lewis eventually earned for *Hitler* came well after its publication date. It is important to remember that in 1930, when the book was published, it caused no major stir and was considered, on the whole, perfectly acceptable.

While Lewis had referred contemptuously to Jews in *Blast*, no. 1 (1914) and in the story "Cantleman's Spring Mate" (1917), they had not so far emerged as a major obsession. With the publication of *Hitler*, the Jews took their place among Lewis's gallery of miscreants. In *Hitler*, as in the subsequent books in which Jews played a prominent role, Lewis envisions only male Jews. To him a Jew was, by definition, a man who, like the invert, straddled the line between masculinity and femininity. Female Jews, who could not be fit into this formula, did not exist in his assumptive universe.

The first part of *Hitler* is devoted to a description of the "Jewish city, Berlin," which is controlled by a cabal of Lewis's favorite people: "tarts," "niggers," "inverts," and "jews." Berlin is "a really first class *mauvais lieu* . . . thrown up by the War out of the earth's bowels, as it were, from sweated cellars, traps, and gutters."[35]

Like the Russian communists and the blacks who mocked the white man with their "Red and Black Laughter" in *Paleface*, this new cabal enjoys playing a particularly vicious trick on the unsuspecting male tourist, one which, like the "insidious proposal" of *The Art of Being Ruled*, is designed to blur the essential boundaries between male and female and to force the persecuted man to abandon his masculinity and become a child or a homosexual. The female tart whom the trusting tourist picks up in order to assert his masculinity may turn out to be a man! Lewis describes in some detail his own experience of being tricked in this way, concluding that the tourist who has such an experience will profit from it by henceforth remaining on guard against all women:

> [T]he feminine will never never be quite the same for him again . . . it will have caused him to regard with a certain sceptical squint, all specifically feminine personality. This may . . . be of great use to him . . . in the subsequent conduct of his life. (*Hitler*, 25–26)

Lewis gleefully cites one hundred and sixty such establishments, and, with great relish and fascination, describes "every variety of Perversion" which exists within them. In Meyers's view, he is "utterly repelled and absorbed with the grotesque *frisson* of sexual degeneracy" (Meyers, 187). But, in a pattern which will reoccur in *The Apes of God*, Lewis becomes threatened by the force of his own attraction. In order to safely split it off from himself, he needs another figure who will authoritatively represent his divorce from the scene. He finds him in the young Nazi, a triumphant representative of the erect white male. The Nazi avoids all such places. They are for him

> the squinting misbegotten paradise of the *Schiebertum*. "Jude verrecke!" he would no doubt mutter or shout, if he got into one. Sooner or later he would desire to . . . roll this nigger-dance luxury-spot up like a verminous carpet and drop it into the Spree—with a heartfelt Pfui! at its big sodden splash. (*Hitler*, 27–28)

Meyers writes, with no apparent irony, "The same perverse spectacle that revolted Lewis, who hated homosexuality and praised Hitler for promising to extinguish vice, attracted the Left-wing Auden, Isherwood and Spender to Berlin . . . in the early 1930s" (Meyers, 187). In fact, the same phenomenon that drew Lewis, Auden, Isherwood, and Spender to Berlin—its open acceptance of homosexuality—also attracted Lewis.

Most of the rest of the book is devoted to a description of Hitler, whom Lewis clearly sees as an extension of himself and whose Nazi ideology he equates with his own position, as a defense against the feminizing aggression of communism.[36] While he acknowledges that Berlin is a violent city, he characterizes the violence as a process in which "the

Communists help the police to beat and shoot the Nazis," rather than the reverse (16). Similarly, the Horst Wessel song portrays a typical ambush by "the marxist gangs [which] take their orders from Moscow" (19). The Nazis themselves go unarmed, except in response to "extreme provocation and in face of the certainty of death if they are not in a position to defend themselves" (20).

Lewis does not ignore Nazi anti-Semitism in this book. Calling it "Judenfrage," he explains it as the German's "deep animal antipathy" against "a glib metropolitan product whose ancient and dissimilar culture seems to threaten the integrity of his own traditional ideals" (34). He goes on to describe it as a "hard-headed" resolve to " 'keep out' at all costs the 'alien' whom the peasant-mind suspects (whether rightly or wrongly, and no doubt sometimes it is one, sometimes the other) of having designs upon its patrimony" (34).

As we have seen, Lewis's accusation that his father had cheated him of his patrimony implied that through his abdication, his father had robbed him of the ability to feel confidence in his masculinity, thus forcing him to maintain a constant vigilance against the alien forces which were in league for that prize. He interprets "the German's" antipathy for the Jew as the same thing: a fierce defense against those aliens who "have designs" on *his* patrimony or manhood. In line with the discourse of the time, Lewis distinguishes between English Jews, who are "disinfected and anglicised," and those of Germany and America:

> The anti-semitism that does exist [in the United States] is sustained solely by the extremely bad manners and barbaric aggressiveness of the eastern slum-Jew immigrant, dumped into America yearly in such great numbers. That is more even than human beings . . . the most stoical and patient of all the animal creation—can comfortably bear. (36)

He approvingly quotes Goebbels on the Jewish control of "Jazz, Nigger-dances and similar amusements (which are completely alien to us)" and concludes, "[I]t is only fair to the Nationalsocialist to say that the Jew has often lent colour to those accusations" (80).

Even the sanitized Jew of England is a would-be woman, and a dominating and engulfing one: "the brilliant and bossy Hausfrau of this stolid English hubby" (41). The German Jew too is "Feminine, and in many ways very unpleasant—all people have their bad sides" (41). The coy tone continues, as does the association of Jews and women, in Lewis's recommendation to the English Hitlerite, at least when at home, to express his anti-Semitism in a lowered voice and accompany it with denial:

> The Hitlerite must understand that when he is talking to an Englishman or an American about "the Jew" (as he is prone to do) he is apt to be talking about that gentleman's *wife*! Or anyhow *Chacun son Jew*! is a good old English saying. So if the Hitlerite desires to win the ear of England he must lower his voice and coo (rather than shout) *Jude verrecke*! if he *must* give expression to such a fiery intolerant notion. Therefore—a pinch of malice certainly, but no "antisemitism" for the love of Mike! (42)

Lewis's recommendation here is accurate enough; we have seen this lowered voice and unnamed anti-Semitism in the Foreign and Home Office memos in chapter 1 and in the code of the English public school described in chapter 3. Having solidly cemented the two concepts "Jew" and "Woman," Lewis then appeals to his fellow Englishmen in a call for male solidarity with their German brothers, against the alien aggressor and Other—the Woman-Jew: "[S]till allow a little *Blutsgefühl* to have its way . . . towards this other mind and body like your own—in favour of this brave and very unhappy impoverished kinsman. Do not allow a mere bagatelle of a *Judenfrage* to stand in the way of that!" (42). The appeal of "Blutsgefühl" is stated even more clearly later:

> [T]he doctrine of the Blutsgefühl . . . desires a *closer* and *closer* drawing together of the people of one race and culture, by means of bodily attraction. It must be a true bodily solidarity. Identical rhythms in the arteries and muscles, and in the effective neural instrument—that should provide us with a passionate *exclusiveness*, within the brotherly bounds of which we could live secure from alien interference, and so proceed with our work and our pleasures, whatever they may be. That is the big idea. (106–7)

The rather passionately homosexual content of this passage by the sworn enemy of the invert is notable here. Just as in *The Art of Being Ruled*, Lewis recommended the segregation of men and women, except for brief sexual contacts, as the only way to provide men with safety from female engulfment, here the concept of "Blutsgefühl" offers a world of brotherly safety from "alien interference," a place where Lewis, tormented by his need for and dependency on women and by the paranoid vigilance required by that need, could finally feel one with other "masculine" men, and do his work in peace.

Hitler for the most part recapitulates Lewis's familiar system, with some important differences. While in *The Art of Being Ruled* Mussolini and fascism offered rather a pale and ineffective counter to the far stronger forces of feminism and homosexuality, in *Hitler* the alien forces are for the first time opposed by an equally strong masculine counterforce in the form of Adolf Hitler and National Socialism. Lewis bewails the Jewish control of the banks and the economy, presided over by "the Jew Karl Marx," but claims that Hitler's program offers a strong defense of Europe at a time when it is under threat by feminine, communist Jews. In *The Art of Being Ruled* women and homosexuals bore the projective burden. In *Paleface* it passed to the "dark" races. In *Hitler*, though these other targets are not forgotten, Jews and communists together bear the projective weight. In Hitler Lewis finds "a sort of inspired and eloquent Everyman" (*Hitler*, 33). He concludes the book with an appreciation of his hero:

> I myself am content to regard him as the expression of the current German manhood— resolved with that admirable tenacity, hardihood and intellectual acumen of the Teuton . . . to seize the big bull of Finance by the horns, and take a chance for the sake of freedom. (202)

In 1938 Virginia Woolf would describe Hitler with a very different emotion but in similar terms as "the quintessence of virility, the perfect type" of manhood (*Three Guineas*, 187).

By 1932, in *Doom of Youth*, Lewis has shifted his terminology from "the white race" to "the aryan race." He continues to emphasize the necessity to keep this entity intact, for, just as the epira will swallow its mate, "[i]n intermarriage, with Jew or Indian, it is the other race that absorbs the European, not the reverse. . . . With his 'borrowed religion' and 'mongrel culture' the Jew will 'absorb' spiritually within half an hour."[37]

Doom of Youth contains a horrified and by now familiar account of how modern youths are infantilized and prevented from achieving manhood by women and feminized homosexuals. In it, Lewis also makes a bitter attack on Alec Waugh, whose *Loom of Youth* (1917), which I examined briefly in chapter 3, he satirizes in his title. Lewis repeatedly attributes his own obsessional structure to Waugh, childishly taunts him by calling him a homosexual and a woman, and even employs one of his own bêtes noires, psychoanalysis, to label him—a "mother."

> The characters Mr. Waugh creates are feminized, as it were, to an obsessional extent . . . Mr. Waugh must have the soul of a nannie . . . I should

> say that all the feminine, maternal attributes were excessively developed in him, and . . . thwarted . . . I think it is fair to say that there is something of an obsessional nature at work; I think that psychoanalysis would reveal the fact that *motherhood* in its most opulent form was what Mr. Waugh had been destined for by nature, and that cruel fate had in some way interfered, and so unhappily he became a man. (114)

In fascist Germany and Italy, unlike in Waugh's England, Lewis asserts, youths are masculine. This leads Lewis to the Jew, who "according to the standards of european masculinity—is feminine—that is clear enough" (117). The Jew is also childish:

> Indeed, that very racial longevity could scarcely have been compassed without a cultivation of all that was primitive, immature and emotional in the human being. . . . Call it a second—or a third—Childhood, if you like: but there it is—it is an essential sly buoyancy, beneath a traditional mask of oppressive gloom. (118–19)

Lewis concludes this chapter with a long quotation about how the Jew, Albert Einstein is "mothered" by his wife who acts as "a doting parent towards a precocious child" (121).

Doom of Youth hardly pretends to coherence. Dismissed by one critic as "a handful of cuttings waved in the face of the public" and by Meyers as "one of his shoddiest efforts," it was withdrawn by his publishers after legal actions by both Alec Waugh and Godfrey Winn, another of the authors the book attacks (Meyers, 215).

Left Wings over Europe (1936) and *Count Your Dead: They Are Alive!* (1937) were written and published at a time when such events as the remilitarization of the Rhineland, the annexation of Austria, and the occupation of the Sudetenland had turned English public opinion firmly against the Nazis. Nevertheless, in both books, Lewis continues to praise and exonerate Hitler and to blame the world crisis on "Jewish financiers."

In *Left Wings over Europe*, Lewis's concentration is on the conspiracy of Russian Marxists and Jews, and in particular on the destruction of Europe by Jewry: that "bird of prey . . . of International Finance" (37). As in other popular anti-Semitic texts of the time, he uses the terms "usury," "international cabal," and "international finance" interchangeably for "Jews."[38]

In an interesting historical foray, he accuses "the ingenious Mr. Disraeli" of liquidating the landed society of England and of pushing the unsuspecting Englishman into "co-citizenship with the Redskin and the Blackamoor, the Jew and the Maorie [*sic*]" (35, 44). He calls Mussolini's invasion of Abyssinia a war of liberation and accuses Britain's "leftist" government of being in league with "an oppressive international cabal, which presumes to condemn all but a very few nations to a status of economic serfdom and inferiority in order to be able to coerce and enslave them" (302). Lewis names members of this cabal: the publishing house of Gollancz, the bishop of Durham, who "seems to be enraged by the elimination of Jews from German public life" but does not care about his own miners, and the Russian ambassador, Mr. Litvinov, whom he accuses of looking like a Jew:

> How can anyone in their senses and with a good pair of eyes in their head suppose . . . once he has had a good look at the photographs of Mr. Litvinov and his associates—that these men . . . are running the communist international for anybody except their own sweet selves and their masters? (321)

As in Lewis's earlier books, the forces of the oppressors are dauntingly organized and powerful. International Jewry is a "money king" who "goes about with his tail between his legs—furtively, and yet bursting with an enormous sense of power—of necessity concealed and in some measure frustrated power. He lives for power—therefore he is rancorous and jealous" (318).

If Lewis's system no longer belongs to the central or dominant English discourse, it has nonetheless found a friendly home. Rosenberg traces the metaphor of the Jew as cowering dog back to medieval texts, and paragraphs almost identical to the one above can be found in anti-Semitic tracts of the twenties by John Wolf, George Bolitho, Nesta Webster, Hilaire Belloc, and G. K. Chesterton, as well as in the pro-Nazi anti-Semitic press of the 1930s. Moreover, Lewis's note of helpless victimization at the hands of unscrupulous and powerful Zionist forces intent on shamefully embarrassing the British is exactly the note we have heard in chapter 1 in the many minutes and letters exchanged by the officers of the Foreign and Colonial Offices, throughout the war.

Lewis's defense of Hitler in *Left Wings over Europe* has a similarly wistful, almost plaintive note. He predicts that when every other country has turned its back on England, "the faithful Adolf will still be there—offering her his strong right arm (if she will not accept his heart and hand) for her defense against her enemies" (331). In *Rude Assignment* (1950) Lewis described the impulse behind his political books of the 1930s:

"With candour, and with an almost criminal indifference to my personal interests, I have given myself up to the study of the State" (69).

In 1936 he portrayed Hitler as a similarly martyred victim:

> This celibate inhabitant of a modest Alpine chalet—vegetarian, non-smoking and non-drinking, has remained the most unassuming and simple of men. He is a man in mortal danger, every moment of his life, who has sacrificed himself, literally, to a principle, that of national freedom. This man does not conform to the popular conception of a tyrant. . . . He is more like one of the oppressed! (*Left Wings*, 280)

In the reviews of *Left Wings over Europe* in 1937, we see that, for the first time, English reviewers have become attuned, though not necessarily sensitive, to the issue of anti-Semitism. The *Times Literary Supplement*, which had defended Lewis's *Hitler* in 1930, now found him guilty of Hitler worship and claimed that "he has learned his doctrines in the Nazi school." The reviewer still acquits Lewis of anti-Semitism, however: "Perhaps the fact that Mr. Lewis is free from any touch of anti-Jewish feeling has caused him to be unaware how completely he has adopted the Nazi outlook."[39] L. M. Horton of the *London Mercury* found Lewis's arguments reasonable for the most part, claiming that "now as always he is worth reading," but rather self-righteously criticized him for overlooking the British incapacity to tolerate anti-Semitism: "There are certain moral scruples particularly affecting Englishmen which exist, whether he approves of them, or not. For instance, it is a fact overlooked by him that Englishmen cannot tolerate German persecution of the Jews and suppression of thought."[40] In a scathing review in the *Spectator*, the first openly to accuse Lewis of anti-Semitism, E. H. Carr took the occasion to condemn the racist right-wing "Die-Hards" who secretly approve Hitler's anti-Semitism but are too hypocritical to proclaim their own. Carr identifies Lewis as a known racist who supports Germany because of the Nazis' attitude toward

> coloured men, even including in that category (the Good British Die-Hard would not have gone so far himself, but it showed the right spirit) the Jews . . . Germany which had for so long been merely a territory inhabited by Huns, now suddenly became a White-Man's Paradise, a land fit for Die-Hards to live in.[41]

Lewis, says Carr, has missed the boat. By now even the Die-Hards have "shuffled off after Mr. Churchill," leaving Mr. Lewis alone "against the

Red Menace" (234). He assures the reader that this book should supply him with "plenty of amusement." Even Meyers does not attempt to rescue *Left Wings over Europe*; he calls it "anti-democratic, anti-Communist and anti-Semitic" (Meyers, 228).

Count Your Dead: They Are Alive! (1937), which Meyers feels is "superfluous" and Lewis's worst book (229), continues the attack. Even more than in *Left Wings over Europe*, it is now the Jews who receive the full weight of his paranoia. Perhaps aware of this, Lewis declares his impartiality: "I'm as little pro-German as I am an anti-Semite."[42] He assures us, "I have often felt compassion for the Jew (This was before he became so important and began taking his own part so effectively everywhere)" (41).

In this, probably his most virulently anti-Semitic book, Lewis wishes that England, like Germany, had "been wise [enough] to understand the Jew. Then we should have no Jewish problem." As it is, "Some offspring of an asiatic bazaar-tout" has become master over those of the blood of Chaucer and Shakespeare (43). He feels that in regard to the Jews, England, "could with advantage take a leaf of the German book" (44). As if this were not explicit enough, he urges: "[G]ive me the hot pogrom every time. These new cold pogroms without a drop of bloodshed get me down" (341).

Hitler is once again again represented as the victim of Britain's "Hitler complex." Lewis warns us, "I will be thoroughly naughty" (83), and the tone of this book, which takes the form of a dialogue between two equally moronic public school men, is indeed written in the voice of a childish bully. At times the author even takes on the tone of a cranky child who is fully aware that he has gone too far and will be punished, but nevertheless feels a compulsion to continue:

> I can understand that Mr. Stalin should dislike Hitler, because the latter is very rude to Communists. I can understand M. Blum disliking Hitler, because the latter is impolite to Jews. But . . . I cannot see what Mr. Baldwin should feel so incredibly deeply about. (76)

The sarcasm is embarrassingly crude:

> I can see we have to kill Hitler. . . . Look what he's done. (1) He's muzzled the Press. Monstrous! (2) He sentences Bolshies to death. Barbarous! (3)

> He prevents Jews from making money. Cruel, I call it! (4) He's apt to seize Danzig, an awfully pretty city on the Baltic. Abominable! (339)

The publication of *Count Your Dead: They Are Alive!* marked the climax of Lewis's anti-Semitic writing. While not completely absent from the book, women and inverts remain in the background, taking second place to "Don Moses Rosenberg," the sinister Marxist-Jew whose poisonous tentacles reach from New York to Moscow and enfold all of England in their grasp. In *Count Your Dead*, Jews are inscribed with the engulfing and murderous qualities of women and the threatening ambisexual qualities of feminine inverts. But the switch of symbolic priorities would be only a temporary one.

A Martyr to His Country: The Jews, Are They Human? *(1939) and* The Hitler Cult *(1939)*

While Lewis's political books, especially the last two, did damage his reputation (Julian Symons tells of a meeting of the Left Book Club in which a boycott was called of his work), he has always had his defenders. I have already cited some of the defenses modern critics have mounted for *Hitler*. Right-wing supporters such as Ezra Pound, whose approbation probably did nothing to help his friend's reputation, were always in evidence. T. S. Eliot, a more powerful right-wing ally, also defended Lewis against the charge of fascism and after his death called him "one of the few men of letters in my generation whom I should call without qualification, men of genius."[43] Lately, the Black Sparrow Press has reprinted several of Lewis's books, and new editions of four more of them, including *Tarr* and *The Art of Being Ruled* (though not *Hitler* or *Left Wings over Europe*), came out from that press in 1990. Never content to leave his defense to others, Lewis attempted to exonerate himself for the opinions expressed in the books we have just examined with two revisionist texts, *The Jews, Are They Human?* (1939) and *The Hitler Cult* (1939).

The Jews, Are They Human? (its title is a parody of Gustaf Renier's *The British, Are They Human?* and hardly a neutral choice) is a fascinating study of the process of splitting. In it Lewis confronts some of his own obsessional structures in an unsuccessful attempt to reason himself out of his anti-Semitism. This book, like *Count Your Dead*, is written in the form of a conversation, this time between Lewis himself and a character he calls "the antisemite," who appears, to any reader of the earlier books, to be Lewis's alter ego. Nevertheless, he never acknowledges any past or present relationship to this "zealot." Instead, he declares himself to be, as "a person who can scarcely be suspected of mercenary intentions, or of courting popularity," in an ideal position to convey "an attitude of common sense regarding the Jew."[44]

Interestingly, one of the foremost characteristics of this "rabbit-toothed weakminded little man," the "antisemite," is his paranoid obsessiveness: he "catches sight of his enemy at all hours of the day." "Of course if you are absorbedly interested in anything," Lewis reminds us, clearly speaking from experience, "you seek opportunities of being near it; of studying it, or enlarging your knowledge of it" (*Jews*, 33–34). The "antisemite," then, is often surrounded by Jews as though by a kind of "animal magnetism." He is "a gentile of disordered mind who has become what he is by brooding upon a bogey" (35). The "antisemite" also shares with Lewis a curious tendency to confuse Jews and women. "Sex-generalities enter a good deal into his hostile analysis of the Jew. The Jew, it is asserted, is *feminine*-receptive rather than creative, over-emotional . . . and he is a parasite too, as the woman is" (61).

Lewis mentions an "antisemite" who married a Jewess: "horror abetting sensuality" (32). He cites Otto Weininger, a "Jewish antisemite," whose "main contention was that the Jews were the *female race*. And he was consumed with a ferocious antipathy for all females—as well as being extremely sensual. You may imagine his predicament. Eventually he committed suicide" (55). It is, of course, his own predicament Lewis is unconsciously describing here in his very accurate description of Weininger.

Lewis's main objection to the "antisemite" is his tendency to drive unsuspecting Gentiles to the opposite extreme: "At the end of a grueling couple of hours, of intensive antisemitism, he almost succeeds in turning one into a pro-Jew" (28). Only almost, however. Speaking for himself, not for "the antisemite," he advises ignoring Jews as a way to make them disappear and comments, four months after Kristallnacht, on the Jew's masochistic tendency to dwell on his own trouble, which "he has quite got used to" and has learned to enjoy, just as many Jews "enjoy Herr Hitler" (21, 55). He dwells on the smell and bad manners of poor Jews, on the intolerable ugliness of the Jew in general and the immediate distaste he provokes:

> To lack of grace, it is further felt, this swarthy stranger adds a bumptiousness, a push, a vulgar swagger, which is irresistibly provoking. . . . A man begins by disliking instinctively a waddling strut. . . . Next he resents the arrogance so provokingly painted upon the "oily" countenance . . . (39–40)

And yet, the Jew has his good points. He is bright, has a pathetic desire to be friendly, and a strange way of coming out on top—so "let us assure him that he's all right with us, so long as he observes our laws and respects our funny little ways" (21).

Through the use of an alter ego, "the antisemite," Lewis approaches in *The Jews, Are They Human?* real insight into his own paranoid system. It is possibly the proximity of that insight which threatens him so much that it leads him to undermine his own conscious intent in this book: to demonstrate that he is not in fact an anti-Semite. *The Jews, Are They Human?*, an attempt to dispel his reputation as an anti-Semite, merely cemented it. Only his faithful supporter, the *Times Literary Supplement*, found *The Jews, Are They Human?* as instructive as Lewis's previous books. The reviewer commented: "In our usual rounds the Jew, especially if he be orthodox and freshly arrived from some Central European State, strikes us often as a grotesque figure, and Mr. Lewis' book is most valuable in those chapters in which he expounds successfully the attitude in which we should regard and treat these strangers to English ways."[45]

In *The Hitler Cult* (1939), although he appears truly disillusioned with his former hero, Lewis once again undermines his own attempts to defend himself against the charge of anti-Semitism. He explains that in England anti-Semitism has always been "[*sic*] a pastime—in the nature of a parlour sport" and that his understandable mistake in the former books had been to assume that it was the same in Germany.[46] Furthermore, who could blame him for failing to feel sympathy for a people who enjoy their own persecution? Lewis explains that his senses

> were not exactly afflicted by what happened to this not very tactful member of society (as is the average Jewish bagman) in the way of insulting badinage . . . and anyway the latter seemed rather to enter into the spirit of it. (17)

Again, the Jews are "a people . . . who have an exasperating idea that they have been especially picked out by the father" (19).

Just as Lewis had not bothered to read *Mein Kampf* before writing *Hitler*, he wrote his recantation of that book without bothering to inform himself of the fate of European Jewry. *The Hitler Cult* appeared in December 1939, after Lewis had left for Canada and three months after war had been declared. Both the events of the Kristallnacht pogrom and the plight of Jews in the Warsaw ghetto had been well publicized in the British press at that time. In one of many such reports from Germany, a *Times* correspondent wrote, "[T]he condition of most Jews here is one of misery, terror and despair." Ignoring this, Lewis speaks of "insulting badinage" and "cold pogroms" and in general reveals a complete ignorance of current events. While, as we have seen, such determined ignorance was not unusual among the British people at that time, it does stand out in a book whose formal purpose was to recant its author's former support of Nazism.

In *Rude Assignment* of 1950, Lewis made one last attempt to simultaneously disown and reclaim his earlier books and to counter the various charges (of racism, fascist sympathizing, and anti-Semitism) which had arisen against them by that time. He explained that *Paleface* contained "nothing antipathetic to the Red and the Black" but was merely an effort "to attack the Paleface sentimentalizing about the dark skin." That book was attacked by intellectuals, he explains, not for its racism, but because Lewis was not "in the pro-Black racket" (*Rude*, 219–21).

Lewis exhibits particular ambivalence about *Hitler*, the book which he felt to be the cause of his ostracism. In a chapter of *Rude Assignment*, which was suppressed when the book appeared in 1950, but was included in the 1984 reprint, he calls his former theory of Hitler as a man of peace "painfully absurd" and "an inexcusable blunder."[47] In the same unpublished chapter, however, he quotes and then justifies several of his more offensive passages, including the one in which he first calls the Jew "the brilliant and bossy Hausfrau of the stolid english hubby," then asserts that "the Jew has often lent colour to the Nazi accusations" (256–57). This passage, he claims in 1950, "shows, with I think judicious insight, the exact relation of these two races, most unfortunately thrown together at this juncture" (257). In the final version of the book, Lewis leaves out this chapter. *Hitler*'s anti-Semitism is completely ignored, and instead of regret for his blunder, Lewis defends a book, which, he explains in his most grandiose manner, was intended to "break the European ostracism of Germany, call in question the wisdom of the Versailles Treaty and get it revised . . . attempt to establish healthy relationships in Western Europe" (224).

Similarly, Lewis defends *Count Your Dead* as "a first rate peace pamphlet" and claims that *Left Wings over Europe*, while mistaken in many ways, was "a violent reaction against Left-wing incitement to war" (226). Far from being anti-Semitic, all three books were efforts to subvert the very spirit which led "to the Gas-ovens at Belsen" (73). This, one of Lewis's few references in all his work to the fate of the Jews, is preceded by another, more personal reference to a private version of the concentration camps: "Any member of this 'intelligentsia' who challenges the system, is relegated to what is little better than a concentration camp and condemned to impotence in this way" (23). Lewis's role of beleaguered male victim whose very manhood is under attack is an important foundation of his own system, and he is reluctant to assign it to anyone else. As he asserts over and over again, "The personal loss entailed . . . by my stand against war was incalculable" (225).

Unlike his friend Ezra Pound, who before his death acknowledged and apologized for his anti-Semitism, Lewis continued to deny his own, admittedly less virulent attitude. In any event, by 1950 Jews had lost their central position in his system. Instead, he warns of "the conjunction of the woman and one of these ubiquitous perverts [which] boded no good for the normal male" (*Rude*, 191) and the "epidemic of homosexuality in England since World War II . . . the feminisation, or neutralisation of the White European . . . [and] the feminist [who] had been followed by the feminising male" (182, 188). We learn once more how the normal male, who must "live cooped up with a snarling woman, or a slatternly lazy one . . . who adds child after child to the household . . . half of them adopting the habits of scavenger dogs," would be far happier "in a men's communal dwelling . . . liberated from the crushing responsibility of sex, of fatherhood and the upkeep of a dirty little 'castle' " (190).

After Lewis repudiated Hitler, as he had repudiated his other male heroes, Jews quickly lost their focal place in his authorial structure. They were relegated, with blacks, to a category of inferior but unimportant aliens. Women and homosexuals had now returned to their proper symbolic places—as the key objects in his paranoid obsessional system.

Impartial Malignity: "Cantleman's Spring Mate" (1917) and Tarr *(1918)*

Even before *The Art of Being Ruled* of 1926, the first didactic book in which Lewis displayed his system; a look at his early fiction reveals it already fully formed. This early fiction, like *The Art of Being Ruled*, contains no major Jewish characters, but presents the script in which Jews would take a leading role in the openly anti-Semitic didactic books of the late 1920s and 1930s and in Lewis's longest fictional production, *The Apes of God* of 1930. A brief look at two earlier works, the short story, "Cantleman's Spring Mate" (1917) and the novel, *Tarr* (1918), will reveal this pattern.

"Cantleman's Spring Mate," intended for publication in Margaret Anderson's *Little Review* of 1917, was found obscene, and the entire issue was suppressed.[48] The censors' objection was, of course, not to the brutality of the sexuality in the story, but rather to its explicitness. The story takes place in England during the First World War, and its hero, like Lewis at that time, is in army training camp in the Northern countryside. (Lewis often used the name "Cantleman" when writing about himself at this time; it seemed to represent a fictional alter ego.) The brilliant young man, walking alone in the spring fields, notices the animal kingdom's "sex-hunger" as well as "the fact that many of its members showed their fondness for their neighbours in an embarrassing way: that is they killed and ate them. But the weaker were so used to dying violent deaths and being eaten that they worried very little about it" (304–5).

Here, nine years earlier than its appearance in *The Art of Being Ruled* of 1926, is the epira whose habits Lewis explored so exhaustively in that book.[49] Sex is a hunger which must be satisfied—but in experiencing that satisfaction one risks being devoured. Perpetual vigilance is required in order not to give in to the longing for aggression which can result in offering oneself as a meal.

The young man rails against his country, which is preparing to send to war a person who is as close as might be found to "the human entirely" and who is endowed with "more human, as well as a little more divine understanding than those usually on his left and right" (306). "Should such allow himself to be disturbed by the quarrels of Jews . . . ?" asks this grandiose embodiment of his author, echoing the "Jews' War" theme (306). He passes a girl and dismisses her as "a crude marsh-plant," but "he had his programme . . . he would live up to his part" (309).

Cantleman hates and despises not only women but his fellow officers. The spring season produces "nothing but ideas of defiance" in his mind, and he understands that "the hypocrisy of Nature and the hypocrisy of War were the same" (309–10). He is determined not to enter into any understanding with life, but instead to be killed or to "remain in it unreconciled." But his hard, rigid surface is threatened by the appearance of the girl, Stella: "With a treachery worthy of a Hun, Nature tempted him towards her" (310). Although he cannot be deeply attracted to as lowly a creature as she is, he finds his need for her deeply humiliating and fantasizes revenge:

> He could throw back Stella where she was discharged from (if it were allowable, now, to change her into a bomb) first having relieved himself of this humiliating gnawing and yearning in his blood. . . . As for Stella . . . all women were contaminated with Nature's hostile power and might be treated as spies or enemies. The only time they could be trusted . . . was as mothers. So he approached Stella with as much falsity as he could muster. (310)

In this one passage, Lewis's system is faithfully recapitulated. The hero's rigid and carefully maintained boundaries are threatened by his sexual need as well as by his humiliating emotional yearning. Equally strong is the need to "live up to his part" or prove his masculinity. Enraged by this need, a "humiliating gnawing and yearning in his blood," he envisions changing the female who has provoked it into a bomb and hurling her as a mass of exploding fragments; an image of extreme phallic violence much like those which Theweleit found over and over again in the writing (and actions) of the Freikorpsmen. As Lewis emphasizes in his next paragraph, such annihilating hostility is a defensive measure against the enemies all women, with the possible exception of a mother in regard to her son, are to men. The falsity Cantleman musters up is the necessary defense to use against such an enemy or spy, who cannot be simply avoided, because she is needed to provide sexual release. That release, when it comes, is a process of discharging rage:

> That night he spat out, in gushes of delicious rage, all the lust that had gathered in his body. . . . He . . . once more turned to the devouring of his mate. He bore down on her as though he wished to mix her body into the soil, and pour his seed into . . . the brown phalanges of floury land. As their two bodies shook and melted together, he felt that he was raiding the bowels of Nature: he was proud that he could remain deliberately aloof, and gaze bravely . . . up at the immense and melancholy night . . . (310)

Once again, one short paragraph recapitulates Lewis's system. Like the Freikorpsmen, who described the sexual act as "a trancelike act of violence" and who "had little to do with a sexuality understood as the desire for physical love with another person" (Theweleit, 2: 61), Lewis describes sexual intercourse with a woman in "Cantleman's Spring Mate" as a process of release, not of desire, but of rage. It is also a devouring—the male in this case having triumphed over the engulfing female. He bears down on her in a murderous way, as though he wishes to mix her body into the soil. The brown phalanges suggest a formation of infantry, ground in death into the soil, and the color brown followed by the "bowels of Nature" suggest fecal matter: he is not only devouring her and killing her in an act of war but also turning her body into excrement. In the end Cantleman feels pride; this act has allowed him to retain his own boundaries, to "remain deliberately aloof." An intact man, he is now able to gaze bravely into the "immense and melancholy" female night without being engulfed by it.

In the last paragraph of the story, Cantleman, on the battlefield, receives a letter from Stella telling him that she is pregnant. Instead of answering it, he "beats a German's brains out . . . with the same impartial malignity that he had displayed in the English night with his Spring mate" (311).

If "Cantleman's Spring Mate" is a metaphorical account of Lewis's own experience in army training camp, his first full-length novel, *Tarr* (1918), is clearly derived from his early years as an artist in Paris and his relationship with the German woman Ida, about whom he wrote so voluminously to his mother. In contrast to the suppression of "Cantleman," *Tarr* was published, at Ezra Pound's urging, by Harriet Weaver's Egoist Press, and it received the more favorable notice than any of Lewis's subsequent work. T. S. Eliot gave it a glowing review in the *Nation*, calling Lewis "[t]he most fascinating personality of our time," a writer whose work revealed "the thought of the modern and the energy of the cave man."[50] In the *Little Review*, Pound called *Tarr* "the most vigorous and volcanic English novel of our time" and compared Lewis to Dostoevsky.[51] Rebecca West also made the comparison to Dostoevsky. She found the character of Kreisler a "figure of great moral significance" and found *Tarr* "a beautiful and serious work of art . . . with permanent value."[52] Despite these rave reviews by his famous friends, *Tarr* only sold six hundred copies, perhaps because, as a work of fiction, it is decidedly unreadable. The characters in the book are as lifeless and unlikable as those in all of Lewis's fiction, and the plot is overshadowed by Lewis's sexist and violent philosophizing.

Tarr is about two young and struggling artists in Paris, one German and one English. The young Englishman, Tarr, like Cantleman, is special. He is "one of the only people who *see*," has "great capacity written all over him," and is, like Lewis, "the only child of a selfish vigorous little mother" (19, 22). Like Cantleman, Tarr is able to take what he needs from women, while maintaining a rigid boundary between himself and them. "In this compartment of my life," he boasts to his friend Butcher, "I have not a vestige of passion" (14). Tarr, like Cantleman, loathes women, who, he complains, instead of staying in their places and providing safe receptacles for "the passions, intuitions, all the features of the emotive life" (*Art*, 246), are pressing and penetrating "everywhere—confusing, blurring, libelling, with their half-baked gushing tawdry presence. It is like a slop and spawn of children and the bawling machinery of the inside of life, always and all over our palaces" (14–15). Tarr, whose own softness and vulnerability are rigidly sealed off, is sickened by "women's psychic discharges which affected him invariably like the sight of a person being seasick" (52). He is especially threatened by the large, beautiful Russian, Anastasia, who "always appeared on the verge of a dark spasm of unconsciousness . . . to have on your hands a blind force of those dimensions! He shuddered . . . " (221). His only warm and uncomplicated relationships are with other men, like his friend Butcher, "the sweetest old kitten" (20), who "was always surly about women, or rather men's tenderness for them: he was a vindictive enemy of the sex" (27). Butcher, who refers to Tarr as "the young master," adores his friend, and is ready to do his bidding, is not, of course, a proper sex object. Tarr needs a female mistress, but as he tells his friend, he only allows himself "to philander with *little* things" (25). Accordingly, he has chosen Bertha, a woman below him in class and education: "a high grade aryan bitch, in good condition, superbly made . . . a succulent, obedient, clear peasant type . . . with a nice healthy bent for self-immolation" (24–25). As an extra precaution, he resolves to "gaze on Bertha inhumanly" (29) as a "machine . . . to take . . . to pieces, bit by bit" (221). In a passage strikingly similar to the Freikorpsmen's fragmented objectification of the female body, Tarr takes care not to see her as a whole person, but rather to look only at the separate "bits" of her, as when "the dressing gown was half open and one large thigh, with ugly whiteness, slid half out of it. It looked dead, and connected with her like a ventriloquist's dummy with its master" (43). Tarr finds Anastasia more interesting than Bertha, but knows she would disturb the rigid boundaries of his world. In a striking restatement of Horney's and Chodorow's theories that both men and women perceive the female as the first, or "generically human," gender (Chodorow, 11), he reasons:

> God was man, the female was a lower form of life. Everything started female and most so continued: a jellyish diffuseness spread itself and gaped. . . . Above a certain level sex disappeared . . . everything below that line was female . . . he enumerated acquaintances palpably below that absolute line: a lack of energy, permanently mesmeric state, almost purely emotional, they all displayed it, they were true "women." (345)

As in *The Art of Being Ruled*, masculinity is not a given. Men are made, not born, and are constantly at risk of becoming permeated with that primordial "jellyish diffuseness" and slipping back into womanhood. Association with Anastasia, who is "in every way too big" (344) and who fits neither the role of "housewife" nor that of the "mother of men," is far too dangerous.

> I do not understand attraction for such beings . . . not being as fine as men . . . not being as fine as housewives or classical Mothers of Men . . . they appear to me to occupy an unfortunate position on this earth. No properly demarcated person as I am, is going to have much to do with them[.] (26)

Like Karen Horney's analysands, who were unable to desire women whom they perceived as equals, Tarr knows he cannot risk a relationship with a woman as powerful as himself, who might threaten the precious "proper demarcation" which keeps him intact (Horney, 359). The phrase "jellyish diffuseness" is the same one Orwell used to refer to the state of young boys sent to school for the first time. For both men, it inscribes the terror of dissolving boundaries.

If Tarr represents the safely sealed-off part of Lewis, Kreisler, the German, is his alter ego, the rageful, psychotic self that Tarr's vigilance keeps at bay, and which Lewis himself hovered perilously near in his own life. Paranoid, permanently enraged, and always penniless, Kreisler frantically begs from the acquaintances he despises. Like Tarr, he regards women as "a natural resource . . . an asset to be harvested and mined" (Dinnerstein, 36–37), but he makes the mistake of turning to them in his need, and entrusting them with his emotions:

> [T]here they were all the time—vast dumping grounds for sorrow and affliction— a world-dimensioned Pawn-shop, in which you could deposit not your dress suit or garments, but yourself. . . . Their hope consisted, no doubt, in the reasonable uncertainty as to whether you would ever be able to take yourself out again. (99)

Kreisler fails in vigilance. He believes "in the efficacity of women" (100) and "falls in love" with Anastasia. As Tarr could have told him, "surrender to a woman was a sort of suicide for an artist" (221). When Anastasia rejects him, he can never "take himself out" again. Without the needed relief, the volcano self-destructively implodes. Kreisler becomes more and more bizarre and enraged, physically attacking women at parties and calling them sows. He rapes the gentle Bertha and, in an increasingly psychotic state, challenges Soltyk, a supposed rival for Anastasia's affections, to a duel. He arrives on the scene too disorganized to fight it, in a state of paranoid homosexual panic:

> He loved that man! Na ja! It was certainly a sort of passion he had for him! But mystery of mysteries!—because he loved him he wished to plunge a sword into him, to plunge it in and out and up and down! Oh why had pistols been chosen? (290)

Kreisler, who seems to have taken off in a mad flight from Lewis's unconscious, asks the horrified Soltyk for a kiss and then "thrust his mouth forth amorously . . . as though Soltyk had been a woman" (292). While on the conscious level Lewis probably intends this act as simply an ironic attack (to approach another man as a woman is to deliver the worst possible insult to him, the equivalent in action of Lewis's textually labeling Alec Waugh a "mother"), the unconscious homosexual activity here, from the plunging and thrusting of the sword to the kiss, is evident. Kreisler proceeds to kill Soltyk, and in a state of numbness in which he wonders "if it were not he that had died," wanders to the German border, where he is captured and humiliated by the police (300). In the cell, he hangs himself and is finally "thrust savagely into the earth" (309).

After splitting off, killing, and finally thrusting his troublesome and terrifyingly unpredictable alter ego deeply into the earth, Lewis offers Tarr, the safely protected self, Kreisler's spoils. Tarr inherits Anastasia, whom he quickly cuts down to size by insult and humiliation, first leading her on, then abruptly refusing her sexual advances, calling her a cheap whore and offering her twenty-five francs. Charmed by this treatment, she shrinks into the proper womanly shape and will from now on follow him docilely. Kreisler has also left Bertha pregnant, and Tarr secretly marries her and from then on "takes" her "in carefully prepared doses of about an hour a day: from say half past four to quarter to six" (315). He maintains separate establishments and treats both women with careful falseness. Unlike Kreisler, who has allowed a woman to destroy him, Tarr prospers. In proof of this, the book ends with the names of three more of his conquests.

Tarr's marriage with Bertha is much like the one Lewis himself would achieve with his "Froanna," whom he met in the year of the book's publication, kept in a separate establishment, and married twelve years later. In fact, we can view *Tarr*, with its split protagonists, as a morality tale in which Lewis warns himself of the dire consequences of relaxing his vigilance. Just as in *The Jews, Are They Human?*, Lewis used an alter ego, "the antisemite," to explore his own more violent and uncontrolled feelings, so Kreisler fulfills this function in this early novel.

Nightmares and Dreams Come True: The Apes of God *(1930)*

Lewis spent seven years on the mammoth *The Apes of God*, which he published himself in 1930 in a 625-page first edition, weighing in at five pounds. *Apes*, which appeared in the same year as *Hitler*, is a conducted tour of the literary world of London given by the artist and connoisseur of young men Horace Zagreus to his besotted and moronic Irish protégé, Dan Boleyn. It contains vicious satires of most of Lewis's benefactors and of many members of the Bloomsbury group, and it gained him countless enemies. T. S. Eliot had told Lewis, after reading early chapters, "[Y]ou have surpassed yourself and everything. It is worthwhile running the *Criterion* just to publish these" (Lewis, *Letters*, 140n. 1). Even he, however, when faced with the final product, felt that Lewis had been "breaking butterflies upon a wheel."[53] Lewis was, as usual, dissatisfied with the amount of publicity received by his huge book, which he compared to Joyce's *Ulysses*, and he was especially furious at the rejection by the *New Statesman* of a review of *The Apes of God* by his friend and admirer Hugh Porteus. Convinced that "Bloomsbury" had suppressed this and other reviews in an organized press boycott, he characteristically published his own pamphlet, *Satire and Fiction* (1930), which he describes on the title page as "The Scandal of an Attempt to Sabotage a Great Work of Art!'"[54] *Satire and Fiction* is a compilation of (positive) contemporary reviews of *The Apes of God*, including Porteus's review and others, as well as letters in praise of the novel. Lewis supplemented these with an explanatory essay on the meaning of art. The selected reviews are interesting not only in themselves but because they give a good indication of the image Lewis wished to project in the world.

The contested review by Porteus describes Lewis as a "masculine intelligence . . . which can survey our generation from outside its two main cults of childishness and femininity" (*Satire*, 16). A letter from Meyrick Booth applauds his attack on "the barbaric cults which now increasingly dominate our social life: back to childhood, back to matriarchy, back to emotion and the unconscious, back, in short, to almost anything that is sufficiently barbaric and irresponsible" (26). More negative reviews which complement the self-image to which Lewis aspires, that of a cruel, unfeeling, and powerful masculine intelligence, are also included. Richard Aldington, for example, calls *Apes* "an amazing example of the power and limitation of pure intelligence" and comments, "You have the feeling that Mr. Lewis would like to kill anybody . . . who enjoyed anything so glandular as a mere kiss" (32). Lewis also includes a review by his friend Naomi Mitchison in *Time and Tide*, in which she calls the book an "exceedingly well written, sometimes brilliantly funny cold bath," and adds:

> [H]e hates more thoroughly and efficiently than any writer living . . . at the moment he specially dislikes homosexuals of both kinds, the war generation still pretending to be young, messy-minded people such as Jews and Irish[.] (33)

The Jewish Mitchison, whose tone wavers between sarcasm and admiration, may have felt some discomfort at her friend's anti-Semitism but declares herself pleased with his homophobia: "As for homosexuals, there are too many of them—and too well pleased with themselves for any stable society" (33).

While many modern critics have found *The Apes of God* "virtually unreadable" (Jameson, 5), others agree with Meyers's evaluation of the book as "a modern Dunciad, a massive but sharp-edged catalogue of literary evils that arrives from contemporary urban chaos" (Meyers, 160). Both Meyers and Paul Edwards, in his afterword to the Black Sparrow edition, offer "definitive" charts that explain which contemporary figure

Lewis intended to parody with each portrait, but the two have some significant disagreements. For the purposes of this study, identifying the originals, while of some interest, is less important than what the text reveals about Lewis's paranoid structure as it involves the representation of Jews and women.

In *The Apes of God* Lewis is finally inside the all-male society he so wistfully envisioned in his polemical books. Though the book opens and closes with a Pope-like scene of an old and ugly woman making her artificial toilette, and there are several other minor (equally repulsive) female characters, most of the book takes place in a homosexual world. Just as in *Hitler*, Lewis was drawn to the homosexual scene in Berlin, and led by the force of his own attraction violently to abuse that scene; here effeminate men are the main subjects as well as the main targets of his system.[55] Perhaps because of the relative absence of women in the book, and because it was written during a time when Lewis was increasingly under the influence of Nazism, Jews provide the other main focus. The book's anti-Semitism, while spread throughout, is most concentrated in the sections on Archie Margolin, James Julius Ratner, and Lionel and Isabel Kein. I will accordingly focus on these chapters in the ensuing discussion.

Archie Margolin, one of the first characters on the scene and one who makes appearances throughout the book, is a "jew-boy from the slum" who is waiting in the ancestral hall to "service" the aristocrat Dick Whittingdon.[56] Standing in a wing of Dick's family castle (the rest has been "rented to rich Jews"), Archie listens to "sewer people" singing jazz—"account[s] of nigger heavens—the lives of other idiot slaves, in cotton fields" (44, 43). In *Paleface*, the book in which blacks were the target of his projective energy, Lewis reviled jazz as primitive "Hottentot" music. In *The Apes of God*, jazz serves as the musical backdrop to the book, in which "niggers" appear as primitive and childlike emblems, imbued with stereotypical masculine virility. Equally despicable but far more dangerous is the feminized male Jew, with his links with communism and high finance and his secret control of the world. In *The Apes of God*, as so often in Lewis's work, historical and mythic stereotypes are tailored to fit his particular needs. In the character of Archie, he combines various stereotypical attributes of the Jew, making him a figure both despicable and powerful. The impoverished slum dweller is also a "sham-yid," who cleverly and shamelessly uses the familiar stereotypes established by Dickens and Shakespeare to ingratiate himself with his keeper:

> [H]e made his eyes shine obligingly, as he gazed into the foolface, with the pleased glitter expected, at the thought of gain. . . . —After considering for a moment, Arch looked archly up . . . and in the most sinister growling guttural he yet employed he repudiated his blood relation absolutely . . . " . . . he's what you'd call awful, Dick, is my brother Isadore, he's a proper old shark. . . . He sells tin watches to poor kids like Ethel, the old Skylark— I mean Shylock— . . . " (46–47)

Sander Gilman notes that stereotypical signifiers may be incorporated within a work of art in a way which is either naive or quite conscious (Gilman, *Difference and Pathology*, 26). In this case, Lewis is not only conscious of the historical power of his stereotypes: he attributes this consciousness to his character as well. Part of this Jew's power lies in his very modernist awareness. In Lewis's construct, instead of being the victim of literary stereotypes, Archie is the conscious and malicious manipulator of them. In his self-naming, Lewis deconstructs the word "Enemy," his self-endowed title reversing the word's usual meaning and changing it to mean "persecuted victim." Similarly, here he deconstructs the construct of Jew as victim. Self-parodying, self conscious, and manipulative, Archie is far from powerless.

Like the female, whose softness masks her lethal powers, Archie is effeminate. His croaking voice "is ill assorted with the feminine gold of the crimped head and the insignificance of the body" (45). Just as the behavior of similarly abject women in other Lewis texts masks their intentions, Archie's groveling, sycophantic behavior has a dangerous ulterior purpose: to use and destroy "the happy British male dupe," Dick. He surveys the ancestral castle, plotting its destruction and, symbolically, the destruction of British (white male) civilization: "This culture was dead as mutton but its great carcass offended him—it would take a hundred years to melt. He grinned and yawned" (43). Archie is not only the feminized invert and the Jew but also the despised and feared child: "His slightness was delicious—he rejoiced in his neat pygmy stature. It was the child height!" (42).

Archie Margolin appears again later in the book, dancing monkeylike on the table to please his new mentor, Horace Zagreus. With Zagreus too, he plays the fool, reassuring him of his class privilege and safety while all the time stealthily plotting his extinction.

Even more than Bertha in *Tarr*, with her "healthy bent for self-immolation" (24), Archie's masochism is at heart a trick to foster dependence in his lover and thus to gain his own ends. "Do you like a servant Horace?" he asks suggestively. "Servants ought to be kept down!" (429). As we saw in chapter 1, the theory of Jewish masochism was popular with British anti-Semites of the period, who reasoned that inherently masochistic Jews virtually compelled helpless Gentiles to mete out the punishment they required. Through his espousal of the theory, Lewis manages to retain the Jew, like the woman, as an emblem of despised weakness *and* of frightening strength. This textual doubleness allows Lewis himself, the real central figure of the book, to continue to retain his own double role as strong, masculine aggressor and conspired-against victim. This strategy fits neatly with that of the Home Office administrators who felt that the Nazi persecution was a plot by "whining Jews" to earn public sympathy and make them (the administrators) look bad.

Like Ratner, the other Jewish homosexual in the book, Archie is rotten through and through, in a decidedly female way. He embodies the most loathsome aspects of the female body. Gilman notes that in Renaissance Europe, male Jews were believed to menstruate "and thus shared with women the ability to contaminate through the menses."[57] Archie, too, seems to have menstrual periods: "Margolin stretched himself and yawned out of his pink-and-white doll-lungs of saw-dust . . . (stretching his mouth-muscles, displaying his midget boxer's reach with curled-up fists) in order to expel the period-heat that was drugging his tissues" (429).

In my earlier discussion, I mentioned Lewis's simultaneous aversion to and belief in the powers of psychoanalysis, which he associated with mother-son incest and endowed with frightening, almost supernatural powers. He pictured psychoanalysis as a Jewish spy network with uncanny means of gaining knowledge, which could and would reveal secret unpleasant truths about people. He often recommended it to his enemies for that purpose, as when he suggested that psychoanalysis would reveal Alec Waugh's effeminacy and his true vocation as a mother. In *The Apes of God*, the Jewish analyst Dr. Frumpfsusan is seen in league with his homosexual patient, Matthew Plunkett, a character both Meyers and Edwards agree is based on Lytton Strachey, whom Lewis often identified as a prime example of the feminine invert and to whom, in 1926, he wrote a strangely seductive letter, suggesting an incognito meeting "in an unfrequented part of town" (Meyers, 109).

The "jewish witch doctor's" advice to the homosexual Plunkett, who has come to him for "extroverting," is to try "overmatching"—that is, to take on a mentally and physically diminutive woman. This advice is identical to Tarr's decision to confine himself to philandering with "little things" (*Tarr*, 125) and also fits Lewis's choice to marry the small, uneducated, and submissive Froanna rather than Nancy Cunard, Iris Barry, or any of the more powerful and intellectual women with whom he had affairs.[58] Frumpfsusan advises his patient:

> In choosing a friend, ascend a step. In choosing a wife, descend a step. When Froggie-would-a-wooing-go, when Froggie is you, my dear boy, he must step down, as many steps as there are beneath him—even unto the last! To be frank with yourself, Matthew . . . an animated doll is all . . . you can really hope to take on. (83)

Frumpfsusan further urges his protégé to *"learn how to bully! . . . be rough!"* (87). He then offers another comforting piece of information particularly relevant to Lewis, who, like Salzman's rigid male clients, Kernberg's borderline patients, or Lewis's dark alter ego, Kreisler, in *Tarr*; alternated periods of grandiosity in which he proclaimed himself a genius with nagging periods of self-doubt and inferiority: "Inferiority-feeling may result from an actual superiority. The handicap of genius, isn't it?" (85).

As in *The Jews, Are They Human?* Lewis dispels his own approaching insight with invective. When Matthew Plunkett asks the doctor if he is himself an invert, Frumpfsusan responds by linking "inversion" to Jewish masochism:

> I am a Jew. . . . When I possess such a first-class source of "inferiority" as that, in the eyes of my fellow-men, what need have I of any other? Does it not put all and any in the shade at once? . . . I am a Jew. I am immune[.] (86)[62]

Impressed and envious, Plunkett asks, "You cannot supply me homeopathically with such a counter-complex as that, to eclipse all complexes?" (86). We have seen how Lewis projected his own masochism onto the Jew. Here Plunkett attempts to do the same thing.

It is interesting to note at this juncture how much Lewis's male Jew differs from the powerfully sexual, castrating Jew in the phallocentric Freudian myth which Fiedler evokes in "What Shall We Do About Fagin?" The danger in Lewis's personal myth is not from a virile, heterosexual father who may castrate the son and steal the coveted female prize, but rather from the female herself, who like the Jewish psychoanalyst, has the almost magic power to penetrate everywhere in her many guises. Here we find her in the effeminate male Jew/invert, whose purpose is to swallow the male, or to render him helpless and begging, a fawning, stomach-up dog.

A later section of the book, "Chez Lionel Kein Esq.," is based on Lewis's patrons, Violet and Sydney Schiff, who bought Lewis's work and consistently supported him financially. In this section, Zagreus takes Dan to visit Isabel and Lionel Kein and makes numerous mocking references to their Jewishness. After calling his host "an impudent old Whore" and referring to his hostess's nineteen face-lifts, her paraffin injections, and her obesity, Zagreus tells Dan that Isabel Kein comes from "the famous Covent Garden misfit shop, Lazarus . . . the mendicant leper" (306). His main attack, however, is on the Keins as patrons of the arts. Sydney Schiff was an admirer of Proust and a translator of his work, and after much ugly banter about Proust's Jewishness and homosexuality, Zagreus resorts to the old image of the engulfing female epira which swallows its mate: "But what generally is that *interest*, about which we hear so much? An 'appetite for people' would describe it? Your 'self-feeling' grows fat upon the people you can intellectually devour or dominate" (254). Lewis experienced "self-feeling" in anyone but himself as a powerful threat of domination and engulfment. The theme of devouring cannibalism is seconded by a French writer, Vernede, another ungrateful protégé and guest of Kein's.

> "Always I find myself afraid—I am afraid that he will swallow zem up! . . . When I see some new person at his house, I am frright-tent at zee way Li opens his *eyes*! And—his mowss!" He made saucers of his eyes and mouth, like a nurse engaged in an an account of the story of Red-Riding-hood . . . "[H]e devours zem, he sucks sem in—he *inhales* zem! (314–15)

In "Little Red Riding Hood," a classic story about the childhood fear of engulfment, the child enters the room unsuspectingly to find the big bad wolf and the benevolent grandmother merged for an awful moment in a combined and disguised wolf-grandmother figure with enormous features, especially the mouth: "The better to eat you with!" Wyndham Lewis, for whom the big bad wolf was indeed female, could not have come up with a better myth with which to embody his adult terror.

Zagreus agrees with Vernede about their common benefactor and adds to the picture by likening him to a louse, or "bloodsucker," a familiar literary metaphor for the Jew. "I always feel more anxiety for the objects of Kein's parasitic interest when the stage of the first breathless inhalation is over. When he has thoroughly warmed himself under the skin and begins to make himself at home" (315).

In creating Shylock and his bloody demand, Shakespeare referred to the myth, embodied in the culture by medieval drama and ballads, in which the Jew kidnaps (and sometimes castrates) small boys and uses their blood in his rites. Lewis's image, based on the same castration fear and the same cultural reference, is tailored to fit his own paranoid system with its ever-present yawning female mouth. The Schiffs refused to be offended and continued to help Lewis financially well after the publication of *The Apes of God*, supporting him through an especially long and debilitating bout of gonorrhea. Perhaps they had after all some touch of the masochism Lewis projects onto all Jews.

The Jewish character who takes up the most space in the *The Apes of God* (indeed he takes up over three hundred pages, and I will be able to mention only a small fraction of his appearances here) is Julius Ratner, the Jewish homosexual writer. In the Afterword, Paul Edwards identifies him as John Rodker,[59] but Meyers identifies him as James Joyce, a match which I find more convincing. Lewis was exactly Joyce's age, and Lewis's initial friendship and intense admiration for the relatively unknown author was soon replaced by a bitter envy of his success. He mocked Joyce's class background, repeatedly called *Ulysses* "mechanical" and "dead," and even accused Joyce of anti-Semitism, claiming that he had "certainly contributed nothing to the literature of the Jew, for which task he is in any case quite unsuited" (Meyers, 140). Lewis was not alone in associating Joyce with Jews: in 1940 the Swiss Alien Police refused the Joyces permission to enter the country on the grounds that they were Jewish, a claim which James Joyce refuted.[60] Finally, though this identification was certainly unconscious, Ratner, with his grandiosity, his homosexuality, his profession as a second-rate, derivative writer, and his virulent self-hatred masked by conceit and self-aggrandizement, also evokes Lewis himself—or at least that hidden and despised side of himself which he spent so much frantic time and energy keeping under wraps.

Whomever Lewis had in mind, he seems to have consulted the catalogue of anti-Semitic types in his creation of this character. Ratner is a homosexual, a coward, a pervert, a scavenger, a plagiarist, a cheat, and an arriviste. His "history" links psychoanalysis, homosexuality, and stereotypical Jewish traits:

> R's career opened not long before the War when he emerged from the East End, with Freud for his talmud and . . . manoeuvered sexually up and down. During the War he went away. That over, he marched out upon what was left of life . . . a promised land (purified by bloodshed and war-debts) lay stretching to the horizon. (137)

In his use of the Jew-as-animal metaphor, Lewis adds several new entries to Rosenberg's impressive inventory.[61] Ratner has the teeth of a wolf and the gums of a rabbit. He is a one-eyed cyclops, a boar with a single yellow fang, a dung beetle, a rat, a lizard, a fish, and an octopus. Even the notorious *Protocols of the Elders of Zion* come into play with heavy-handed references to "*a Lost Tribe*" and to "the elder [of] the Mediaeval Zion" (165). Ratner is also the Jew as moneylender, pornographer, pervert, masochist, communist, filthy disease-carrier, and child-killer. He gloats at the memory of the pornography he has sold at great profit. His feet are planted "to place the holy city at Moscow instead of Mecca" (153).

In one of the most bizarre passages in the book, more reminiscent of Charles Williams, the next author I shall discuss, Zagreus excites Ratner by invoking a kind of Yiddish-tinged black magic and claiming that among other repulsive objects, he owns a box containing a phallus, taken from a child killed on "the Moor." At the mention of this, "Ratner's countenance was lighted with the sultry covetousness of the dung fly" (340). In fact, Zagreus has been leading him on and now mocks him: "Poor Julius! Nothing doing!—I'll make up for it one of these days. . . . I'll have a Sex-morsel there, yum-yum—certainly I have! I've been keeping it especially for you: if you will stand up on your hind legs and beg nicely" (341).

Like Stella, whom Cantleman grinds into the ground like fecal matter, the Jew Ratner is continually associated with excrement. Zagreus instructs Dan: "Do not omit to feel some compassion—such as you would experience, it may be, if you met a dung-beetle and it had just had what it believed to be the last ball of excrement taken away from it" (138). When naive Dan meets Ratner, "he believed that he smelt—there was a smell" (169). Then he realizes where the smell comes from: "He had never seen a Jew before—and, he hoped from the bottom of his great Irish heart that he might never see one again!" (171).

Our first view of Ratner, which involves a great deal of excretory and other loathsome detail, catches him waking up in bed, body rotting, eyes caked and filthy, rattling and "moving his neck a little, circumspectly, like a snake" (145). Lewis's own particular preoccupations soon emerge. Ratner keeps a captive charwoman, Mrs. Lecher, and pays her to play a revolting and incestuous game of infant and mother. "It is love, it is the woman loving, always loving the lucky and so lovable 'great baby' that all Ratners lovingly are" (148). Lewis pursues this theme doggedly for pages:

> No I shaaant Mrs. Lochore! Joo wailed in teasing gritty growl, very pleased—very very Spoiltboy at this, very Naughty-man. . . . Beneath the crafty swollen eyes of the salaried british bonds-woman foster-mother, he cuddled his pillow openly. For two pins he would pluck a pis-en-lit in his bed, under the old grog-blossom nose of her he would. Becoming very siamese-kittenish Joo cooed, with the runculation of the matutinal catarrh. (146–47)

Once out of bed, "Joo" boasts of venereal disease, which unlike his creator, he is not virile enough to possess. He feels that "the Old Muse wanted to excrete a little" and types a few pages of puerile borrowed prose, "this obscene diarrhoea of ill-assorted vocables," then turns on himself with "that bitter Conscience . . . of the last of the pure pre-War Jews" and recognizes his writing as the secondhand fecal matter that it is (159–62). Later, he brings a pimply woman to his flat where his need to prove his masculinity forces him, against his inclination, to "clip and peck and glue the lip" (164). Ratner's filth goes hand in hand with his masochism and cowardice. Before setting off for Lord Osmund's party, Zagreus spits three times in his face, "for luck," and Ratner accepts it without a murmur. Spittle, like excretion, plays an important role here. Ratner himself spits "with the stealth of a cat" and feels that "everyone was repelled by and had a down on his spittle" (446).

At the "Great Lenten Freak Party" at Lord Osmund's house, attended by all of Bloomsbury, Ratner's disguise is the "Split Man." This image, signaling an awareness of inner doubleness, was an important one for Lewis's rival, Joyce, as well as for another of Lewis's particular targets, Gide. Such doubleness, which would later become a signature of the modern male antihero and a sign of his intelligence and awareness in the face of an absurd world, has a deeply negative connotation for Lewis, who was unable to integrate his own "good and bad introjections and identifications" (Kernberg, 34). The "split-man" disguise represents Ratner's impotence and his ability to "only half-live—the eternal imitation person." It is also indicative of his half- manhood as a homosexual and his half-humanity as a Jew.

After an attack of indigestion "which would have to be blasted out the morning-after with charges of pink female pills, nothing less," Ratner retreats to the kitchen, a setting which combines a medieval vision of Jew as devil with Lewis's loathing of the female reproductive system and of women:

> The heat of this nether cook-house found favor with his chilly bones, his body took like a duck to water to the hell-heat. He drew near to the distant fireplace, between the pillars, a whipped under-devil or sub-demon scheduled to play a domestic animal part,of an unwanted doctored cat, spinally sectioned black-sided and white sided. . . . It was the cheer of the period-fire, in the period-kitchen. (422)

Near the end of the book, Ratner is threatened by Starr-Smith, a fascist Blackshirt who has stormed the party to save the day. Although the sorely tempted Blackshirt does his best to restrain himself, Ratner masochistically teases and coaxes him into violence. In one of the uglier passages of anti-Semitism that I have encountered, Lewis tells us clearly that the Jews invited and enjoyed pogroms:

> [T]he pogromed animal of another day came out, and the grinning face was frankly used as a bait . . . to draw blood—an auto-bloodletting—he ogled the other inviting a good stiff blow and the Blackshirt felt it being drawn out of him by that hypnotic fish-eye . . . he started back as he felt that infernal attraction . . . [S]everal full seconds he held back but Ratner's eye had the better of the argument. Steadily it milked away at him in puissant glances of seductive insult—drawing the famous *violence* out of him. (596)

Needless to say, Ratner is beaten up and enjoys it.

Zagreus is eventually unmasked as himself an "ape," thus allowing defenders of Lewis such as Paul Edwards to argue that, because of this "disclaimer" we as readers are to understand that Lewis stands behind none of Zagreus's statements. In fact, the narrative style of *The Apes of God* does not depend in the least on anything so subtle as the established fictional device of a shifting narrative viewpoint. As another look at the quotations above should make amply clear, the reader is never urged to filter statements through the questionable mind or consciousness of an unreliable narrator and to emerge with his or her own conclusion. Instead, in a departure more typical of a polemical essay, all the narrative stems from one erupting consciousness—that of Lewis himself, who shouts at his reader: YOU WILL BE MADE TO HEAR IT! (*Tarr*, 9). The frenzies of anti-Semitism in the book are not so easily rationalized.

As if Lewis's authorial omnipresence were not enough, he several times refers to himself by name within the text, calling himself the "solitary high-brow pur-sang Lewis" (401) and referring to his own "war-jargon of german peace-politics" (402). He is also quite consciously self-referential in the character of Pierpoint, an off-stage "genius" whom Zagreus worships and constantly quotes, and whose philosophy is presented in an "Encyclical" and a series of long "broadcasts" which in many places closely echo *The Art of Being Ruled.* On one occasion only, the remote Pierpoint becomes strangely human, as Lionel Kein discusses him:

> Isabel and I will never change in our regard for him—our deep regard! But there are things about Pierpoint which even his most devoted friend would find it difficult to defend. . . . Poor Pierpoint! I wish I could have helped him to—to, not to lay himself open to so much hostile criticism. What he will do now I really wonder. . . . He has no money. What I'm terribly afraid of is that he may—well really go under—a man like that depends so much upon the support of a few friends—*good friends*! (299)

It is as if Lewis has slipped for a moment and introduced a realistic portion of his friends' talk about him into his idealized portrait of a masculine and uncaring genius, too remote and noble to even make an appearance in the book.

If Pierpoint, except for the passage above, is a careful and consciously idealized self-portrait, Dan Boleyn, who was probably intended as a parody of Stephen Spender, embodies Lewis's unconscious self-loathing and his fear of infantilization and engulfment by the female. Dan's tour ends in the company of heroic fascists who beat up Jews, but it begins, as does Lewis's paranoid system, in the nursery. Early in the book a weeping Dan, having been rejected by Zagreus, retires to the home of his motherly friend, Melanie, who, in typical female fashion, takes advantage of his weakness, abusing him with her "army of maternal fingers."

> You're only a child Dandarling aren't you now but a big baby, I'll be your nursemaid this time honey and put you to Bye-Bye, I know how to do

> that—no let Melanie do this for you . . . let me pull off this jacket, and the little waisty. (107)

Melanie forces Dan, who has now metamorphosed into an infant with lolling head, to lie down with her, and pursues him with her voracious female mouth. "Side by side like mother and new-born infant . . . she held him. . . . His head rolled away, to escape these attentions. The other mouth came after him as if it had been hungry" (107). Advancing on her "virgin victim," Melanie is "as strong as a boa constrictor" (108). She brings him to a reluctant climax in a passage which captures the full extent of Lewis's horror and terror of female sexuality:

> Almost he shot his bolt of terror in one agony after another. . . . Off with your lips the harlot-woman! Off with the sticky and shameless mouth of you! His disgust knew no bounds, he spat on the pillow . . . he . . . desired to vomit upon the whole machine, so fell and rhythmic and untiring. He was about to cat—in a moment he would be retching. And then his entire body fell down and gaped, it was sunk in a hot wallow of new shame . . . had he been sick or what, that there was this pulsing agony? (109)

It is perhaps no wonder, after this rape (for there is no other name for it) by the devouring woman, who first turns him into an infant and then violates him, that Dan Boleyn (and Lewis) feels a need to withdraw for the rest of the book to a world of homosexual men.

Such a withdrawal, has, of course, its own dangers. At Lord Osmund's party, a fire lashes at Dan's loins, almost castrating him and destroying his male costume (425). Zagreus, in another version of the "insidious proposal" in *The Art of Being Ruled*, tells him, "For the rest of the evening you'll have to be a girl Dan" (425). In *The Art of Being Ruled*, Lewis reasoned that a man "*does not want, if he can possibly help it, to be a man*, not at least if it is so *difficult*" (280). Lewis's assumption, which, like all his assumptions, is based on his own experience of reality, is that each man has a secret homosexual longing; that is, a deep desire to give up the battle and passively allow himself to be engulfed by/eaten by/turned into a female. Here the passive and obedient masochist, Dan, feels terror and aversion at the proposed transformation, but he has no choice. He must (deliciously) give in:

> All must go by the board (sex he would not consent to think of directly but it was *sex* must be sacrificed his sex whispered and he could not stop it) in such an emergency all had to go . . . yet he would not, it stood to

> reason, choose to take a female part. What man would wish to be got up as a girl? No man would. It was the last thing of course . . . (425)

Dan is transformed into a woman in an appropriate place for such a dire operation, "Mrs. Bosun's Closet." Another one of Lewis's horrible charladies, Mrs. Bosun, the "period nurse of gigantic tots," rules Lord Osmund's household from a suitably filthy boudoir, surrounded by such female trappings as "bloodbaked sheaths" (178, 179). Mrs. Bosun strips Dan, who is once again trapped in the nursery, and he feels the full misery of his victimized masculinity:

> [G]irls lucky devils were protected . . . at least had he been a girl there would have been no question of his being manhandled . . . or washed down like a public stallion with no mind of its own. Sometimes to be *a man* was awful nothing short! . . . He was fully alive to all the danger that he ran in the room of this terrible old lady. (438)

Despite his feeble effort to escape, "the hearty old hen would have her way" (181), and Dan is once again raped (this time symbolically) by a woman. Not surprisingly, this idyll is interrupted by several chapters of abuse of Ratner.

Dan is finally rescued, not once but three times by the Blackshirt, "the protector of his youth." If Mrs. Bosun's Closet represents Lewis's sexual nightmare and the punishment he constantly holds over his own head as the price of indulging his "homosexual" desire, then Dan's rescue represents his dream come true.

> Dan felt the officious finger relax, the pressure of the arms grow less oppressive. Through his tear-dimmed eyes Dan was just able to perceive a new figure . . . who had thrust himself suddenly into the picture. He heard himself asked in a voice of the coldest command, in accents that immediately dispelled the treacherous mists of period-illusion . . . Are you Dan Boleyn? (468)

"This is a man!" the Blackshirt proclaims, restoring Dan to his proper status while simultaneously commanding him to retain his passive role. "For the remainder of the evening you are to regard yourself as under my charge" (473). Starr-Smith, or Blackshirt, "masculine to a fault" (563) and "occupied with his private thoughts as a young man should be" (470), now tells Dan, "I have been looking for you the entire evening" (472). Enthralled, Dan admires his black moustache and "found he wanted off and on to put out his hand and pull it" (471). The two young men drink champagne, and Dan becomes drunk and must be held in Blackshirt's strong and masculine arms. He falls asleep and is awakened by two other Blackshirts who seize him brutally, but he is safe: "his head rolling upon the bosom of his own particular Blackshirt . . . ever so comfortable, he smiled. If they only knew!" (583). In gaining his position on the loving male "bosom" of the Blackshirt, Dan has countered the loss he suffered at the hands of the false female "Bosun." Unlike the destructive and engulfing female bosun, this male rescuer provides the only moments of peace and pleasure in the 625 pages. The Blackshirt, "masculine to a fault," offers female tenderness without its risks and homosexual adventure without its stigma. If they only knew indeed!

Dan is captured by Ratner and Zagreus once more, and rescued once again by Blackshirt, who beats up Ratner, defeating the forces of combined Jewry and femininity. In fact the book continues for fifty more redundant pages, but the climax has been reached. The prince has come to the rescue, the forces of Jewry and femaleness have been vanquished, and Dan rests safely on the "bosom" of his heroic friend, a man in a man's world. A close reading of *The Apes of God* helps us understand why Lewis was so entranced by Mosley and his glamorous Blackshirts, by the Hitler Youth movement, and finally by Hitler himself, and why he continued to sing his hero's praises after Hitler had ceased to be popular in England, even when such a stance must mean his own ruin.

Conclusion: The Vicious Cycle

If my discussion of *The Apes of God* does not rely on a linear movement of plot or action, it is because the book itself is similarly nonlinear. Much more than *Ulysses*, the modernist text with which Lewis repeatedly attempted to class his own book, *The Apes of God* subverts the established fictional conventions. With no movement of plot, exclusively one-dimensional parodied characters, who are unreal and unlikable and who certainly never change or grow, its shape may be found only in the system which we identified first in *The Art of Being Ruled* and which preoccupied Lewis all his life. A circular plot has no real beginning or ending, but we can join this one in the nightmare nursery, where a young boy is swallowed up by a large and powerful woman whom he needs to escape from but depends on for his survival. We watch him search, usually in vain for the father-rescuer, who comes only in rare fantasy, or in the guise of homosexuals who, like the woman, are out to capture his precious manhood. We watch him toughen himself, learning to reject the female comfort and softness he longs for, attacking it wherever he finds it, in men, in women, or in his own despised self. We watch him search for a woman he can dominate enough to feel safe with, and observe him in his difficult journey as The Enemy, battling friends who betray, men who turn into women, and women who unite with homosexuals, blacks, and Jews, in a plot to swallow him, infantilize him, and feminize him. We see, too, how this system, which evolved as a survival mechanism and a means of self-defense, at times diverges and at times merges with the dominant cultural and political discourse, leaving the "Enemy" at first inside the mainstream, later outside it, banging and shouting at the exclusion he knew all the time was coming.

In tracing Wyndham Lewis's system through twelve texts in which he tirelessly recapitulates and reinterprets it, we begin to understand how, in this author, as in the Nazis and their predecessors, the Freikorpsmen, the fear and hatred of women and of Jews was part of a deeply embedded psychic structure which, as Kate Millett writes, was "a way of life with influence over every other psychological and emotional facet of existence" (229).

FIVE

Charles Williams's Extrusion Machine

Introduction: The Mechanisms of Protection

Poet, novelist, and theologian Charles Williams was a tremendously fertile writer who produced thirty-eight books of poetry, drama, biography, theology, religious scholarship, literary criticism, and fiction in his fifty-nine years. His productions have an outwardly less driven quality than Lewis's, but his system is equally pervasive and all-encompassing and is reproduced in virtually the same form in all the genres in which he wrote. As we have seen in the previous chapter, Wyndham Lewis's authorial structure was essentially a paranoid and narcissistic one. He saw himself as the victim at the center of a ring of conspiring hostile forces bent on the destruction of his masculine autonomy. Williams, like Lewis a narcissist who saw himself as the key figure in his universe and had trouble conceiving of other people as fully real, embodied in his texts and his life an obsessive-compulsive system whose primary goal was to "retain control and avoid disaster."[1] Cameron and Rychlak could be describing Charles Williams in their description of the obsessive-compulsive personality:

> The major conflicts deal with problems of love and hate, right and wrong, cleanliness and dirt, orderliness and disorder. Sadism and masochism find free expression and . . . strong feelings of guilt appear. . . . Magical thinking and superstition appear more clearly than in the manifest symptoms of any neurosis . . . the patient is conscious of being in conflict. . . . Sometimes all feelings seem to be replaced by a cold intellectual detachment[.] (203, 207)

Charles Williams was, in the words of an ex-disciple, always "conscious of the necessity of holding an infinitely delicate balance which if lost, would precipitate him into the realm of madness." The complicated screen of duality through which he filtered the world was his means of maintaining that balance.[2]

Although Williams was a devout Anglo-Catholic whose Christian convictions pervade all of his writing, hierarchical structures which originate outside of the Christian framework are even more central in his own personal system. For example, the story of King Arthur and the Holy Grail plays a much larger part than does the story of Jesus, while the offices of the Oxford University Press provide a much more crucial setting than does Jerusalem or any other biblical site. Numerology, magic, and other methods associated with the occult also play surprisingly important roles in this "Christian" worldview. The saying "This also is Thou: neither is this Thou," a kind of magical formula or incantation which Williams coined and quoted continually throughout his life and in all his writings as a way to ward off evil, emphasized the "doubleness" which was a key to his system, as well as his sense of the mutability of his own boundaries.[3]

As Salzman and Shapiro stress, the rigid man suffers from the need to control the universe and the grandiose fear that he might do so. Williams's obsessive structure enabled him to split off his own enraged, murderous self, which he experienced as powerful enough to take over the world (the intention of at least one main character in each of his novels) and to subject it to constant vigilance and supervision. In this structure, each person has two natures, a good and an evil one, and a complicated transferral process is necessary in order to separate the evil from the good and to embrace the latter while vanquishing the former. The system functions like a kind of extrusion press into which Williams feeds the molten libidinal metals of rage, hunger for power, and sexual sadism: those disowned parts of himself. Inside this press, various mechanistic operations, including role playing, arrangement into rigid hierarchies, exchange, coinherence, and substitution, convert these raw materials and extrude them out in the form of Christian goodness. Williams's reassuring or self-protective concepts inevitably have a double: an evil or frightening counterpart which consists of the same idea as it exists before the mechanistic "extrusion" operation.

Williams's system offered him a sense of autonomy and control over what he perceived as his own inner chaos and evil and over the chaotic, frightening, and invasive world. Gilman emphasizes that stereotypes arise from the need to control the uncontrollable universe; the pathological personality, whose boundaries are more than ordinarily shaky, "sees the entire world in terms of the rigid line of difference" and consequently has an exaggerated need to stereotype (Gilman, *Difference and Pathology*, 18). Williams's dualism depended on just such a rigid line and encoded a particularly rigid network of projective stereotypes.[4]

Williams, like Lewis, desperately needed women while at the same time experiencing them as dangerously alien, intrusive, and teeming with evil and repulsive female carnality. These contradictory needs caused him, as they caused Lewis, considerable anguish. Through his system, Williams manages to distance or disarm women as needed. It classifies them into two categories: evil, grasping bitches who are instruments of the devil and Slave-Goddesses. The evil women must be hunted down and destroyed before they can achieve their aim of destroying men, while the Slave-Goddesses must be worshiped from a safe distance and punished for their own good. Karen Horney's neurotic patients tried to cope with their dread of women and regain their lost self-respect by either disparaging women or glorifying them in an objectifying way. Their relations with women often took "on a sadistic tinge" (356). Charles Williams's ritualized sadism toward women is reflected in his life and in all the texts we will examine in this chapter.

Jews, who are once again less central to Williams than women, fit into only one category. Inevitably male, they are symbols of the Antichrist, containers for the rage, greed, and hunger for power Williams struggled with and disowned in himself.

Lewis's system found a home or location first in mainstream misogynist and racist ideology and later in the ideology of several defined fascist groups. In contrast, Williams fit his dualistic obsessive-compulsive system into the socially acceptable framework of Anglican Christianity. Such dualistic Christian concepts as good and evil, purity and carnality, Christian and Jew, heaven and hell, God and the Devil, body and soul were of key importance to Williams. He utilized Christian vocabulary and concepts to convert obsession into devotion, ritual repetition into prayer, magical transactions into religious ritual, and sadomasochistic ritual into religious counseling. The obsessive-compulsives described by Shapiro, Salzman, and Cameron and Rychlak kept their compulsions secret. In a far more successful adaptation, Williams formalized his mechanisms of defense as a unique Christian philosophy which he imposed on his own life and the lives of his willing followers, and expounded in all his work.

A charismatic figure, Williams served as a guru, or religious leader, to a group of disciples, mainly women, who adopted his system as their own. To some others, as well as to those followers who later became disillusioned, he appeared bizarre and distasteful—a cult leader whose "Christian goodness" masked a need to dominate and control others, whom he bent to his often perverse will.

Masculine Angel or Sadistic Anti-Semite: The Critical Reaction

Like those who knew him, critics and biographers of Charles Williams take no middle ground, tending either to the fervently enthusiastic or the contemptuously wrathful. Highly positive, often doting essays and biographies have been written by former pupils or protegées, by members of Williams's inner circle ("The Companions of the Co-Inherence"), and by members of the Oxford-based group "The Inklings," to which Williams belonged toward the end of his life and which also included such right-wing Anglo-Catholic luminaries as J. R. R. Tolkien, Dorothy L. Sayers, and C. S. Lewis. Williams's highly individualized and romantic Anglo-Catholicism and his hierarchical and deeply conservative ideology, which champions royalty and the rule of the elite over the mob, have attracted and continue to attract support from diverse individuals. Both Hilaire Belloc and G. K. Chesterton were prominent admirers, as was Ezra Pound. To T. S. Eliot, Williams "seemed to . . . approximate, more nearly than any man I have ever known familiarly, . . . the saint."[5] Eliot personally championed Williams's work as he championed Wyndham Lewis's, but he felt a great deal more personal warmth for Williams and mourned him at his death. C. S. Lewis, who agreed as to the saintliness, called his friend a "masculine angel."

Williams's admirers were not all politically conservative. On meeting Williams, whom he partially credited with his religious conversion, W. H. Auden noted, "[F]or the first time in my life I felt in the presence of personal sanctity."[6] The left-wing American Catholic writer James Agee also found Williams "one of the very few contemporary writers who moves me and interests me to read."[7] To his followers, Williams's work provided and still provides religious comfort and sustenance. To them, he is "one of the most original and spiritually perceptive authors of our time," whose work "puts into fresh contemporary language the age-old truths about God, the soul, the mystic experience, sin and salvation."[8]

Even today, Williams and his work continue to attract students and devotees. Regular essays about him appear, for example, in the American journal *Mythlore*, a journal of the Mythopoetic Society devoted to the works of Tolkien, Lewis, and Williams, and in the publications of the active Charles Williams Society in Britain. All six of Williams's novels remain in print in accessible paperback editions, and his work as a whole seems to exert the same cultish attraction as he himself did when alive. To give one example, at the small progressive university where I teach at the time of writing (in 1990), two female graduate students have chosen to concentrate their research on their favorite author: Charles Williams. Although one is an observant Jew and both define themselves as radical feminists, Williams's attitudes toward Jews and women do not deter them from revering the man and his work.

In the other camp fall those who see Williams as a modern example of the most shocking and virulent anti-Semitism. In 1962, in *An Age of Enormity*, Issac Rosenfeld commented on Williams's novel *All Hallows' Eve* (1945): "In a last minute rescue, Betty is saved (she is half English: it is worth the trouble), Simon is vanquished, Christian love prevails over the Jewish lust for power, and the living and dead go their separate, indistinguishable ways."[9]

Edgar Rosenberg, who takes Williams rather more seriously than does Rosenfeld, calls him one of the worst of the modern anti-Semites and comments with some force on *All Hallows' Eve*:

> The ghastly figure of Clerk Simon . . . is a creature at once so acutely horrible, so minutely and graphically defined, and at the same time so vastly distorted by the totemic and symbolic uses to which Williams puts him . . . that in reading the book one has the impression of dreaming the whole thing. . . . Williams has recaptured some of the primitive sensations of religious fright that the Jew must have inspired in his early sub-literary manifestations. . . . Williams' appeal is direct, instinctive, the nineteenth century had nothing like it to offer. (290)

Leslie Fiedler agrees with this assessment, labeling Williams and his cohorts "childish in their wickedness" ("Fagin," 417). While the majority of Williams's modern supporters have ignored these accusations, others have felt the need to defend him against them. Thomas Howard employs the old defense of authorial intention; Williams did not intend to be anti-Semitic, consequently he was not.[10]

> Williams at times invites the suspicion of anti-Semitism. . . . But anti-Semitism is far from his intention. He uses *all* facts and characteristics in a highly "visionary" way, and his sole point about Judaism is that it never accepted the Incarnation. Hence . . . it has opted for a divided world. . . . If there is a quarrel between Williams and the Jews it is not racial. It is solely theological. . . . Readers worry about anti-Semitism here, but this concern stems from a misreading of Williams' intentions.[11]

Nancy-Lou Patterson, one of the editors of *Mythlore*, while asserting Williams's nobility of intention, sorrowfully admits his anti-Semitism, concluding:

> The making of a person or of a whole people into "the other"— the target against which to project the shadow of our own unacknowledged weaknesses: this is the pit continually set at the feet of writers who follow the Way of the Affirmation of Images. . . . The powers with which writers of fantasy have to deal are real, but they are in each one of us [and] should never be attributed to anyone else.[12]

Life, Prose, and Poetry: The Figure of Beatrice, Witchcraft, Letters to Lalage, The Region of the Summer Stars

Unlike the other authors in this study, Charles Williams has as yet attracted no major biographer, and at the time I write, there exists no collected edition of letters or diaries. Much of the biographical material which does exist is authored by Williams's followers and tends more toward hagiography than literary biography.[13] Alice Mary Hadfield, the only biographer who had free access to the many letters Williams wrote to his second love, Phyllis Jones, was a colleague of both Williams and Jones, a friend and disciple of Williams's, and one of the founding members of his group, "The Order of the Companions of the Co-Inherence." Glen Cavaliero, Anne Ridler, Mary McDermott Shideler, and Kathleen Spencer, while also Williams enthusiasts, and in some cases his personal friends, are less protective of his reputation and thus more helpful. Cavaliero also edited the very revealing *Letters to Lalage* (Lang-Sims, 1989).

Although he would certainly have been horrified at my conclusions, I believe that Charles Williams would have approved of the approach I will take in this section, in which I will discuss his life in the context of three of his books, including religious scholarship (*The Figure of Beatrice* and *Witchcraft*), poems (*The Region of the Summer Stars*), and letters (*Letters to Lalage*). He saw his personal life, the public appearances he made as a teacher and a religious guru, his work at the Oxford University Press, and his literary productions as parts which formed one overweening and congruent religious whole, a view which his friendly critics also adopt.[14] T. S. Eliot can be said to speak for all of them when he writes of "the unity between the man and the work," and adds, "I can think of no writer who was more wholly the same man in his life and his writing."[15]

More recently, less friendly critics have also found unity between the man and his work. Valentine Cunningham wonders what T. S. Eliot must have made of the "troubled ecstasy of violence" which runs through Williams's spiritual thrillers and his book on witchcraft:

> Williams resorts repeatedly to nailed flesh, gnashings of teeth, the black pangs of hell, the clashing turmoils of evil, to murders and suicides and to supernatural grisliness in his fictions, just as he was drawn to the torturous details of witchhunting—the red-hot iron plates, the beheadings and strangling. . . . It was, as we know, Williams's own nature to try to tame the nature of woman by also offering punishments to the ladies who fell into his clutches as a spiritual adviser. (68)

Charles Williams was born in North London in 1886, to lower–middle-class parents, an only son with a sister three years younger. His parents were deeply devout, prayed several times a day, and brought their children to the two Anglican church services they attended every Sunday. Charles won early praise for his religious devotion and his ability to memorize church texts. Like many other obsessive-compulsives, he was a docile child who was subject to occasional attacks of seemingly irrational temper in which the shell of goodness cracked open.[16] These "turns," as his sister called them, worsened when young Charles reached adolescence and were later labeled with the convenient and all-encompassing term "neuralgia." In Williams's novels, the good, Christian characters are often subject to similar "turns." As a child, Williams earned praise for his religiosity and "goodness," while as an adult he was admired and even worshiped for his saintly qualities. Understandably, he felt considerable investment in this image of himself. With few outlets for his less-than-saintly qualities of rage, aggression, envy, and striving for power, Williams split off "his enormous ground swell of feeling" and projected them onto the Others in his dual system: most particularly women and Jews (Salzman, 29).

When Charles was eight, the firm where his father worked as a clerk closed down. At the same time, Walter Williams apparently received medical advice that a country setting would be beneficial for his failing eyesight. As Hadfield puts it, "it had become clear to Mary that she was better at controlling the family finances than her husband and that decisions about the future would depend on her."[17] The family moved from London to nearby St. Albans, where the mother opened an art supply shop and the father lapsed into a permanent state of guilt and depression. Charles, who shared his father's literary and historical interests, his absent-minded clumsiness, and his bad eyesight, became his depressed father's confidant.

Although Walter Williams, unlike Lewis's father, was present throughout his son's childhood, his depression, guilt, and passive inactivity did not provide a hopeful or positive model of adult masculinity. Unlike Lewis, whose aggression always bubbled near the surface, Williams's equally powerful aggression remained forcibly suppressed, emerging only, both in his texts and in his life, in split-off and passive-aggressive stances, and in ritual activities. While his sister Edith helped in the shop, Charles withdrew into the hierarchal, rigidly defined "historical-romantic world of courts and ceremonies" (Cavaliero, *Charles Williams*, 2). Edith Williams later wrote that, with the father frustrated by increasing blindness and the mother by overwork, "there was bound to be tension and some disagreement" in the family. She adds that this early trauma may have been partly responsible for "the nervous explosions which Charles developed during his adolescence, which in turn may have accounted for the shakiness of hand which lasted for the rest of his life."[18] All who knew Williams remember his shaking hands, prominent facial tics and grimaces. T. S. Eliot recalls, "He was never still: He writhed and swayed" (*Hallows*, Eliot, xii), and Lois Lang-Sims describes the "constant jerky movement of his limbs and the muscles of his face" (*Lalage*, Lang-Sims, 31). This writhing, for which no physical factor could be found, may be seen as a parallel to Lewis's inner volcano, whose force often caused him to feel that the top of his head would explode. It seems possible that Williams, an outwardly sweet but inwardly enraged man, shook and writhed with the force of his suppressed anger.

Unlike Greene and Lewis, middle-class boys who attended public boarding schools, Charles Williams attended the local Abbey School. For two years he commuted from his home to London University, but the art shop was doing poorly, and he was forced to leave without a degree.

A largely self-educated man, he always read widely, and after leaving university, attended lectures at the Working Men's College. When he began to publish his poems and scholarship, and as his books acquired a small but enthusiastic group of readers, he became a part-time lecturer in both London and in Oxford, speaking on Milton, Shakespeare, and Dante, and on his own literary-religious philosophy. He always regretted his lack of a public school education, and his later identification with the Oxford University Press included an enthusiastic adoption of the public school and Oxford values which he revered so much. As Cunningham puts it, "Williams was as devoted an honorary Oxonian as A. L. Rowse became the epitome of All Soulishness" (137). In fact, his less privileged class status probably saved Williams from what would have been an excruciating experience for the delicate and clumsy dreamer, with his twitches and compulsive behaviors. The image Williams later presented to the world was of a saintly and otherworldly religious scholar, delicate, spiritual, and bookish. He preferred the company of women as disciples and seemed to experience none of the frantic need to prove his heterosexuality or the counterphobic avoidance of effeminate or homosexual men which characterized both of the other public school–educated writers under discussion here. As we have seen, even a writer, like Isherwood, who later identified as homosexual remained preoccupied with the "test of masculinity" he was exposed to in public school. Charles Williams was spared at least this kind of agony.

After failing the civil service exam and spending a short time packing books at the Methodist Book Room, Williams found a job as proofreader at the Oxford University Press, where he remained for the rest of his life. Proofreading, and later close editing, tasks which require attention to "meticulous detail, extreme orderliness . . . exact repetition or systemic doubting," provided the perfect job for him (Cameron and Rychlak, 207). Shapiro, too, notes that the obsessive-compulsive is "intensely and more or less continuously active at some kind of work . . . inasmuch as the compulsive person identifies with that regime and identifies its purposes as his own, he feels entitled by his work and accomplishments to self-respect and a sense of personal authority" (*Autonomy*, 83).

The Oxford University Press (hereafter OUP) became Williams's "own little niche or bailiwick," in which he devoted himself to carrying out his "established duties ordained by higher authorities" (Shapiro, *Neurotic Styles*, 41). Not only the painstaking work he performed, but also the

Press's strictly defined hierarchical structure, which included a fixed place for him, provided the containment and safety he needed so badly. In Katherine Spencer's words: "He genuinely liked routine and the clear structure of hierarchy; they seemed like assurances of stability in the midst of what he sensed to be an uncertain existence."[19] Like Lewis, Williams experienced "the absence of a differentiated sense of self and other" (Benjamin, 73). For him, boundaries of self were shaky and could dissolve at any time. The ritualized and orderly routine of the OUP provided him with an outside structure to bind and contain a self which he, like Orwell and Lewis, felt could dissolve at any time into a jellylike diffuseness.

The OUP, the real center of Williams's existence, also provided a setting for the myth which had now begun to dominate his fantasy life. His more general interest in kings and courts had by this time been transformed into a fantasy world based upon the legend of King Arthur and the Holy Grail (or Graal, as Williams and his followers spelled it), and the OUP was transformed into a latter-day setting for King Arthur's court.

I have noted Williams's success in channeling his obsessive countermeasures in productive and acceptable ways, and this success was notable in his relationship with the Press. While his slowness and perfectionism disqualified him for promotion to a better-paid editorial position, his meticulous work and clockwork presence (like other obsessive-compulsives, he was always on time and never took holidays) were prized by his employers, and in particular by the Press's publisher, Sir Humphrey Milford. Shapiro notes the great importance of rigid hierarchies for the obsessive-compulsive, who has been unable to internalize autonomy and must "constantly and forcibly impose it on himself, often through the idealization of some outward authority figure or institution" (*Autonomy*, 73). Williams worshiped Milford, whom he referred to in one poem as "the divine John out of heaven, great Sir" (Hadfield, 53).

Williams was also able to translate his fantasy world into quasi-Arthurian poems in which the world of the Press was used as a metaphor for the world of the Round Table, which in turn referred to the New Testament. These poems were published by the OUP and achieved minor successes. He also composed, for performance on holidays and other occasions, a series of masques in which the employees of the Press actually played the Arthurian parts he had privately assigned to them. Williams himself directed these masques and introduced the performances, activities which were sources of great satisfaction to him. Cavaliero writes of Williams at the press:

> Not only did his fantasy world issue in poetry and fiction, it was also imposed upon the circumstances of his daily life and in due course even upon the people who shared in them. He thus sought to combine the roles of both poet and magician. . . . He needed a life with limitations in order to support the myth, and he fed his own experience of fellowship and sharing into the master pattern, treating the Press's Editor in Chief, Sir Humphrey Milford, as though he were Imperial Caesar, and interpreting his own work and that of his colleagues as metaphorical enactments of divinely appointed law. (*Lalage*, Cavaliero, 4–5)

Ridler describes the privately printed masques as "at once a game and something to be taken seriously: they [the employees] were acting parts and yet they were being themselves" (xxvi). Lois Lang-Sims found them less benign and describes Williams's habit "of manipulating his friends into fulfilling the roles created for them in his private myth" (*Lalage*, Lang-Sims, 16).

Williams assigned the role of Taliessin, the king's poet and lieutenant to himself, an identification biographers such as Ridler, Sibley, and Hadfield accept as a charming whimsy and faithfully adopt in their language and references.[20] More perceptively, Cavaliero suggests that "Williams' identification of himself with Taliessin, the king's poet, was more total than he himself was perhaps aware" (*Lalage*, Cavaliero, 4). He adds that Williams's preoccupation with the myth amounted to an obsession, which enabled him to distance himself from the real people in his life (*Lalage*, Cavaliero, 5). This elaborate concoction spun of Arthurian legend and the OUP and held together with occult and Christian ritual enabled Charles Williams to live and to work productively, but it could not fill his inner emptiness, any more than his ritualized and hierarchical relationships could finally conceal his inability to genuinely connect with others or conceive of them as other than projections of himself. Like Kernberg's narcissistic patients, he hid a self which was hungry and enraged, "full of impotent anger at being frustrated, and fearful of a world which seem[ed] as hateful . . . as the patient himself" (233).

At twenty-three, Williams met Florence Conway at a children's Sunday school party. He dedicated his first book of poems, *The Silver Stair* (1912), to her, and biographers note Florence's bewilderment when presented with these poems, which Cavaliero describes as "fervent but impersonal, full of ideas, but devoid of intimacy and particularly of reference. Falling in love was the subject, not the loved woman in herself" (*Charles Williams*, 2). Kathleen Spencer agrees that "the subject of the sequence was surprisingly, not love, but the renunciation of love" (13). Williams prefaced this book with a quotation from Yeats:

> It is love that I am seeking for,
> But of a beautiful unheard-of kind
> That is not in the world
>
> (Hadfield, 16)

When Florence asked for more than obscure poems and distant worship, Charles became increasingly tortured and indecisive. During their nine-year engagement, he made frequent references to a horoscope which had been made for him which recommended that he remain celibate and ruminated about whether he should in fact follow that advice (Ridler, xviii). In 1914, when the war broke out, he was rejected as unfit for active duty because of his poor eyesight and probably also because of his nervous condition. Several of his friends who did serve were killed, and he became devastated by grief and guilt, claiming that he should have died instead of them. As a consequence of this crisis, his marriage was put off again.

Indecision and rumination are one of the most common symptoms of the obsessive-compulsive cycle. Attacks of doubt and rumination are followed by periods of intense guilt in which the sufferer feels that he or she is worthless, has contaminated others, and deserves punishment. This in turn is followed by a series of countermeasures, such as compulsive hand-washing or the repetition of numbers, phrases, or private rituals (Cameron and Rychlak, 220). While undergoing his long crisis of indecision about marriage, Williams was once again able to find a socially acceptable measure of containment which provided him with a communal rather than an isolating experience. During his engagement, he began to study the writings of A. E. Waite, a Christian scholar of the occult. In 1917, a few months after his marriage, he joined Waite's "Fellowship of the Rosy Cross," formerly the "Hermetic Order of the Golden Dawn."[21] Williams was a member of this secret group, which studied freemasonry, Jewish and Christian mysticism, the Kabbalah, the Tarot, "black" magic, and Rosicrucianism, for eleven years. According to Spencer, the group appealed to his need for order, authority, and obedience. Williams's

Christian devotees are understandably defensive about this membership. All of them stress that Yeats himself was a member of the same group in his later years, that the Order can be viewed as a branch of Christianity, and that Williams never left the Anglican church.[22] Both Ridler and Cavaliero, however, have found that Williams was more deeply involved than his friends and critics were aware, and that the Order's influence on his work was a very deep one. Cavaliero maintains, "he was involved for over ten years in the study of occult and cabbalistic lore and of its corresponding rituals; for him the wisdom of alchemy and magic... provided a viable method of interpreting the spiritual laws of the universe" (*Lalage*, Cavaliero, 4).

Anne Ridler mentions the delight Williams took in the rituals which he recited from memory rather than read, as did the other celebrants. Her description of an initiation in which "the novice is threatened with death by a hostile current... if he broke the oath of secrecy" suggests that the Order did significantly depart from ordinary Christian practices (Ridler, xxiii). Nancy-Lou Patterson agrees that Williams's participation was enthusiastic: "Charles Williams, who was quite enraptured by it all, seems to have accepted everything into his passionate mind and from it fashioned high fantasies of his own, in a sort of 'twentieth century Gothic' style" (28). Patterson points out that while genuine Jewish mysticism can indeed involve the ritual pronouncement of sacred words, letters, and numbers (and even ritual hand washing), Waite's version of Kabbalah was not in fact remotely connected with Judaism.[23] Nevertheless, it was labeled as a Jewish rite by the group. Jews first claimed an active place in Williams's obsessional system during his involvement with the Rosy Dawn. Occult practices, associated with sexual guilt, terror, and the unholy assertion of power, are featured in each of Williams's novels; always associated with women, and very often with Jews. In *Shadows of Ecstasy* (1933), Williams portrays the occult with admiration, but in his later novels, he condemns the black magic he has learned and carefully splits off the role of evil magician, assigning it to the Jew. In Williams's most common plot, the Jewish magician, working in league with the evil woman, turns his evil powers on the good woman, punishing her sadistically.

After nine years of tortured indecision, Florence apparently put her foot down, and the two were married in 1917. Charles, who was thirty-one, wrote a poem about the day when "Our young virginities together went." Expressively titled "Black Letter Days," the poem is filled with images of doom, doubt, and engulfment. "Adventuring all we doubted on a day," Williams writes, "Who should our selfhoods mystically slay."[24]

Even his disciples agree that sexuality did not come easily to Charles Williams, who felt a deep loathing of the female's "fleshly mortality . . . a fear that she is untrustworthy and malevolent" (Dinnerstein, 36–37). Hadfield, abridging tactfully from Williams's letters to a wealthy mentor, Alice Meynell, writes: "The first evenings in the flat, and the first nights . . . cannot have been easy. Charles . . . self-described virgin at thirty, was . . . petrified in practice" (26). Cavaliero comments dryly, "[I]n domestic matters his overpowering belief in a transcendent mystery may have proved embarrassing" (*Lalage*, Cavaliero, 6), and Anne Ridler concludes, "[H]is sense of revolt against the flesh was at times very strong" (Ridler, xxiii). Biographers agree that Williams's marriage was always tempestuous, and the birth of a son did not improve things. In a tone of ill-achieved lightness, Williams wrote of that event in a letter to his friend John Pellow:

> In the Divine and only true World of Eternity there exist (we find) a spirit who now thrusts himself into Time. . . . I have no conscious change of emotion: a child is a guest of a somewhat insistent temperament, rather difficult to get rid of, almost pushing; a poor relation. . . . His little voice pulls at my ears; my heartstrings are unplucked. (Hadfield, 39)

While Williams, unlike Lewis, did allow his wife to have one child, he experienced his son as an unwanted, pushing guest, who deprived him of the coveted maternal attentions. Like Kernberg's narcissistic borderline men and like Lewis, he felt a dislike of children and a horror of childbirth and of "the primal scene," which he presented in various distorted and frightening ways in various texts.

For Lewis children were a reminder of a time when he had been helpless, undefended, and at the mercy of women. For Williams they functioned in addition as a symbol of his inner evil, unrestrained and unconverted. In his study of the occult, *Witchcraft* (1941), for example, he stresses the role played by children in the accusations of innocent people and comments sarcastically: "There is a physical appearance of innocence about many young children—no-one who has had much to do with them will suppose it is more than physical."[25]

Not only did the physical aspects of marriage prove overwhelming, but Williams discovered that his goddess was all too human—and was not ready for enslavement. No "Froanna," Florence Conway lacked awe for her husband's spiritual leadership and resented his absorption in the world of the OUP. Williams, like Kernberg's narcissistic patients, had unrealistically idealized and longed for his love object, rather than feeling real empathy. Kernberg notes that such idealization is a mask against primitive rage and is liable to rapid breakdown, followed by rage or withdrawal. Soon after the marriage, Williams withdrew physically and emotionally from his wife, although he remained narcissistically dependent on her. He renamed her "Michal," after David's wife who mocked David when he danced before the Ark of God; she assumed the name for the rest of her life. In *Orientalism*, Edward Said points out the power of naming as a way to redefine and objectify the "Other" (21–27). It is notable that both Lewis and Williams renamed the women in their lives—and that both women became known thereafter by these names. While Williams's name for his wife reflected his anger at her stubborn individuality, Lewis's "Froanna" (a contraction of Frau Anna) was based on his often-expressed conception of her as a lowly German peasant "hausfrau."

In 1924 the Press moved its offices to a grander building, an event heralded by a flood of religious poetry from Williams. The new building boasted a library, and he fell romantically in love with the librarian, Phyllis Jones. He named her "Phillida" and "Celia" and addressed all his new poetry and masques to her. This new, strictly platonic love enabled him to finally detach himself from his wife and her unwanted carnal demands. In 1930 he wrote to Phyllis Jones: "It is months and months since any kind of married intercourse took place—O ages. And I am not at all certain that this is not done for me. On the other hand, she may think my nature is *so* and that's that" (Hadfield, 86).

Williams treated his love for Phyllis Jones as a religious phenomenon and an occasion to practice one of his most important mechanistic operations: transfer. In this case the term referred to the transfer of love from the specific or carnal sphere to one more universal and godly. His platonic worship of Jones continued through her affair with another married colleague at the Press and her eventual marriage; it lasted, in fact, to the end of his life. As Hadfield romantically puts it, "He could not escape his choice to love and serve her for ever, though she had removed herself to Java and another man's bed" (127).

Williams could not understand why his wife held a different view of things. In his disquisition on romantic love, *The Figure of Beatrice* (1943), he explains the recoil that accompanies the loss of "the Beatrician quality" in the first love object, who turns out to be "not always celestial" and surprisingly "other."[26] In addition, if one marries the first love, one must contend with the problem of "co-ordination of the physical and mental satisfactions" and the troublesome "habit . . . of physical intercourse," which, while necessary for the production of children and the "coinherence of married bodies (if fortunate)," is sure to end romantic love (37). This symbolic "death of Beatrice" clears the way for a new, more perfect love: a "second image" toward which "we must wholly practice passion without concupiscence" (50). Such a second platonic passion is not sinful on the part of the man; the only sin involved is on the part of the first woman, whose limitations lead her into unbecoming female jealousy and resentment. Williams muses: "If it were possible to create in marriage a mutual adoration towards the second image . . . and also a mutual limitation of the method of it, I do not know what new liberties and powers might be achieved" (50).

Florence Williams had no interest in joining a mutual adoration society for Phyllis Jones. After his death she referred to Williams alternately as her lord and as her cross and spoke bitterly of Phyllis, of Charles's colleagues at the OUP whom she felt had encouraged her husband's mental unfaithfulness, and of the many other "predatory . . . chew-string gaseous" female disciples who flocked to him in adoration (*Lalage*, Cavaliero, 7).

Just as Williams's "theory" in *The Figure of Beatrice* provided a textual justification for his loss of interest in his wife and his platonic attentions to Phyllis Jones, a great portion of his work can be seen as an attempt to rationalize or textualize his loathing of female sexuality and his terror of his own "female" or evil nature. Ridler describes "his lifelong attempt to develop an adequate theology of marriage," explaining that we all have "the need to relate our physical nature to some great principle of order" (Ridler, xxv). In his first book of theology, *Outlines of Romantic Theology* (1924), Williams painstakingly goes through each step of the Communion service "with sexual love in focus," in an attempt to show that in making love to his wife, a man, if he practices the principles of "transfer," need not be in actual contact with the carnal female body, but can instead make love to or receive the body of Christ—which is universal love (Hadfield, 43; Shideler, 75–85).

In *Witchcraft* (1941) Williams is more specific about the nature of the man's recoil from female otherness. This bizarre book, in which he dwells at great length and with some complacence on the torture of female witches, who he implies deserved their punishments, offers a great deal of information about what Williams called his own "darkness." He describes a "fairly common experience" in a passage which, as Kathleen Spencer notes, "has the ring of personal experience about it, experience so compelling that Williams believed it to have been fairly common" (15). This is the moment when

> it seems that anything might turn into anything else . . . one will be with a lover and the hand will become a different and terrifying thing, moving in one's own like a malicious intruder, too real for anything but fear. . . . There is in our human centre, a heart-gripping fear of irrational exchange, of perilous and malevolent change[.] (*Witchcraft*, 77–78)

Like Lewis, who feared that his fragile male boundaries might be destroyed, causing him to turn into a woman or child, Williams experienced a "heart-gripping fear" of the malicious (female) intruder, "too real for anything but fear," who would destroy his careful boundaries, causing "irrational, perilous, and malevolent" change. The word "exchange" stands for one of the more reassuring (to the male) operations in Williams system: a mechanism in which the Slave-Goddess takes on the man's pain or trouble in a kind of willing and joyful submission. In the paragraph above we see the converse of this concept, as it is employed against the male by the malevolent female on the other side of the divide.

In his preface to *All Hallows' Eve*, T. S. Eliot describes Williams's unusual relationship with the supernatural: "To him the supernatural was perfectly natural, and the natural was also supernatural. . . . Williams is telling us about a world of experience known to him: he does not merely persuade us to believe in something, he communicates this experience that he has had" (xv). Williams's description of the "Lamia" legend in *Witchcraft* conveys just that sense of felt experience and eloquently sums up his terror of women and of the lethal trap they present:

> [T]he cruelty of her blood-lust changed her face from the beauty which Zeus had loved to mere bestiality. And though there was only one of her, yet there were many of her; the horrible mad figure of creatures neither quite woman nor quite beast wandered through the night. Witches were like the Lamia; they were *lamiae* . . . [who] could take again the appearance

> of beautiful young women. . . . They have amorous appetites, but their chief appetite is for human flesh, and they ensnare their intended victims with the bait of love. (60–61)

Man's fear of the lamiae and other witches, Williams tells us, is the fear of "a great and awful blasphemy—of the sexual union of alien and opposed natures" (35). At the end of the book, he makes another attempt to name "the image of an almost abstract perversion," that thing he knows exists "underneath all the tales":

> [T]he thing which is invoked is a thing of a different nature, however it may put on a human appearance or indulge in its servants their human appetites. It is cold, it is hungry, it is violent, it is illusory. The warm blood of children and the intercourse at the Sabbath do not satisfy it. It wants something more and other; it wants "obedience" it wants "souls" and yet it mines for matter. It never was, and yet it always is. (310–11)

The description of the lamiae's blood lust, their need for "the warm blood of children and the intercourse at the Sabbath," evokes the medieval blood libel of the bloodthirsty Jew, while Williams's musings on the awful blasphemy of the sexual union of alien natures evokes the "specifically 'Jewish' crime to which the Germans have since given the name Rassenschande" (Rosenberg, 256). As Fiedler perceptively notes, "both female witchcraft and Jewish usury . . . reflect the male Gentile's fear of loss of potency" (*Stranger*, 125). Finally, Horney describes how the man attempts "to rid himself of his fear of women by rationalizing: "It is not . . . that I dread her; it is that she herself is malignant, capable of any crime, a beast of prey, a vampire, a witch, insatiable in her desires" (347). It is easy to see how, through the train of associations which accrue around a projective stereotype, Williams's primal fear of the female was entwined and conjoined with his fear and hatred of witches—and of Jews.

As we have seen in the example of the lamia, women were indeed "Other" for Williams: alien and dangerous creatures who hide their bestial nature beneath a mask of female appeal and use the mask of love to conceal their appetite for human (male) flesh. We are also reminded of the cannibalistic, engulfing women we met in Lewis's work and in the works of the Freikorpsmen.[27] For Williams, the "almost abstract perversion" is located in the sexuality between human man and beastly woman. And neither the mechanistic operations of transfer, substitution or exchange, nor the firm placement of the woman in a role of Slave-Goddess is sufficient to restrain the beastliness underneath the surface. As Theweleit and Chodorow demonstrate, the most threatening "beastliness" is that which is found within the self. For Shapiro's rigid men, and for Williams, women "embody what the rigid individual is ashamed of, defensively repudiates, and therefore hates" (Shapiro, *Autonomy*, 101–2).

Unlike Lewis, whose open support of Hitler got him into serious trouble, Williams remained serenely unconcerned with the events of the day and emerged unscathed by criticism. He regarded his founding of the "Companions of the Co-inherence" in late 1938, as his contribution toward the "greater Order." When war was declared, he wrote to his friends in the Order urging them "to know co-inherence, including the enemy, including Hitler and he with us, and all in Christ" (Hadfield, 176). No mention was made of co-inherence with the Jews of Europe, or of Jews as anything but historical and religious symbols of the Antichrist.

In an essay called "The Jews" written in 1943 and first published as a *Time and Tide* review of Jacques Maritain's *Redeeming the Time* (1943), Williams praises Maritain's conclusion that the Christian hates and execrates the Jew because of the Jewish need to "quarrel with the world" in which he is "*supernaturally* a stranger." Williams then declares that Christians and orthodox Jews cannot in fact approach "the Jewish problem" except theologically.[28] He recommends extreme courtesy toward Jews, especially toward Orthodox Jews, as good manners are especially important "whenever we are right" (163). Such politeness, however, is not easy:

> [T]he relation of Israel and the Church—like it or like it not—must be more intense. It is something in our blood which springs; it is a hatred. . . . There is a Fact between us, and neither side can forget the Fact. When the Sabbath and Sunday come we remember The Jew hears the Christian declaring that the High and Holy one took flesh; the Christian sees the Jew crucifying the God-Man. How at bottom can there be peace? (162)

The phrase "took flesh" evokes the cannibalistic lamia, as do the references to crucifixion and blood. Unlike women, who were sometimes the recipients of his aggression, sometimes the embodiment of it, male Jews were the Antichrist, vessels for Williams's own suppressed rage and sexual sadism. To speak of Jews, in 1943, as the recipients of a natural "hatred in our blood which springs" is more than negligent; it is reprehensible. While Williams prided himself on his political uninvolvement, it must have taken some effort to ignore news which was available everywhere.

Wyndham Lewis produced the body of his anti-Semitic writing between 1926 and 1938, attempted to deny his anti-Semitism in 1939, and for the most part excluded Jews from his work after that date. In contrast, Williams wrote *All Hallows' Eve*, his most blatantly anti-Semitic novel, in 1944. An obsessive and guilty man, he was not troubled by any worry or guilt about his textual treatment of a group he never saw as human, or identified as the victims of the Holocaust. In Williams's bipolar system, with its rigid line of difference (Gilman, *Difference and Pathology*, 18), the Jew provided the necessary counter to the Christian. No outer events could change or modify that inner reality.

What did trouble him about the war was the moving of the OUP from London to Oxford in 1939. Williams moved to Oxford with his beloved Press, leaving Michal and his son in war-torn London, but the move shook the foundations of his myth. He wrote to Anne Ridler in some panic: "There is no-one (NO-ONE) in Oxford to whom I can talk about Taliessin. This is a serious blow, and I only found it out yesterday" (Hadfield, 181).

In Oxford, Williams began his association with C. S. Lewis, J. R. R. Tolkien, and the other members of the Inklings group. C. S. Lewis in particular seems to have loved Williams with some of the enthusiasm of the female disciples, but for Williams himself the Inklings association remained peripheral. He was unable to become deeply involved with a group of men to whom he was no guru, and with whom he was forced to be simply Charles Williams, not Taliessin. The association with the Inklings, as well as his continued literary productivity, led to some material success. He was nominated to give a series of lectures at Oxford, where he was awarded an honorary degree in 1943, and his books began to provide him with a substantial income. These honors did not make up for the loss of Taliessin. The final war years in Oxford were a most productive period for Williams, but also a period of great instability. He became increasingly tense and preoccupied with geometrical symbols, found his son's temporary presence in Oxford agitating and tormenting, and resorted to his old fits of uncontrolled temper (Ridler, xxxiv). As in childhood and adolescence, his "good" self threatened to crack open, revealing the enraged and power-hungry man beneath. He wrote to his wife: "I want to be nice and good, but I'm not feeling so a bit. . . . There are wells of hate in one which are terrifying—wells of suspicion and even malice" (Hadfield, 189).

Perhaps as a way to contain these terrifying inner wells of hate, the Company of the Co-Inherence assumed an increasingly important position in his life, and he began to attract a growing number of female disciples. C. S. Lewis commented fondly about his friend: "Women find him so attractive that if he were a bad man he could do what he liked, either as a Don Juan or charlatan." Anne Ridler also writes of his relationship with students and disciples at this time:

> His friends, to tease him, would call him promiscuous, and perhaps would wish him to be more selective, but would then recall that the saints were not selective. And in fact, however freely he seemed to give of his energies and even of his personal confidences, he had always a certain inner detachment. (Ridler, xxii)

Anne Ridler, who first met Williams in 1918, when she was an admiring schoolgirl, and was close to him until his death, is not blind to her friend's "impulse toward violence" and even notices "a certain sadism in a few of the Taliessin poems" (Ridler, xxxii). She feels, however, that the struggle against these impulses made him an even better spiritual advisor: "[T]he very difficulties of his nature he made a source of strength; they became a synthesis of power. . . . Those who came to him for help felt that no experience could be outside the range of his understanding, no sin or misery could defeat his reconciling power" (Ridler, xxxii).

Williams believed in disciplining his female followers in order to "exchange" the "malicious intruder" inside them for Christian godliness. In *The Region of the Summer Stars* (1944), the second volume of Arthurian poems, inspired by Phyllis Jones, Taliessin despairingly laments his own state:

> It is a doubt if my body is flesh or fish
> hapless the woman who loves me,
> hapless I—flung alive where only
> the cold-lipped mermen thrive among staring creatures

of undersea, or lost where the beast-natures
in a wood of suicides lap at the loss of intellect.[29]

Williams pictures himself here as a sexless, impotent, and isolated creature of the deep. So inwardly empty he is scarcely human, he is flung in among bestial women he is unable to satisfy, and flung as well into his own bestial female nature, which threatens to explode, unseating his reason and leading him toward "a wood of suicides." Shapiro comments that, for rigid men, strength consists of "the capacity to struggle against, resist, and overcome one's own feelings . . . to resist doing what one actually wants to do or desires. . . . The authority of the rigid person's will . . . estranges him from his own feelings and motivations."[30] Such a person is unable to experience or even to visualize relationships other than those "between superior and inferior—the degradation or humiliation of one by another, the imposing of will by one, the surrender of the other. . . . This contemptuous punishment of weakness or inferiority . . . is what we call sadism" (Shapiro, *Autonomy*, 107).

In a passage reminiscent of Orwell's slogan in *1984*, "Freedom is Slavery," a slave girl in the poem is given the choice to be set free after seven years of servitude or to "compact again with a free heart's love," that is, to freely choose to remain a slave in the house of Taliessin (*Stars*, 29). She observes how, in her mistress, Dindrane, who has also chosen slavery, "all circumstance of bondage [were] blessed in her body" (31). The slave girl then becomes "at one in her heart, servitude and freedom were one and interchangeable" (*Stars*, 31). Predictably, she too chooses her "newly treasured servitude," slavery, and begs for one more thing, although she is too humble to name it openly:

" . . . to choose
were insolence too much and of too strange a kind;
my lord knows my mind." Her eyes were set
upon him, companion to companion, peer to peer
He sent his energy wholly into hers . . .
Lightly he struck her face; at once the blast
of union struck her heart. . . . (46)

The themes of ritualized bondage and flagellation, touched on in this poem, were also ritually enacted in Charles Williams's life and are available to us in the constructed text *Letters to Lalage*. Charles Williams wrote these letters to one of his disciples, twenty-six-year-old Lois Lang-

Sims, between 1943 and 1944, at the same time he was completing *The Region of the Summer Stars.* In 1989 Lang-Sims published the letters, along with a commentary on them written thirty-six years after their receipt, and an introduction by Glen Cavaliero. (She does not include her own letters to Williams.) When read together, *Region of the Summer Stars* and *Letters to Lalage* show that there is indeed a "unity between the man and his work" (*Hallows*, Eliot, xiii) and also raise "the critical question of . . . the nature of Charles Williams's relationship with his disciples" (*Lalage*, Cavaliero, 7).

When she first met him, Lois Lang-Sims found Williams's magnetism such that "it turned the ugliness of his voice and features to no account" (*Lalage*, Lang-Sims, 32). She remembers the first letter she wrote to the fifty-seven-year-old author after having read *The Figure of Beatrice*, in which she praised the book but complained that Williams neglected the individual person of the beloved. Williams responded with a seductive letter in which he invited her to join "a Company . . . scattered and unknown to each other . . . called the Co-inherence" (*Lalage*, Williams, 27). In his next letter, he sent her the "Promulgation of the Company." This document, written in pseudobiblical language, with much use of the royal "We" and of the phrase "As it was said," recommends:

> that its members shall make a formal act of union with it as of recognition of their own nature. . . . Its concern is the practice of the apprehension of the Co-inherence both as a natural and a supernatural principle . . . the study of the Co-inherence of the Trinity, of the Two Natures in the Single Person . . . and on the active side, of methods of exchange, in the State, in all forms of love. . . . It concludes in the Divine Substitution of Messias all forms of exchange and substitution and it invokes this act as the root of all. (*Lalage*, Lang-Sims, 30)

The "promulgation" emphasizes each person's double nature and proposes a series of devices with which to transform or rein in this double nature. What Williams in fact had in mind "on the active side" would become increasingly clear as the relationship continued.

Lois Lang-Sims describes her first meeting with Williams in his office at the OUP, after the exchange of several more letters: "He was standing over me in an attitude that was somehow at the same time deferential and authoritarian" (*Lalage*, Lang-Sims, 31). She remembers her conclusions after this first meeting, perhaps claiming some retrospective insight:

> I felt that I had committed myself to Charles, without in the least understanding what the commitment was going to involve... I was aware of being enspelled... I knew even then that Charles was incapable of what I at least understood as being a human relationship on a personal basis. I sensed that he was totally identified with, and enclosed with, his own myth. (*Lalage*, Lang-Sims, 33)

In a subsequent letter, Charles calls Lois a girl slave, assigns her various tasks of "substitution," and writes: "You are engaged to report—as a mythical slave or schoolgirl should—yes? on your four jobs. . . . If you are lazy or inattentive or negligent or a truant... I warn you I will have you, frankly, pay for it" (*Lalage*, Williams, 36). He concludes the next letter by giving her passages to write over: "[A]nd at the end you will add half a dozen times: 'and I shall have my ears soundly boxed for disobedience' (which you shall, next time you come). And send it to me" (*Lalage*, Williams, 39).

The next letter contains a poem he has written for her in which he refers to "the free turn in bondage" and "freedom living in bondage" and calls her a "negligent slave" (*Lalage*, Williams, 40). In her next visit to him at his office at the OUP, he ceremonially strikes her hand with a ruler and she thanks him for it. She has told him that her favorite name is Lalage, a Greek name found in Horace, and in the following letter Charles suggests a plot: Taliessin owns a Greek slave girl called Lalage, who has carelessly neglected her work of lighting the candles: "[O]ccasionally the Lord Taliessin, wishing to write verse, found his own room dark—after which (as might be expected) Lalage spent some time in general discomfort, though no one lost any joy" (*Lalage*, Williams, 53). In the same letter, he announces: "[I]t occurred to Us that... you were pre-designed by Almighty God to be of use to God, to Us, and to Our household" (*Lalage*, Williams, 52). He informs her that Alice Mary Hadfield (the author of the biography we have cited) will be returning by sea from Bermuda, and it will be Lalage's job to bear her seasickness "in exchange for her."

In the ensuing correspondence the master-slave theme escalates, and Williams repeats and formalizes his attitude of worshipful deference combined with authoritarian command. He informs her, "What you need... is a sound thrashing at once" and instructs her to tie a cord around her ankle: "after all if slaves will dither, they must expect to be chained" (*Lalage*, Williams, 58, 60). He refers to her own power over him, telling her, "[Y]ou— for all your docility, have a certain lioness-effect calculated to scare most . . . Masters?" (*Lalage*, Williams, 60). Lois Lang-Sims comments:

> [T]he mythological structure within which Charles had enclosed me was a perfect globe, a bubble that must not be pricked. . . . Within that enclosure I possessed him—or felt that I did—in a particular manner that . . . was delectable[.] (*Lalage*, Lang-Sims, 68)

At their next meeting, Williams tells her to lift her skirt and beats her with the ruler. Next, "he paused in front of me and, putting his arms about me, held me close to him in a strange stillness" (*Lalage*, Lang-Sims, 68). Lang-Sims explains, and Cavaliero corroborates, that Charles Williams was attempting through "exchange" to gain access to her sexual energy, which he could convert and use for holy and creative purposes. She adds that this use of her was by no means unique:

> He once confessed . . . that his work demanded these practices; only so could his creative powers be released. He made these demands because, from some cause hidden deep in his nature, he needed the creative power that he derived from their fulfillment. Without that power he could not work. Essentially it was a power derived from the consciously directed holding in check of the passions associated with romantic love. (*Lalage*, Lang-Sims, 17, 70)

Lois Lang-Sims had apparently contracted for a rather more traditional sadomasochistic relationship in which the master's beating would endow the subject with power over him. Her plan had not included ritual drainings of her energy, a process she describes as both exhausting and terrifying. Both she and Williams clearly believed in this draining process in quite a literal sense, describing "electric" forces as in the vocabulary of mesmerism. In a more symbolic sense, the vampirelike image of a male draining energy from a female can be seen as an exact reversal of Williams's "lamia" image. Equally, that dread can be seen in terms of projective identification, as a projection of Williams's own rage. Desiring to engulf and "drain" women himself, Williams disowns his desire and attributes it to women, then fears and loathes the object of his projected need. More concretely, the image serves as a metaphor for both Lewis's and Williams's materialist use of women "as a natural resource . . . to be . . . harvested and mined" (Dinnerstein, 236). It is not really surprising that Lois Lang-Sims became seriously ill after her last visit to Williams.

Upon her recovery, some weeks later, she wrote him a letter in which she asked to be called by her real name instead of "Lalage," and also asked for some acknowledgment of herself as a person. Williams's response was speedy and severe. In his next letter he writes: "You will . . . be aware that a certain Riseness works in you; I will go further and say that your You-ness is risen" (*Lalage*, Williams, 77). "Lalage" had insisted on her individual identity and had stepped outside of his myth. Her "You-ness" was intolerable to Williams, who immediately and angrily severed the connection. Just as Lewis found his patrons' "self feeling" unacceptable (*Apes*, 245), Williams refused to tolerate this demand for recognition in his Slave-Goddess.

Freud first made the the connection between sadism and obsessive compulsiveness in 1913.[31] Shapiro notes the highly ideational, role-playing aspect of sadomasochistic sexuality; what Simone de Beauvoir called "the will bent on fulfilling the flesh without losing itself in it."[32] He concludes: "It is to the rigid person—to whom the *actuality* of sexual abandonment is inimical to the will, to self-control, and to self-respect —that the *idea* of subjugation seems so erotic" (Shapiro, *Autonomy*, 131).

Like Wyndham Lewis, Charles Williams regarded his own mother as the source of power and nurturance but saw her power as annihilating to his father. Like Lewis, he felt unable to exist without the all-important female and was enraged by his own dependence. Lewis managed his conflicting needs and feelings through compulsive heterosexual, genital sexuality, and through a long-term relationship with a woman he regarded as inferior and treated as his servant. Williams, who found genital sexuality abhorrent, played out his needs through long-term primarily nonsexual relationships with his wife and with his object of romantic adoration and, in a more ritualistic fashion, with his disciples. The rigid boundaries of these relationships helped him to confine his own unacceptable libidinal impulses and assert his fragile boundaries while functioning within the safe confines of his private myth. He was able to chastise and beat down invasive and evil women as well as the evil and invasive female inside himself, while simultaneously gaining access to the female energy or force which he so badly needed. As Lois Lang-Sims said, "without that power he could not work."

Theories as to the reason for Williams's premature death in 1945 are fittingly mystical and dichotomous. In her commentary, Lang-Sims suggests that the process which made her ill was equally debilitating for Williams, and that indulging in similar activities with far too many young women led to his early death. Hadfield prefers the theory that "he had worn his thread almost through. He was coming in to 'peace and the perfect end' " (235). Theories aside, Charles Williams died at the age of fifty-eight of a stomach operation which had not been expected to be serious, on 15 May 1945, soon after the end of the war which he had hardly noticed.

The Outrageous and the Foul: Charles Williams's Novels

Between 1930 and 1944 Charles Williams wrote seven novels, which represent only a fraction of his enormous literary output. In this discussion I will limit myself to the three novels with the most prominent Jewish characters: *Shadows of Ecstasy* (1933), *War in Heaven* (1930), and *All Hallows' Eve* (1945). In his introduction to *All Hallows' Eve*, T. S. Eliot protests rather too hard in his effort to defend his friend from the charge of morbidity:

> The stories of Charles Williams . . . are not like those of Edgar Allan Poe, woven out of morbid psychology—I have never known a healthier-minded man than Williams . . . had he himself not always seen Evil, unerringly as the contrast to Good . . . there are passages in his book and in other books . . . which would only be outrageous and foul. (xvi)

Just as Lewis's novels and didactic books all recapitulate his paranoid, narcissistic system, Williams's novels recapitulate the obsessional system which we have already observed in his poems, his scholarly books, and his life. Williams's novels are extremely homogeneous, each one employing the same basic plot. All utilize an ostensibly "Christian" framework, and all are set in the worlds of the occult. Today they would be labeled religious fantasy or science fiction. We have noted that other people had little reality for Charles Williams, aside from the functions they could perform, and the characters in these novels are one-dimensional and flat. As in medieval morality plays and didactic religious novels like *Pilgrim's Progress*, characters in these novels serve didactic rather than realistic purposes, with each character functioning as a representative of some Christian or anti-Christian quality. Place and time are vague and undeveloped. Language, including dialogue, is stilted and long-winded. As in Williams's own life, ritualized symbols are far more important than any representation of outer or inner reality.

In six of the seven novels, the plot is identical. A male antagonist begins an occult operation to work his will for power upon the world. Evil forces gain a foothold, but Christian heroes and helpers arrive just in time to restore the rightful hierarchy of Christianity. The variation in plot in the remaining novel is slight.[33] In all of them, a Christian world of good in which Williams's mechanisms of exchange, transfer, substitution, and co-inherence are practiced is contrasted with a parallel world of evil, in which the same mechanisms exist in a distorted or twisted form. Though good wins in the end, most of these books actually inhabit the world of evil—the one Eliot called the outrageous and the foul.

Shadows of Ecstasy, though published in 1933, was actually written in the early 1920s and is thus the earliest of the three novels I will examine. Like the others, it concerns a man who strives for power over the world and is eventually defeated by the forces of Christianity. However, this novel departs significantly from the others because in it, Williams consistently privileges the forces of the Antichrist over the forces of Christianity. The novel, which Williams called "The Black Bastard" before his publishers wisely renamed it *Shadows of Ecstasy*, was written during Williams's membership in The Fellowship of the Rosy Dawn and reflects his enchantment with magical as opposed to Christian powers. *Shadows of Ecstasy* celebrates the powers and theories of Nigel Considine, the first and most appealing of Williams's Antichrists. Considine has mastered the art of immortality, and as the book begins he is embarking on an attempt to take over the world through occult practices. Having previously endowed a chair at London University in "Ritual Transmutations of Energy," he has recently returned to London to give a lecture on the subject and to observe the effects of his plan. He has already taken control of Africa, and under the name of "The High Executive" issues a proclamation freeing Africans from white rule and inviting all those who "exist in the exchanged or unexchanged adoration of love" to come forward.[34] If Europe will not submit he plans to direct Africa to defeat Europe and then the rest of the world, which he will then rule in the name of love and freedom. As the people of London take this in, an African king, Inkamasi, a former Christian, now under Considine's spell, shows up in

Hampstead. A vicar, Caithness, appears and pledges to win Inkamasi's soul back to Christianity, and the fight is on. Next, we learn of the death of Rosenberg, a rich and powerful Jew, who has left his wealth and collection of jewels to his Orthodox nephews. Considine, who has been gaining ground, assumes control of both the nephews and their jewels, but in an anti-Semitic riot in war-torn chaotic London, one of the nephews is killed.

Meanwhile, in the cozy family group headed by the retired surgeon Sir Bernard Travers, everyone must take a side for or against the new order. While Sir Bernard and his son Philip reject it, as does Philip's evil wife Rosamund, young Roger Ingram, a disaffected teacher of literature who admires Considine's devotion to art and has his own yearnings toward the transmutation of energy, decides to follow Considine. He is supported in this choice by his wife, the faithful Isabel, although she does not follow Considine herself. Considine then transports Roger, the remaining Jewish nephew, Rosenberg, a band of his followers who have mastered some of his skills, and Inkamasi to a house by the sea. Caithness, still in pursuit of Inkamasi's immortal soul, follows him there. In the end, Considine, aided by Caithness, is shot and temporarily thwarted by one of his disciples, Mottreux, who has succumbed to greed and wants the Jew's jewels. Roger returns to London and his wife but feels assured that his leader's magical abilities will ensure that his death is not permanent; he has merely withdrawn to gather his forces for another return.

Shadows of Ecstasy's privileging of the occult over Christianity, like Williams's membership in the Fellowship of the Rosy Dawn, caused embarrassment, consternation, and denial among Williams's Christian critics. Most of these either reinterpret the ending in the light of their beliefs and Williams's later novels or dismiss it as a mistake.[35] Typically, Agnes Sibley writes of the ending:

> The reader now begins to understand religion and love, or God *as* love to be a more certain and comprehensive power than Considine's ecstasy or Sir Bernard's reason. By ignoring religion, Considine fails, not only in ruling the will of Inkamasi, but in his whole attempt to dominate the world. (46)

In fact, the reader understands no such thing. Considine, the master of the occult and the figure around which the novel revolves, is a much more powerful, compelling, and even likeable character than the rather puny representative of the church, Caithness, who cannot save Inkamasi from being killed and who allies himself with Mottreux, the Judas-figure who betrays Considine for a handful of jewels. Even this might have been acceptable to the Christian critics if Williams had damned the Antichrist at the end and restored the proper balance. But Considine is neither condemned nor punished at the end of the book. A grandiose image of Williams himself, Considine is "man conscious of himself and his powers, man powerful and victorious, bold and serene, a culmination and a prophecy" (*Shadows*, 81). Through his mastery of the transmutation of energy, he has achieved an immortality that even Christ, doomed "to look for resurrection in another world," never mastered.

Considine embodies the Williams system, not, like the later Antichrists, in its twisted form, but in a thoroughly majestic way. He shares with Williams and with the king Inkamasi an "intense appreciation of royalty"—what Caithness calls "the making visible of hierarchic freedom, a presented moment of obedience and rule" (184, 96). His "Proclamation" is very like the "Promulgation" Williams wrote and distributed for the Companions of the Co-Inherence in 1939, and Considine's Inner Circle, with its emphasis on renunciation, love-exchange, and obedience to the leader, resembles Williams's group even in its membership:

> "The Devotees," the Zulu answered. "It's a high circle of those who having achieved much choose to render their lives wholly into the will of the Deathless One that he may use them as he pleases. . . . Most of them . . . are women." (110)

When Roger asks Considine how he has managed to defeat death, his answers invoke the Williams extrusion press. In Considine's transmutation, energy is transferred from "poetry or love or any manner of ecstasy, into the power of a greater ecstasy" (73). Members of Considine's Circle, like the members of Williams's order and like Williams himself with his female disciples, "have learned to arouse and restrain and direct the exaltation of love to such purposes as they choose" (108). His followers have "learned by the contemplation of beauty in man or woman to fill themselves with a wonderful and delighted excitement and to turn that excitement to deliberate ends" (108). Sexual love, like religion and art, explains Considine, is only "the shadow of ecstasy." It is the transcendence of sexuality which brings real power—and immortality. When Philip asks Considine how to cope with his sexuality, he assures him,

"You can know your joy and direct it . . . when your manhood's aflame with love" (72).

Over and over again, Considine tells his admiring disciple Roger, how he has managed to use women to achieve his ends:

> I myself carried out the great experiment, and I laid my imagination upon all the powers and influences of sex and love and desire. . . . I have gathered from many women all that imagination desired, and I have changed it to strength and cunning and length of days . . . the delights of mere bodily love are but shadows beside the rich joys of the transforming imagination. (154)

Like Williams, Considine has managed to transcend the dreaded contact with female carnality.

> I have endured love and transmuted it. I have found . . . that the sensual desires of man can be changed into strength of imagination. . . . I have transmuted masculine sex into human life. I am one of the masters of love. . . . Now I need love and hate no more. (83)

Considine, who speaks in the enigmatic phrases suitable to an immortal, tells Roger that it all started when a boy was jilted by a girl:

> [T]he boy said, "Why do I suffer helplessly? This also is I—all this unutterable pain is I. . . . " The girl's dead long ago; she was a pretty baby. . . . Then—a little later . . . the boy found another girl and loved her. But . . . he remembered the vastness of his pain . . . and asked himself whether love were not meant for something more than wantonness and child-bearing and the future that closes in death . . . he poured physical desire and mental passion into his determination of life. Then he was free. (202)

In this passage, a man, suffering under the wanton and overwhelming power of women, invents a system to "transmute" his love, moving it from the sordid femaleness of "wantonness and child-bearing" to freedom and a triumph over death, time, and place: the special enemies of the obsessive compulsive. The woman who caused the boy to suffer and made him helpless has been punished by death. Speaking in Considine's voice, Williams allows himself the cynical contempt of "she was a pretty baby." Considine invokes the magical "This also is Thou," but significantly substitutes "I" for Thou. In the other novels, such heresy will be punished, but in *Shadows of Ecstasy*, Considine, the embodiment of Williams's libidinal, power-hungry self, is shot but does not quite die. Instead, he leaves his body and is last seen in Roger's rapt vision, awakening in the sea in a state of "shining lucidity" to prepare his conquering return (223–24).

Like practitioners of the occult, Jews and blacks are treated more gently in this novel than in any of the others. Inkamasi, "the Zulu," seems to be a genuine enough, though rather comical king, who dies nobly rather than be subsumed by Considine. The other blacks, however, referred to as "swarming negroes," "screaming Africans," "this crowd of bats with negro faces," is loosed on London by Considine as a warning of things to come and a reminder of the white crowds' own inner savagery (187). In this case blacks serve as an especially frightening embodiment of the "mob," which for Williams, as for Lewis and the Freikorpsmen, shares some of the characteristics of women: it is a raging, uncontrolled mass, threatening to break boundaries if not controlled. On the other hand, in *Shadows of Ecstasy* blacks, along with Jews, are also the victims of the mob, which pursues both the two Rosenberg cousins and Inkamasi with cries of "bloody niggers" and "lowsy old Jews" (138).

Jews, like blacks, play a double role in *Shadows of Ecstasy*. The Rosenberg cousins' uncle, "a certain Simon Rosenberg," owned Africa before Considine. He has interests in "railways and periodicals and fisheries and dye-works, in South African diamonds and Persian oils and Chinese silks, in textiles and cereals and patent-medicines, rubber and coffee and wool" (*Shadows*, 21). Rosenberg has made the mistake of seeking power through the collection of material things and has made a fetish of decorating his wife with costly jewels. When she dies, having "externalized in that adorned figure all his power and possession," he has nothing more left and commits suicide (28). Incapable of love, dominated by insatiable greed, and with a finger in every concern, he is (Edgar) Rosenberg's "Jew as Parasite," the miser who "threatens the survival of the body politic" (5). On the other hand, the two cousins, "devoted students of Kabbalistic doctrines," "fanatical in their vision and desire" (30, 32), are, like the blacks, victims of the crazed mob who are both martyred for their faith. Williams never asks us to take Inkamasi's kingship or the Rosenbergs' religious devotion seriously, presenting them as comic and foolish representatives of blackness and Old Testament Jewry. Nevertheless, they are seen as victims rather than victimizers, unlike the other Jews in Williams's novels.

While Jews and blacks are not rigidly fixed stereotypes in *Shadows of Ecstasy* as they will be in the later novels, women have already assumed their set roles. Rosamund, Roger's sister-in-law, and the fiancée of Sir Bernard's son, Philip, has a "deceitfully soft voice" and generally embodies stealthy, feline, female evil: "She was small and dainty, and she moved, as it were, in little pounces. And yet she was so strong; it was as if strength pretended to be weak" (63, 36). Rosamund refuses to keep quiet in the company of men, and takes every opportunity to assert that You-ness which so repelled Williams when he saw it "rise" in Lois Lang-Sims. She sneaks to the police and reports Considine when he is a guest in her father-in-law's house, breaking all the laws of hospitality and English good manners. When she calls Philip's name it is in a commanding tone which contains "scorn and hate and fear" (63). Rosamund's good sister, Isabel, keeps remembering a time when Rosamund "had once secretly and greedily devoured a whole boxful" of chocolates, then tried to blame Isabel. Rosamund had been punished by "appalling physical results," which had made her guilt clear (63). Inside Rosamund there lives: "an octopus, the tentacles of which she had seen waving at a distance at night . . . a huge something whose form lay hidden in the darkness and the distance . . . an octopus that lay not merely without" (63).

"Appalling" and "abominable" are Williams's most frequently used words for female carnality. The octopus within, with its invasive female tentacles, is a recurrent symbol which appears in *Witchcraft* and again in the title of his verse drama of 1945, *The House of the Octopus*. Like the character Kreisler in Lewis's *Tarr*, Rosamund provides a nightmare or warning vision of what might happen to Williams without a defensive system—and without a well-defined outlet for his longings. In her chocolate orgy, she is a child "giving way to the thrust of its secret longing and vainly trying to conceal from others' eyes the force of its desires" (135). Williams might have been talking of himself in his description of her need to maintain an image of goodness and to keep a lid on her hidden self.

> She had cheated herself for so long, consciously in childhood with that strange combination of perfect innocence and deliberate sin which makes childhood so blameless and so guilty at one and the same moment; less consciously in youth as innocence faded and the necessity of imposing some kind of image of herself on the world grew stronger, till now in her first womanhood . . . her outraged flesh rebelled and clamoured from starvation for food. (135)

Considine has "transmuted" his overwhelming sadosexual urges into a method of achieving immortality. Rosamund, whose urges are equally strong, has achieved no such mastery. "Power was in her and she was terrified of it" (135). She has evil carnal longings for the black king, Inkamasi. Trying to decide whether or not to marry Philip, she finds herself stuck in an obsessive crisis much like Williams's own when he felt torn between the two women in his life: "[N]ot being there, she was determined to get back there. She would run there, and then run away, till the strait-jacket of time and place imprisoned her as it imprisons all in the end who suffer from a like madness" (136). It is his own self-hatred as well as his loathing of women which Williams expresses in Roger's prescription for Rosamund: "What she needs . . . is prussic acid" (137).

If Rosamund is Williams's evil woman or "lamia," Isabel is his Slave-Goddess. Calm and soothing where Rosamund is shrill and demanding, she, unlike her sister, knows when to make herself scarce. She tells her sister, "[A] man needs you to get away from," and explains that women have less need of Considine's transmutation services because they have already "turned everything into themselves," which is also why they have "never made great art." When Roger becomes envious of female power, she assures him, "We only live on what you give us—imaginatively, I mean; you have to find the greater powers" (55). Unlike Williams's wife, who refused to support his love for other women no matter how transmuted, Isabel warmly supports Roger in his need to follow Considine, although it contradicts her own values and also means that he will leave her. She explains this to Sir Bernard:

> I wanted him to, since he wanted to. . . . More; for I wanted him to even more than he did, since I hadn't myself to think of and he had. . . . I want it—whatever he wants. . . . And then since I haven't myself to think of, I'm not divided or disturbed in wanting, so I *can* save him trouble. (163)

Amazed by this "triumphant contradiction," Sir Bernard asks Isabel what she gets out of it, and she explains that it makes her utterly happy: "O of course it's dreadfully painful, but—yes, utterly" (163). In *The Figure of Beatrice*, Williams explained that mere renunciation is not enough; one must renounce with pleasure. Isabel fulsomely illustrates this principle:

> I'm a fool at knowing things, but when there's something in you that has its way, and when Roger's doing what he must do, and I too—O every fibre of me's aching for him and I can sing for joy all through me. Isn't that all the ecstasy that I could bear? Come and let's do something before it breaks my heart to be alive. (165)

Fittingly, the "something" which Isabel proceeds to do consists of feeding and offering shelter to some weary refugees passing outside her window. Isabel's renunciation, Sir Bernard notices, "curiously agreed" with Considine's enthronement of the self: "They were both beyond the places of logic and compromise" (163). In this "match" there is only room for one selfhood—the male's. The matched positions in a sadomasochistic system, with the woman as slave and the man as master, also "curiously agree."[36]

Shadows of Ecstasy, the most cheerful of Williams's novels, ends with comfort all around. Considine is killed, but not permanently. Roger, who has experienced vicarious ecstasy through following him, is reunited with gentle Isabel. Even Rosamund survives to do more mischief. Only the most expendable characters, the Jews and blacks, are definitively killed. In allowing his aggressive, power-hungry self not only to emerge but to triumph in this novel of wish-fulfillment, Charles Williams achieved a fantasy escape from his rigid, self-punishing boundaries, his private "strait jacket." It is noteworthy that *Shadows of Ecstasy*, the most gentle and the least sadistic of all the novels, is dismissed as a minor effort by Williams's Christian critics.

War in Heaven (1930) begins with the discovery of a murdered body by a young family man, Lionel Rackstraw, a worker in the publishing house owned by Gregory Persimmons, specialist in the occult. Persimmons has just published a book by his fellow practitioner of the occult, Sir Giles Tumulty, which claims that the Holy Graal, the chalice of the Arthurian legend, is now to be found in the English parish church of Fardles. Sir Giles and Persimmons want the Graal in order to use its great power to make contact with evil, but the Archdeacon of Fardles, a mild and saintly man, is determined to resist the evil and retain the chalice for the forces of good, synonymous in this novel with Christianity. The Archdeacon is aided in this aim by two young helpers, an editor from the same publishing house, Kenneth Mornington, and the Roman Catholic aristocrat the Duke of Riding. Tumulty and Gregory are joined by *their* co-conspirators, a powerful, nameless Greek and his master, the Jew Manasseh. While the Graal is stolen and restolen by the forces of evil and good, Gregory obtains a foul ointment from Manasseh and the Greek, and with its aid, embarks on a nighttime visit to the land of darkness. During his sojourn there, he realizes that in order to work the ultimate evil, he needs a child, and for this purpose he chooses Adrian, the son of Lionel Rackstraw and his sweet and innocent wife, Barbara. After luring the Rackstraw family down to his country estate near Fardles, Gregory takes advantage of Barbara's proximity to attack her with the ointment, sending her into a paroxysm of wanton madness. Just as the forces of evil seem to be gaining the upper hand, the angel Prester John, the true guardian of the Holy Graal, appears on the scene, cures Barbara, and claims Adrian's soul back for God. In the final conflict, the Jew, the Greek, Persimmons, and Tumulty lure the Archdeacon to their slimy hole and attempt to use him, along with the soul of the murdered man, Gregory's victim, in their ultimate rite, which will result in the destruction of Christian civilization. But between the intervention of Prester John and the Archdeacon's serene love and faith, the evildoers are destroyed and the Graal returned to its holy place. The Archdeacon, exhausted by all the commotion, dies happily and is welcomed into his heavenly home.

Through his use of the OUP setting and of the Arthurian legend, Williams locates this book squarely inside his own structure, and *War in Heaven* contains two clearly delineated but parallel worlds of foreign evil and Christian good, separated by the Williams extrusion machine. Perhaps because Williams was no longer involved in the Fellowship of the Rosy Dawn at the time of writing, he thoroughly condemns the forces of the occult in this book. These forces are equated with the devil, shown up as far weaker than the forces of good and punished roundly at the end. It is the Christian rather than the occult forces who practice the Williams system in *War in Heaven*. The Archdeacon especially is very prone to hum, "Neither is this Thou" and "Yet this also is Thou" as he goes about his pleasingly ritualized tasks. While he loves the Graal for its holy associations, he knows it is only material and that true power is to be found in the everyday exchanges of love and such larger substitutions as he himself contributes when he offers his body at the end of the book. This time it is the group of Christians who join together to protect the Graal who form an order of co-inherence, "an arranged order—people whom we can trust . . . an Order. . . . A new Table!"[37]

While Williams consciously locates himself in the character of the sweet and humble Archdeacon, the figure of Gregory Persimmons is a less conscious reflection of his suppressed self. Gregory's hatefulness has sent his wife into the asylum and worn down his son. He is a mass of enraged lust for power, which threatens, like Lewis's volcano or Rosamund's outraged flesh, to erupt when he meets Prester John:

> His fingers twitched to tear the clothes off his enemy and to break and pound him into a mass of flesh and bone . . . his being was absorbed in a more profound lust. It aimed itself in a thrust of passion which should wholly blot the other out of existence. (154–55)

The lust for power is evident in all of Gregory's speeches. Even when he is masquerading as a benign neighbor in an unsuccessful effort to trick the Archdeacon into selling him the Graal, he betrays his greed through talking of his desire to send out "a sort of magnetic thrill" by sending a friend the chalice (44). As we have seen, Lois Lang-Sims repeatedly used similar language in relation to Williams, whose hand, when it touched hers, "quivered as from a succession of electric shocks," and Williams himself often described the exchange of love as "electric" (*Lalage*, Lang-Sims, 33).

Like Lewis's foul Jew, Julius Ratner, the dung beetle, Gregory Persimmons has an excremental smell which he carries everywhere and which attaches to every object he touches. Kenneth Mornington comments, "I'm sure you've got Gregory here, it smells like a dung-heap" (215). Like the Archdeacon, who chants ritual prayers and like Williams himself, Gregory is obsessed with ritualistic numbers and geometric figures. This is especially evident in the scene in which he anoints himself with the magical salve, certainly one of the more "outrageous and foul" passages which Eliot assured us Williams included only in order to highlight the good.

After making his purchase in the beastly terrace of slime which is Manasseh the Jew's natural habitat, Gregory goes home to his country estate to apply the ointment, which has the smell "of some complete decay." This smell reminds him of his "power to enter into those lives which he touched and twist them out of their security into a sliding destruction" (71). He opens the tin of ointment which "seemed almost to suck itself upward round his fingers," and, chanting the "hierarchal titles," marks ritual figures on "the chosen parts—the soles of the feet, the palms of the hands,the inner side of the fingers, the ears and eyelids, the environs of nose and mouth, the secret organs" (73). He then lies naked on his bed in orgiastic abandon:

> [T]onight the powerful ointment worked so swiftly upon him, stealing through all his flesh with a delicious venom. . . . He accepted the union in a deep sigh of pleasure . . . he lay given up to that sensation of swift and easy motion towards some still hidden moment of exquisite and destructive delight. . . . Suddenly . . . there rose within him the sense of a vast and rapid flow, of which he was part, rushing and palpitating with desire. He de-

sired—the heat about his heart grew stronger—to give himself out, to be one with something that should submit to him and from which he should yet draw nourishment. . . . He was hungry—but not for food; he was thirsty—but not for drink; he was filled with passion—but not for flesh. He expanded in the rush of an ancient desire; he longed to be married to the universe for a bride. (74–75)

Although Gregory does achieve "the wild rhythm of that aboriginal longing" that night, his need for "something that should submit to him and from which he should draw nourishment" is not yet satisfied (75). He realizes that he will not manage to achieve a final climax until "this god also who was himself and not himself" obtains a child. He recalls Lionel Rackstraw's child, Adrian, and this realization does the trick:

Nailed, as it were, through feet and hands and head and genitals, he passed utterly into a pang that was an ecstasy beyond his dreams. (77)

Williams's theories of co-inherence, substitution, and exchange, are here embodied in a sadomasochistic pedophiliac fantasy which brings its host to orgasm. Williams writes of Christ's crucifixion as the first "exchange," and Gregory's experience is a masochistic parody of the crucifixion: the image of himself nailed "through feet and hands and head and genitals," together with the thought of the child, is what finally brings him to climax. Because Gregory and his world are safely split off and presented as embodiments of evil, Williams can allow himself to revel in what he himself experienced as his own outrageous and foul self: power-hungry, enraged, and sexually sadistic (*Hallows*, Eliot, xvi).

Similarly, through Gregory, Williams textualizes his rage and loathing against the hated female. Although the child Adrian rather than his mother is his intended victim, when Gregory sees Barbara he cannot resist striking out at her, slashing her with a sharp edge of the electric train he has bought to seduce Adrian. When she is bleeding, Gregory applies the ointment, knowing that she will experience it like "an invader, a conqueror, perhaps even an infernal lover. . . . Unless indeed she also became that" (161). Gregory, who is far too fastidious and repulsed by female sexuality to desire actual sexual contact, achieves instead a kind of voyeuristic rape, capped by a ceremonial bondage. Under the influence of the ointment, the restrained Barbara erupts:

Barbara, still moving in that wild dance, threw up her hand and, carelessly and unconsciously tore open her light frock and underwear from the breast downwards. It hung, a moment, ripped and rent, from the girdle that caught

> it together; then it fell lower, and she shook her legs free without checking the movement of the dance. . . . It . . . needed the three of them to bring her into some sort of subordination, and to bind her with such material as could be obtained. (161–62)

The doctor manages to quiet Barbara's outer movements with morphia, but her flagrant female sexuality is still "working inward." Gregory, who realizes this, gloats with some of the feeling Considine displayed when he told Roger of the death of the "pretty baby":

> Was the inner being that was Barbara being driven deeper into that flow of desire which was the unity and compulsion of man? What an unusual experience for a charming young housewife of the twentieth century. And perhaps she also would not be able to return. (164)

When Giles Tumulty arrives on the scene, Gregory tells him gleefully: "Pity you weren't here; you'd have liked to see how Mrs. Rackstraw went on. Quite unusual, for an English lady" (170).

In *War in Heaven*, rather than creating two women, an evil and a good one, Williams manages to embody his need for "a rigid line of difference" (Gilman, *Difference and Pathology*, 18) by situating both types in Barbara Rackstraw. The Jew's ointment reveals the "lamia" that Williams knows is lurking beneath the surface of that most sexually demure of beings, "a charming young English lady." What has been revealed is an incarnation of shameless and frenzied female sexuality, an apparition so hellish that the shocked doctor hastens to get away, and Barbara's loving husband, Lionel, who assumes that Barbara will harm her son, immediately worries about the cost of removing her from him. "He couldn't afford to keep Barbara and a housekeeper . . . but . . . after such an attack she couldn't for a long time be left alone with Adrian" (166).

Lionel has realized what Williams and Lewis both understood: that inside even the most loving mother there lives a murderous female, "malignant, capable of any crime . . . the personification of what is sinister" (Horney, 349).

In the good Christian world, Barbara Rackstraw is one of Williams's idealized Slave-Goddesses, concerned only with the happiness of her male son and child: exactly such a wife as Alice Mary Hadfield would wish to be. In that hidden world which the ointment reveals, "anything can turn into anything else," and a seemingly loving, innocent girl can change into the fearsome creature which lives beneath her surface.

Gregory, like Williams's other villains, is especially drawn to such "moments of malevolent change," when souls and bodies are invaded and penetrated. He smiles in pleasure when he comes up with the plan to "marry" the body of the dead devil-worshiper he murdered (the body which was found in the Press offices in the beginning of the book) to the Archdeacon: "we will marry it to this priest, body and soul, so that he shall live with it by day and by night, and come indeed in the end to know not which is he" (213). As always in Williams's bipolar system, each "good" is opposed by an evil which consists of virtually the same thing reversed. The energy-draining ritual Williams used with Lois Lang-Sims provided an antidote against the female "lamia." Similarly, the various mechanisms of Williams's extrusion machine provide protection for the male body with its vulnerability to invasion. But these mechanisms when used by Gregory Persimmons have the opposite effect: they destroy the bodily boundaries of the female. The ultimate nightmare for both Lewis and Williams consists of being transformed forever into their carefully hidden and split-off female self. For Lewis's Kreisler in *Tarr* such a moment comes when, after giving up his powers to Anastasia, he finds he "cannot take himself out again" (100). Williams visits a similar transformation on a female character, Barbara Rackstraw.

While Gregory is the split-off representative of Williams's power-hungry self and the main agent of the evil side of the dual structure, Giles Tumulty's is the cynical inner voice in which Williams mocks his own efforts at goodness, or system-conversion. Tumulty finds the Archdeacon one of those religious extremists who "wandered in a borderland . . . of metaphysics, mysticism, and insanity" and understands that for such people the whole world is nothing but a sadomasochistic ritual: "[G]iven in the Jew's mind the delusion that he loved the world, what else was the Passion but masochism? And the passion of the communicant was, of course, a corresponding sadism" (83). These doubts are expressed by evil Giles Tumulty, who signals his contempt for Jesus by calling him "the Jew," and Williams does not intend his reader to buy the argument. Nevertheless, the pleasurable grandiosity of *Shadows of Ecstasy* is gone here. The bipolar worlds of good and evil are frighteningly close, and even the good world is attended by a mocking inner voice.

This threat of the collision of the good and evil worlds and the dissolution of the wall which separates them appears elsewhere in the novel. Lionel Rackstraw and Kenneth Mornington, who, like Williams himself, work at "the Press," are both subject to terrifying "spells" in which the ground swell of evil threatens to break through their careful Christian boundaries. To write the scene in which Gregory fires Kenneth from his job, Williams evokes one of his own "neuralgic turns" and perhaps imagines how he himself would have felt if fired from the Press, the precious home of his fantasy life:

> He wanted to smash; he wanted to strangle Gregory and push him also underneath Lionel's desk; for the sake of destroying he meant to destroy. The contempt he had always felt leapt fierce and raging in him; till now it had always dwelt in a secret house of his own. (134)

Lionel Rackstraw, a less stable character than Kenneth, is a man who, like Williams, feels dependent upon his wife for his sanity and bitterly resents his dependence. He requires Barbara's serene and unselfish love to calm him down on a daily basis. On the day he finds the body under his desk, he has an experience which has "the ring of personal experience" about it (Spencer, 46). Upon arriving home, he finds that his boundaries seem to have vanished. "His usual sense of the fantastic and dangerous possibilities of life, a sense which dwelled persistently in a remote corner of his mind . . . —this sense now escaped from his keeping, and instead of being too hidden, became too universal to be seized" (17). While in this state, Lionel is subject to a paranoid anxiety attack. He imagines that Barbara is a whore who has just entertained another lover, that Adrian is not really a child but a horrible, prodigious, and malevolent man of forty, and that he will be poisoned by his wife who has up to now concealed her murderous hatred "under the shelter of a peaceful and happy domesticity." Finally:

> [I]t was not the possibility of administered poison that occupied him, but the question whether all food, and all other things also, were not in themselves poisonous. Fruit, he thought, might be; was there not in the nature of things some venom which nourished while it tormented, so that the very air he breathed did but enable him to endure for a longer time the spiritual malevolence of the world? (18)

Fantasies of being poisoned by chemicals in the air, by food, water, and life itself, are common among obsessive-compulsive people in crises when the mechanisms of compulsive hand-washing, ruminating over decisions, or numerical or other repetitions are no longer sufficient to stave off the massive unpredictability of the world.[38] While under the influence of his "turn," Lionel sees the evil Barbara lurking beneath the good veneer, thus anticipating her later malevolent transformation when Persimmons attacks her. Through Lionel, Williams textualizes his own rage against women (specifically against his wife, on whom he was dependent) and his fear of their power. In the first episode, Williams presents that rage and fear as an actual projection in Lionel's disordered mind, but in the second, he sadistically visits his rage upon her and transforms her into a dangerously malevolent "lamia."

In *War in Heaven*, while the Jew still holds the place carved out for him by centuries of myth and stereotype, he has also moved to a more prominent place in Williams's own system. An unearthly magician figure, he moves between Williams's two worlds and, as an agent of malevolent change, lures unsuspecting humans into the world of evil. The first reference to a Jew in the book evokes the image of a carnal beast, existing in a concrete version of Williams's own agony of indecisiveness—a limbo of torture. Tumulty warns Gregory not to try the ointment: "Better leave it alone . . . a Jew in Beyrout tried it and didn't get back. Filthy beast he looked, all naked and screaming that he couldn't find his way. That was four years ago and he's screaming the same thing still, unless he's dead" (64).

The sadistic brutality of this first image of the Jew is followed up with the information that the ointment is to be found in a chemist's shop, located in "one of those sudden terraces of slime which hang over the pit of hell, and for which beastliness is too dignified a name. But the slime was still only oozing over it" (68). The whole neighborhood is infected by this slime. Even the chocolates in the sweet shop are "more degradingly sensual than the ordinary kind" (66).[39] The Greek in the shop hesitates as he sells Gregory the ointment: "[W]hat will my master say if I mistake?" (67). After the Archdeacon has recovered the chalice, Gregory returns to the slimy shop, this time meeting its master, and the real originator of the ointment: Manasseh, the Jew. As owner of the ointment, Manasseh is the agent of the other world. He at first agrees that the Graal must be stolen back—so that he can destroy it.

> Because it has power . . . it must be destroyed. Don't you understand that yet? They build and we destroy. . . . One day we shall destroy the world . . . to destroy this is to ruin another of their houses and another step towards the hour when we shall breathe against the heavens and they shall fall. The only use in anything for us is that it may be destroyed. (144)

In Manasseh, whose name Williams took from the Old Testament king of Israel who was rumored to deal with familiar spirits and wizards and to practice other abominations involving sacrifices, we find the stereotype of the international financier merged with that of the medieval demon.[40] He approves of the kidnapping plot, and agrees that instead of destroying the Graal, they should take it and the child to meet the devil in the Jewish kingdoms of the East, "the high places of our god." They will travel by "the hidden road to the East . . . the furniture ship in Amsterdam or the picture dealer in Zurich . . . the boat-builder in Constantinople and the Armenian ferry . . . the vortex of destruction is in the East" (152).

After bewitching Barbara with Manasseh's ointment, Gregory tells her husband that the only man with the ability to cure her is Manasseh. As Rosenberg suggests, Williams's view of Jews is a medieval one, and this use of Manasseh is reminiscent of the years between 1290 and 1664, when Jewish physicians, the only Jews allowed into England, could be summoned, then accused of witchcraft if they failed to cure their patients. It is Manasseh's ointment which activates the release of female carnality in Barbara, and he arrives pretending that he intends to cure her but actually intent on fixing her in her madness. He intones, "[P]ossession is nothing besides destruction," and in a speech reminiscent of Shylock, declares, "I must have my price. Unless I have it I will not act" (184). When Prester John intervenes to save Barbara before the Jew can get his hands on her, Manasseh grinds his teeth in a very Shylock-like manner: "I don't like her getting away. She was on the very edge of destruction; she might have been torn to bits *there*—and she wasn't" (188).

Unlike the nihilistic Greek and Gregory, Manasseh is never satisfied. Death itself only feeds his terrible greed. This quality disturbs even Gregory, whose evil, unlike the Jew's, is human. He begins to have second thoughts about his plan and is alarmed at what he has unleashed: "no power of destructions seemed to satisfy Manasseh's hunger" (236).

When the Archdeacon arrives at the shop, Manasseh catches his arm "with a little crow of greedy satisfaction" and fills the Graal with blood, in preparation for a suitably medieval ceremony (240). Indeed, Manasseh is one of the medieval Jews Trachtenberg describes: a stand-in for "the mysterious, fearsome evil forces which . . . have menaced the peace and security of mankind . . . his inherited dread" (52). The Archdeacon, now prone on the floor, must fight three different forces or "shafts": Gregory's human, English evil; the Greek's powerful rejection and negativity; and the terrible malevolence of the Jew. This last is comprised of

> the knowledge of all hateful and separating and deathly things: madness and tormenting disease and the vengeance of gods. This was the hunger with which creation preys upon itself, a supernatural famine that has no relish except for the poisons that waste it . . . it ran . . . on a hungry mission of death. (241)

Like other fictional and mythic Jews, Manasseh ends his days "shaking and writhing on his back," presumably contemplating his final home (245).

In its final scene, *War in Heaven* returns to the world of the good in a church service over which Prester John officiates, using the Holy Graal as his chalice. He is served by Adrian, and the entire cast of good people are in attendance. The Archdeacon dies, and, in vivid contrast to the death of the Jew, goes peacefully and happily to his Maker. Barbara, whose feeble female mind cannot follow the service, does take in the words:

> "[I]n the image of God created He him, male and female created He him, male and female created He them." The very sound inclined her every so slightly towards her husband; her hand went out and found his, and so linked, they watched till the end. (253)

The chaotic, hungry forces of Jewry are defeated, and female cupidity has been subdued and tamed. All has returned to the proper Christian hierarchy. The war in heaven is over.

In the preface to *All Hallows' Eve* (1945) which Eliot wrote in 1948, he praises Williams for his portrait of the Jew, Clerk Simon, who, he writes, "is defined by his function of representing the single-minded lust for unlawful and unlimited power." Eliot also approves Williams's portraits of the two young women, Lester and Evelyn, which "reveal his understanding of the depth and intricacies of human nature" (xvii). Williams's portraits of both Jews and women are indeed revealing in this book; among other things, they reveal the inextricable connections between these two Others in the Williams system.

All Hallows' Eve, which was published twenty years after Eliot's *The Waste Land*, shows clear traces of Eliot's poem. One of its sentences, "He did not know how great the multitudes were who followed those unreal Two; nor how unreal the Two were," even echoes *The Waste Land* in a kind of stylistic parody.[41] As we have seen in chapters 1 and 2, Eliot often used the Jew as a symbol of society's putrefaction, and in *All Hallows' Eve*, Williams takes this symbolism several steps further.

In the beginning of the book, whose entire action takes place on All Hallows' Eve, a young woman, Lester Furnival, finds herself wandering in a postwar London which bears a striking resemblance to Eliot's "unreal city" in which "I had not thought death had undone so many."[42] Lester, although she does not know it yet, is one of the undone; she and her companion Evelyn, who is wandering with her, have been killed by a plane that crashed into Westminster Bridge. (In *The Waste Land* London Bridge is featured.) When alive, Evelyn was an evil, sadistic girl whose main pleasure in life had been torturing her schoolmate, the meek, slave-like Betty Wallingford. Lester herself, though not intrinsically evil like Evelyn, has been selfish and willful. While she loved her new husband Richard Furnival, and has even sacrificed herself for him on occasion, she did it proudly, rather than out of the kind of joyful sacrificial exchange practiced by model wives Isabel Ingram and Barbara Rackstraw. Now that it is too late, she bitterly regrets this and tries to make up for it throughout the book in a series of postmortem visits to her husband. Meanwhile, Richard, who works in the Foreign Office, and his painter friend, Jonathan Drayton, call on Betty Wallingford and her mother, Lady Wallingford, to show them the painting Jonathan has just finished of Lady Wallingford's beloved leader, Clerk Simon. Simon is a charismatic Jew who has been attracting attention all over the world, and the portrait is of a sinister beetle holding sway over a crowd of other beetles. Lady Wallingford is understandably offended and forbids her daughter from ever seeing her suitor, Jonathan, again. Later, Clerk Simon himself comes to Jonathan's studio to see the painting and finds that it suits him perfectly. Entering into his mind as he returns to his hall, we learn of his ancient antecedents, all Jewish practitioners of the occult; and also that he has already created two images of himself, who are now ruling China and Russia and with whose aid he plans to take over the world. We learn too that Betty is the daughter of a sinister union between Lady Wallingford and Clerk Simon, and that he created her for his own dark purposes, although so far he has confined himself to taking over her body and sending her on unholy spying missions throughout dead and living London.

On one of these missions, Betty encounters a repentant Lester, who bitterly regrets her offhand treatment of her when they were both alive and is determined to make up for it. They return together to Clerk Simon's slimy hall, the residence of many repulsively crippled people whom he has temporarily healed, and who remain there as his disciples. Simon attempts a final operation on Betty, whose soul he must destroy to obtain the use of her body for his final evil plan, but Lester interposes herself in a courageous act of exchange. Stymied by Lester, Simon turns to lesser arts and creates a deformed female body out of his saliva. Climbing into this body, which she must share with the repellent Evelyn, Lester visits her ex-husband and Jonathan, who reclaims Betty.

They all return to the hall in Holborn just in time to intercept Simon in the act of busily draining Lady Wallingford's blood, and inserting it into still another female homuncula. Once again, the good combine their forces in order to defeat Simon. He summons his other two images, but they cannot help him, and all three disappear in a cloud of foggy blood. Lester goes to heaven; Evelyn to hell. Betty finishes healing the cripples, who are in need of this service again now that Simon is gone, and then marries Jonathan.

All Hallows' Eve, like *War in Heaven*, contains two clearly delineated but parallel worlds of foreign evil and Christian good, separated out by the Williams extrusion press. As in the earlier book, Williams's system exists here both in its purified state in the good world and in its unregenerate state in the evil world. In *All Hallows' Eve*, however, the forces of evil are not spread around as they are in the former book among Gregory Persimmons, Giles Tumulty, the Greek, and the Jew, but are instead completely concentrated in the hands of one man, whose power is repeatedly identified as the power of Jewry. Perhaps because of this concentration, the two worlds do not threaten to coalesce as they did in the former book, but remain in safely dichotomous categories.

In his essay of 1943, Williams declared that the only way for a Christian to approach a Jew was "theologically" and talked of the hatred which "springs in our blood" at the knowledge that the Jew has crucified the God-Man ("Jews," 1943). The Christian Gregory Persimmons's need for power and his sadistic behavior toward Barbara Rackstraw were somewhat difficult for Williams to disown, and Gregory, unlike the immoral Jew Manasseh was subject to nagging guilt and rumination much like his creator's. Clerk Simon is a far more remote and convenient villain than

Gregory and a safer container for the author's disowned and feared grandiose, power-hungry self. As the archetypal Jew Villain or Antichrist, he stands in opposition to Williams's own Christian identity. Williams, who constantly proclaimed, "This also is Thou, neither is this Thou," seems here to be shouting at the top of his voice, "This Jew is not I!"

We first see Clerk Simon as the repulsive beetle in the painting by Jonathan. His beetle followers comprise the hated mob or mass and are, like Considine's followers in *Shadows of Ecstasy* and the followers of Williams himself, largely female. Like Williams, Simon both needs and despises them. "They aren't insects," he tells Jonathan, "they are something less. . . . It's quite good for them to be hypnotized; they're much happier" (57). The last war, he continues, was nothing compared to what he has in mind: "The war, like Hitler, was a foolery. I am the one who is to come, not Hitler" (59).

It is soon clear that the destruction this Jew intends for the Christian world will indeed make Hitler's destruction look like foolery. In addition to minimizing (almost denying) the Holocaust, Williams here attributes the role of victim to the Gentile and that of victimizer to the Jew. Fisch, Kernberg, and all the objects relations theorists describe the process of primitive projective identification, in which the patient "attributes to the other an impulse he has repressed in himself" and then, "under the influence of the projected impulse," experiences fear and loathing toward that Other (Kernberg, 17). It is a small step from this reversal to the implication that Hitler was merely and justifiably defending his country against the inexorable Jewish hunger for power. Indeed, Williams consistently develops this theme throughout the book.

When Simon leaves Jonathan's studio, "the Jewish quality in his face seemed to deepen" (61). He represents "the second climax" of that august race, which had killed its own prophet:

> deception had taken them; they had, bidding a scaffold for the blasphemer, destroyed their predestined conclusion, and the race which had been set for the salvation of the world became a judgment and even a curse to the world and to themselves. (62)

Speaking from his "theological" point of view, Williams, like the British Union of Fascists, is labeling World War II the "Jews' War." He reasons that the Jews, by killing Christ, not only brought upon themselves the punishment they received in World War II, but also brought down the curse of the war on innocent Christians. Because of the crucifixion by the Jews of their own, "there arose in Europe something which was neither . . . [Gentile nor Jew] . . . and set itself to destroy both" (62–63).

Simon remembers his birth, which, much like Lewis's Ratner's, took place "in one of those hiding places of necromancy" at the time of the French revolution (63). Like Considine, Simon has mastered the art of living forever, but in this book immortality is an art "private . . . to the high priestly race. . . . Only a Jew could utter the Jewish, which was the final, word of power" (64). It takes a Jew, too, to speak with the devil as Simon does, and to understand his "high piping sound" (150).

Although Clerk Simon is the most powerful, he explains that he is only the latest in a line of evil Jews who have attempted to overthrow the world. The operation he intends for his daughter Betty was attempted by another Jew, but "the living thing that had been born of his feminine counterpart had perished miserably" (65). Earlier, another Simon, Simon Magus, the magician whose history Williams traces in *Witchcraft*, slew a little Christian boy for the same purpose. Williams repeatedly identifies Simon with both the older and the newer stereotype of Jewry: the castrating mutilator of the medieval ballads and the power-hungry international financier of the Chester-Bellocs and the *Protocols of the Elders of Zion*. As he looms over her with a needle, preparing to drain her blood, Simon is a personification of the medieval Jew. Lady Wallingford sees his great face: "the face of the Exile of Israel, of the old Israel and the new . . . the face of all exile, the face of the refusal of the Return . . . it seemed to her as imbecile as it had been in the painting" (246).

Simon's more modern face emerges when we learn that the Foreign Office, itself under the influence of the Jewish conspiracy, is preparing to offer the modern world to him and his two images.

Simon, like Williams's other Antichrists, practices the evil version of Williams's system. In his evil and sadistic concupiscence and in his grandiose greed for power, he is a fitting container for Williams's suppressed self. Throughout the book, Simon shares Williams's own geometrical and numerical obsessions, as well as his bodily ones. This is especially noticeable when the clerk is under stress and rapidly repeats the "backward intoned Tetragrammaton," the key to power. Just as in *Shadows of Ecstasy* Williams attributed his own forbidden sexual urges, including the angry punishment of female carnality, to Gregory, here these urges, in a more extreme form, are Simon's. Like Williams and Considine, Simon has avoided sex, "except for rational purposes" (*Shadows*, 64). He is disgusted by female carnality, and "grimaces ignorantly" at the thought of Jonathan and Betty's love (*Hallows*, 65). He intends Betty for "another purpose." The operation he plans for her, which will be the means of "his coming empery in the world," has incestuous as well as sadistic elements (65).

The only scene of genital sexuality between a man and a woman in any of these three novels by Williams is the scene of Betty's conception. Lady Wallingford, who, like Gregory is evil but human, remembers the occasion with horror:

> She could hear a heavy breathing, almost a panting, and almost animal . . . it became so low a moan that the sweat broke out on her forehead . . . a moan of . . . compulsion. The temperature of the room grew hotter; a uterine warmth oppressed her. . . . She had given herself to his will . . . the room was full of a great tension; the heat grew; she lay sweating and willed what he willed[.] (111)

"Since that night," Lady Wallingford remembers, "there had been no physical intercourse between them. She—even she—could not have endured it" (112–13). If one examines this sexual passage out of context, it is curiously innocuous; one can imagine a similar passage in the work of D. H. Lawrence, for example, as a description of successful return to our lost animal nature. But for Williams, genital sexuality with woman, the alien, is a horrifying, unclean, and magical act, rather like having sex with the devil. Although it is Simon who controls Lady Wallingford, the scene is pervaded by a female, "uterine" heat. In this scene the woman and Jew literally mingle, and the Jew's evil is subordinate to the female's. Even the evil Jew could not embark on such a scene for enjoyment, but only to beget a creature of his own.

Simon's needy dominance of women, like his repugnance for their sexuality, echoes Williams's own needs and habits. Simon's relations with his daughter and his mistress consist of ceremonies in which he inhabits their bodies and compels them to act: rituals which gain him the power he needs to "work." As the forces of good combine and things begin to go wrong for him, Simon turns to ever more bizarre ways of dominating women. Out of his spittle he creates two different female figures, one a deformed creature: "a little under two feet high and with the head gradually forming . . . more like a living india-rubber doll than anything else but then it did live. It was breathing and moving" (194). The other is the "endoplasmic doll" which he attempts to fill with Lady Wallingford's blood, in order, in one of Williams's mechanisms reversed, to substitute or exchange her for Betty.

At the end of the book, when the walls of Simon's house turn into slime like the walls of the Jew's house in *War in Heaven*, his female creatures dissolve into their essence: revolting pools of female carnality.

> [T]he doll on the chair at once melted; it ran over the woman's hand and wholly disappeared, except for a thin film of liquid putrescence which covered them, pullulating as if with unspermed life. She saw it and under it her hands still bloody; she shook them wildly and tried to tear at them, but the thin pulsing jelly was everywhere over them and her fingers could not get through it. (262)

The other doll too, melts and oozes, and indeed the Jew himself loses all his boundaries and dissolves into an oozing cloud of stinking blood. Williams's terror of dissolution, of dissolving into "jelly," is here embodied in all its horror and is visited first on the female, then on the Jew.

The images of female "liquid putrescence" is a familiar one in the Freikorps texts, and Theweleit identifies the lack of boundaries and the terror of dissolution as basic to the Freikorpsmen's psychology. Sander Gilman too identifies similar imagery in Zola's *Nana*, in which the prostitute Nana dies of smallpox and is described as suppurating, carrion, and putrefying: "The decaying visage is the visible sign of the diseased genitalia through which the sexualized female corrupts an entire nation of warriors and leads them to the collapse at Sedan" (Gilman, *Difference and Pathology*, 105).

Rosenberg points out that Simon the Jew is "both demiurge and beast, anti-Christ, as well as satyr" (289). His urge for power involves not only the anesthetizing of the will but also "the Clerk's own withdrawal into a preconscious area, sacramental and bestial, shrouded in secrecy and hemmed in by power taboos" (Rosenberg, 289). In the light of our discussion it is clear that this area is the world of Williams's own rejected self, split off and distanced by the label "Jew."

Just as *All Hallows' Eve* presents a more clearly demarcated world of good and evil than do either of the previous novels, the portraits of women in this book lack any authorial ambivalence. Every female character in *All Hallows' Eve* is portrayed in sadomasochistic terms, with the evil women acting as masochists in relation to the male Jew and as sadists in relation to other women. Lady Wallingford's role in relation to Clerk Simon is one of sexual masochism and submission. She is his "instrument," whose only purpose is to be used. Toward her daughter, on the other hand, she functions as a cruel mistress, forcing her ritually to enact a role of submission and slavery. At the end, Lady Wallingford moves from the world of evil to the world of good. To protect her daughter, she interposes herself between Betty and Simon in an act of love-exchange. But in the case of this loathsome female, the two worlds prove to be not all that different. Lady Wallingford's reward for good behavior consists merely of a switch of masters. Williams explains that "since in that gift she had desired the good of another . . . since she had indeed willed to give her self," she will be rewarded by being allowed to spend the remainder of her days as a paralyzed infant completely dependent for food and care on her daughter Betty (270).

A whining and grasping woman like Rosamund in *Shadows of Ecstasy,* Lester's friend Evelyn is drawn to Simon through "spiritual suction." Looking at her, Richard sees "a slight thing and so full of vileness that he almost fainted" (116). Evelyn advances toward Simon with the "semi-bestiality of her movements" and her "muddled and obsessed brain," desperate to give herself over to evil (173). Evelyn's prime motive in life has been the abuse of Betty. Indeed, her desperate need to find Betty and continue to abuse her is what keeps her, though dead, alive. Evelyn approaches Simon as a creature masochistically panting and thirsting for abuse. He uses her, then sends her back to her personal hell, where she will wander alone, with no object for her sadism.

The best woman in *All Hallows' Eve*, as in the other novels, is the Slave-Goddess. Betty Wallingford, with her immaculate soul, is Williams's ultimate woman, more highly praised than even the docile Isabel Ingram in *Shadows of Ecstasy* or the unselfish Barbara Rackstraw in *War in Heaven*. Betty is so profoundly passive that she has no self at all. Docility, sweetness, and cheerfulness are natural to her, and these qualities, along with the low intelligence which is always a characteristic of Williams's Slave-Goddesses, make her accept her role of slave and victim to her evil parents without ever thinking of escape.

> Someone had once told her that her mind wasn't very strong, and "indeed it isn't," she thought gaily, "but it's quite strong enough to do what it's got to do, and what it hasn't got to do it needn't worry about not doing." (79)

Fathered and then invaded (dominated is too mild a word) by Simon, Betty is also her mother's slave: "her mistress-mother, her mother-mistress, told her what to do" (67). In a plot-twist which Williams must have inserted for his own satisfaction alone, as it is unrelated to anything else in the novel, Lady Wallingford has a habit of taking poor Betty out into the country for a bit of sadistic role playing; calling her daughter "Bettina," she abuses her and forces her to play the role of an under-housemaid. When Lester removes Betty from her evil parents, she passes directly into Jonathan's control: "I'm not very intelligent, and I've got a lot to learn," she tells him. "Jon, you must help me" (210). Betty models "The Law of Exchange" for Lester. Although she had at first not wanted to remember her bad times at school, "as soon as she knew that Lester wanted it, she too wanted it; so simple is love-in-paradise" (132).

In the beginning of the book, Lester is Williams's most lively and assertive woman, described in similar terms to those which his followers used to describe Williams's wife, Florence. We learn that when alive she did not like her husband, Richard, to keep her waiting, and that she was capable, proud, and fond of her own way. Lester's punishment for this unforgivable "you-ness" only begins with her death, which takes place before the book begins. It continues when she meets her living husband and realizes that she herself is "dead, and she had done it [asserted herself] once too often. Dead, and this had been their parting" (6). Lester's enraging female assertiveness is further punished when she masochistically inserts herself between Betty and her sadistic father and receives his invading needles and evil curses on herself. Next, her "Riseness" is properly humiliated when she is forced to inhabit the body of one of Simon's deformed dolls for a final visit to her ex-husband, who cannot bear to look at her. In the end of the novel, having attained a Betty-like willingness to sacrifice herself, Lester fades into one of the quiet dead.

If the female characters in *All Hallows' Eve* provide an opportunity for Williams, in the persona of an evil Jew, to exercise his sadistic fantasies against women, even such rituals do not provide adequate protection against female carnality. Just as a voracious whore lurked behind the surface of the sweet English mother Barbara Rackstraw in *War in Heaven*, ugly carnal smells and images lurk behind the sacrificial meekness of all the women, good and evil, in *All Hallows' Eve*. A repulsive (female) smell of fish hovers in Simon's dank hall. The deformed and anonymous homunculae or dolls, with their dank palms, heavy hanging hands, and dead flesh (220, 230) are femaleness incarnate and, as we have noted, finally melt down to the putrescent essence of femaleness itself. Despite its happy ending, it is this foul and female world which is the real setting of *All Hallows' Eve*.

Conclusion: When the Goddess Is a Slave

Women play a number of parts in Williams's system. They are hateful symbols of his own libidinous self or idealized love objects which he bitterly resents because of his dependence on them. The evil ones must be destroyed, the good ones enslaved and suitably punished. Because Williams does not need Jews as he needs women, Jews play a less complex role in his system. Symbolic repositories of his evil, split-off self, they are also instrumental in releasing the carnality and evil which lie beneath the female surface.

Of the two authors, Williams seems to me to be the more dangerous. Wyndham Lewis's anti-Semitism is disturbing but predictable. A clumsy, trampling elephant, Lewis trumpets his paranoid vision loudly enough for us to get out of his way. In contrast, borrowing from his own imagery of malevolent transformation, we can picture Williams as a house cat which waits until one is asleep, then reveals pantherlike fangs which he plunges into our neck with a sweet purr. The venom and hatred toward women and Jews which Charles Williams reveals is especially disturbing because it is hidden under the saccharine religiosity and gentle loving-kindness which are so central to his self-image.

Similarly, Lewis warns us of his misogyny by loudly proclaiming his anger against women. Williams, on the other hand, offers women obeisance, gentle attention, and the appealing doctrines of co-inherence and exchange. Only later does one realize that in his system, the Goddess is a slave.

SIX

Escaping the Inner Void: The Early Novels of Graham Greene

Introduction: The Cracked Bell

Graham Greene, like the other two authors in this study, experienced the world as an evil and dangerous place in which constant vigilance was necessary for survival. However, Greene, unlike either Lewis or Williams, located the problem inside as well as outside of himself. A self-diagnosed manic-depressive, he frequently referred to himself as soiled goods or as a cracked bell, images which recur in his work to indicate a potentially fine man who has been damaged or destroyed by childhood trauma.[1] A hunted, guilt-ridden man like the many hunted and guilty men he created in his fiction, Graham Greene spent much of his life in efforts to outrun his pursuer—suicidal depression. When overtaken by "this horrid climbing down," Greene felt himself to be inhabited by a "wriggling germ of misery" (Sherry, 158, 276), a restless, depressive boredom which threatened, rather like Wyndham Lewis's inner volcano and Williams's explosive inner evil, to boil over or explode. Greene's frequent suicide attempts as a boy, the Russian roulette he resorted to as an adolescent and young man, his abasement at the altar of a loved woman and his conversion to Catholicism at her behest, his compulsive travel into dangerous and unknown places, and finally his many productions as a fiction writer, were all more or less adaptive ways of outrunning or staying one step ahead of this intolerable feeling.

Though Greene refers to isolation and loneliness, phobic terrors, guilt, and suicidal despair, he most frequently resorts to the word "boredom" to describes these states, a word which implies an absence of inner space or resources: an emptiness or void. Greene's chronic and torturous boredom is typical of Kernberg's narcissistic borderline personality, as is his nagging doubt and inferiority and his tendency to idealize women, then reject them when they become available. However, Greene lacks the grandiosity which allowed Lewis and Williams to picture the world as revolving around them. While neither Lewis nor Williams was capable of conceiving of other people as real, neither of them experienced their inability to connect as a problem. Greene, on the other hand, experienced a conscious and agonizing feeling of inauthenticity: "the desperate anguish of those who feel dead and empty, unable to connect to themselves or others" (Benjamin, 19). This sense of falseness and of alienation from a world which is morally as well as physically shabby and corrupt is the almost tangible atmosphere which all of Greene's characters inhabit, and which critics have named "Greeneland." Though outwardly empty, it is never a neutral space, but is instead constantly open to habitation by Greene's "Personal Evil . . . that sends those ghastly dreams and whispers things" (Sherry, 276).[2] This personal inner evil, which Greene called original sin after his conversion to Catholicism, is a corporeal quality which lives in, and is embodied by, the physical existence of the body: it is greedy and lustful, cynical in its needs, shameless, and selfish.

Greene is more explicit than the other authors about his traumatic childhood. As I will attempt to demonstrate in this chapter, this trauma had its roots in his headmaster father's obsessions about homosexuality and masculinity and originated even before Graham was sent as a boarder to his father's school, the event he identifies as the source of the trauma. At school, Greene was stigmatized for failing to live up to the requirements of the male gender role and was devalued as a male and consequently as a human being (Chodorow, 22). His resultant struggle to repudiate his own "feminine" attributes, and the ensuing "loss of inner space," were particularly fierce (Benjamin, 19). Not only is each man who lives in Greeneland pursued by his own inner emptiness and evil, he is also hunted by the constant threat to his precarious manhood. These two needs, to escape boredom and emptiness and to compulsively prove himself a man, were dominant and interlocking themes in Greene's life and in his early fiction. The betrayals, guilt, doubleness, cowardice, and sexual inadequacy common to the characters we will examine in the early novels are inevitably the results of failing to pass one or both of these tests. Greene's system can be seen as his attempt to outrun his two pursuing monsters.

This system, which divides the world into two as firmly as do Williams's and Lewis's systems, is recapitulated in some form in each of the five books I will examine here. In each one, a flawed young man, pursued by an internal or external bad father and struggling against his inner emptiness, is offered a choice of two worlds: a good one, exemplified by a the love of a virginal woman and a substitute or alternative good father, and an evil one, exemplified by a whore, a bad father, and in most cases, a Jew. In some cases this choice is coterminous with the test of masculinity the young man is set; in others the test undermines or opposes the choice. Greene's structure, like that of the other two authors, requires a strict splitting-off of the "woman" inside himself. For Greene, as for Williams, women are either virgins or whores. The whores, embodiments of selfishness, greed, and sinful lustfulness, often act in collusion with male Jews, who embody many of the same characteristics. The virgins, outwardly weak and self-sacrificing, exert deadly pressure on the hero by challenging him to pass the two tests of goodness and masculinity, and are almost inevitably punished for this by death. Greene's Jews, direct descendents of their literary forebears, share greed and perverse, lustful concupiscence with their colleagues, the whores. In addition they are avaricious, murderously knife-wielding, and cowardly. Together, the Jew and the whore tempt the hero into their world.

For each of the three authors, male Jews served as a receptacle for the parts of themselves they found most unacceptable and needed most to disown. Williams, who did not attend public school, felt comfortable with his less-than-macho image of saintly sweetness, but needed to disown his unacceptable aggression and sadism. His male Jews were consequently aggressive sadists in a strictly masculine vein. Lewis accepted and enjoyed his aggression, but felt terrified that he might prove insufficiently virile and "masculine." His Jews were impotent and effeminate cowards. Greene, like Lewis, experienced a constant struggle to maintain his masculinity, but, like Williams, found his own aggression and sexual rage unacceptable, experiencing himself as numb and empty rather than angry. His Jews combined cowardice and effeminacy with sexual lustfulness. The stereotype of the cringing, self-loathing hypersexual Jew fit well with the pervasive self-loathing which accompanied his depressions.

The Freikorpsmen destroyed the women they classified as whores and preserved those they classified as virgins. In Greene's early novels, by contrast, the virgins are allowed only a brief existence, while the whores and the Jews with whom they collude live on forever. But Greene understood that to split oneself in two and destroy the soft, feeling part is a kind of death. In killing off his good women, Greene simultaneously kills off his male heroes' only chance for goodness and for a life which contains the possibility of genuine feeling rather than emptiness, connectedness rather than alienation and solitude. Men are empty bubbles or balloons which can be filled only by women. When the good women are destroyed, the men are left to their own evil. In a world dominated by whores and Jews, the bubble will invariably be filled with evil and torment. The victimized man longs in vain for peace, but finds it only through the oblivion of sleep, drink, or death.

"Why Escape? Because I Don't Like Myself": The Early Life and Loves of Graham Greene

The Sources. Unlike Wyndham Lewis or Charles Williams, Graham Greene was fascinated by his own psychology and wrote several books in which he attempted to frame his life. *A Sort of Life*, (1971) and *Ways of Escape* (1980) are autobiographical sketches. *The Other Man* (1983) is a constructed text: a series of interviews with Greene by Marie-Françoise Allain, edited by Greene himself and mostly concerned with his past life.[3] Greene's travel books, *Journey without Maps* (1936) and *Lawless Roads* (1939), also offer important autobiographical material. Greene, who was a film buff and screenplay writer, textualizes memory as a series of illuminating images or flashbacks. The writing of *A Sort of Life*, the most revealing of the memoirs, was Greene's alternative to shock therapy during one of his acute depressions (*Other*, 17). In a description of the process of trying to recapture memory in order to write *A Sort of Life*, he remarks, "[T]he fragments remain fragments, the complete story always escapes" (*Sort*, 33). For that "complete story," at least of Greene's first thirty-five years, I was lucky to be able to refer to volume 1 of Norman Sherry's excellent and definitive biography, *The Life of Graham Greene* (1989). While it would have been possible, though more difficult, for me to write about Greene's childhood using only his own autobiographical material, Greene was careful to protect the people in his adult life and published no such in-depth record of his marriage and other adult relationships.

Sherry worked closely with Greene, and had access to his otherwise unpublished diaries and letters, and I depended on his book for my discussion of Greene's later life, in particular his early relationship with his wife. Graham Greene died as I completed one draft of this chapter, on April 2, 1991, at the age of eighty-six. Perhaps volume 2 of Sherry's biography will soon be forthcoming.

Greene often quoted the lines "In the childhood of Judas/ Christ was betrayed."[4] Born two decades after Lewis and Williams, into a generation which had begun to assimilate the Freudian view of human nature, he was a Catholic Freudian, whose belief that the experience of childhood determined adult character coexisted with his belief in original sin. In his famous essay on Dickens and Kipling, "The Burden of Childhood," he notes:

> There are certain writers . . . who never shake off the burden of their childhood. . . . All later experience seems to have been related to those months or years of unhappiness. Life, which turns its cruel side to most of us at an age when we have begun to learn the arts of self-protection, took these two writers by surprise during the defenselessness of early childhood.[5]

Greene was quite consciously speaking of himself as well as of Dickens and Kipling. In *A Sort of Life*, he describes Berkhamsted, the small town one hour from London where he grew up: "Everything one was to become must have been there, for better and for worse. . . . Here in Berkhamsted was the first mold of which the shape was to be endlessly reproduced" (15). While our knowledge of the multiple forces which shape personality makes it difficult to trace clear correlations between specific childhood experiences and later life, Greene's conviction that his *writing* at least stemmed from his early life experiences can indeed be borne out. It is possible to trace most scenes in the early fiction to his recorded childhood experiences, whether of dreams (after psychoanalysis at fourteen, he made a habit of recording them) or of waking reality. I am accordingly following Graham Greene's own lead in exploring his childhood as a source of the all-encompassing system that appears in his early novels. I will also describe Greene's courtship of his wife Vivien in some detail, as this information has, it seems to me, direct bearing on Greene's treatment of women and of romance in the early novels. For a complete and fascinating account of Greene as a writer and of other aspects of his first thirty-five years, I recommend the reader to Sherry.

The Burden of Childhood. Graham Greene was born in 1904, eighteen years after Charles Williams and twenty-two years after Wyndham Lewis. He was the fourth child in a family of six children. Of his birth, Greene's sister recalled, "My mother had a number of miscarriages and she had been appalled to find herself pregnant again" (Sherry, 3). Both of Greene's parents were from solid middle-class English families with long recorded lineages. His father, Charles Greene, was then housemaster of St. John's house, Berkhamsted School, where he would later hold the office of headmaster, and his mother, Marion Greene, was in charge of the house's catering. In *A Sort of Life*, Greene declares that his unhappiness began at thirteen, when he became a boarder at his father's public school. Before that, his life was "luminous with happiness." There could be "no loneliness to be experienced however occupied the parents might be," in a family of six children, numerous aunts and uncles, and many servants (72). In *The Other Man* too he recalls "only happiness, a state of contentment" (30). But these cheerful statements are undermined by the memories Greene records of his childhood before thirteen. "Unhappiness in a child accumulates," he writes, "because he sees no end to the dark tunnel" (*Sort*, 80). And "In childhood eternity has no meaning—a child has not learned to hope" (*Sort*, 61). It is most probable that despite the adult denial, Greene's despair and hopelessness were in evidence long before the disastrous boarding school experience. His statements echo those of the abused children studied by Alice Miller and by Davis and Bass: these children cannot acknowledge their own pain because it would mean blaming the parents on whom they are dependent for nurturance and survival. Greene avoided that blame through "identifying [himself] as bad" (cf. Bass and Davis, 42), through emotional numbing, and through a dualistic splitting of his childhood into a time of perfection while living with his parents and a time of hell after entering boarding school at thirteen.

Graham Greene's first memory is of sitting in a pram with a dead dog lying at his feet. His first recorded words, "poor dog," were connected to this incident (*Sort*, 17; *Journey*, 31). Although Greene recounts this image in at least five different places, he hastens to disown its effect on him: "There was no emotion attached to the sight. It was just a fact. At that period in life one has an admirable objectivity."[6] Another early memory which Greene reproduces over and over again in both his autobiography and his fiction is of a man "who rushed out of a cottage near the canal bridge and into the next house; he had a knife in his hand; people ran after him shouting; he wanted to kill himself" (*Journey*, 31). Later, Greene remembered the man as "having no hope and without God in the world."[7] Greene's own feelings of despair and isolation are evident in this early identification with a dead dog and a suicidal man.

For many young children, the mother is the source of warmth and comfort. Most upper–middle-class mothers at that time did not assume the primary care of their children, but Greene's shy and undemonstrative mother, Marion Greene, is described by family, friends, and schoolboys at Berkhamsted as "astonishingly remote," even by the standards of the day (Sherry, 46). While the emotional bond between Marion Greene and her fourth son was close in later life, her daughter describes her as a mother who never touched her children. Other respondents remember her as painfully awkward and silent in the presence of the husband to whom she was strongly bound, and who dominated her. In all of Greene's memories of his mother, a statement about her coldness is followed by a quick rebuttal in which he disowns her fault or disclaims his own pain. Thus, "I associate my mother with remoteness, which I did not at all resent" and with "a particular kind of wheaten biscuit with a very pale pure unsweetened flavor—I am reminded now of the Host—which only my mother had the right to eat" (*Sort*, 19). He remembers her "remoteness, her wonderful lack of the possessive instinct," which was achieved with the assistance of an old and bad-tempered nanny, who does not appear to have provided an alternative source of warmth or affection (*Sort*, 29). He tells Marie-Françoise Allain:

> My mother was very remote and showed no interest in our affairs. . . . You saw a little notebook in which she began noting down the age when I started to walk, my childhood illnesses, et cetera. She soon gave it up—I suppose it bored her. But I never suffered from her indifference. (*Other*, 32–33)

Sometimes the denial precedes the statement: "I was very fond of her, though I realized that I could go happily for months without seeing her" (*Journey*, 33).[8] The pattern of quick denial becomes apparent when we set the statements in two columns:

a remoteness	which I did not resent
a biscuit	which was pure/pale/unsweetened/ out of reach

her remoteness	her wonderful lack of possessive instinct
her boredom	I did not suffer from her indifference
I was fond of her	I could go for months without seeing her.

Like many children of that class and time, the six Greene children's only contact with their mother was on formal evening occasions; as Greene put it, "She paid occasional state visits to the nursery" (Sherry, 35). Of these visits, Greene remembers principally his dread of a story Marion Greene read about children whose parents had abandoned them: "[T]he murderer repented and left them to die of exposure and afterwards the birds covered their bodies with leaves. I dreaded the story because I was afraid of weeping" (*Sort*, 18).

Just as the adult Wyndham Lewis looked for women who would offer him the same unconditional and nonreciprocal nurturing that his mother had given him, the adult Graham Greene met women with all the force of his unrequited longing for his remote and idealized mother, as well as with his suppressed rage against her. For him, the only truly desirable woman was the unattainable one. Once he had won his object, his attention soon shifted. Greene identified his untouchable mother with the Virgin, and in his early novels he repeatedly idealizes, and then kills off, his young and untouchable virginal female characters. Like Wyndham Lewis, Greene continued to write letters to his mother throughout his adult life until her death. In an interesting parallel, as a young man at Oxford on a trip abroad, he too wrote to his mother describing a French matron who schemed to marry him to her daughter, describing himself as "a poor fly hopelessly entangled in the web, powerless even to struggle" (*Sort*, 136). Greene, like Lewis, saw women as dangerous and powerful victimizers and himself as the helpless victim. Also like Lewis, he felt the need to pledge his allegiance to his mother. But Greene's letter differs from Lewis's in its wistful tone. Commenting on it years later, he notes: "I had one respectable chance of adventure . . . someone at least had considered me old enough to marry" (*Sort*, 136). It is as though Greene must prove his desirability as a love object to the mother who never loved him enough. Greene's relationship to his mother can be described as a lifelong unfulfilled passion. He experienced her as remote, beautiful and out of reach, and always felt unable to live up to her impossibly high standards. He worshiped her, but resented her unavailability and coldness and what he experienced as the pressure of her judgmental purity. Like the other two authors in this study, Greene would be riven by the violent force of his need for women and his simultaneous rage against the objects of his dependence.

If Marion Greene's strongest bond was to her husband, Charles Greene was bonded as much to his school as to his wife. His son notes: "The only separation that really existed was from his children. As a headmaster, he was even more distant than our aloof mother" (*Sort*, 28). About his father, Graham told Allain, "I had no feeling. . . . He embodied Authority too much" (*Sort*, 28; *Other*, 33). In a recurrent dream after his father's death, Greene visualized him as "shut away in hospital out of touch with his wife and children—though sometimes he returned home on a visit, a silent, solitary man, not really cured, who would have to go back again into exile" (*Sort*, 27). In a denial similar to his reversals about his mother's remoteness, Greene adds, "There was no truth at all in the idea of his loneliness and unhappiness . . . perhaps the dreams show that I loved him more than I knew" (*Sort*, 28). In fact, the adult Greene was unable to experience any warmth for his father and cut off all communications with him until shortly before his death. The bell-jar vision of a man set apart from other humans, exiled and solitary, is an accurate psychological image not only of the father with whom he deeply identified but could not love but also of the son's feelings about himself.

Sherry's research is extremely helpful in understanding what went wrong between Graham Greene and his father. Through many interviews with former masters and students at Berkhamsted, Sherry established that the school Charles Greene ran was organized around one main principle: "to prevent the possibility of homosexual relationships developing" (40). While this principle was already in place when Charles Greene inherited the school from his predecessor, Dr. Fry; it matched Charles Greene's own obsessive hatred and fear of homosexuality and became an even more central theme under his control. A strong advocate of "muscular Christianity," with its emphasis on sports and cold showers, Charles Greene believed that homosexuality would occur, in former Berkhamstedian Claude Cockburn's words, "between any two boys who might conceivably be alone together for more than twenty minutes." He carefully organized the school in such a way that such a temptation could never appear (Sherry, 42). Boys could never be left alone either, as they would immediately begin to masturbate, an action which Charles Greene believed, with a fervor which belonged to a slightly earlier era, would lead directly to madness and perhaps to blindness as well. As a headmaster, Charles Greene was an authoritarian man whom respondents describe as ruthless in his pursuit of his "purity campaign," his ceaseless effort at "dampening down the sexual urge" (Sherry, 40). The boys at Berkhamsted were kept always in groups and constantly active, and Charles Greene set up a system of perpetual watchfulness, spying, and reporting.

The system was successful in that homosexuality was apparently unknown at Berkhamsted during Charles Greene's reign: as Sherry says, "It was one of the least corrupt of schools" (40). Of course, corruption may have many faces. Sherry's respondents speak of several boys who were mysteriously removed in the night after having been reported for masturbating and of one who received the same punishment after having been seen kissing a girl. On his last day at school, Charles Greene gave each boy a private lecture on keeping pure for their future wives. He regularly preached on "filthiness," and all respondents, even the most affectionate, agree that he was a man "obsessed."

It is not hard to imagine the effects of life with such a father on a sensitive boy who fainted at the sight of insects or blood, wept often, and was, by his own and all other accounts, quite outstandingly physically uncoordinated. Dorothy Dinnerstein discusses the tendency to "renounce the sensuous emotional world of early childhood, to seal off the layer of personality in which the primitive erotic flow between the self and the surround has its source" (32). This splitting off of the feminine or feeling part of himself, which all the object relations theorists have identified as one of the tasks and the dangers of growing up male in our society, became even more consuming for Graham Greene in the face of his father's obsession; an obsession Greene fought but was finally unable to escape.

While Greene only began to attend Berkhamsted as a boarder at almost fourteen, he attended the school as a day boy from the age of ten and encountered his father there as well as at home. In his essay on the public school as an institution in his collection of school memories, *The Old School*, Greene writes, "One is alternatively amazed at the unworldly innocence of the pedagogic mind and at its torturous obscenity."[9] As Sherry points out, "His criticism is of the system, but his father was in charge of that system" (88). Zoe Richmond, the wife of the analyst to whom Graham was sent after his suicide attempt and breakdown at school in 1921 at the age of sixteen, told Norman Sherry:

> His father had a frightful instinct against homosexuality. Graham wasn't homosexual but he was feminine. . . . To be sensitive is feminine. . . . In Graham's case he wanted to commit suicide in the end because he couldn't love himself or anybody else, and he was never openly loved and you see he was frightened of his own sensitivity. Lack of love creates the kind of disability Graham had. . . . His father was barmy. He had an obsession. (Sherry, 103)

Chodorow writes of the paramount importance the task of achieving adequate masculinity assumes in a male-dominated society in which, as in all societies, boys "begin life with a primary female identity." Just as Greene's later sense of alienation was in part an identification with or incorporation of his father's own emptiness and alienation, Greene incorporated his father's values and obsessive, dualistic system concerning women and sexuality and his father's negative judgment of his son's manhood. His sense of himself as a pursued, hunted man, an image which appears so often in his work, can be seen as an effort to outstrip this harsh parental condemnation, while the compulsive tests of manhood to which he subjected himself (and all his characters) contain many of the threatening questions Charles Greene must have posed to his "feminine" son. The desperate and lonely need to split off the inner female also became a major life theme for Greene, and one central to his texts.

Although it is difficult to determine the extent of this pattern, it is clear that one way this distant and authoritarian father did connect with his son was through beatings. Greene writes, "I have an impression my father used to smack me as a child," and remembers an incident of being beaten by him for calling his aunt a bugger, a name he did not understand; this "woke a sexual interest in me" (*Sort*, 34). He remembers another caning, in his nightshirt, for missing school. He describes his father in his role as headmaster caning a certain stigmatized 'house boy' in public "for some offense which was never made clear to any of us, but we were accustomed at that age to the moral confusion of adults and we didn't trouble to ask him the reason" (*Sort*, 49). The young men in Greene's early novels inevitably feel the same sense of an immoral and senseless world lacking in any kindness or reason. It is easy to understand the appeal of Catholicism to one whose experience of life fit the words of the blinded Gloucester in *King Lear*: "like flies to wanton boys are we t'the Gods, / they kill us for their sport" (4. 1. 36–37). In Greene's case, the gods were fathers, and many Catholic critics have been troubled by the malevolence of the Christian God he portrays.

While memories of beatings by his own father are vague, Greene recalls several other male adults (or "fathers") at the school who obtained sexual pleasure through beating children. One of these, Simpson (described in *The Lawless Roads* as a Mr. Cranden, with three grim chins and "a kind of demoniac sensuality"), obviously enjoyed beating his boys, who reciprocated in kind: "It seemed to me even then that his boys were collaborators in a pleasure" (*Lawless*, 4; *Sort*, 65). Greene also recalls another "anal flogger," his father's "sinister, sadistic predecessor," Dr. Fry (Sherry, 50, 59; *Sort*, 69). Greene's scathing portrait of Dr. Fry in *A Sort of Life* led to many angry letters from old Berkhamstedians who pointed out that Greene must have been fabricating, as Fry had left the school when he was still quite a young child. Very much like the old St. Cyprianite, who protested angrily at Orwell's unmasking of his school, writing "YOU SOD!" in the margin of his essay and calling the author of "Such, Such Were the Joys" "a wretched, sniveling little neurotic," these old Berkhamstedians accused Greene of lacking grit, letting the side down, and spitting into his own soup . . . ("schoolboys fart and what's the fuss about") (Sherry, 90).

Norman Sherry, unlike Orwell's biographer, Bernard Crick, feels no need to deny or denigrate his subject's story, but he does wonder at his venom toward Fry. Sherry identifies the source of Greene's information about Dr. Fry as his tutor at Oxford, who attended Berkhamsted during Fry's reign, and suggests that Greene's anger "is a reaction to his father's admiration of Fry and his perpetuation of Fry's traditions in the school" (51). I would go one step further and propose that Graham Greene's hatred of Dr. Fry was a transferral of his feelings for his own father, an unacceptable target for hatred.

"Memory," writes Greene, "is like a long broken night. As I write, it is as though I am waking from sleep continually to grasp at an image which I hope may drag in its wake a whole intact dream, but the fragments remain fragments, the complete story always escapes" (*Sort*, 33). Victims of childhood sexual abuse often remember—and forget—in just this way. Using similar imagery, Bass and Davis speak of the necessity of forgetting, of the vague and dreamlike sense of recovering occluded memories, and of the "constellation of feelings, reactions, and recollections" which come back in fragments as the adult begins to remember (22, 70–72).

Whether or not Charles Greene actually beat his son and obtained sexual enjoyment from this activity, or instead confined himself to the mental abuse of denigration and contempt, it is safe to conclude that Greene did suffer from humiliation at the hands of a father for whom he, like other abused children, still felt love and strong loyalty. Greene's conflicted feelings about his father emerge in the early novels in the many instances of the split between a good and bad father and in the portraits of abusive or condemnatory fathers who haunt their sons even after death.

His mother, strongly bonded to and dependent on her husband, seems to have remained silent. Alice Miller writes of the mother who

> watches her child being humiliated, derided, and tormented, without coming to his defense, without doing anything to save him. Through her silence she is in complicity with the persecutor; she is abandoning her child. . . . Perhaps this child will love his mother dearly on a conscious level; later, in his relationships with other people, he will repeatedly have the feeling of being abandoned, sacrificed and betrayed. (Miller, 192)

It is no wonder that Greene remembers fearing his mother's story of the children who had been abandoned by their parents. Greene dedicated *A Sort of Life*, the only book in which he describes his childhood at length, to his brothers and sister. The dedication reads: "For the Survivors, Raymond Greene, Hugh Greene and Elisabeth Dennys."

Just as the adult Greene assures his reader that neither his mother's indifference nor the dead dog in his pram bothered him, the child Graham struggled to conceal his tears at his mother's story, as well as his other feelings. These efforts to hide his feelings were part of the ongoing effort to suppress his "feminine" feeling self and to pass the test of manhood. They can also be seen as a way of achieving autonomy. Greene writes again and again of his efforts to protect himself by concealing his inner life from his parents. Even when he learned to read, he concealed this ability all summer, sure that it would be used against him (*Lawless*, 14).

The suppressed feelings, however, came out in other ways. From early childhood and all through his life, Greene suffered from recurrent nightmares. As a young child he also had numerous phobias, several of which also extended into adulthood. He feared drowning and burning, and even as an adult retained "a blinding terror," which he shared with his mother, of winged creatures, including birds, insects, bats, and moths (*Sort*, 31). The strength of this last phobia and its connection with sexuality are evident in the adult Greene's reflection: "Fear and the sense of sex are linked in secret conspiracy, but terror is a sickness like hate" (*Sort*, 31). The terror of birds, bats, and moths, with their furry or feathery bodies and brushing wings, emerged at night. So did the fear of another flying thing, a witch, which in nightmares "would leap on my back and dig long mandarin fingernails into my shoulders" (*Sort*, 32).[10] It is interesting that Charles Williams's uses the similar phrase "heart gripping fear" in his description of the malevolent transformation in *Witchcraft*.

Phobias, linked with depression and nightmares, are frequent in victims of sexual abuse. Phobic anxiety offers a means of control over pervasive anxiety through the displaced focus of that fear onto another object (Cameron and Rychlak, 197). While it is hard to say just what those winged creatures which came out at night to brush against Greene's face represented to him, it seems justified to conclude that they were symbols of forbidden sexuality—the sexuality which his father introduced to him as a terrible secret: filthy, obscene, and never to be acknowledged. Already in childhood, even worse than the phobias was boredom: "Boredom seemed to swell like a balloon inside the head; it became a pressure inside the skull; sometimes I feared the balloon would burst and I would lose my reason" (*Sort*, 120).

In a book review for the "Spectator" in 1933 when Greene was twenty-nine, he wrote:

> Against the background of visits to grandparents, of examinations and lessons and children's parties, the tragic drama of childhood is played, the attempt to understand what is happening, to cut through adult lies, which are not regarded as lies simply because they are spoken to a child, to piece together the scraps of conversation, the hints through open doors, the clues on dressing-tables, to understand. Your whole future is threatened by these lowered voices, these consultations . . . but you are told nothing, you are patted on the head and scolded, kissed and lied to, and sent to bed. (Sherry, 21–22)

Male children in Greene's fiction (there are no female children, just as there are almost no female Jews) are terrified victims, struggling to conceal their feelings from the cruel and arbitrary adult world which they can neither predict nor trust.[11] In fact, much of Greene's early fiction was based on his attempt to piece together the reality behind the lies, to understand the lost clues, and to reclaim the future threatened by his childhood.

Boarding School and Psychoanalysis. In chapter 2, in the section on the public school experience, I discussed the trauma Greene experienced when, at the age of thirteen, he crossed the green baize door which separated home from school. Greene described his father's school as "a savage country of strange customs and inexplicable cruelties, a country in which I was a foreigner and a suspect—a hunted creature." For him, boarding at his father's school was a savage initiation rite intended to "brainwash the primary feminine identity and to establish firmly the secondary male identity" (Chodorow, n. 23). While it succeeded in its aim, the cure almost killed the patient. Greene's experience at school was one of misery and betrayal, which he would attempt to exorcize in novel after novel.

While for some children with cruel fathers, going away to school meant a release into a more rational world than that of the family, for Graham Greene it meant entering into the heart of the familial terror, without the protection offered by mother, servants, brothers and sisters, and the freedom of a large house and grounds. To Greene, school represented his father's intrusion, contempt, and obsession personified in the body of an all-inclusive institution. The spying, the lack of privacy (low-walled cubicles separating beds, toilets without doors), and the whole "scatological world" of the school which Greene found so intolerable, were an intrinsic part of the the Fry-Charles Greene design. At his father's school, the privacy and autonomy Graham had so carefully guarded throughout his early childhood were deeply threatened. Hopeless at games, constrained by his phobias, the butt of bullies, and compared unfavorably to his successful cousin and to his athletic brother, the head prefect, the sensitive boy's confidence and self-concept as a viable male rapidly disintegrated.

At school, Graham's older brother Raymond was considered a fitting son for Charles Greene. As for Graham, in the words of J. B. Wilson, a schoolmate, "Raymond and Ben Greene [a cousin] held their own. They were perfectly normal as regards athletics and everything else. Graham was abnormal. There was no question about it" (Sherry, 70). Referring to men who had known him at school, Greene later wrote to his fiancée, Vivien Dayrell-Browning: "Do you slink by such people with an inferiority complex? I do. It's the one thing that it's impossible to forgive one's parents" (Sherry, 59).

The code of manhood, even more precious at this crisis, prohibited tears or complaint. While other boys could at least complain of school to their parents in letters, Graham's father *was* the school: there was no court of appeal. Like Orwell and many others, Greene felt abandoned by his mother when she allowed him to be sent to school. In his case, the sense of betrayal was even stronger: she had literally given her son up to his father. Other boys had each other. To bond with them against his father would have been, it seemed to the already guilt-ridden Graham, a dreadful betrayal of his family—a "spitting in his own soup" which would violate the precious code of manhood. In fact, it appears that Greene did confide in other boys from time to time, and suffered great guilt as a consequence. In *A Sort of Life*, he confesses that as a day student he "invent[ed] apocryphal stories of having been cruelly flogged" by his father. These stories may not, in fact, have been all that apocryphal (71). As a boarder, he confided in a boy called Watson, who passed his confidences on to Greene's particular torturer, Carter, whose sadomasochistic relationship with Greene I described in chapter 2. Carter "perfected during my fourteenth and fifteenth year a system of mental torture based on my difficult situation," and his sneering nicknames were like "splinters under the nails" (82). Carter, with his "genius for evil," is a recurrent figure who appears in many guises in Greene's novels (Sherry, 75). Even worse than the torture by Carter, which seems to have in some way met Greene's need for self-punishment, was the betrayal by Watson. The desire for revenge against him remained alive in Greene "like a creature under a stone," and he wondered "if I would ever have written a book had it not been for Watson and the dead Carter, if those years of humiliation had not given me an excessive desire to prove that I was good at something" (*Sort*, 82, 84).

The young Greene experienced betrayal by his mother and betrayal by Watson. In turn, he suffered from his own betrayal of his father. In addition, through his shameful vulnerability and his "feminine" misery and weakness at school, Greene felt that he had betrayed the precious values of masculinity which his father upheld and which Greene himself had so deeply internalized. Betrayal, a prominent feature of Greeneland, is stressed over and over again in his obsessive memories of this time.[12]

Greene's first year at school led to his first suicidal gesture, a bungled attempt to cut his leg. This was followed by "a hundred and four weeks of monotony, humiliation and mental pain" (*Sort*, 88). Afterward he made several more serious suicide attempts, involving swallowing aspirin and other medications, and finally ran away to Berkhamsted Common on the last day of the summer term, leaving a note sufficiently alarming to cause his parents temporarily to remove him from the school. For Greene, the experience as a boarder at his father's school was a traumatic event comparable to the trauma experienced by survivors of war, torture, or concentration camps. Symptoms of depression and anxiety, emotional anesthesia, hyperalertness and impulsive behavior, and recurrent dreams and nightmares are all characteristic of post-traumatic stress disorder (*DSM III*, 236).[13] They are also listed by Virginia Terr as symptoms suffered by the traumatized children in her study. Graham Greene suffered from all of these symptoms.

Greene's suicide threat and state of breakdown caused guilt and panic in his family. After finding him in the Common, Marion Greene moved to protect her son: "I put him to bed and told him he should never go back" (Sherry, 87). Greene remembers that his father interrogated him "seriously and tenderly" and concluded that his son's references to the school's "filth" meant that he had been the victim of a masturbation ring, after which "investigations were . . . set on foot among the innocent inhabitants of St. John's" (*Sort*, 92). As I have mentioned, Charles Greene believed that masturbation led to madness. He also feared the mental illness which existed on both sides of the family. Graham's elder brother Hugh, who was studying medicine at that time, was consulted, and recommended psychoanalysis. Fortuitously, Graham was sent to live in London with Kenneth Richmond, a benign Jungian analyst, and his wife Zoe.

Greene later described his time with the Richmonds as "a choice for which I have never ceased to be grateful . . . the happiest six months of my life" (*Sort*, 98). The Richmonds were loving and expressive people who believed that sexuality was pleasurable rather than sinful and that men could show their feelings without turning into women. As parents they were guided by the principle that children should not be thwarted. Every morning Kenneth Richmond listened to Graham's dreams, and the two of them together attempted interpretations. For the rest, he was allowed the freedom to roam London on his own and provided with privacy, comfort, warmth, and love. During this time, Greene began the dream diary which he would keep all his life and which he would use as an important tool in his writing. The Richmonds valued their protégé's intellect and sensitivity, and validated his wholeness rather than forcing him to split parts of himself off. As Greene wrote about this second "good" father, "He patiently waited for me to discover the long road back to myself" (Sherry, 102).

Greene was by no means "cured." Depression, self-loathing, and the inability to conceive of or relate to women as real people would continue to haunt him. But the experience with the Richmonds may well have saved his life, and certainly influenced him to become a writer. On his return to Berkhamsted a year later, he was allowed to live at home and was able to resist the pressure of his father's school.[14] He went on to Oxford, where he made friends and began to write and publish. Greene later claimed that his treatment did not go deep enough. He also suggested that it was the psychoanalysis which caused a kind of numbness which left him unable to appreciate visual or sensory experiences. In fact, "emotional anesthesia" is one of the effects of unacknowledged abuse and one of the most prominent features of post-traumatic stress disorder. In addition, as we have seen, Greene's emotional numbness was a way in which he cut off or disowned his "feminine" self and his unacceptable anger. Just as Lewis blamed psychoanalysis, which he had never experienced, for his uncomfortable closeness with his mother, Greene in this case found an easy scapegoat for a deep symptom.

Alice Miller comments that children who have suffered the effects of unacknowledged abuse during their own childhood often exhibit "an astonishing lack of sensitivity to other children's suffering" (115). This seems to have held true for Greene when it came to his own children. Sherry comments that he "never relented in his opposition to public schools . . . though extraordinarily he sent his own son Francis to one" (107). Greene's detachment toward his children was much like his mother's toward him. In 1981, he described his younger sister and brother as the two family members to whom he still felt close. When Allain asked, "And your children?" he responded: "I think my books are my children. . . . I'm very fond of my son and daughter, but just as I don't want my parents meddling in my private life, I didn't want to intrude into theirs" (*Other*, 35).

Courtship and Marriage

Greene found the experience of unfulfilled longing agonizing, and yet he needed it in order to feel love. Once a woman became available, he no longer desired her. When he was in love, he felt his own boundaries weaken and sometimes disappear, a sensation he found both terrifying and erotic. Benjamin writes that the man who is cut off from the maternal source of goodness and "feels excluded from the feminine world of nurturance" loses access to his own inner space:

> He is thrown back into feeling that desire is the property of the object. . . . His experience parallels woman's loss of sexual agency. The intense stimulation from outside robs him of the inner space to feel desire emerging from within—a kind of reverse violation. (164)

When in the throes of an intense and passionate dependence on a loved woman, Greene was no more able to feel hostility toward her than he had been able to feel angry at his inaccessible mother. Unlike Lewis and Williams, he projected his hostility inward rather than outward at the woman in question, who remained an unreal but worshiped icon. At the same time, however, he directed great contempt and anger against other "whorish" women.

At nineteen, on holiday from Oxford, Greene fell in love with Gwen Howell, his sister and brother's governess who was already engaged to be married. "It was an obsessive passion," he remembers, "I lived only for moments with her" (*Sort*, 125). Kernberg's borderline patients, like Greene, found relief from their chronic and tormenting boredom in idealized passions. When the idealization broke down, they were again prey to their own emptiness. Greene's passion for Gwen Howell managed to "temporarily ease the burden of boredom," but when she rejected him, the old condition returned in full force: "boredom, as deep as the love and more enduring" (*Sort*, 128–29). Greene's solution was to take a loaded revolver to the same common to which he had run away as a child, and play Russian roulette. Upon beating the odds he felt "an extraordinary sense of jubilation . . . like a young man's first successful experience of sex . . . as if one had passed a test of manhood."[15]

The longing for a woman provided a badly needed respite from his habitual boredom, but it was also a profoundly unmanning experience which brought Greene into contact with his "female" neediness and vulnerability and took him back to the helplessness of his unmothered and unprotected childhood. Rejection, painful for anyone, was for him almost unbearable. The "revolver trick" gave him the kind of control that many suicidal people feel: in playing with death, he asserted control over his own life. Greene took the revolver back to Oxford with him and played this game of manhood five more times before he gave up the drug for the less dangerous drug of travel to unmapped and often dangerous areas of the world. The "revolver trick" retained its significance for him, however. He described it in all his memoirs and often referred to it in his letters to his new love.

Greene met Vivien Daynell-Brown in 1925 while still at Oxford and courted her during the period of his abortive plan to go to China with the British American Tobacco Company, then through his fledgling career as a reporter in Nottingham and as a subeditor for the *Times*.[16] During the courtship, he repeatedly wrote to Vivien telling her of her power over him. At times he used the metaphor of one of his phobias, drowning:

> Loving you is like being drowned in a moment of ecstasy, during a clean swift stroke, when the whole arc of blue is caught up by the eye, & death comes and . . . there is to be no awakening. (Sherry, 219)

"My mind's like a bubble," he wrote in 1925, employing one of his frequently used metaphors for his feeling of emptiness:

> [I]t's getting bigger and bigger & if it it bursts I feel I shall simply shriek and shriek and not be able to stop. . . . It's been your last two letters. I felt that . . . you were feeling less fond of me than ever before and the bubble gets bigger & I want, oh God how I want to be dead, or asleep or blind drunk or anything. (Sherry, 220)

Greene's letters to Vivien do give the impression of a drowning man, hastening toward his fate. For the most part, he idealizes her, calling her a saint and endowing her with life-giving nurturing qualities. His picture of marriage, as Sherry points out, has a distinctly nursery flavor, and, as in his feeling toward his unavailable mother, his rage at Vivien's power over him occasionally surfaced. "It must be rather fun collecting souls, Vivienne. Like postage stamps," he wrote to her in 1925 (Sherry, 185). In a poem similar to one he wrote to Gwen Howell, and prefacing the doom of so many of his female heroines, he romantically pictured Vivien's death and his release. Over and over again, he shamefully acknowledged his desperate need: "I want you to come so frightfully badly, & I'm ashamed of myself. I didn't think I'd ever need any one so badly" (Sherry, 186).

Even though Vivien to some extent reciprocated his love, this did not relieve the pain. His mood swung dangerously between elation—"the absolute pinnacle of happiness"—and depressions during which he repeatedly became suicidal and felt himself "falling over the edge" (Sherry, 196). Because Vivien was a Catholic and disapproved, he swore not to resort to his two usual cures for depression, drink and Russian Roulette. He did have a tooth out to obtain "a few minutes unconsciousness... a holiday from the world. I had lost a good tooth, but the boredom was for the time dispersed" (Sherry, 217). In a poem, Greene calls on God, addressing him as "Constable" and "Sergeant," and asks him to "bring your own manacles and handcuff me" (Sherry, 187). Toward Vivien he is pleading and subservient, referring to himself as a cracked bell and soiled goods, and telling her, "You are so wonderful & I'm so paltry. I crawl about on the ground" (Sherry 188, 218). He claimed again and again, "I'll do anything you want" (192). This assertion proved far from hyperbolic. When Vivien mentioned fears of sex, he offered a celibate marriage, telling her, "I am perfectly prepared to sacrifice one bit of one part of my love" (Sherry, 201). Finally, when Vivien reasoned that she, as a devout Catholic, could not marry him as a Protestant, Greene received instruction in the Catholic faith and converted to Catholicism in 1926.

Greene at first conceived of his Catholicism as a sacrifice to win Vivien, but it soon became deeply important to him. Although Catholic critics like Martin Turnell have criticized his morbid emphasis on original sin and his many portraits of sinful and immoral Catholic characters, and have claimed that Greene is not in fact a "true" Catholic writer, Catholicism was an important bulwark in Greene's inner struggle. It provided him with a stern prohibition against suicide, always a constant temptation for him. It gave him an internalized loving God who could at least argue with his internalized harsh father, and it provided firm boundaries in a world whose moral void seemed to match his own inner emptiness.

The need for a religion which could provide boundaries grew as the relationship with Vivien progressed. "I have been made of your breath," he wrote to her. "If you didn't exist... I should vanish in a breath of mist" (Sherry, 203). In 1927, shortly before their marriage, he wrote:

> You've chipped me about and added and taken away in the most wholesale and reckless fashion . . . I'm quite muddled myself not knowing what's me and what's you. . . . We've got too hopelessly mixed up with each other for anything short of death to untwist it all . . . so prepare to be sacrificed on the altar of matrimony. (Sherry, 291–92)

The marriage was temporarily called off when a doctor misdiagnosed Greene with epilepsy (in fact, he had always been subject to fainting fits at the sight of blood or when in contact with his other phobic objects), and Greene was subject to last minute hesitations in which he wondered if they should marry after all ("sometimes I think you are too fine for love"). But Vivien remained cool and somewhat unavailable and in this way secured Greene's interest. The two were married in 1927. In a letter to Vivien before his wedding, Greene evoked the "hoards of disapproving faces" which he believed would haunt their wedding. Again avoiding any direct mention of his father, he quoted a poem on Stonehenge:

> They sit there forever on the dim
> horizon of my mind, that Stonehenge circle of elderly disapproving faces
> Faces of the Uncles & Schoolmasters who frowned on my youth.[17]

While Greene had soon given up the idea of a celibate marriage, his textual separation of women into the sacred and the profane extended to his life. He protested when Vivien claimed that men married "for animality": "there's really no more connection with animality than the thin connection between an uneducated drunkard's lewd scribble on a patch of wall & a Velasquez." His adoration of her as a fine work of art did not mean turning his back on the "lewd scribble" (Sherry, 294). During his courtship and even soon after his marriage, he and his cousin regularly went to brothels in London and Paris. Greene seemed to assume that virtue lay not in abstention from this kind of activity but in keeping it separate from his relationship with Vivien. In a prenuptial letter to Vivien, he assured her, "My peccadilloes, darling, shall be kept in Paris" (Sherry, 293).

While little information exists at this time on Greene's marriage and on his later relationships with other women, we do know that, although as Catholics the Greenes were not permitted to divorce, estrangement and eventual separation followed a short initial period during which he and his wife were completely inseparable. Sherry suggests that close contact with Vivien in the isolated cottage where the two of them lived when

Greene was still struggling as a writer "seemed to reduce his reverence for her. She was perhaps no longer 'all beauty and all mystery and all wonder' " (Sherry, 444). Greene never took his wife along on any of his voyages, which often included extramarital romances, and in 1977 Vivien Greene told Norman Sherry resentfully about being left alone in unsuitable places while Graham went off and had adventures: "With hindsight she felt that Greene was a person who should never have married" (Sherry, 665). During the course of his life, Greene had several famous mistresses, and the mourners at his death included his estranged wife, his two children, and his mistress of many years, the married Frenchwoman Yvonne Cloetta.

Politics and Jews

It is difficult to assess Greene's attitude toward Jews outside of the evidence of his fiction because of the absence of references to them in his autobiographical work and in Sherry's biography. The small evidence that does exist suggests that in his youth he shared the dominant unreflective anti-Semitism of his times. On the other hand, he was among the earliest to take a strong stand against fascism, and during the war, while his novels continued to reflect his unconscious anti-Semitism, his public stance was one of strong condemnation of the Nazi persecution of Jews.

Greene's film reviews reflect his ambivalence in this area. In a *Spectator* film review of 5 June 1936, he echoes Lewis's view of the film industry as "an ignoble gang of foreign, semitic 'gutter-people' " (Cunningham, 281). Greene writes: "Watching the dark alien executive tipping his cigar ash behind the glass partition in Wardour Street . . . I cannot help wondering whether from this great moneyed industry anything of value to the human spirit can ever emerge" (Cunningham, 281). Just four months earlier, however, in March 1936, he had criticized a Polish film, *The Day of the Great Adventure*, because of its fascist quality: "the Boy Scouts' 'handsome brutish faces,' their Aryan righteousness and flag-waving purity, were just Hitlerite, Greene thought" (Cunningham, 185).

Unlike Lewis, who was an open Mosleyite, and Williams, who believed that Jews must be regarded as Christ-killers who had earned whatever persecution they got, Greene was horrified by Mosley and by the police protection offered to his supporters. And unlike Lewis's, Williams's, and many right-wing Anglo-Catholics' early support of Hitler, Greene's reaction to Nazism was unambiguous and swift. "Sometimes it's impossible not to choose one's sides, as in the last war against Hitler," he told Allain (*Other*, 80); and Rosenberg and Fiedler both mention his defense of the Jews in his wartime radio broadcasts and reporting (Rosenberg, 300; Fiedler, 415). For Greene, the concentration camps proved the existence of pure evil, and after the war he became a longtime friend of the Israeli government. While he recently criticized Israeli policy, he never withdrew his strong support of Israel's right to exist (*Other*, 148).

Greene does not mention the treatment of his Jewish characters in any of his own harsh critiques of his early books and makes no explicit textual apology for, or acknowledgment of, his own anti-Semitism. However, when his early novels, which had originally been published by Heinemann, were reprinted by Penguin after the war, he quietly made several significant alterations in them. The most notable of these is the transformation of the criminal gang-leader Colleoni, a Jew in the 1938 edition of *Brighton Rock*, to an Italian in the Penguin edition of 1943. Less evident textual changes are also present in the postwar editions of *Stamboul Train* and *A Gun for Sale*. (These novels, first published by Heinemann in 1932 and 1936, respectively, were issued by Penguin in 1963.) For instance, he repeatedly changed the word "Jew" to "man" in both of these books.[18] These linguistic changes, which do not alter the deeper level of anti-Semitism in the novels, are more indicative of Greene's awareness that he has offended and of his willingness to make textual reparations than of any deep or major change in his attitude.

Perhaps despairing of the possibility of getting it right, Greene virtually stopped using Jewish characters in his later novels, and the only Jewish portraits in his autobiographical writing seem designed to counter the image of the cowardly, gesticulating, and boastful Jew we meet in early Greene. In 1971, for example, he describes "our old Jewish post warden, powerful and imperturbable in his shiny black mackintosh, like a moving statue in malachite, the stone catching the reflection of the flames and flares, one of the bravest men I have known and the most unaware of his own courage" (*Sort*, 87).

While the evidence regarding the younger Greene and Jews is sparse, we do know that as a young man, between the ages of twenty-one and thirty-four, when he wrote the books under discussion, Greene's need to outrun his depression and escape his emptiness took precedence over any more reasoned political stance. In 1924, while still at Oxford, he volunteered to be a courier-spy for a French nationalist separatist organization attempting to set up a separate republic in the Ruhr, one of the occupied zones of Germany. Greene and his friend Claude Cockburn volunteered to spy on the French for the German Secret Service, and Greene reported on this (fortunately aborted) adventure for the notoriously right-wing and anti-Semitic journal *The Patriot*. Greene recalled this episode in 1971: "Today I would have scruples about the purpose I served, but at that age I was ready to be a mercenary in any cause so long as I was repaid with excitement and a little risk" (*Sort*, 143). Some of his unthinking immorality of that time, which could include both racism and misogyny, is evident in an aside about the spying episode: at Bonn, the two young men "encouraged by the atrocity stories we had heard in Cologne . . . followed innocent Senegalese soldiers in the hope of seeing a rape" (*Sort*, 142). Greene's membership in the Communist party for four weeks in 1923 while he was at Oxford was an equally immature action, motivated not by belief but by his desire for free travel to the Soviet Union.

For Greene, a subeditor at the *Times* at twenty-two, the General Strike of 1926 was a game which had been arranged in order to keep him from his dread boredom and a prime chance to assert his masculinity. In 1971, forty-five years later, he remembered the atmosphere of the strike as that of "a rugger match played against a team from a rather rough council school which didn't stick to the conventional rules" (*Sort*, 178). He was a member of the *Times* "shock troops" and also volunteered to be a special constable. Later he remembered doing all this "more from curiosity than from any wish to support the Establishment. . . . A few years later my sympathies would have lain with them [the strikers]" (*Sort*, 177–78). His letters to Vivien during the strike are unusually happy. "I'm feeling fearfully glad to be alive," he told her. "Everything fearfully exciting" (Sherry, 299). He wished for "a little bit of civil war" and enjoyed the "sinister strain" which reminded him of his spying trip to the Ruhr. "I'm rather sorry that it's over," he wrote home when the strike ended (Sherry, 299).

This moral irresponsibility seems to have been restricted to the period of Greene's youth. He liked to talk about the "splinter of ice in the heart of a writer," comparing himself with Little Kay, the boy in Hans Christian Andersen's "The Snow Queen," who has a splinter of ice in his heart and cannot feel. In fact, writing was the method he found to thaw out his frozen and empty inner space and to learn to feel for others (*Sort*, 188). Greene writes again and again of the therapeutic effects of writing. When he "began to write . . . the past lost some of its power—I wrote it out of me" (*Sort*, 83). Writing served him as an escape, as therapy, and as a way to work through old pain. A highly disciplined writer, he learned to use even his depression as copy. In *A Sort of Life*, he explains with great dignity his choice of avoiding irony in writing about the past and his decision to treat his child-self with empathy and love rather than with distance or shame: "Those emotions were real when we felt them. Why should we be more ashamed of them than of the indifference of old age?" (*Sort*, 12).

In his mid-thirties, Greene began increasingly to transform the trauma of his childhood into responsible social action. While he still felt the compulsive need to confront danger as a way to prove his masculinity and to escape boredom, he replaced his random travel to dangerous places (the activity which had replaced his games of Russian roulette) with travel to countries under oppressive regimes, which he would then challenge in books and articles. He became known for his bravery in exposing the regimes he found in Haiti, Nicaragua, Vietnam, and South Africa. Never a doctrinaire Marxist, he became known as a defender of the victimized and the oppressed. As he wrote of the responsibility of the writer, "He stands for the victims and the victims change" (*Other*, 80).

The undeniable anti-Semitism in the early novels must be seen, then, as the production of a young and troubled man. For that young man, as for Williams and Lewis in their maturity, the Jew offered a convenient symbolic receptacle into which to deposit his split-off pain and self-loathing.

Earliest Novels: Self-Loathing Enthroned

Modern Appraisal. Both Rosenberg and Fiedler single Greene out as one of the most anti-Semitic of the modern generation of writers, but both point out the split between his actions and his textual representation. Fiedler, for example, refers to "Graham Greene who writes publicly against the persecution of the Jews, [but] peoples his works with Jews unfailingly sinister: creatures lost to the spirit, devoted only to things" ("Fagin," 415). As I have noted above, Greene stopped using Jewish characters in his novels after 1938. The sinister creatures both critics refer to are accordingly all found in the novels written between 1929 and 1938. I will focus on four of those novels here.

Unlike contemporary reviewers, who praised *The Man Within* (1929) and either disregarded or denigrated *The Name of Action* (1930), modern critics unanimously classify both of these early books as literary failures which helped Greene along on his way to novelistic maturity. Allot and Farris point out in these early novels a "lack of psychological distance" which gives us as readers "the feeling that the author is too personally involved."[19] They especially remark the peculiarity of Greene's attitude toward sexual love. While they note that this "fear of the body" will remain a constant in Greene's later fiction, they find it especially "contaminates" the early books (45, 236–37). They feel that the female characters in these books fail because of "a young man's absorption in the 'otherness' of women" and mention "the remarkable polarity of attraction and repulsion that the sexual act has for his characters and the fixity of the separation he makes between desire and affection" (44–45). Martin Turnell shares this perception. He writes of Greene's "defective attitude toward sexuality," finds in it "something obsessive, something unbalanced," and "cannot remember a single instance of a really satisfactory [sexual] connection" in these early novels.[20]

Norman Sherry describes Greene's early novels as "indulgent and romantic" self-portraits: "There is too much self-love, too little self-criticism in these early portraits of pleasant, anguished young men built up from Greene's own notion of himself as a young man romantically caught in the toils of love" (411). While I agree that *The Man Within* and *The Name of Action* are romantic, I find the self-portraits in these books neither self-satisfied nor pleasant. In my view, *The Man Within* and *The Name of Action*, as well as the later and more assured *Stamboul Train* (1932), are about self-loathing, not about self-love.

For Greene, who needed to "re-earn his maleness every day" (Chodorow, 40), the choice to be a novelist, a profession which is not culturally defined as strongly masculine, was a risky one. In addition, Greene's choice to leave his well-paying job on the *Times* in order to write fiction entailed a financial risk. For his early productions, he chose traditionally male popular genres: adventure novels and thrillers. *The Man Within* and *The Name of Action* are historical adventure narratives which depend heavily on plot and contain plenty of "male" action (spying, the shipment of arms, revolution, war, shooting, rapes, and seduction). Greene labeled the other three books under discussion, *A Gun for Sale*, *Stamboul Train*, and *Brighton Rock*, "entertainments," to distinguish them from his more serious novels. However, unlike more traditional samples of these genres, Greene's books do not rely on chance occurrences or mysterious conundrums. Instead, as in Shakespearian tragedy, the action of the plot is propelled by the characters' psychology—in particular by their failings. The real suspense lies in the question of whether a given protagonist will pass or fail the tests of manhood and of morality. Greene's choice of form, like Lewis's and Williams's, reflects his personal system. His choice of genre classified him as a decidedly "male" writer. The concentration on his protagonists' psychological failings reveals his own obsessional self-doubt and self-analysis.

"His Father Was His Lust": The Man Within. Greene began *The Man Within*, his third novel and the first one published, in 1926, when he was twenty one, during his courtship of Vivien. The novel was published in 1929. Unlike *The Name of Action*, which he omitted from the later edition of his collected works, Greene allowed *The Man Within* to be reissued as an author's "sentimental gesture toward his own past, the period of ambition and hope."[21] Part of Greene's fond memory for his first published novel and second published book (he had previously published a collection of verse) has to do with its reception. *The Man Within* was a publishing success, and received superlative reviews in both Britain and the United States. Greene was hailed as a rising talent and a new literary light. As a result of this acclaim, he decided that he would be able to make his living as a writer and gave up his job as a subeditor on the *Times*, a move he would regret deeply upon the failure of his next two novels. In 1971 Greene called *The Man Within* "young and very sentimental . . . the book of a complete stranger" (*Sort*, 197). Despite this disclaimer, the novel's themes were far from strange to Greene. The book contains no Jewish characters, but it encodes the system which will be repeated in the other three novels I will discuss in this chapter and is worth examining for that reason.

The Man Within is set on the Sussex Downs around 1850, although the historical and descriptive details are vague and it could take place anywhere and at almost any time. We learn that after the death of his father, the leader of a band of smugglers, young Francis Andrews, was rescued from his hated boarding school by Carlyon, his father's kindly friend, and adopted into the smugglers' band. The book begins some years later, after Andrews, driven by hatred of his father, has informed on Carlyon and the other smugglers in the band. A hunted man, he arrives at a deserted cottage where a pure young woman, Elizabeth, is standing watch over the body of her dead guardian. They fall in love, and Elizabeth persuades him to agree to testify against the smugglers in court. When he arrives there he meets Lucy, the prosecuting lawyer's young mistress, who, in order to help the prosecutor, also pushes Andrews to testify, bribing him with the promise of sex. Andrews testifies against his former friends, who are, however, acquitted by a jury of their countrymen. He spends the night with Lucy, then belatedly returns to Elizabeth, and the two of them renew their vows. On a trip to the pump for water, he hears one of the vengeful smugglers entering the cottage where she is waiting for him alone. Instead of returning to protect her, the cowardly Andrews runs away, and the smuggler attempts to rape Elizabeth. By the time Andrews returns, she has stabbed herself to death rather than submit. When the police arrive, Andrews assuages his guilt by saving Carlyon, who has by now appeared on the scene and is under suspicion, by himself confessing to her murder.

When we first meet Andrews he is already a "sort of Judas," whose acts of betrayal stem from his need to get revenge on his abusive father, a need which, like Greene's own, has remained "alive like a creature under a stone" (*Sort*, 82). Andrews's father was "dominating, brutal, a conscious master, not chary of his blows to either child or wife . . . dominant, easily aroused, ready . . . with the whip" (*Man*, 59, 33).

Andrews is especially enraged by the dichotomy between his father's public and private selves, his own inability to live up to his father's image, and the necessity he has felt to uphold the lie. "His crew worshipped him," he tells Elizabeth:

> [A]ll the time I was at sea, I could see how they wondered that such a mountain could bring forth such a mouse. . . . You can't understand what life was like with these men. I could do nothing which was not weighed up with my father and found wanting. They kept telling me of his courage. . . . And I knew all the time things they didn't know, how he had beaten my mother, of his conceit, his ignorance, his beastly bullying ways. (*Man*, 73)

"Life with those men" on the ship which had been ruled by his father, where Andrews "was afraid of being hurt" and hated the noise and the danger, is a clear transposition of Greene's life in the school his father ran. The sensitive, awkward, and "abnormal" mouse-son of the mountain-headmaster had also felt that he could never do anything which was not "weighed up with my father and found wanting." Like Andrews, Graham was forced to listen to such unflattering comparisons in silence, unable to betray his father as a "beastly bully." Like Andrews's, Graham's secret festered. Even his father's death could not rid him of "the schoolmasters and the uncles," whose "circle of disapproving faces" would, he was sure, curse his wedding day. "I thought my father was dead," Andrews tells Elizabeth, "but I soon found that he had followed me on board" (76). Andrews's father, a hero to the crew, had "killed his wife and ruined his son through his abuse." Andrews uses his precious moment in court to testify against him:

> It was because I had a father whom I hated and he was always being put before me as a model. It made me mad. And I'm a coward. . . . Unless I did something it would have gone on for always and always. And I wanted to show those men that I was someone to be considered, that I had the power to smash all their plans. (153)

Andrews's statement, "Unless I did something it would have gone on for always and always," painfully echoes Greene's two statements about the special vulnerability of the child, who has no concept of time: "Unhappiness in a child accumulates because he sees no end to the dark tunnel" and "[A] child has not learned to hope" (*Sort*, 80, 61). When Greene at first attempted suicide by swallowing medications and deadly nightshade, and later ran away to the Common, leaving a note threatening suicide if he should be made to return to school, he too felt the need somehow to take an action, however shameful, which would put an end to his pain. Andrews's self-condemnation, "I'm a coward," as well as his cowardly escape during Elizabeth's rape, reflects Greene's own shame at his childhood vulnerability, and especially the deep shame he felt about his act of fleeing. Andrews's need to "show those men" has its parallel in Greene's need to become a famous writer and thus prove to the schoolmates who despised him "that I was good at something" (*Sort*, 84).

When Carlyon comes to tell him of his father's death, he asks Andrews why he has not left the school he hates. "It's worse at home," Andrews answers. "My mother's dead." When the young Graham ran away from his father's school, he could not run home either. His father was there as well as in school, while his mother's lack of support made her "dead" in terms of her ability to protect him. Graham ran instead to the Common behind both school and home. He, like Andrews, was removed to the care of a benign substitute father, Kenneth Richmond, whose treatment enabled him to "look under the stone less and less often until when he finally raised it he realized that nothing was there" (*Sort*, 82–84).

In later life, Greene's memories of his father are quite mild, but he accused Kenneth Richmond of causing his psychological numbness. For Graham, as for Andrews, the good father arrived too late. The damage, though not fatal in Graham's case as in the case of his fictional representative, Andrews, had been done. As Alice Miller writes of Hitler's father's death: "When Adolf's father died, he had already long since been internalized by the son" (168). After Andrews finds Elizabeth dead, he kneels by her body:

> Was there anything of himself that was not his father? His father was his lust, and his cowardice had been fashioned by his father. (*Man*, 241)

At the end of the book, Andrews works out a "plan for dealing with his father" which will force "his father's spirit to [shrink] into a small space leaving Andrew's own brain more clear and simple than he had ever known it" (239). This plan is his decision to turn himself in for a crime he did not commit but for which he knows he will be hanged; in other words, to commit suicide. If Greene had been forced to stay on at school instead of being sent to live with the Richmonds, his own solution may well have been similar.

"His father was his lust," Andrews realizes. The splitting of the two female characters in *The Man Within* into a sacrificial virgin and a destructive and indestructible whore reflects both the need to split off his own feeling or female self and the inability to regard women as whole people, two legacies Charles Greene bequeathed to his son. This binary opposition also reflects Greene's longing for and idealization of his unattainable mother, and his simultaneous split-off, denied anger at her lack of warmth and protection. As the hunted Andrews runs from his pursuers in the beginning of the book, he longs for an older woman to take him in and act as his confessor. She would open the door and be "like a mother to him."[22] Instead there is a peer, Elizabeth, mother and beautiful virgin in one, who has the power to transform Andrews from a corrupt and cowardly criminal to a man capable of good. Elizabeth is described throughout in remote, ethereal images of light. When drunk, Andrews visualizes her as "a saint surrounded with white birds." She is scarcely allowed a corporeal frame: her body is "a fragile and beautiful casing, which just succeeded in enclosing her lightly poised spirit." He declares, "I don't believe that any man will ever touch her" (107). Elizabeth's remote, white goodness is reminiscent of Greene's symbol for his mother: that pale pure unsweetened biscuit which no one else was allowed to eat, with its associations to the Host.

Like Vivien, Elizabeth returns Andrews's declaration of love, but withholds sex until they are married. She also offers him protection: "I will stand now for ever between you and them" (209). In a paroxysm much like the letters Greene wrote to Vivien, Andrews declares his dependence on her, and his corresponding loss of self:

> You must stay with me always. You must not die before me. If you did I should fall away. It would be worse than before if I should lose you now. . . . You must possess me, go on possessing me, never leave me to myself. (209, 212)

Not surprisingly, Andrews fears this love which is "so strong that I feel that it could fling me at any moment into Heaven or Hell." He tells her, "You are filling me with yourself. That means courage, peace holiness," but he seems far from peaceful (207). In a somewhat hostile leap into the future, he imagines her in childbirth: "It must bring you pain" (211). A few hours later he leaves her in the cottage to be attacked. The virgin has been punished, not by a future painful childbirth, but far more quickly and more efficiently.

No such fate is allotted to Lucy, the manipulative and knowing whore who is the object of Andrews's immoral lust. Andrews recognizes in her his own "lustful body and despicable heart" and thinks, "I could make her wriggle" (117). He damns himself for a swine for his desire for Lucy but realizes that he wants her as he cannot want the untouchable Elizabeth:

> Never before had he desired a woman so much—no, not Elizabeth. There was a kind of mystery in Elizabeth, a kind of sanctity which blurred and obscured his desire with love. Here there was no love and no reverence. The animal in him could ponder her beauty crudely and lustfully . . . with the added spice of a reciprocated desire. (129)

In Greene's system, mothers and virgins, by their very nature, cannot feel lust or reciprocate desire. They are holy, but not very sexy. On the other hand, any woman who can experience sexual desire must be a whore.

In addition to his need to classify and objectify women, Andrews suffers from a desperate and doomed need to prove his masculinity. He is about to resist temptation and return to Elizabeth when Lucy teases him: "I'll go into Harry. He's old and tired but I believe he's more of a man than you" (181). This taunt to his fragile manhood is too much for him. His better self (the man within) abandons him, telling him, "Now your body has chosen and your body shall stand alone" (130). In fact, it is not Andrews's body but his harsh inner father which makes the choice, and we hear Greene's own angry self-hatred in the condemnation of a character who has fallen "back into the slime from which he had emerged" (182).

For all its romanticism, Greene's tone in *The Man Within* is far from self-satisfied. From the beginning of the book Andrews is shown to be the empty and weak creature Greene feared he was himself. The book begins with an epigraph from Sir Thomas Browne: "There's another man within me / that's angry with me." Most critics interpret this as Greene's view of the dualistic (good and evil) nature of man. In my reading, the "man within" is not so much a better self but a self-loathing flagellant: an internalized bad father.

Greene describes Andrews's inner emptiness as that of a puppet—an image which Wyndham Lewis also frequently used and which evokes Greene's recurrent sense of a balloonlike vacuity, easily filled by a malevolent outside force. Andrews, like Lewis's "split man," Ratner, is thoroughly false, with assumed stage gestures and "strings that put his speech and mouth in servitude to others" (*Man*, 16). His only act of initiative consists of a strangely motiveless betrayal of Carlyon, the good father who has rescued him. When he tells Elizabeth, "[Y]ou must never leave me to myself," it is because he knows that his inner void or numbness conceals inner rage and evil.

There is no place for reciprocal, mutually satisfying sex in Greene's system as it is presented here, and Andrews, like Kernberg's borderline personalities, derives no enjoyment from his sexuality or from anything else in a world in which "there are only two kinds of people, abusers and victims" (Lew, 73). A virgin like Elizabeth cannot enjoy sex, but must instead be ravished. In his act of sex with Lucy, on the other hand, it is Andrews himself who is ravished by the voracious whore. "Have you enjoyed yourself?" she asks, and he answers grimly, "I've wallowed," and "You've made me feel myself dirtier . . . I could kill myself" (183).

For Lewis, who also experienced sexuality as a filthy compulsion, the sexual act at least served to reassure him of his manhood. In his system, the man remained clean while the woman became filthy as a result of sexual intercourse. Williams, who regarded genital sexuality with a woman as filthy, redefined the sexual act as a religious one and found other means of satisfaction which he duly encoded into his system. For Greene's young male characters, the offer of sex from an experienced woman was a test they could not afford to pass up, but one they could not possibly pass either. To refuse would provide proof of impotence (of failure at the test of manhood), but success meant defeat and emasculation through ravishment and moreover provided proof of one's own inner filth and degradation. Lucy's simple, unthinking evil is insignificant compared to that of the more complex Andrews with his persecutory man within. "I have spoiled everything I touch," thinks Andrews, reflecting the young Greene's own despair (206).

Andrews's final betrayal of Elizabeth is even more despicable because she has entrusted (and burdened) him with her fate. "Listen and believe this if you never believe another word I speak," she tells him. "I trust you absolutely" (213). Andrews, who knocked on her door hoping for motherly protection, is thrust instead into the role of manly protector—presented with another, even more impossible test of manhood. Foreseeing the worst, he prays for courage, which God does not provide. When the brutal Joe enters the cottage, Andrews abandons Elizabeth, proving forever and beyond a doubt that he is no man. This failure, within the frame of the novel, is far more devastating than Elizabeth's death. It is her impossible demands on him which destroy Andrews, and his abandonment of her is not only an attempt to save his own life but also a way to punish the cold and pure woman who has claimed and then shamed him. Additionally, in killing off Elizabeth, Greene is killing off Andrews's last hope for human connection and love and is silencing his (loving, trustful) female self. As Andrews runs away, Greene conveys his terror and shame and also evokes his mother through the image of their shared phobia: "The flickering wings of a bat dived at him and he put up fingers, tingling and jumping with nerves, to guard his face" (228).

As we have seen in the works of both Williams and Lewis, the authorial obsessions can sometimes become so pressing that minor characters must step out of their set positions to express them. In *The Man Within*, Carlyon, whose position throughout most of the book is that of the good father who arrives too late and whose courage and chivalry toward women serve as a contrast to Andrews's deficiencies; twice steps out of his role. Upon his first meeting with Elizabeth, whom he ostensibly admires, he suddenly turns on her and accuses her of inner carnality:

> I think that you are lovely, good, and full of pity, but that is only a dream. You know all about yourself, how you are greedy for this and that, afraid of insects, full of disgusting physical needs. You'll never find a man who will love you for anything but a bare, unfilled-in outline of yourself. (66)

Speaking through the only "good" and strong male character in the book, Greene accuses Mother/Elizabeth of the inner cupidity which is also a characteristic of all of Williams's and Lewis's women. Just as charming, innocent Barbara Rackstraw contained a voracious whore within, who only needed a summons to come out, the pure Elizabeth contains a greedy, abhorrent inner self. Greene usually confines such attribution to his whores, keeping his virgins clean. Carlyon's accusation, which involve Greene's own phobias and "disgusting physical needs," show very clearly that the femaleness Greene loathed and attacked in his women characters was the same quality he persecuted so unceasingly in himself.

Once again, after Andrews has betrayed his friendship, Carlyon steps out of character and speaks of him in a way which is reminiscent of Greene's own reflections about Watson, the boy who betrayed his confidences:

> Was he laughing at me the whole time . . . while we were friends? He's a coward and cowards are cunning. I told him all the things I liked. I read him things, shared what I loved with him. I can only make him forget what I told him by killing him. (69)

For Greene, as for Lewis, the world is populated by "potential persecutors representing the nonintegrated sadistic superego" (Kernberg, 282). They smile sweetly but secretly plot betrayal of the defenseless and victimized boy-child.

For Greene, as for both Williams and Lewis, manhood is a precious and tenuous quality, to be guarded, fought for, betrayed, and, in Andrews's case, lost. *The Man Within* contains no Jews, blacks, or other strangers to "take the weight" of Greene's system. Consequently, Greene's preoccupation with his father, his bipolar division of women as virgins or whores, his need to punish the virgins; and his overwhelming self-loathing are all displayed in their most naked form. *The Man Within* is, accordingly, a strangely bare book. The haunted characters, unreal and seemingly unmotivated, play out their primal drama on a stripped stage.

When the Virgin Is a Whore and the Winner Is a Jew: The Name of Action. In both his autobiographies and interviews Greene describes his next two books, *The Name of Action* and *Rumour at Nightfall* (both 1932), as being completely without merit: "My two books, *Rumour at Nightfall* and *The Name of Action*, were bad because I had left too little distance between them and myself. The umbilical cord was left unbroken, you might say . . . the romantic young author I was at the time was too recognizable in the characters" (*Other*, 45,130).

In *Ways of Escape* (1980) he expands on this criticism of *The Name of Action*: "[T]he author at twenty-six was as unreal to himself, in spite of psychoanalysis at sixteen, as Oliver Chant . . . is to the author. Chant is only a daydream in the mind of a young romantic author."[23] Contemporary critics agreed with this appraisal.[24] *The Name of Action*, which Greene found the only one of his books which never gave him "at least once a momentary illusion of success," is fascinating for the purposes of this study not because of its meager literary interest but just because of that unbroken umbilical cord to the young and troubled author's mind (*Sort*, 202). It is also in this book that Jews first take their place alongside women as important actors in the bitter play.

The Name of Action is the story of the young and wealthy Englishman Oliver Chant, who, like his creator, experiences his life in London as excruciatingly boring, meaningless, and enervating. This nonlife is interrupted when an acquaintance at a party recruits him to help the opposition cause in Trier, where a dictatorship has been established. He is especially interested in the proposition because he has heard of the dictator's beautiful wife, Anne-Marie. When Chant arrives in Trier, he meets Kapper, a Jewish poet, and leader of the opposition. Kapper hopes to overthrow the dictator, Demassener, through propaganda, but Chant finds the idea of shipping in arms more romantic, and as he has money, he gets his way. He is invited to the palace, where he meets Anne-Marie, and eventually has sex with her. She reveals her husband's impotence to him, and Chant leaks this information to Kapper, who uses it in a satirical song which causes Demassener's overthrow before the arms can be used. In 1980, Greene wrote: "The book ends with Chant leaving Trier by train, in charge of the defeated, wounded and unconscious dictator. What happened to the wife? It is only a matter of months since I drove myself to reread *The Name of Action* and I've already forgotten her fate, so little does she live or matter" (*Ways*, 20).

Greene later called his imitation of Conrad in his early novels "bastard Conradese tortuosity," and Chant's recruiter is named Kurtz, evoking the nihilistic explorer in Conrad's *Heart of Darkness*, a representative of the collapse of romantic ideals when faced with the evil in the heart of humanity (Sherry, 411). Greene had converted to Catholicism four years before and had become increasingly religious: Chant's name evokes the plainsong liturgy of the Catholic church. Chant himself, a boy-man figure like Andrews in *The Man Within*, is as innocent and as romantic as his name. He accepts his commission much in the spirit that Greene himself accepted his early spy mission, and his eager need for armed struggle as a way to fight depression is similar to Greene's enjoyment of the General Strike and his wish for "a little bit of civil war."

As we shall see, in many ways *The Name of Action* recapitulates the pattern introduced in *The Man Within* . However, there are some important differences. In *The Man Within*, Greene offers Andrews a clearly dichotomized choice between the virgin, Elizabeth, and the whore, Lucy. In *The Name of Action*, however, as in Williams's *War in Heaven*, one woman plays both parts. In *War in Heaven*, the saintly Barbara Rackstraw becomes a whore under the influence of Clerk Simon's potion, while in *The Name of Action* Anne-Marie, whom Chant at first mistakes for a virgin, turns out to be a whore.

The Name of Action also differs from *The Man Within* in its central characters, Chant and Andrews, who, though brothers, are not twins. Chant is an unlikeable character and a silly fool, but he is morally a vast improvement over the despicable Andrews. Chant seems to be haunted by no evil internalized father, and his faults are consequently more the result of youthful folly than of deep internal sin. It is the added figure of the Jew in *The Name of Action* which assumes most of the weight of Greene's self-loathing and guilt, removing it from the central protagonist.

In London, Chant walks through "narrow ordured streets" to the party where he meets Kurtz, the Ruritanian exile who recruits him for the cause. After pledging himself to the adventure, which promises to be "the first Eden," he returns through streets which now appear "spacious and extravagantly lit with stars."[25] Chant's enervation and boredom, much like Greene's own, cause him ordinarily to see his world through excrement-colored glasses. The chance of an adventure, complete with a secret password, romantic possibilities, and a schoolboy's ideal test of valor, temporarily removes the ordure from the streets. This daydream is much like the one in which Isherwood imagined himself as an austere young prefect "surrounded by sneering critics and open enemies, fighting slackness, moral rottenness . . . finally passing the tests, emerging—a Man" (*Lions and Shadows*, 48). Chant's daydream differs from Isherwood's only in that *his* Eden includes a pure and idealized woman rather than a pure younger boy. But Chant's Eden has its Jewish snake, and an Eve who is more than ready to collude with it. Ordured streets, it turns out, are not so easy to clean.

Chant's daydream and his naivete receive a blow when he goes to the arranged place to meet Kapper. He finds that the shabby conspirator in the shoemaker's shop has forgotten the password, the recitation of which has been such a delicious part of his fantasy, "the moment of which he had dreamed almost continually during the last week" (*Name*, 29). When he finally gains entrance, Chant sees

> a thin Jew, who started nervously forward, though forward was not the word to express his sidelong advance which ended at Chant's side and in its course offered to the gaze no more than a profile or a single eye. (*Name*, 29)

The crab, another addition to Rosenberg's list of animal metaphors for the Jew, sidles forth with a shifty, cringing approach, and the Jew soon demonstrates his narcissistic and grandiose character by his continual repetition of his name ("I am Kapper the poet"), his excitement at the sound of his own voice, and his illusions of power (36). He, like Lewis's Ratner and other literary Jews, is a pornographer, whose perverse attitude toward women is shown by the obscene verses and pictures which litter the walls of his room. Kapper's name suggests the Latin *capra*, or goat, a common animal metaphor for unbridled, unselective sexuality, and for the male Jew. Kapper is, like Lewis's and Williams's Jews, immediately identifiable on sight. Like Shylock or Fagin before him, he is usually referred to as "the Jew" by Greene and by the other characters. Just as Lewis evoked Fagin and Shylock in his description of Archie Margolin, Greene takes extra care to locate his Jew firmly within the tradition: "Through the guttural German came faintly the nasal note that spoke of deserts and a doubting people and the flight from Egypt" (31).

Vain and posturing, greedy (though for fame, not money), cowardly, murderous in a sneaking, feminine way, and sexually lustful, Kapper is Rosenberg's Jew as villain, as degenerate, and as clown. In his person he embodies "the passionate avarice, the nihilism, and the desire to mutilate" that Fiedler describes ("Fagin," 418). Just as the Jewish crab's approach is diametrically opposed to that of the straightforward romantic schoolboy, with his password and his illusions, so Kapper's defects exist in direct opposition to the values upheld in Thomas Arnold's and Thomas Hughes's concept of Muscular Christianity, embodied by the upstanding band of youths in Kipling's *Stalky and Co.*, and measured in Isherwood's schoolboy test of manhood. Kapper's profession is, of course, no coincidence. Just as the failed Jewish writer Ratner was an unconscious portrait of his creator, Greene's rather more conscious identification is as much with Kapper, the boastful, cowardly, lustful, and ambitious Jewish writer, as with Chant, the innocent young man.

Clerk Simon and Ratner represent attempts by Williams and Lewis to split off and isolate their unacceptable parts by depositing them in the person of the despicable Jew. Greene's self-hatred does not allow him such an easy solution. In *The Name of Action*, inner evil cannot be confined to Kapper the Jew, who is only a temporary intercessor between Greene and his self-contempt. Instead, Chant and Kapper are inextricably textually linked. Greene's effort to place Kapper squarely inside the literary tradition of evil Jews is an attempt to fashion him into an airtight container which might stop the overflow of evil into Chant. In fact, most of the "action" in *The Name of Action* concerns Greene's unsuccessful effort to split off and isolate the inner Jew, who, in league with the woman, consistently invades his young protagonist, refusing to give him any peace. We are reminded of Otto Weininger, who, failing at his attempt to "overcome the woman and the Jew in him," finally killed himself (Decker, 39).

Chant's romanticism hides a sinister emptiness similar to Andrews's. When Kapper urges him to descend into the cellar, where there are spider webs which threaten to brush his face like the insect and bat wings of the Greene phobia, it is clear that the voyage into the basement of the house of the Jew is a voyage into the author's own "dark cellar." Chant is easily drawn into the "Jewish" darkness:

> Chant started at the voice behind him and caught his first glimpse of what was happening behind the black, shifting curtain of the Jew's eyes, dark halls, and clammy mysteries and perpetual night. Must I, too, he wondered, become a part of that dream and let myself be shifted here and there by that imagination always in darkness? (34, 35)

When there is a knock on the door, Kapper steps back into stereotype, dissolving in fear, and snaps at Chant "in the tone of a harassed housewife" (38). The invader turns out to be Anne-Marie Demassener herself, and Kapper, no English gentleman, refuses to give her brandy, even though she is shaken from a car accident. As Kapper assumes a sinister position behind Anne-Marie, Chant notices the flash of metal, indicating the weapon of the mythic Jew: a knife. Chant, who is less cowardly than Andrews, attempts to protect her, but Anne-Marie wants none of it. She can defend herself, and even seems drawn to the knife-wielding Jew: "They regarded each other if not with friendship at least with a kind of mutual understanding" (42).

When Anne-Marie looks at *him*, Chant imagines that she can see the "Jew" he feels in himself and that she is thinking: "How well you fit with your companions, that shifty-eyed mean-bodied Jew and his fat friend. You are not yourself, you are only one of three" (40). The dark halls, clammy mystery, and perpetual night in the Jew's eyes are stereotypical—but they belong to Chant as well as to the Jew. This ocular image recurs many times. Chant hates the idea that Anne-Marie "was a woman in the eyes of the German Jew, a woman to be examined by those dark, desecrating eyes" (113). Later, as Kapper tries to persuade Chant to betray the dictator's impotence, the Jew's eyes become inhuman, devilish. "The lacquered eyes approached his, points of light gleaming at the pupils" (277). When Chant looks into the Jew's eyes and finds "a passage leading straight to a sanctuary which was too dark to be comprehended," it is once again his own inner darkness or void which he is viewing with horror (114).

Kapper's knife is not his only weapon. Soon after Chant's arrival, Kapper, creeping up from behind as usual, shoots a young and friendly policeman who has been petting a cat and is now in the act of reaching toward Chant in friendship (96). Chant, who has colluded in this death, must join with the Jew in the disposal of the body. The empty balloon of moral void, only thinly covered by his romanticism, is quickly being filled with Jewish evil, and the daydream test of manhood is fast turning into a nightmare.

Unlike his literary predecessors, this Jew has a wife, a bedraggled and masochistic creature who acts as Kapper's instrument much as Williams's bedraggled female homunculae followed the bidding of their master, Clerk Simon. In order to hide the bloodstains on the street, Kapper orders his wife to spread bloody liver on them. Too cowardly to do the job himself, he stamps, screams, and gesticulates with stereotypical hysteria until she goes to cover his tracks. Bertha Kapper, one of only two female Jews in the texts in this study, "seemed to have no substance, to blow back before his approach" (102). She is a cringing, ugly "cowardly and characterless woman," whose sex is not needed and who is unnecessary "for any purpose whatever" (107). She cares more for a few marks than for the murder of a man and is at once the Jew's cringing, abused victim and a rapacious, money-loving Jew herself. Although she is an abused woman, Chant's code of schoolboy chivalry does not extend to Bertha Kapper. Dropping the Jew's ordure in place is a fitting activity for this creature, who combines the worst traits of the female and the Jew.

When his wife has left, Kapper reminds Chant that it is he, not Kapper, who has chosen the way of violence. The Jew tells the young man in so many words that he will not be allowed to escape, through projective identification, from his responsibility for murder:

> "*Your* way, Herr Chant," and his twisted mouth seemed to call bitter attention to a young face dead, a body twisting with upturned rump upon the Moselle, and a pile of raw liver flung on a dirty street. Ordure. But my way was not ordure, Chant thought, his memory catching at a brief belief in barricades and shots fired openly in a good cause. (113, emphasis mine)

Kapper, like Clerk Simon and Du Maurier's Svengali, fascinates women, whose inner evil he understands and matches. While Chant is still lost in his meaningless fantasy of the pure and saintly Anne-Marie, "the chief beauty of life and the chief attraction of... death," Kapper recognizes her for the trollop she is by her voice and tells her, "I'm not interested in your name... I know the voice of every trollop in Trier. I don't need to know their names . . . I am a man and you are a woman. We all meet in the same place sooner or later . . . between the sheets" (236–37). Just as in *The Man Within* Carlyon stepped out of his role to accuse Elizabeth of inner cupidity, in this passage Kapper the Jew is the mouthpiece for an insight common to Lewis and Williams as well as Greene: that even the most romanticized woman contains a suppurating trollop underneath. Anne-Marie feels seen by Kapper and is attracted by his brutality: "I like a man who is proud and unhappy. Dark, musical, liking women . . . I like your Kapper. His frankness interests me. I believe it even excites me a little" (237). Chant tells Kapper to "keep your dirty fingers off, . . . Jew," but the Jew's dirty fingers have already been there (275). The beautiful woman conceals the inner whore, and the Jew and the woman are drawn together in a pact of mutual darkness.

While Kapper recognizes himself in whores and feels comfortable with them (just as Andrews felt comfortable with Lucy, in whom he recognized his own "lustful body and despicable heart"), he cannot tolerate the presence of virgins. Perhaps to make up for the absence of any virgin in the flesh, the Madonna herself makes several appearances in *The Name of Action*, and the Jew encounters her with horror and defeat, in the way a vampire encounters a cross. He repeatedly looks out of a window at a bronze Madonna, "the mother of his eternal enemy," and, as if at her bidding, his men begin to speak of Catholicism and going to Mass, and turn against him.

Greene's Kapper, like Williams's Clerk Simon, is a sexually virile man, although his cowardice is "female." By contrast, Chant, like Andrews in *The Man Within*, approaches sex without desire, but with the need to prove his manhood. When Anne-Marie has engineered their one sexual encounter and the two of them are in an empty room in an inn, he is overtaken by anxiety. He uneasily repeats that he loves her, then evokes the name of her husband, Demassener. Anne-Marie tells him that Demassener has never made love to her, even though, no virgin, she was another man's mistress before marrying him. She will not tell Chant that she loves him but insists, "I want you." Like Greene himself, who lost interest in available women, and like Horney's neurotic men who became "very indignant with a woman who takes their intentions too seriously" (359), Chant loses interest. "Chant stared at the floor and wondered where desire had gone and why it had left him. 'I love you,' he said, with perplexity and without passion" (247).

It is only when Anne-Marie, like Lucy in *The Man Within*, taunts Chant that he manages to approach her. "There's only one mark of a man," she tells him, likening him to her impotent husband. At the sound of the contempt in her voice, he grabs her, and intercourse is achieved (246). But for Chant as for Andrews, the encounter is not pleasurable but devastating. Not only has his virgin proven a whore, but Chant, like Andrews, has himself been ravaged. Anne- Marie, like Lucy, like Melanie, the rapacious female who rapes young Dan Boleyn in *The Apes of God*, and like the women who threatened both Lewis and Greene with marriage when they went abroad, is an embodiment of that yawning female mouth which threatens to swallow the victimized male.

At first, Chant endeavors to hold on to his illusions about Anne-Marie. "I love you as men have loved God!" he tries to convince himself (259). But in the end, Anne-Marie forces him to face facts. In the incongruent holiness of the Catholic church where they meet for the last time, she tells him, in a voice which "sounded less lovely than shrill":

> Last night . . . was nothing. Anyone would have satisfied me . . . if I thought you were dangerous . . . I would have reported you to the police days ago. You would have been shot. I care just that much for your body. (271)

Chant's insight after this revelation reminds one of Lewis's engulfing epira in *The Art of Being Ruled*: "He had believed in love. Love now was the struggle of two bodies to possess each other" (*Name*, 264).

In *The Man Within*, Greene gave Andrews a bad father, whom he internalized, and a good one, whom he betrayed. In *The Name of Action*, there is no good woman, and no good father either. If Kapper the Jew embodies Greene's lust and bestiality, Demassener the dictator embodies his terror and loathing of the female body and the shameful end of those who fail the test of manhood. A cold, dignified figure enthroned in "the loneliness inevitable to power," Demassener has used his reign to clear the country of pornography and prostitution. He also denies his subjects music and dancing, as these can lead to sexual feelings and indulgence (69). He apparently refrains from sex with his wife not because he is impotent but rather because "all that disgusts him," or, as he tells Chant, "my love is not of that kind" (246, 289–90). This puritan dictator opposes "freedom for the animal in man. I would bind man in clean chains" (71).

As Chant grows more and more disgusted by the Jew, Demassener's clean austerity proves increasingly appealing. In an early meeting, Chant recognizes the dictator, his supposed enemy, as "his kind," as the Jew and his (Jewish) associates can never be (74). After his own devastating encounter with Anne-Marie, Demassener's abstinence makes even more sense to him. But whether or not it is really caused by impotence, that abstinence leads to the dictator's downfall. One who has failed the test of manhood cannot hide; he will be recognized and found out. The news of the dictator's failure, spread through town by Kapper's mocking song, causes him to be laughed out of office, then shot in a part of the body which is not named, but which one of the Jew's more sinister supporters, "the man with the syphilitic scar," hints to be the genitals (300). The punishment for impotence could not be more clearly spelled out: it is castration. Anne-Marie predictably elects to stay in Trier with the new head of government, the Jew, and Chant chooses to leave on a train with the castrated dictator, who, in a final moment of humiliation, weakly moans for the wife he could not manage to keep. At the last moment, Anne-Marie seems about to yield and wants to know if her husband has asked for her, but Chant lies to her and denies that he has. On the train, to add insult to his injury, the dictator is symbolically raped by "the representative of the New World," an American reporter from the *Chicago Tribune*.

Although Chant finally chooses cold purity over evil lust, it is a choice with no glory in it. The emasculated dictator and the young man, who, emptied of his fine illusions and his innocence, has now become a liar and a whoremaster, are not much better than the Jew and the whore to whom they yield the field. The dethroned Demassener asks Kapper, "Can you imagine anything more laughable than me beaten by you?" and the laughter which closes *The Name of Action* is hollow indeed.

The Jew Within: Stamboul Train. In *Stamboul Train* (1932), published in the United States as *Orient Express*, Greene, who had begun to review films, abandons the genre of the historical romance for that of the contemporary thriller and increasingly relies on cinematic rather than romantic writing. Greene always emphasized that he wrote *Stamboul Train*, an "entertainment" to make money.[26] *Stamboul Train* indeed made money for its author, as well as receiving almost uniformly excellent reviews. It was chosen as the monthly selection of the Book Society, although its explicit sexuality, and especially the lesbian characters, shocked many of the Book Society members. The only contemporary censures of the novel dealt with this "coarseness" and made no more mention of Greene's use of Jewish characters than had the reviews of *The Name of Action*.

Some modern critics do discuss the import of the Jewish character in *Stamboul Train*, though they disagree as to his significance. Grahame Smith regards the political atmosphere and the anti-Semitism Greene portrays in the novel as evidence of his political clairvoyance. He sees the train where most of the action takes place as a vision of Nazi Germany in the year before Hitler's accession to power. In his view, "Myatt is literally a wandering Jew and Greene does all he can to accentuate his position 'as the centre of a hostile world.' " Smith concludes, "The soil which nurtures the growth of Jewish persecution could hardly be more tangibly presented."[27] Fiedler and Rosenberg, on the other hand, see Myatt as one of Greene's most offensive Jewish stereotypes.

Judging from the changes he made in the postwar editions, Greene must later have felt some awareness of his anti-Semitism in *Stamboul Train*. Although he makes no direct apology, in *Ways of Escape* he explains, "Hitler had not yet come to power when *Orient Express* was written. It was a different world and a different author—an author still in his twenties. I am not sure that I detect much promise in his work." Yet the same paragraph ends with his appreciation of "Mr. Stein, a fraudulent businessman," a character for whose creation "the old writer can salute his young predecessor with a certain respect" (32–33). When we consider Mr. Stein, who uses surgery to hide his crooked nose and subterfuge to hide his crooked identity, who enjoys a refined "little bit of smut in female company," and who brazenly sells off his niece in a marriage to suit his convenience, we cannot help but hear a note of defiance on Greene's part toward those who have accused him of anti-Semitism.[28]

Stamboul Train is set on a train bound for Istanbul. The young Anglo-Jewish currant merchant, Carleton Myatt, en route to Constantinople to buy up a rival business for his father's firm, meets Coral Musker, a virginal chorus girl with a heart condition. Coral faints, Myatt takes pity on her and offers her his first class berth; and they have an affair. Coral is revived from her faint by Dr. Richard Czinner, an exiled socialist leader, returning to his country, after an absence of many years, to participate in a revolution. Mabel Warren, a drunken lesbian journalist, has boarded the train in pursuit of Czinner and of her companion, the lovely but whorish Janet

Pardoe. At Vienna, a criminal German, Joseph Grünlich, fleeing after having brutally murdered a man in the course of a robbery, also gets on. At the Subotica border, Dr. Czinner is recognized by the authorities and stopped. He hands a paper to Coral, and she and Grünlich, who has been caught with a gun, are also taken off the train. After a mock trial in which Czinner is condemned to death, Coral, Czinner, and Grünlich are locked in a jail cell together. Grünlich picks the lock, and the three attempt to escape across the snow. Czinner is shot, and he and Coral hide in a shed. Meanwhile, Myatt, who has returned in a car to look for Coral, encounters only Grünlich, who denies that Coral is there. Myatt has been frightened by the anti-Semitism of the officials he has encountered in his rescue effort, and, though he knows that Grünlich is lying, he rescues him instead of Coral and goes on to Constantinople on the train. There he decides to marry Janet Pardoe, who turns out to be his colleague's half- Jewish niece. After spending the night in the shed with the dying Czinner, Coral is rescued the next day by Mabel Warren, but dies when her heart gives out, on the floor of Mabel's car.

In *Stamboul Train*, we find the system in *The Man Within* recapitulated quite closely. Once more the empty young man, pursued by his past, is faced with a binary opposition between the worlds of good and evil and the necessity to make a choice between them. The world of good is embodied here by a pure virgin, a good father, and the possibility of sacrificial love; and the world of evil by a whore, a bad father, and the encroaching larger world of corruption and greed. Once more the young man, influenced by the virgin, makes an initial move toward goodness, but, failing the test of manhood, betrays her through his cowardice. The virgin is killed off; and evil, embodied in the alliance of the Jew and the whore, is left to rule.

In *The Man Within*, Andrews himself contained most of the evil in the book, while in *The Name of Action*, the Jew was the prime repository of that evil, although the more conscious authorial representative, Chant, was also tainted. In *Stamboul Train*, Myatt the gesticulating Jew, contains within himself the stereotypical qualities of greed and avarice, cowardice, servility, and sexual concupiscence. At the same time, he is also the authorial representative, the empty young man who, in each of Greene's early novels, must undergo the test of manhood. Of all the characters, it is only Myatt who contains duality: the possibility for good or for evil. It is Myatt who, like Greene, is haunted in his dreams by accusations of some nameless guilt, and Myatt who is offered redemption through Coral's love, so strong that it might change his acquisitive lust to tenderness and unfreeze his frozen heart. The real action in this book concerns Myatt's moral struggle between the good and evil in himself. In creating Myatt, Greene did not free himself from the stereotypes attached to the Jew: Myatt embodies them all. However, he places the Jew in a central position, as his own authorial representative. To a great extent, this is Myatt's book, and, at least for most of it, Myatt appears to be a flawed human being rather than a metaphor of projection.

Carleton Myatt, like Kapper, is immediately identifiable as a Jew. Greene refers to him throughout the book as "the Jew," "the moneylender," or "the young Jew." But Greene as sender is communicating a different message to us as receivers and sharers of a common code of morality than he formerly did through his use of this label (Suleiman and Crosman, 8). As readers, we automatically discount the stereotypical handles which are offered to us by the other passengers, because Greene quickly teaches us to disapprove of them. The three characters in the book who most fully embody evil—Joseph Grünlich, the German thief and murderer; Mabel Warren, the lesbian journalist; and her whorish companion, Janet Pardoe—are also the most virulent anti-Semites. Grünlich, whose mind works like an evil, highly efficient machine, considers using his chisel to blind the servant of the house he is robbing (one of Greene's many useless and repulsive older women), but decides it would be superfluous. He is full of obscene sentimentality and grandiose boastfulness. In a dream, he tells himself, "I am President of the Republic" (149). Grahame Smith is certainly correct in his assessment of this character: "Destiny, violence, and emotionalism are all key elements in the Nazi mentality . . . Grünlich is surely a proto-Nazi" (26–27). In contrast to his treatment of Grünlich, the German murderer and anti-Semite, a figure of absolute and unrelieved evil, Greene offers Myatt the Jew at least the choice of redemption.

Mabel Warren, Greene's nightmare woman, is almost as unrelieved a symbol of evil as is Grünlich. Here, as in the ending of *The Name of Action*, reporters symbolize the shameful invasion of the male boundaries of self, which for Greene, as for Williams and Lewis, represents an omnipresent terror. The female reporter is Greene's equivalent of Williams's lamia: the ultimate engulfing female. As a lesbian, Mabel has attempted to usurp male territory or boundaries in yet another way. As a drunk, she has yet again transgressed her proper role as a woman. Mabel Warren meets Janet Pardoe at a theatre, where their "mutual disgust of the chief actor," an "oiled man" like Myatt, brings them together. Later Mabel tells Janet, "I don't like Jews," and Janet, in a response that is doubly blameworthy, as she is Jewish herself, responds, "[N]or do I, darling" (*Stamboul*, 55).

A Judas to her own people and a whore to the lesbian, Janet Pardoe is the second Jewish woman in this study, and one of the most evil of Greene's hardened whores.

The other passengers on the train share these characters' evil—and their anti-Semitism. When Coral has the misfortune to sit next to the Peterses, respectable English "shopkeepers on a spree," they reveal a depth of depravity which Greene indicates is tied to their anti-Semitism. When the exhausted and ill Coral falls asleep, Mr. Peters fingers her legs and thighs, and when Myatt offers her his sleeping car and she leaves their third-class carriage, Mrs. Peters shouts at her, "A dirty little Jew, that's all you're good for . . . Jews and foreigners. You ought to be ashamed" (127–28). The pseudo-Cockney writer, Savory, and the unctuous clergyman, Mr. Opie, are equally vain, depraved, and anti-Semitic.

Just as the evil characters reveal themselves through their anti-Semitism, the good ones distinguish themselves by their freedom from it. When Mabel Warren, who wants Coral for herself, tells her to avoid Myatt, she warns her: "Jews are not to be trusted" (66). Coral is horrified at the idea that Myatt may have attributed anti-Semitic feelings to her. "I shall go and tell him that I like him, that I've always liked Jews," she tells Mabel, and it is in part her pity for him as a victim of anti-Semitism which causes her to "sacrifice" her precious virginity to him later (60).

Richard Czinner, though he is incapable of caring for Myatt as an individual, loves him as a member of an oppressed group and as one of the masses who are the objects of his life's work. Czinner comes out of hiding too late to save his people, and, like Greene's other good fathers, he arrives too late and is himself not whole enough to provide the fathering that Myatt would require in order to become a whole man. Czinner, like the rigid, alienated men described by Kate Millett and Virginia Woolf, is cut off forever from "the layer of personality in which the primitive erotic flow between the self and the surround has its source" (Dinnerstein, 32). A more sympathetic version of Demassener, the self-alienated dictator in *The Name of Action*, he too has failed to embrace the people in their individuality or their wholeness—dirt and sins and all. He longs as much to clear away the unsightly "ordure" of the poor as to end their hunger (118). But Czinner's failure, unlike Demassener's and most unlike Myatt's, is a heroic and manly one. There is no question that, as Coral tells Myatt with absolute conviction, "he's good" (27).

On the conscious level, then, we must agree with Smith that Greene has indeed condemned anti-Semitism in *Stamboul Train*. Myatt, the wandering Jew, provides a kind of mini–morality test for the other characters, a test which all but Coral and Czinner fail. Just as Greene is the first author in this study to use a Jew for a central character of authorial identification, so is he the first to make such a conscious statement.

It is only when Myatt's Jewishness becomes the embodiment or representative of Greene's self-loathing that we flinch at Greene's unconscious anti-Semitism. This process begins as soon as Greene invites his implied reader into Myatt's consciousness, and we realize that Myatt himself regards his Jewishness as the bad past or evil father which stalks him as surely as Andrews's evil father stalks him in *The Man Within*. When we first meet Myatt, preparing to enter the train in France after the crossing at Dover, he is creeping away from a customs officer who has called him "Juif, Juif." Wounded, he retreats into the history of his people and into the familiar stereotype of the greedy financier, a stereotype which Greene urges us to valorize by presenting it to us as originating from a privileged source: Myatt's own consciousness. The smoke surrounding the train reminds him of: "grey nomad tents . . . [where he was] at home and required no longer the knowledge of this fur coat, of his suit from Savile Row, his money, or his position in the firm to hearten him" (4–5).

Myatt senses himself (perfectly accurately, considering the others' reactions to him) "at the centre of a hostile world" (5). He has a perpetual chip on his shoulder and shuns others because of the probability of a snub. He bribes the purser to obtain a single carriage because of "his hatred of undressing before another man," an anxiety Greene himself developed after his experience of group nakedness and the lack of privacy at school (5). In his self-consciousness and fear, his sense of being an outsider in the world, and his constant need to compensate, Myatt is a clear stand-in for the young Greene, whose schoolmates labeled him "abnormal."

In my discussion of George Orwell's "Such, Such Were the Joys" in chapter 2, I distinguished between Orwell's externalized and acknowledged anger at the way he was treated at school and the internalized self-hatred which left him with a picture of himself as a disgusting, smelly, and ugly child. Alice Miller too makes the distinction between abuse which has been acknowledged and externalized and that more dangerous, unacknowledged abuse which is forced underground. Greene, like Orwell, was able to identify and acknowledge some of the abuse he suffered at school, but he too internalized the image of himself as a "leper who had to ring his bell while approaching people" (*Other*, 27). In his presentation of Myatt's Jewishness to us, he invites us to share Myatt's perception of it as a kind of inner leprosy, a disease which inspires the less worthy passengers with hatred and disgust and the most worthy with Christian pity. Most importantly, we are invited to perceive it as a disease or disability which is located not inside the spectator, where Fiedler placed it, but rather inside the sufferer (the Jew) himself.

Once safely in his compartment, Myatt begins to finger the currants he always carries in his pocket. Like T. S. Eliot's "Mr. Eugenides, the Smyrna merchant / Unshaven, with a pocket full of currants," he is at home only with commerce and must use his only currency to buy himself culture, luxury, companionship, and sex (Eliot, *Waste Land*, l. 43, in *Complete Poems and Plays*). Eliot labels his unsavory currant merchant as a Syrian, not necessarily a Jew, but the Jew Myatt is definitely his relative, just as Williams's unreal city is clearly related to Eliot's. As Myatt fingers the currants in his pocket with the obsessive relish of Shylock fingering his coins, the image of the stereotypical Jew merges with Greene's own memory of childhood greed:

> It was . . . before I went to school, that I began regularly to steal currants and sultanas out of the big biscuit tins in the School House storeroom, stuff my pockets with them, currants in the left, sultanas in the right, and feast on them secretly in the garden. (*Sort*, 36)

Myatt, shifting his currants and testing them, compares his firm's product with the rival's and attempts to assures himself that he is not in fact a despised Jew, but instead "one of the lords of the world, carrying destiny with him" (*Stamboul*, 9).

In the restaurant car, Myatt obsessively and cunningly reviews his intrigues with other criminal Jew-merchants who are waiting for him in Constantinople: the enigmatic and cunning Stein and the wolfish Eckman, with his "sharp prominent teeth" and his "intricate hidden relations" with Stein, "skirting the outer fringe of the law" (12). Myatt also visualizes his own father, an old, emasculated man, drinking the food of infancy, "the glass of curdling warm milk" (16). Stein and Eckman are stealthy tricksters like Myatt himself, but they are more despicable than he is because they, like Janet Pardoe, pretend to Christianity. Eckman attempts to establish his Christianity by keeping a Bible chained to the lavatory in his pretentious home, and when we remember Greene's horrified memories of school lavatories with open doors and the dreaded odor of farts, it is clear just how deeply such attempts at "passing" disturb him. To Greene, a Jew who attempts to be a Christian is as incongruent and wrong as a Bible in the toilet. Such an attempt is a trick; an effort to break down the lines or boundaries which prevent a chaotic collapse into "jellylike diffuseness." Such an effort to rob the world of its moral and symbolic content resembles the effort of the whore who tries to trick innocent men by passing herself off as a virgin.

While Myatt, unlike Stein and Eckman, makes no attempt to hide his Jewish identity, he has thoroughly internalized the hatred directed at him. Like Kapper, he combines a most ungentlemanlike boastfulness with a distasteful cringing whenever he approaches Christians: "the excessive humility of the bowed head in the desert" (15). When Coral sends him a friendly look, he feels grateful that she has shown "no distaste, no knowledge of his uneasiness in the best clothes that money could buy" (20).

Coral Musker's ability to love such a cringing Jew is a saintly action comparable to Elizabeth's love for the despicable Andrew in *The Man Within*. Coral combines Elizabeth's motherly, nurturing qualities with a physical fragility and low status which save her from Elizabeth's (and Marion Greene's) daunting remoteness. Like Elizabeth, however, and like Williams's angelic slaves, Coral's drive to sacrifice herself for others is instinctual. She fends off Peters's obscene groping and never complains, though her face is blue with cold. Her pluck and forbearance move Myatt to his first act of generosity: giving her his sleeping car and sleeping in the corridor.

Elizabeth could only fill the empty Andrews with her goodness while in his immediate presence. Similarly, Myatt's inner bad father—his Jewishness—emerges as soon as he leaves Coral. He mentally converts his act of kindness to her into an act of self-conscious pride: "Parsimony was the traditional reproach against his race, and he would show one Christian how undeserved it was." Once again he remembers the deserts, the "flesh pots of Egypt, the tent in the oasis," and begins to measure up Coral's cost to him (28). When she wakes up, he has trouble restraining himself from "a spread of the hands, a slight bow of the hips . . . tricks of his race which he was consciously repressing." When he shrugs his shoulders, he "might have been a pawnbroker undervaluing a watch or vase" (47). When Coral emerges and looks at him, even she cannot help but recognize and hate the Jew in him:

> She had seen this man too often . . . the too familiar features, the small eyes, the large nose, the black oiled hair . . . the world of the theatre vibrated with his soft humble imperative voice; he was mean with a commonplace habitual meanness, generous in fits and starts, never to be trusted. (49)

But just as Elizabeth refused to see Andrews's cowardice and inner void and concentrated instead on his inner goodness (and ended up raped for her trouble), Coral refuses to see Myatt as merely the "familiar" Jew, and her goodness begins to transform him. From the beginning, as the light she sees streaming through the window when she awakens shines on both Czinner and "the young Jew," she sheds light on his darkness (24). Later, when he approaches her in his role as "the moneylender," she puts out her hands to him, resting them on his knee, and "hiding the rows of numerals, Mr. Eckman's calculations and subterfuges and cunning concealments, offer[s] herself" (87–88). In exactly the same way, Williams's ideal women interposed their own bodies, taking the evil forces meant for their men onto themselves through the mechanisms Williams named "exchange" and "transfer."

Myatt continues to be torn between Coral's goodness and his inner Jewishness. He generously takes her to dinner, but boasts there of his expensive ring. When she impulsively and gratefully tells him that she loves him, he dismisses it—"What a joke"—but later begins to think of her "as he had never thought before of any woman who was attainable: she is dear and sweet, I should like to do things for her" (143).

During the actual seduction scene, his inner battle continues. In his cynicism he had never suspected that she could be a virgin, and he is moved when "lying in the berth she proved awkward in a mysterious innocent fashion which astonished him" (145). She cries out in pain, and he realizes the great treasure she has given him, and for a moment, understands her true worth.[29] Greene allows Myatt a moment of tenderness.

> "I never knew. I never guessed." There was such warmth in the carriage now between them that, without closing the window, he knelt beside the berth and put his hands to her face, touching her features with curious fingers. Again he was overwhelmed with the novel thought, "How sweet, how dear." She lay quiet, shaken a little by quick breaths of pain or excitement. (146–47)

But the world with all its evil vulgarity enters in the form of somebody (probably Grünlich) in the third-class carriage, cursing in German at the fiddler who has been gently playing during the sex scene. Myatt's thoughts too turn immediately to the medium he knows best: money. He contemplates the cost of keeping Coral in Constantinople and boastfully plans an expensive party to celebrate his conquest: "It'll cost two pounds a head" (147). After she leaves the compartment, he is free to return to his all-consuming money-making schemes: "now she was relegated to her proper place" (184). And just as Andrews turns to the whore, Lucy, as soon as he has left Elizabeth, Myatt immediately catches sight of Janet Pardoe, and compares her favorably to Coral, his pearl of great price: "[t]his girl was silver polished goods, while Coral was at the best a piece of pretty colored glass, valued for sentimental reasons; the other had intrinsic worth" (193). Like Groucho Marx, he decides that anyone who will have him must be worthless: "I am a Jew, and I have learned nothing except how to make money" (193).[30] In a typical Greenian double bind, virginity is for Myatt an indication of unavailability, a quality which automatically increases a woman's value and makes her more attractive, but is at the same time a desexualizing sign. Through "giving up" her virginity, a woman became more sexually appealing, but less valuable. Unlike Myatt, Coral values her lover more rather than less after sexual consummation:

> His face no longer resembled that of all the Jewish boys she had known with half intimacy; even the gestures with which he gave and gave, the instinctive spreading of the hands, was different, his emphasis on how much he would spend, on what a good time he would give her, was unique because she believed him. (166)

While in extreme danger in the freezing jail cell, she tells Dr. Czinner: "He's quite different from other Jews. They're generally kind, but he—well, he's quiet" (172).

In loving and trusting Myatt the Jew, Coral is performing an act like Christ's when he washed the feet of the leper: offering love and forgiveness even to the lowest of the low. As she sits in the shed by the dying Czinner, she seems to have some awareness of Myatt's actual unworthiness, but she prefers to hold on to her vision of him. Just as Greene signified that Myatt's Jewish darkness resides inside *him*, he now emphasizes that his goodness resides in Coral, not in her unworthy love object:

> [H]er thoughts returned with a stupid fidelity to Myatt himself, to her last sight of him in the restaurant-car with his fingers caressing his gold cigarette case. But she was aware all the time that there as no quality in Myatt to justify her fidelity; it was just that she was like that and he had been kind. (228–29)

Myatt's struggle is not yet over. He is unable to completely forget Coral, and when he realizes, after the unforeseen stop in Subotica, that she is no longer on the train, he feels some concern. At the train's next stop, motivated in part by that concern and in part by a need to act in a manly or un-Jewish fashion, he hires a car and goes back to look for her. Myatt wastes precious time when his Jewish nature makes obstacles along the way. First, he is tempted by "the smell of the ancestral market place" and stops to indulge in "the joy of bargaining"; next he stops to send a business telegram to Eckman (189). His cowardice, which emerges when he encounters the officials' anti-Semitism, prompts him to turn back, and his moral emptiness and inability to appreciate Coral or to feel love for her provide little motivation to continue:

> Myatt knew suddenly that he would not be sorry to accept the clerk's word and end his search. . . . He thought of Coral for a moment as a small alley, enticing a man's footsteps, but blind at the end with a windowless wall . . . there were others, and he thought for a moment of Janet Pardoe, who were like streets lined with shops full of glitter and warmth, streets which led somewhere. (211)

But Coral's love is a strong force which, even at a distance, appears to him from time to time, offering him borrowed courage. He persists in his search even though the guards in the dark station and the passing country people call him a dirty Jew, and he correctly senses the possibilities of evil in "this dark cup of the earth" and sees in the soldiers' attitude "the spirit which made pogroms possible" (206, 222).

He is engaged in the great test, and we believe that he has at least a chance of passing. In the end, however, it is evil in the person of Joseph Grünlich which he takes into his car instead of good in the person of Coral. Even though he knows that it is a lie, he allows himself to believe Grünlich's assertion that there is "no girl" in Subotica and retreats, leaving his salvation, who still has faith in him, crouching in a freezing shed next to a dying Czinner.

Like Elizabeth, who could not survive the desecration of rape, Coral dies before she can be taken over by Mabel Warren and subjected to a fate worse than death at her hands. When her heart gives out in the back of Mabel Warren's rented car, her last thoughts are of her unworthy lover:

> She had a pain in her breast . . . she wondered with an obstinate fidelity where Myatt was. The pain made breathing difficult, but she was determined not to speak. To speak, to describe her pain, to ask for help would be to empty her mind for a moment of his face; her ears would lose the sound of his voice. . . . I won't be the first to forget, she thought with obstinacy, fighting desperately at last against pain . . . I remember. I haven't forgotten . . . (238)[31]

An alternative ending of the book might have seen Coral going off with Mabel; after all, a woman with mercy and love in her heart for a Jew might conceivably find some for a lesbian, and Coral longs for relief from her hard life. But Greene could not allow this to happen. Apart from the inevitable sullying the association with Mabel would bring, the newly deflowered Coral fits nowhere in Greene's structure. Having sacrificed herself to the Jew, she has lost the goodness which can only belong to a virgin. As virgin and whore are the only two possibilities available for women in this system, she must die.

Another reason for Coral's early demise lies in the challenge which even she, the most unthreatening of women, poses to the young man. In *The Man Within*, Elizabeth challenges Andrews to act bravely—a test he fails pitifully. In *The Name of Action*, the supposed virgin, Anne-Marie, challenges young Chant to prove his virility; he manages to do so, but only because she is not the genuine article. Coral, like Elizabeth, challenges Myatt to prove his courage, and on a larger plane, to leave behind his bad internalized father, his Jewishness. But Greene's virtuous woman is a schoolmistress whose test cannot be passed, a mother whose standards can never be lived up to. She presents a constant reproach in her very being, and killing her off is the only way to finally get her off one's back. In killing Coral, as he killed Elizabeth, Greene is also reenacting the choice he made as a self- hating male child: to destroy the female part of himself.

Once in Constantinople, with "the nightmare of Subotica faded" and Coral all but forgotten, Myatt is overjoyed to be back in the world of figures—"something that he could understand and that had no feelings" (241, 244). Relieved to fall back into being an unfeeling Jew, he begins to "unfurl . . . his peacock tail" of Jewish stealth and bargaining. He makes a bid to Stein for his niece, Janet Pardoe, even using the amount of money he spent to "buy" Coral's favors as a card in this vulgar and loveless transaction. In his selection of the soiled and evil Janet Pardoe as a mate, Myatt chooses evil as surely as when he took Grünlich instead of Coral into his car. As in the end of *The Name of Action*, in the end of *Stamboul Train* the representatives of good have been killed, and the world is left in the hands of the Jews, the Grünlichs, and the whores.

Just as Myatt hovers throughout *Stamboul Train* between some kind of humanity and the ugliest and most vengeful kind of stereotyping, so Greene hovers in this book between condemnation of such stereotyping and using it to achieve his needs. And just as Myatt abandons Coral and turns back to his comforting figures with relief, Greene himself turns in the end of the book back to the anti-Semitic stereotype which he consciously despises. Myatt fails the test of manhood in the particular way that he does, not because he is a flawed man, but rather because he is a Jew. At the end, Mabel Warren's assertion, "Jews are not to be trusted," proves perfectly true. Greene could have given us a Myatt who made the wrong choice and was afterward haunted by his own cowardice, as are many of Greene's flawed-but-human Gentile characters. Instead, in the book's final line, "He wondered whether Mr. Stein had the contract in his pocket" (264), Greene places Myatt squarely and safely back in the "archetype inhabiting the collective unconscious of the English-speaking people" (Fiedler, "Fagin," 413).

Inside the World of the Bad Fathers: A Gun for Sale. In *Stamboul Train*, Greene had slowly begun to move toward a more human and less symbolic view of the Jew. With *A Gun for Sale* (1936), another financially and critically successful thriller, he retreated drastically from this position.

A Gun for Sale revolves around the young hired killer Raven, whose poverty and harelip have doomed him to a life of evil criminality. In the beginning of the book, Raven has already killed the peace-loving Czech war minister, a death whose repercussions threaten to set off a new world war. After having shot the minister and his servant, Raven learns that he has been betrayed by his unknown English masters, who have paid him for the job with marked notes designed to tip off the police.

Raven follows the man who hired him, and who goes by the aliases of Cholmondeley and Davis, from London to "Nottwich" in order to track down the powers behind the set-up. In the station in London, he takes a hostage, Anne. A chorus girl who is also traveling to Nottwich to perform in a pantomime there, she happens to be the fiancée of Mather, the police inspector investigating the crime. Raven tells Anne what he has discovered of the plot, and after ingeniously getting away from him, she determines to find out more herself and to halt the coming war by making her knowledge public. In order to do so, she goes out to dinner with Davis, one of the backers of her pantomime. Afterward he takes her to a bawdy-house kept by a filthy defrocked Anglican priest and his repulsive wife. When Davis learns of her knowledge, he strangles her inefficiently and stuffs her up a chimney there. Raven follows Anne to the house and removes her from the chimney just in time. They spend the night hiding together in a cold hut, where he confides in her, telling her the sad story of his life. The next day the threat of war occasions a citywide gas-mask drill, and Raven escapes from the hut in the fog and manages to steal a gas mask, which disguises his deformed face. Wearing it, he follows Davis to the real seat of power, the Midland Steel building, where the armament dealer and magnate Sir Marcus has his offices. By now Raven realizes that Sir Marcus is the one who hired him to kill the good war minister, in order to enrich himself by the ensuing world war. Raven confronts and shoots first Davis, then Sir Marcus; but Anne has reported him to the police, and he too is shot and killed. Because of Anne's timely information, the war is prevented.

Andrews, Chant, and Myatt are offered redemption and refuse it, but in *A Gun for Sale*, although he proves to be braver and more capable of love than any of the other young heroes, Raven's "lost childhood" has effectively doomed him from the beginning, preventing any such redemption. Andrews is pursued by his internalized bad father and Myatt by the Jewishness which serves the same function, but Raven's past is with him constantly, in the repugnance with which people turn from his badly repaired harelip and in the terrible flashbacks which never leave him alone. In *A Gun for Sale*, as in the later *Brighton Rock* (1938), we inhabit the world of the bad fathers. And this time the bad father is, unmistakably, a Jew.

Raven's harelip, "a badge of class [which] revealed the poverty of parents who couldn't afford a clever surgeon," sets him even more apart than Myatt's Jewishness.[32] We learn early that "Raven had never had a girl. The hare-lip prevented that" (1). As if poverty and disfigurement are not enough, Raven was born when his father was in jail and his mother in a state of despair. "You get sort of mad," Raven tells Anne, his sympathetic confessor, "when everything reminds you of what's over and done with. Sometimes you want to begin fresh, and then someone praying, or a smell, or something you read in the paper, and it's all back again, the places and the people" (159).

The story of childhood betrayal and violence which Raven tells Anne begins with the betrayal of his mother's purity which resulted in his conception. As for Kernberg's borderline narcissistic patients, for Lewis, and for Williams, the primal scene is a location of horror and disgust:

> They have a good time and what do they mind if someone's born ugly? Three minutes in bed or against a wall, and then a life time for the one that's born. . . . Mother love . . . the kitchen table, the carving knife on the linoleum, the blood all over his mother's dress. (156)

As Wyndham Lewis and Charles Williams also conclude, a life which begins with female concupiscence is a life hardly worth living. Raven's father, who was himself a murderer, was hanged, and his son, who has helplessly internalized his evil, feels bound to follow his pattern. He repeats over and over: "They aren't going to get me. I'm not going to prison. I don't care a damn if I plug one of you. I don't care if I hang. My father hanged . . . what's good enough for him . . . " (20). His mother has committed the ultimate betrayal by slashing her throat with a carving knife and leaving her son to find her. "She hadn't even troubled to lock the door: that was all she cared about him" (129). After her death, Raven was sent to an industrial school: "one of her majesty's homes." He remembers "solitary confinement for a kid that's caught talking in the chapel and the birch for almost anything you do. Bread and water. A sergeant knocking you around if you try to lark a bit . . . the cold stone stairs, the cracked commanding bell, the tiny punishment cells" (158–59).

It is this lost childhood which has made Raven into what he is: a man for whom "there's always been a war"; a hired killer who, "like Kay in *The Snow Queen*... bore the cold within him as he walked... felt no pain from the chip of ice in his breast" (57, 9).

A comparison of this monstrous childhood to Greene's own and the accompanying assumption that Raven is a mouthpiece for Greene may seem farfetched. Greene himself mocked the suggestion when Allain brought it up in relation to Pinkie, the boy-murderer in *Brighton Rock*, for whom Raven was a preliminary sketch. "Say what you will," he told her, "I doubt whether any parallel can be drawn between Pinkie... and myself" (*Other*, 24). In fact, one does not have to look far to find parallels between Pinkie, Raven (his fraternal twin), and Greene. Raven's sliver of ice is chipped from Greene's own block, while Raven's rage at the parental betrayal is like Greene's own murderous rage, which, when turned inward, led him to attempt suicide. The events in Raven's childhood closely mirror the feeling content if not the material reality of Greene's childhood: Greene's punishing father appears as Raven's murderous one; Greene's remote mother is transformed into one so uncaring that she withdraws all the way into death. Especially the portrait of Raven's industrial school fits the interior reality of Greene's experience in that "savage country" in which he was "a hunted creature, a leper." Raven, the depraved killer, screams in the voice of Greene's abused inner child.

Critics have blamed Greene for what they see as his excessive sympathy with characters like Raven and Pinkie, and it is true that Greene carefully invites his implied reader to understand that it is not in Raven but elsewhere we must look to find the real murderer.[33] Early in the book, we see Raven tenderly caressing a kitten, always a signal of Greene's fondness for a character,[34] and our sympathy grows when we witness the way in which his landlord and the landlord's daughter, Alice, betray him to the police: "I shan't be sorry when you've locked him up.... He's ugly through and through. That lip of his. It gives you the creeps.... Him, friends—what would he do with friends?" (17).

"Why can't you play fair?" Raven asks Alice, and his other persecutors. It is the hopeless question of the betrayed and powerless child, to whom life has never given a fighting chance (20).

Kapper in *The Name of Action* keeps running into Madonnas, a juxtaposition which points up his own Jewish evil. The action of *A Gun for Sale* takes place just before Christmas, and Raven repeatedly runs into cribs or creches, symbols which Greene manipulates in order to increase our sympathy for Raven by leading us to compare him to the Christ who was refused a shelter at his birth and was later tormented, as Raven is tormented throughout the book. Raven remembers the Christian mercy which was shown to him at school: "Nobody was beaten on Christmas Day: all punishments were saved for Boxing Day" (113). After the murder, still in London, he buys a dress for Alice and is mocked by a cruel, "genteel" Jewish salesgirl. He then returns to his lodging to find a crib beneath a Christmas tree. He picks up the Jesus, made of cheap painted plaster, and immediately identifies with the Christ child, like him homeless and like him betrayed:

> "All this business of no room in the inn. They used to give us plum pudding. . . . You see I know the stuff, I'm educated. They used to read it us once a year". . . . Raven picked up the bambino. The cradle came with it all of a piece: cheap painted plaster. "They put him on the spot, eh?" (14–15)

Later, in Nottwich, he sees another crib and stands

> staring at the swaddled child with a horrified tenderness, "the little bastard," because he was educated and knew what the child was in for, the damned Jews and the double-crossing Judas and only one man . . . on his side when the Roman soldiers came for him in the garden. (89)[35]

Up to now, Raven has had no one at all on his side. But, like Hans Christian Andersen's Kay, whose inner sliver of ice is melted by the tears of his virginal little sister, it requires only the love and sympathy of a virginal, motherly woman to melt the ice chip Raven carries in his heart. When Anne, whom he has captured as his hostage, seems not to reject him but instead listens to his sad story and offers him sympathy and protection, the melting begins at once. Like the Greene who wrote to Vivien, "[I]f you didn't exist I should vanish in a breath of mist," or Andrews, who tells Elizabeth, "You must stay with me always. You must not die before me. If you did I should fall away," Raven quickly becomes completely dependent on Anne, the only person who has even pretended to care for him. Dependence on a woman, for Greene as for both Lewis and Williams, is a constant temptation and a lethal danger. As we have seen in Greene's previous novels, such dependence carries its own burden and risks. As Andrews tells Elizabeth, "It would be worse than before if I should lose you now" (*Man*, 212). When Anne treats Raven kindly, "It was as if something sharp and cold were breaking in his heart with great pain. He sat there under the sink with the automatic in his hand and began to cry" (56).

In a freezing cold shed like the shed in which Coral comforted the dying Czinner, Anne suggests that they tell stories—"It's about the children's hour," but the deprived Raven, who has never been a child, knows no stories. Instead, "He sat in the dark feeling tears like heavy weights behind his eyes" (153). Only a determinedly hard-hearted reader would fail to feel sympathy for this child-criminal.

In *The Man Within*, Elizabeth reassured Andrews, "I will stand now forever between you and them" (209). In *A Gun for Sale*, Anne cannot stand between Raven and the world, but she can act as his confessor/psychoanalyst. In case we miss the reference, Greene has Raven tell Anne about an article he has read about "psicko— psicko—":

> It's like you carry a load around you; you are born with some of it because of what your father and mother were and their fathers . . . seems as if it goes right back, like it says in the Bible about the sins being visited. Then when you're a kid the load gets bigger; all the things you need to do and can't and then all the things you do . . . you tell these doctors everything. . . . And when you've told everything it's gone. (160)

Anne tells Raven that the war minister he had been hired to kill, whom he had been told was "one of the high and mighties," was instead a poor man whose father had been a thief and whose mother had been a suicide, like Raven's own mother. He had even attended a school like Raven's. Even worse, the minister spent his whole life "trying to alter all that" for the poor (156). Like Andrews, who testified in court against his good father, Carlyon, Raven has turned, not on his actual betrayers, but on the good father who, like Carlyon and Czinner, arrived too late, but was one of the very few to take his side.

In an endless cycle of betrayal, Raven is not only Jesus the betrayed but also Judas the betrayer. In return for killing the war minister who "loved humanity" and wanted only to help the oppressed, he has received thirty pieces of contaminated silver. The war minister, like Jesus, was betrayed by one of "his own people" or disciples. Again like Judas, and like all Greene's weak boy-men, Raven has victimized himself more than anyone else through his treachery. When he realizes this, he is even more determined to punish those who used him for their evil purposes—those "damned Jews."

Raven's real betrayer, and in fact the force behind the betrayal that has been his whole life, is the sinister Jewish arms dealer, Sir Marcus, the president of Midland Steel. In Sir Marcus and his crowd, more than in any Jewish character we have encountered so far in Greene, we recognize the myth of the international Jewish conspiracy found in the *Protocols of the Elders of Zion*, in the propaganda of the fascist and right-wing groups in Britain whose ideology I described in chapter 1, and in its culmination in Nazi ideology. In *A Gun for Sale*, we meet Sir Marcus's henchman, the greedy, sadistic, and cowardly Davis, alias Cholmondeley; but we only hear about the the hidden army of Cranbeims, Rosens, Ziffos, and Cohens who have betrayed Raven and his kind for centuries, who are the hidden power behind the world's corruption, and who are in the process of planning a world war for their own profit.

It is Davis, Sir Marcus's flunky, who actually hires Raven to kill the war minister. Although he attempts to hide his Jewish identity through numerous aliases, Greene identifies him clearly as the worst of those criminal Jews whose "soft humble imperative voice[s]" haunted the world of Coral Musker's theatre, and who were "mean with a commonplace habitual meanness, generous in fits and starts, never to be trusted" (*Stamboul*, 56). Davis is introduced in a stereotypical portrait which even includes an image of the medieval horned Jew:

> He was fat and wore an emerald ring. His wide square face fell in folds over his collar. He looked like a real estate man or perhaps a man more than usually successful in selling women's belts. . . . His great white face was like a curtain on which you can throw grotesque images: a rabbit, a man with horns. He was fat, he was vulgar, he was false, but he gave an impression of great power as he sat there with the cream dripping from his mouth. He was prosperity, he was one of those who possessed things. (*Gun*, 12)

On the train to Nottwich, Davis piggishly stops Anne from signaling to her lover by blocking the train window in order to buy chocolate to stuff his fat face. He is a backer of the show in which Anne will be performing in Nottwich, one of a network of petty, avaricious Jews behind the scenes, all connected, related, and criminal. The harassed director of the pantomime tries to remember whether "Davis was the man Cohen had quarrelled with or . . . the uncle of the man Cohen had quarrelled with" (67–68).

In a restaurant with Anne, Davis consumes food with revolting greed. On his way to the bawdy house where he will strangle her, he passes a group of children singing Christmas carols, and with a Faginlike gesture (or possibly with the glee of a Jew kidnapping a Christian child at Christmas to take home and roast), he "suddenly rounded and seized the hair of the boy nearest him; he pulled it till the boy screamed; pulled it till a tuft came out between his fingers. He said, 'That will teach you. . . . They can't play with me' " (74). After this, "his mouth was open and his lip was wet with saliva; he brooded over his victory in the same way as he had brooded over the lobster" (74).

Although his lust for sex is subordinate to his lust for food, Davis is quite ready to rape Anne, in between bites of his Turkish delight, when she makes the mistake of revealing that she knows too much about Raven's crime. The necessity of killing her fills him with Jewish self-pity: "He began to sniffle, sitting on the bed nursing his great hairy hands. 'I don't want to hurt you . . . I've got a weak stomach' " (79).

In a truly grotesque scene, this bogeyman smothers Anne with a pillow, his hands "strong and soft and sticky with icing sugar" and then stuffs her up the chimney (80). In contrast to Raven, whose death later in the book is a courageous one, filled with images of Anne and of Jesus, Davis meets his own death screaming in a high, feminine, peacock voice (like Myatt's peacock tail at the end of *Stamboul Train*) that it is all his boss's fault.

Davis gives an "impression of great power," but he is insignificant in comparison to his master, Sir Marcus—a figure of mystery and threat rather like Williams's Simon the Clerk, with his three international replicas and his plans to take over the world. Although we have seen Sir Marcus's photograph on the desk of the good war minister killed by Raven, and know that he is a Jew who grew up in the same orphanage as the war minister, his prior origins are obscure. He does seem to come from that same Jewish backwater which spawned Williams's Simon the Clerk and Lewis's Ratner: "If there was a touch of Jerusalem, there was also a touch of St. James's, if of Vienna or some Central European ghetto, there were also marks of the most exclusive clubs in Cannes . . . [he] might have been pawnbroker to the Pompadour" (137).

Sir Marcus is from the ghetto and from the brothel. When armament shares go up, so do his fortunes. The killing of the peaceful minister represents merely one small link in the inclusive plot, hatched with his associates, the other international Jews, to arrange for war. When we meet him, he is outwardly old and feeble, sucking at hot milk and rusks like Myatt's old father, another successful Jewish businessman. Even in his enfeebled state, his Jewish traits of greed, concupiscence, and the desire for Christian death and blood are still present:

> The deaths he had ordered were no more real to him than the deaths he read about in the newspapers. A little greed (for his milk), a little vice (occasionally to put his old hand inside a girl's blouse and feel the warmth of life), a little avarice and calculation (half a million against a death).... these were his only passions. (215)

Sir Marcus gives orders that Raven be shot on sight, referring to him as a waste product. Even his valet of years hates him and upon seeing him dead, wishes he had had the courage to kill him. In case the reader has not already noticed the contrast between Raven, the outlaw Christian, and Sir Marcus, the respectable Jew, Greene emphasizes this point in their death scenes. When Raven has trapped Sir Marcus, he determines to make him suffer more than the old woman he (indirectly) hired Raven to kill. He asks Sir Marcus, "Don't you want to pray? You're a Jew, aren't you? Better people than you... believe in a God" (216). But Sir Marcus only responds, "I have the West Rand Goldfields filed... the East African Petroleum Company" (217). When Raven actually shoots him, it is because these words "seemed to be disturbing some memory of peace and goodness which had been on the point of returning to him when he told Sir Marcus to pray" (217). Sir Marcus's Jewish evil, not content to despoil the world, has invaded Raven's new discovery of his own Christian innocence and faith, and sullied the last moments of his life.

The atmosphere of *A Gun for Sale*, even more than that of *Stamboul Train*, evokes the atmosphere of T. S. Eliot's poem *The Waste Land*.[36] The characters of Sir Marcus and his gang are not to be found in *The Waste Land*, but we can find them in "Gerontion" (1920) in the lines "My house is a decayed house, / And the jew squats on the window sill, the owner" (Eliot, "Gerontion," l. 21, in *Complete Poems and Plays*).

It is difficult to understand what caused Greene to move from the ambivalent but still conscious condemnation of anti-Semitism in *Stamboul Train* in 1932 to the inescapable implication in *A Gun for Sale* that the Jews are behind the coming war and the blatant though somewhat less central anti-Semitism of *Brighton Rock*. One possible explanation for this backward movement lies in the force of Greene's conscious denial of parental blame for his childhood misery. The abused children described by Alice Miller, who were not free to hate or condemn their actual persecutors, grew numb and empty. They surrendered their own sense of self and either projected their anger and hatred inward in suicidal self-hatred or outward onto some Other. Greene availed himself of all of these options, turning his own hatred on himself and, in these texts, on women and Jews. While the grim worlds of *A Gun for Sale* and *Brighton Rock* are far removed from Berkhamsted's middle-class ease, on the unconscious or feeling level they are uncomfortably close to Greene's own experience. Raven's murderous cry of rage against the parental world may well have aroused the censor in his creator and pushed him back to the comfort of safely established Jewish stereotypes.

Another, more speculative solution has to do with the upset of Greene's established bipolar system of virgin and whore in the character of Anne in *A Gun for Sale*. In *The Man Within* and *Stamboul Train*, the young man fails in courage and betrays the innocent virgin who trusts him, and she dies as a result of that betrayal. In *The Name of Action*, the supposed virgin is allowed to survive only because she turns out to be a whore. In *A Gun for Sale*, Raven does not and would never betray Anne. She, on the other hand, while a certifiable virgin like the others, is a tough survivor. When Raven takes her hostage, she tries to escape by throwing a cup of hot coffee in his face, something one can picture the whore Anne-Marie doing, but which is far more enterprising and violent than anything the self-sacrificing and passive Elizabeth or Coral might attempt. Even after being strangled, stuffed up a suffocating chimney, and left for hours, Anne miraculously revives the moment she is taken out. Unlike Elizabeth and Coral, whose faithfulness is such that they are willing to lay down their lives for men they know to be unworthy, once Anne finds out that it is Raven who has killed the beloved war minister, she rejects him, regarding him with revulsion and contempt. She wants to retch when she looks at his hare-lip, and regards him not as a fellow human being in pain but rather as a "wild animal who had to be dealt with carefully and then destroyed" (170).

As we have seen, in *Stamboul Train* Greene maintains close control over his implied reader. In *A Gun for Sale*, we are directed to react in ways contrary to the ordinary expectations of the thriller genre, in which we normally sympathize with the victim and condemn the criminal. This leads to an incongruence between Anne's ostensibly sensible action of rejecting Raven and turning him into the authorities and our reaction of sympathy for Raven. If we submit to Greene's direction, we blame Raven's mother for his first and irrevocable trauma, and blame Anne even more for destroying him after bringing him painfully back to life. "She had said to him: 'I'm your friend. You can trust me' " (220). When he learns of her betrayal, Raven's despair is complete, and he is ready to join his mother in suicide:

> He was only aware of a pain and despair which was more like a complete weariness than anything else . . . he had been marked from his birth for this end, to be betrayed in turn by everyone until every avenue into life was safely closed. . . . How could he have expected to have escaped the commonest betrayal of all, to go soft on a skirt? . . . The only problem when you were once born was to get out of life more neatly and expeditiously than you had entered it. . . . For the first time the idea of his mother's suicide came to him without bitterness. (221)

After allowing the virgins in the two previous novels to exert pressure on their morally empty lovers, Greene promptly killed them off. But Anne, who is neither a virgin nor yet, quite, a whore, and who is good by societal standards but morally blameworthy, is allowed to live. In Anne, the whore/virgin dichotomy no longer holds. Greene's other young male heroes were ravished by the whores and themselves raged and/or killed the virgins. This time it is Raven, the outwardly evil but morally innocent and Christlike man, who assumes the part of the sacrificial virgin who must be killed. Greene's system, like those of Lewis and Williams, served to protect him from his terrors. Here, we see it, at least as it applied to women, in fragments. Gilman believes that the need to stereotype becomes especially strong in situations in which our sense of order and self-integration is threatened (Gilman, *Difference and Pathology*, 18). It is possible that Greene may have experienced his own attempt to reverse his bipolar system as it applied to women as sufficiently threatening to cause his regression into a less ambivalent, more unthinking stereotype of Jews in this book and in *Brighton Rock*.

Whatever the reasons for Greene's reversion to stereotype in *A Gun for Sale*, there is no doubt about the identity of the bad fathers here. It is Sir Marcus and his forces who have turned Raven, born with so much inner potential, into a hired murderer. It is also the Jew and his machinations who have forced Anne to leave her role as faithful virgin and to betray Raven rather than to rescue him. Despite the superficially happy ending, the world will continue on shaky foundations. "The rats are underneath the piles./ The jew is underneath the lot" (Eliot, "Burbank With a Baedeker: Bleistein with a Cigar," ll. 23–24, in *Complete Poems and Plays*).

This regression is even more marked in *Brighton Rock*, published two years later, in 1938. I will limit myself here to a brief discussion of this novel, in many ways a more emphatic, less ambivalent recapitulation of *A Gun for Sale*.

The book's antihero, Pinkie, or "the Boy," another maimed boy-man with a past which he remembers as "a cracked bell ringing, a child weeping under the cane," is a Raven increasingly embittered and stony-hearted.[37] Unlike Raven, who was capable of selfless love for Anne, Pinkie is so overwhelmed by his bitter revulsion at the horror of female sexuality that he can feel nothing for even Greene's ultimate unthreatening and victim-like woman: the pale, shrunken, sixteen-year-old Catholic virgin, Rose. Rose is entirely loyal to Pinkie and even agrees to kill herself at his bidding when he proposes a fake mutual suicide pact (a kind of parody of Greene's early games of Russian roulette). She is saved from this death only at the last minute by the overripe busybody Ida Arnold. Ida is as strong and energetic as Anne, and like her, lives on the "right" side of the law. No virgin, she hunts down Pinkie and finally has him killed, not to prevent more deaths (Anne's reason for destroying Raven), but rather out of her need to penetrate to every corner in the ultimate female engulfment.

Greene's simplification of his treatment of female characters in *Brighton Rock* applies equally to his treatment of Jews. Even more than the world of Nottwich in *A Gun for Sale*, the criminal underworld of Brighton which is the setting for *Brighton Rock* is literally infested with corrupt and evil Jews: little bitches in fur coats who parade their wares in the rich hotel; an oily-haired young moneylender; a sidling gangster named, appropriately, Crab; and the members of Colleoni's mob—nameless, vicious, and knife-wielding Jews, who laugh in glee as they attack helpless Christians. Attacked by this mob, in a nightmare vision, Pinkie sees "Semitic faces ringing him all round. They grinned back at him: every man had his razor out; and he remembered for the first time Colleoni laughing up the telephone wire" (152).

In *Stamboul Train*, Davis was only a front man for the real power behind the scenes, Sir Marcus. In *Brighton Rock*, it is Colleoni, the "small

Jew with a neat round belly," who holds the real power (84). Pinkie, like Raven, is a homeless wanderer in a world of poverty and deprivation, while Colleoni is snug and at home in his huge moneyed hotel (87). Fiedler calls him "the gangster with the razor blade" ("Fagin," 414), but like Sir Marcus, Colleoni has bought removal from the world of razors and knives: as he tells Pinkie, "I'm just a business man" (88). Like Sir Marcus, Colleoni is removed from the bitter Catholic world of good, evil, guilt, and punishment. He floats instead in a vacuum of Jewish immorality:

> His old Semitic face showed few emotions but a mild amusement, a mild friendliness; but suddenly sitting there in the rich Victorian room, with the gold lighter in his pocket and the cigar case on his lap, he looked as a man might look who owned the whole world, the whole visible world, that is: the cash registers and policemen and prostitutes, Parliament and the laws which say "this is Right and this Wrong." (89)

Colleoni, though a criminal, is no outsider but instead a representative of the dominant society. He works hand in hand with the police, and, as Crab tells Pinkie, "[H]e'll go in for politics one day. The Conservatives think a lot of him—he's got contacts" (232). Colleoni is less individual than Sir Marcus. He is an almost random representative of the type who is taking over the world. Throughout the hotel, a Semitic hissing and whispering can be heard, and all the faces are dark and Semitic. A "Sir Joseph Montagu" is paged, and we have the sense of a rotten world in which Colleonis are penetrating everywhere. Pinkie at one point thinks he may see Colleoni but then realizes that it could be "any rich middle-aged Jew" (157).

We have noted the fragmentation of Greene's system in *A Gun for Sale*. At the end of that book, the corrupt Jews have been vanquished, and the Jews' War avoided. Power seems to rest for the moment in the hands of Anne and Mather, solid if unimaginative citizens, whose only fault lies in their lack of real empathy and vision.

None of the other books ends in such ambivalence. In *The Name of Action*, the pornographer-Jew, Kapper, and his whore, Anne-Marie, inherit the world. In *Stamboul Train*, it is the cowardly Jew, Myatt, and his whore, Janet Pardoe, who are the heirs. In *Brighton Rock*, the gangster-Jew, Colleoni, and the engulfing female Ida Arnold are the new inheritors of an increasingly bleak and inhuman world. As one of Pinkie's wiser cohorts warns him, "Colleoni's going to take over this place from you" (305).

Brighton Rock was published in 1938, the year of Kristallnacht and the annexation of Austria, and one year before Britain entered the war. Graham Greene, who had taken an early stand against Mosley and his movement and who had already publicly condemned Hitler at the time of the writing of the book, seemingly remained blind until after the war to the anti-Semitic content of this and his other novels. When Greene did make changes in the postwar editions of *Brighton Rock*, they consisted, as they did in the case of *Stamboul Train* and *A Gun for Sale*, of appeasing shortcuts rather than thoughtful revisions. However, the changes in *Brighton Rock*, unlike those in the other two books, make a significant difference in the way we interpret it. By changing Colleoni into an Italian and removing the words "Jew," "Jewish," and "Semitic" throughout the novel, in contrast to the earlier edition, where they are repeated in a building chorus of invective, Greene effected a "quick fix." Unsuspecting readers of the Penguin *Brighton Rock*, the only version which is in print and readily available for sale today, may encounter Colleoni and his cohorts and wonder at Greene's strange venom against Italians, and at the oddly familiar racial stereotypes he seems to attach to this group.[38]

As I have noted, Greene nowhere in his writings refers to these revisions, instead quietly introducing them into the new versions of the books. While it is probably preferable to change offending passages rather than simply allowing them to stand, an explanation of the changes and of what occasioned them would have been useful to us as readers. Still another option for Greene would have been to leave the original text as it stood, and to add an introduction in which he acknowledged his own textual anti-Semitism and explained how his consciousness had been raised since the time of writing. As it is, the revisions Greene made seem an attempt to rewrite textual history rather than a true effort by an author to own his own history of anti-Semitism.

Conclusion: A Cracked and Fragile System

Kapper, Davis, Sir Marcus, and Colleoni could swagger into the pages of Charles Williams and feel at home. Greene's Jews turn to revolution and fiscal conspiracy, while Manasseh and Clerk Simon prefer necromancy, but all six are trying to take over the world, and all are decidedly more masculine in their orientation than are Archie Margolin or Julius Ratner, those cringing quasi-females who inhabit the pages of Lewis. While the male Jews of all three authors closely conspire with the whorish females, Lewis's Jews are sisters to the whores, while Greene's and Williams's are whoremasters. Once again, Greene's dichotomy of virgin and whore bears a somewhat closer relation to Williams's dichotomy of Slave-Goddess and bitch than to Lewis's somewhat undifferentiated engulfing female. However, even the best women in all three authors' systems, whether they are Slave-Goddesses, nurturing mothers, or pure virgins, have an unsettling tendency to leave one assigned category and enter the other. Greene's good women, especially, are in some ways more threatening than his whores and must be destroyed whenever possible.

Despite these similarities, in Greene much more than in either Williams or Lewis, we have the sense of an author who is actually struggling with the weight of self-knowledge and with the guilt and complicity which it implies. Myatt in *Stamboul Train*, a Jew and Greene's authorial representative, is the embodiment of this self-knowledge and would find himself out of place in either Lewis's or Williams's productions. While the splitting, projection, and attribution we have found in the other two novelists' systems are still present in Greene's, his structure here is more fragile, more open to self-examination and self-doubt.

Even in the early books, Greene's inevitable central figure, a tortured young man faced with a corrupt and immoral universe and burdened with a traumatic past, must take some degree of responsibility and make a choice. When this young man fails the tests of manhood and morality, as he almost always does, the responsibility rests at least partly on him, rather than being located entirely outside of him, in either the past which torments him, the virgins who pressure him, the whores who tempt him, or the Jews who lead him into evil ways. It is this self-consciousness which forbids Graham Greene the kind of total split that both Wyndham Lewis and Charles Williams achieve with their loathsome Jews and engulfing women. The Jew and the woman are only temporary intercessors between Greene and his own confrontation with himself. In Greene's work, inner evil cannot be confined to the Other. It lies everywhere, beneath the surface.

Greene also has less success than do either Williams or Lewis in splitting off the "female" or feeling part of himself, and he is far more conscious of its loss. Like Raven, whose contact with Anne taught him how to feel and how to love and consequently meant increased pain as he faced the absence of these things in his life; Greene's own consciousness of his inner split only intensifies his pain. In these early novels, Greene mourns the death in life which comes from denying the "female" within himself. Greene, like his morally weak young men, wavers between a more responsible use of his Jewish characters and a reversion to well-worn and ugly stereotypes. In his later fiction, he would eliminate the Jewish stereotypes, and although his female characters would never become wholly human, they would at least escape the two restrictive choices of the early novels. As it is, even the early Greene we meet in these pages is a more complex writer and thinker than either Charles Williams or Wyndham Lewis. This is perhaps why, when he falls, it hurts us more.

SEVEN

Conclusion

As I attempt to draw this lengthy study to a conclusion, what surprises me most is its cohesiveness. The book which began as a broad survey widened in its scope before it narrowed. At one point I feared that my various sorties into the fields of historical literary criticism, Anglo-Jewish history, and psychoanalytic theory had been a waste of precious time, a self-defeating method of prolonging an already lengthy process, and a diversion from my main task of close textual analysis. Looking back now, it is clear to me that far from wasting my time, in my various ventures "outside" of textual analysis I was moving gradually but firmly away from the New Critical approach I had been taught, an approach which treated each text as a unique and frozen object, floating alone in its own pure vacuum. Each voyage away from my texts brought me back to them with a new understanding and a new context. My thinking began to escape the confines of fenced-off fields of knowledge called "history," "psychology," and "literary criticism" and moved toward a model of concentric, multidimensional spheres of knowledge, in which all these fields are connected.

This growing sense of connection took many forms in my study. My survey of the previous literary criticism on the representation of Jews in British literature allowed me to take a more objective look at my own methods and to see my own study as one link in a long chain, rather than as an isolated and unique event.

I emerged from my venture into Anglo-Jewish history with a pervasive image of silencing and denial, a sense of a virulent anti-Semitism which remained unspoken, a potent yet at times invisible force which was no less lethal because it existed beneath the surface. This awareness matched the very similar sense of denial, silencing, and hypocrisy which I found in my fictional texts when they touched on Jews and things Jewish. It allowed me to understand, for instance, the existence of undercurrents of vicious anti-Semitism in works whose ostensible or overt message was philo-Semitic.

I encountered a similar cohesiveness when I turned to psychoanalytic theorists in order to construct or verbalize a theoretical basis for the study and to deepen my understanding of the forces at work in my three authors. I had expected and feared that the different theorists would lead me in widely divergent directions. Instead I found different but converging roads, leading me to locations which felt deeply familiar, as I had already visited them at length through my fictional texts. All my theorists, whether they were male or female, literary critics, diagnosticians, or psychoanalysts, agreed that Western men are brought up by a female parent in the context of a misogynist and woman-hating culture. During the process of becoming socialized as males, they (to different degrees) suffer damage which leaves them split off from their feelings, rigid, divided, and on guard, unable to relax from their stance of unbending vigilance, often unable to love, and at times prevented from attaining full humanity. They are forced, as the price of their entry into adult manhood, to split off or deny the soft, feeling parts of themselves, which are relegated to and associated with the mother, and with all females. The pain of this severance, which means a kind of death of the spirit, causes those more badly damaged to split these parts off, to name them "woman," "foreigner," "Jew," or "nigger" and to turn on them with hatred and disgust. Traumatic abuse, either familial or on an institutional level, reinforces this damage, which is especially lethal when it is not acknowledged, as in the societally accepted institution of the public school.

In another example of the kind of connection which I mentioned above, my readings on the public school system and the effect of hidden abuse brought me back to my lessons in Anglo-Jewish history. The men who ran the governments and the civil service, and who thus made the policy decisions which sealed the fate of the European Jews, were the same men who were victimized by the unacknowledged, hidden abuse of the public school system and who imbibed its ideology. In the interoffice memos they sent each other, these men spoke of themselves as victims of encroaching, engulfing Jews. In the decisions they made to attack boatloads of Jewish refugees and to close Britain's territories against the Jewish hordes, they treated their country as a similarly besieged and victimized man, who must attack in order to survive. The same note sounds repeatedly in all the fictional texts I examined. As all the theorists explain, such damaged men have no sense of inner space and no sense of firm outer boundaries. They experience themselves as victims, easily invaded, swallowed, or engulfed, at the mercy of women and of other groups, such as male Jews, whom they see as alien or Other and whom they identify with the persecuted forces inside themselves. Cut off from their own feeling selves, such men desperately need women to feel whole, but such need implies female weakness and dependence, which cannot be tolerated. The resultant persecutory rage is directed either inward or at the woman or at her stand-in, who is often the Jew. In order to defend themselves against this invasion, they rigidify increasingly, protecting themselves with defensive dualistic systems that draw strict lines between male and female, Jew and Gentile, good and evil. And so the vicious cycle continues.

After my sortie into psychoanalytic theory I returned to my fictional texts with a sharpened understanding of these texts, and a new appreciation of how childhood and the school experience had shaped the authors and their productions. While each text still held its own shape, I increasingly recognized an authorial core system which seemed to encompass an individual author's early life as well as his work and to be repeated over and over in each of the texts I studied. Because I have already summarized these systems in the introductions and conclusions of chapters 4 through 6, I will allow myself a more imagist approach here.

For the system of Wyndham Lewis, my image is of a man running on a treadmill, swinging his fists wildly at himself and all around him as he runs, using up a vast amount of energy to barely escape the combined forces which threaten to capture him and turn him into a woman or a child. To us, these forces may appear to be merely people going about their business, but to him they are an army, led by women, with feminine homosexuals in the second rank, and with Jews, blacks, and a vast horde of unwashed and communistic masses bringing up the rear.

For Charles Williams's system, my image is of a magician in a seedy parlor which attracts respectable clients with unacknowledged sadomasochistic urges. The magician's main power lies in his trick of splitting the world into two parts and in his mastery of certain rituals involving dominance and submission. As a magician, he cannot operate without his woman assistant, who must be available to lend him her energy when needed, to allow herself to be stuffed into cupboards, and to lie down and be sawn in two pieces. But this same assistant has in herself a chaos of evil and corruption, which by her own magic powers she knows how to remove from the secret places of her own female body and locate inside his. Other sources of chaos and evil can be found in the audience, in particular in wicked Jews who threaten to run away with the assistant and otherwise disrupt the show, and thus to bring down the forces of evil corruption which will envelop the world.

In my image for his system, Graham Greene, like the other two authors, is constantly in motion, a weary and vigilant traveler, whose job is to map out such bleak and barren areas as arid deserts, arctic wastes, and ghost towns which have been abandoned by their former inhabitants. As long as he remains alone, empty, and isolated, the explorer can continue with his work. But when he encounters women, to whom he is drawn with all the force of his tremendous loneliness, a kind of centrifugal whirlpool opens in front of him and attempts to suck him in. These women often walk hand in hand with, or in the footsteps of, their companions, the Jews. When the explorer encounters such a pair, he is in for the worst nightmare of all, for it is then that he notices the foul whirlpool, with its deadly centrifugal force, opening inside himself.

Reading over these three images, gathered from years of waking and sleeping hours spent with each author, I notice that each one is distinct and different, but all three bear the same disquieting quality, like different nightmares dreamed by one miserable and preoccupied person, or by three brothers in one dysfunctional, unparented family. To take the last metaphor one step further is to visualize Wyndham Lewis as the boldest, oldest brother, Charles Williams as the strange middle brother, and Graham Greene as the youngest and shyest brother. The Enemy, Wyndham Lewis; the Saint, Charles Williams; and the Manic-Depressive, Graham Greene—they are indeed brothers under the skin. All three were rigid men whose productions demonstrate their preoccupation with relationships of power and dominance. All three constructed systems to counter what they experienced as the pervasive threat of invasion and disintegration of their fragile boundaries. And all three provided women with key and Jews with comparatively minor roles in their all-encompassing systems.

Until very late in the process of writing this book, I visualized women and Jews as playing complementary and equal roles in the work of my three authors. Somewhere toward the end of my work, however, I realized that in fact my findings would be similar to those made by Klaus Theweleit in his study of the writing and lives of the German Freikorpsmen. Theweleit found that for his subjects, the hatred and loathing of women was an overwhelming unconscious and conscious preoccupation, from which stemmed the Freikorpsmen's other hatreds, including the hatred of those people they murdered most often: working-class socialist men. As Theweleit's conclusions demonstrate, the targets of hatred of the Other may be far afield from the original object. I too found that in the systems of my three authors, the Jewish characters existed mainly, though not exclusively, in relation to the women characters. I had to conclude, as Kate Millett does in *Sexual Politics*, that "sexual politics, while connected to economics and other tangibles of social organization, is, like racism, or certain aspects of caste, primarily an ideology, a way of life, with influence over every other psychological and emotional facet of existence. It has created, therefore, a psychic structure, deeply embedded in our past" (229).

I found this conclusion and its possible implications rather staggering and immediately began to question it. My first concern was that such a conclusion might be interpreted as a minimizing of anti-Semitism, a force with its own history and mythology and its own terrible consequences. When I say that anti-Semitism plays a secondary role in these authors' work, I am referring to the role played by Jews as it relates to the role played by women in these texts, not to the relative effects on the victims of these prejudices in real life. In the face of our history, I appreciate the pressing need for separate studies of anti-Semitism, and understand why many authors have decided to restrict their focus to it.

Next I asked myself whether my identity as a woman and a feminist had informed my reading of these texts so that I saw women where another reader might have seen only Jews, and yet another might have seen differences in class. While one's readings are indeed indisputably tied to one's identity and perspective, my conclusion cannot be completely attributed to my particular slanted focus. I began this study as a result of my discomfort in England as a Jew, not as a woman, and I continued to view my work as a way to explore my assimilated Jewish identity. From the beginning, I named and defined this book as a study of the representation of Jews in British literature. Such efforts to privilege one part of one's diverse identity over another are not particularly useful. I am merely trying to establish that the conclusion I reached was in no way foreseen or consciously sought.

Nevertheless, it appeared unavoidable. In every case in these particular texts, women, with their open, ravenous mouths and their tendency to engulf and victimize men, seemed to be everywhere that Jews were—and everywhere, too, that Jews were not.

Finally, I returned to the critics I surveyed in chapter 2. If authorial anti-Semitism is so clearly linked to misogyny, I wondered, why had so few of these critics made that connection? My answers to this question supported my conclusion, curbed my rising grandiosity, and led to some possibilities for further study. In the first place, I realized, these critics were filling an unmet and important need, and any other focus would have diluted the force of their statements. They never saw the connections between the authorial anti-Semitism they chronicled and authorial misogyny because they had purposely narrowed the scope of their studies, choosing to focus exclusively on the anti-Semitism in their texts. When I turned to critics who *had* chosen to widen their scope of inquiry, I found that they did in fact come to many of the same conclusions that I did.

But my own study, like those of the earlier critics, is narrow in its scope. It examines only two groups, Jews and women, thus eliminating all other groups from its field of discourse. Blacks, gays, children, communists, members of the working class, Greeks, and Germans were only some of the other groups who appeared as Others in these texts, often playing starring roles, which I chose not to investigate. Obviously, I cannot claim a dominant role for gender without looking at race or class, to name only two of the many variables which I excluded. In addition, my study, unlike the wide-ranging surveys in chapter 2, examined the work of only three authors, all middle-class, male, British Gentiles whom I had hand-picked on the basis of their reputed anti-Semitism. I had further narrowed my scope by selecting only those of their works in which Jews appeared. It became clear to me that in order not to be wildly speculative, I would have to limit my concluding statements to the selected work of my three authors.

And yet, to return to the cohesiveness I cited at the beginning of this final section, I do feel able to make one broader claim. Just as the hatred of Jews is intimately linked with the hatred of women in the work of these three authors, I believe that other stereotypes or uses of the Other, often approached separately, are also similarly linked within larger cohesive systems, both within texts and outside of texts. While I continue to believe in the need for issue- and identity- based struggle, I will not be able to look at anti-Semitism, or at misogyny, racism, homophobia, or any other exploitation of the Other, in complete isolation again.

Afterword

In many ways, this conclusion leaves me at the beginning, not the end, of my quest, and I will end by posing some of the questions and unexplored paths which remain with me. Is it possible that what I have described in this book is a purely modern phenomenon? To show that it is not, I would need to go back and look at the early classics of anti-Semitism in the light of this study. Is the anti-Semitism in *The Prioress's Tale*, *The Merchant of Venice*, and *Oliver Twist* an outgrowth of Chaucer's, Shakespeare's, and Dickens's loathing of women? Somehow, I think it is not that simple, but I do not know. I have similar questions about the links between anti-Semitism and woman-hating in the early medieval ballads and miracle plays.

I wonder too what I would I find were I to broaden my focus to the use of all "Others" in the work of my three writers, including but not limited to those divisions imposed by reason of race, class, national and ethnic origin, physical disability, and sexual preference. Would I find that *all* of these factors were outgrowths of the male fear and loathing of women, or, given a truly open focus, would another factor or factors take their place at the forefront? Would I find that, on the contrary, there exists no one dominant factor, but that the preponderant issue depended on the perceived identity of the author? Would I identify the same issues of invasion and engulfment, simply transferred to different groups, or would the issues be different according to the particular identified Other?

How much, I wonder, do my conclusions depend on the British focus of this study, or on its male focus? Would questions like these even be relevant were I to examine the work of women authors? What would I find if I looked at self-reflective writing—fiction in which Jews write about Jews, or in which members of other identified "Others" write about themselves? The permutations are endless.

Appendix: A Historical and Literary Timeline of Jews in England

33	Jesus crucified
400	**Authoritative version of the New Testament gathered in one book: Jew as Herod, as Judas, and as bloodthirsty Christ-killers, "[w]ho both killed the Lord Jesus, and their own prophets, and have persecuted us; and they please not God, and are contrary to all men." (1 Thessalonians 2: 14–16)**
1070	Jews "follow" William the Conqueror from Rouen into England, settling there later than in any other country in Europe.
1100–35	Henry I grants the Jews a charter of protection, which permits them to move freely in the country, protects them from abuse, and establishes their subjection to royal control and no other.
1144–83	First recorded case of blood libel accusation at Norwich, followed by cases at Bury St. Edmunds, Bristol, Winchester. Jews assembled for circumcision and other ceremonies accused of seizing on young Christian boys, torturing, sometimes crucifying them. From this time on, Jews often arrested and fined for these offenses, for poisoning wells or for administering poison to Christians in their role as physicians.
1188	To finance Henry II's crusade, Jews taxed at one fourth of their property.
1189–90	Richard I orders no Jews or women to attend his coronation. Rumor that he has ordered Jews exterminated results in destruction of Jewish communities all over England, including destruction of Jews of York.
1194	Richard establishes Exchequeur of the Jews; "archa," or chest, in which duplicate records of all debts to the Jews kept.
1215	Hostile legislation of Fourth Lateran Council (Pope Innocent II) establishes anti-Jewish code including the wearing of distinguishing yellow badges.

1227	Jews taxed mercilessly as punishment for various ritual crimes: forcibly circumcising men, crucifying children, poisoning wells, mistreating image of Virgin.
1231–53	Edict issued expelling Jews from Leicester, followed by other local expulsions.
1255	Accusation of ritual murder of little Hugh of Lincoln. The king (Henry II) himself supervises hanging and torture of accused Jew.
1255	**In his *Historia Major* Mathew Parris tells the story of Hugh of Lincoln.**
1263–66	Widespread sacking and burning of Jewish communities.
1275	Edward I: Statutum de Judaismo forbids Jews to practice usury, empowers them to enter commerce and farming, but without owning land or entering guilds.
1290	Expulsion: Edward expels all Jews, setting a precedent for other European countries. Jewish population, never more than four thousand, completely disappears from England, except for an occasional physician called in for royalty.
1300–1690	**During absence of Jews, miracle and mystery plays, ballads like "The Jew's Daughter" and "Sir Hugh" and "Sir Hugh or the Jew's Daughter" recount martyrdom of little Hugh of Lincoln. York cycle of mystery plays, Corpus Christi pageants presented by guilds, portray Jews as malicious usurers, brutal Christ-killers, or comic clowns; all devilish incarnations of evil.**
1362	**William Langland, *The Vision of Piers the Ploughman*: Jews as representatives of the Seven Deadly Sins.**
1390	**Geoffrey Chaucer, *Canterbury Tales*, including "The Prioress's Tale": Jew as ritual murderer of small boys.**
1392	**John Gower, *Confessio Amantis*: sinful Jew destroyed by virtuous lion.**
1500s	Small colony of Marranos (Spanish and Portuguese Jews converted to Catholicism) forms in London, fleeing persecution in Spain and Portugal. Breaks up in 1553 on accession of Mary and Catholic reaction.
1577	**In his *Chronicles*, Holinshed reports on the coronation of Richard the Lion-Hearted, and the massacre "because of the hatred generallie conceived against the obstinate frowardness of the Jewes."**
1592	**Christopher Marlowe, *The Jew of Malta*: Jew as poisoner, usurer, murderer of countless nuns and innocents; not even a good father.**
1594	Roderigo Lopez, physician to Queen Elizabeth, is executed for plotting to poison her.

1594 **William Shakespeare, *The Merchant of Venice*: mixed portrait of much-wronged usurer who wants blood revenge but does love his daughter and bleeds like other men.**

1632 **A *Short Demurrer to the Jews Long Discontinued Remitter into England*, William Prynne's answer to the question of the readmittance of the Jews: "The Jews had been formerly great clippers and forgers of money, and had crucified three or four children at least, which were the principal cause of their banishment."**

1655 Manasseh Ben Israel, Amsterdam rabbi and mystic, presents his "Humble Address" to Parliament with support of Oliver Cromwell. Petition turned down but Jews begin to reenter England gradually.

1663 **Samuel Pepys records a visit to a synagogue in his *Diary*; "to see the disorder, laughing, sporting... more like brutes than people knowing the true God."**

1664–73 Charles II authorizes readmittance and promises protection, freedom of worship.

1690–1761 Formation of small Yiddish-speaking Ashkenazi community fleeing persecution in Germany and Poland.

1730–50 Period of relative calm. Jews still cannot own land or leave money to their heirs, are excluded from mercantile and other organizations, considered aliens.

1735 The Jewish Naturalization Bill (Jew Bill), providing for naturalization of Jews resident in England for three years, defeated.

1760 London Committee of British Jews (Board of Deputies) created. Now between 6,000 and 8,000 Jews in England, including those engaged in wholesale commerce, brokerage, stock jobbing, trade in precious stones, shopkeepers, watchmakers, artisans, old-clothes peddlers. Largest community in London; smaller communities in Leeds, Manchester.

1794 **Richard Cumberland, *The Jew*: Jew as helpless saint. "If your playwriters want a butt of a buffoon or a knave to make sport of, out comes a Jew to be baited and buffeted through five long acts for the amusement of all good Christians."**

1807 **In his "Letters From England," Robert Southey visits the Jews: "Anything for money, in contempt of their own law as well as the law of the country.... England has been called... the paradise of women: it may be added that it is the heaven of the Jews—alas, they have no other heaven to expect!"**

1819 **Sir Walter Scott, *Ivanhoe*: the virtuous Jew's daughter, Rebecca, comes into her own; the Jewish plight is treated with historical veracity in Isaac, the Jew as marginal man.**

1831	**Richard Hazlitt's "The Spider of the Mind" on the question of Jewish Emancipation: "If they are vicious, it is we who have made them so."**
1831	**Macaulay's "Civil Disabilities of the Jews": "If it is our duty as Christians to exclude the Jews from political power, it must be our duty to treat them as our ancestors treated them—to murder them and banish them, and rob them."**
1833	**Maria Edgeworth, *Harrington*: effort to put to rest the Jew as bogeyman.**
1833–55	Jewish Emancipation Bill first introduced, rejected repeatedly, finally accepted. Lionel de Rothschild seated in Parliament.
1833–35	David Solomons elected sheriff of London, only public office open to Jews.
1837	**Charles Dickens, *Oliver Twist*: Fagin, the Jew, as evil corrupter and terrorizer of small boys.**
1837	Benjamin Disraeli, Christian convert, early Zionist, visionary, elected to Parliament.
1840	Sir Moses Montefiore serves as ambassador to Damascus, begins Anglo-Jewry's policy of protecting Jews all over the world with assistance of English government.
1844	**Disraeli, *Coningsby*: the Jew as hero and scholar-prince.**
1847	**Disraeli, *Tancred*: the new crusade to Jerusalem.**
1850s	*Jewish Chronicle* (newspaper), Jews College (theological seminary), Jewish Board of Guardians (welfare organization) established. Jews now make up 0.1% of population.
1857	**Thomas Hughes, *Tom Brown's School Days.***
1863	Dickens's famous exchange of letters with Mrs. Eliza Davis, who accuses him of doing "a great wrong" to the Jews: he responds that "it unfortunately was true . . . that that class of criminal almost invariably *was* a Jew."
1864	**Dickens, *Our Mutual Friend*: Riah, the Jew as defenseless and saintly victim.**
1868	Disraeli's first term as prime minister.
1874–80	Disraeli serves as prime minister.
1875	**Anthony Trollope, *The Way We Live Now*: Jew as vulgar parasite and arriviste; symbol of corrupt society.**
1876	**George Eliot, *Daniel Deronda*: Jew as hero and polemicist; early Zionism.**
1878	Joint Foreign Committee formed to safeguard Jews abroad.
1881	Persecution in Russia leads to great increase in immigration: working-class ghettos established in East London, Manchester, Leeds, Liverpool, Glasgow. Much resistance from both established Jewish community and non-Jews.

1880–90	Surge of anti-Semitism accompanies immigration. Foreign Jews held responsible for sweating system in factories, for housing shortages, and for spreading disease and causing race degeneration. Reports in mainstream press and by J. A. Hobson, Beatrice Potter, and many others accuse them of being both merciless capitalists and uncivilized savages.
1894	Dreyfus convicted in France; Zola writes *J'Accuse*; the case makes waves throughout Europe.
1894	**George Du Maurier, *Trilby*: Jew as sexual hypnotist of innocent Christian girls.**
1896	**Arthur Morrison, *A Child of the Jago*: Aaron Weech, a Jewish "fence," destroys life-chances of child Dicky Perrott, in a new version of *Oliver Twist.***
1897	**Rudyard Kipling, *Stalky and Co.***
1879–1911	Unsuccessful campaign by Jewish community to suppress Sir Richard Burton's chapter "Human Sacrifice among the Sephardim or Eastern Jews" in his book *The Jew, the Gypsy and El Islam*.
1897	Theodore Herzl calls the first Zionist Congress in Basel, officially founds the movement for "[t]he establishment of a legally secure homeland in Palestine."
1899–1902	Boer War with widespread claim that it was caused by Jewish capitalist conspiracy, a view held by many conservatives, liberals, and socialists.
1901	**David Philipson, *The Jew in English Fiction.***
1902	British Brothers League founded, including several East End M.P.s in its membership. Other associated groups founded around the same time are Londoners League and the IRA or Immigration Reform Association, a more "respectable" group. All aim "to keep Britain British."
1903	**J. Evans Gorden, *The Alien Immigrant.***
1903	***Protocols of the Elders of Zion* first published in Russia: forgery detailing plans of Jews and Freemasons to take over and enslave the world.**
1903–4	First serious consideration by government of British sponsorship of Jewish settlement in the Sinai peninsula or in East Africa as a way to "divert the flow of Jewish refugees from Britain."
1904	Creagh affair in Limerick, Ireland. Priest raises blood libel against Jews, causing large-scale boycott, violence, relocation of most of Limerick Jewish community.
1905	Aliens Act restricts aliens but retains rights of asylum. Gives rise to anti-Jewish "England for the English" campaign. Flow of Jewish immigration reduced by 40%.

1907	**J. Bannister, *England under the Jews*: describes the menace of the invading "semitic sewerage."**
1909	**H. G. Wells, *Tono Bungay*.**
1911	*Eye Witness*, weekly newspaper edited by Hilaire Belloc, later taken over by Cecil Chesterton, begins publication. Advocate of Jewish conspiracy theory and of recommendation that special laws be established to curb Jews in England.
1911	Violence against Jews in South Wales.
1912	**H. G. Wells, *Marriage*.**
1913	Marconi Scandal: Jewish cabinet ministers accused of trading shares on wireless scheme.
June 1914	Britain at war.
June 1914	**Wyndham Lewis, ed., *Blast* 1.**
1913–15	Leo Frank case in U.S.A.: Young Jew falsely accused of murdering young girl in Georgia and, after fighting the case through the courts, is dragged from jail and lynched.
1914	Alien Restriction Act.
July 1915	**Wyndham Lewis, ed., *Blast* 2.**
1917	Increased wartime anti-Semitism in press and in streets, including violent demonstrations in London and Leeds over nonconscription of Russian Jews "of German extraction."
1917	**Alec Waugh, *The Loom of Youth*.**
Nov. 1917	Balfour Declaration: the British undertake to establish in Palestine "a national home for the Jewish people," with the proviso that "nothing shall be done which may prejudice civil or religious rights of existing non-Jewish communities in Palestine."
Dec. 1917	General Allenby enters Jerusalem: by the end of the war the entire country is occupied by British.
Dec. 1917	Beliss case in Russia (man charged with ritual murder).
1917	Russian Revolution: secretary of state for war warns: "We must not lose sight of the fact that this movement is engineered and managed by astute Jews." Pamphlet directed to British women states that Bolshevik women were "at the disposal of any citizen who applied for them" and mentions Jewish link.
1918	In Israel, an Arab nationalist movement against Zionism begins: leads to riots in 1920–29 in which many Jews are killed.
1918	**Wyndham Lewis, *Tarr*.**
Nov. 1918	War over, with almost one million British and colonial deaths.
June 1919	Treaty of Versailles. German colonies lost, German army restricted and disarmed, reparation provisions made.
1919	"Britons" founded: virulently anti-Semitic group which suggests expulsion or extermination as solution to Jewish problem. "No man can be a patriotic Briton and not be anti-Semitic."

1920 **T. S. Eliot, "Gerontion": "My house is a decayed house/ And the jew squats on the window sill, the owner."**

1920 **First English edition of *Protocols: The Jewish Peril: Protocols of the Learned Elders of Zion,* sponsored by The Britons. Used in propaganda from that time until today.**

1920 **T. S. Eliot, "Burbank with a Baedeker: Bleistein with a Cigar."**

1920 League of Nations established for world peace: widely held to be instrument of World Jewry.

1921 *Protocols* exposed as forgery in *Times* but exposé ignored by *Blackwoods, The Patriot, Catholic Herald, Catholic News, Catholic Gazette, Catholic Times,* all of which cite it during the next twenty years.

1922 **Hilaire Belloc, *The Jews*: "The Jews are gaining control and we will not be controlled by them."**

1922 League of Nations confirms British mandate over Palestine, but government white paper asserts that the terms of Balfour "do not contemplate that Palestine as a whole should be converted into a Jewish national home but that such a home shall be founded in Palestine." Growing Arab discontent and British ambivalence.

1922 Mussolini establishes his dictatorship in Italy.

1923 British Fascists founded by Rother Linton-Ormond. Many landed gentry in membership.

1924 **Adolf Hitler, *Mein Kampf,* proclaims his plans for the Jews. "Gradually I began to hate them. I was transformed from a weakly world citizen to a fanatical anti-semite."**

1924–29 Economic depression.

1926 General Strike.

1926 **M. J. Landa, *The Jew in Drama.***

1926 **Wyndham Lewis, *The Art of Being Ruled.***

1927 **Hugh Walpole, *Jeremy at Crale.***

1928 Arnold Lees's Imperial Fascist League, small but vicious fringe group with much publicity: "It must be admitted that the most certain and permanent way of disposing of the Jews would be to exterminate them by some humane method such as the lethal chamber." Other associated groups founded at this time include Military Christian Patriots, National Workers Party. None had large memberships.

1929 **Wyndham Lewis, *Paleface.***

1929 **Graham Greene, *The Man Within.***

1929 **Aldous Huxley, *Do What You Will.***

1930 **Wyndham Lewis, *The Apes of God* and *Hitler.***

1930 **Graham Greene, *The Name of Action.***

1931	**Charles Williams, *War in Heaven.***
1931	**William Gerhardi, *Memoirs of a Polyglot.***
1929–31	Economic crisis causes Britain to withdraw to isolationist policy, favoring appeasement. Radical Right blames recession on "international Jews."
1931	**Graham Greene, *The Man Within.***
1932	Sir Oswald Mosley founds BUF (British Union of Fascists), only such group to gain mass support. Prominent members include A. K. Chesterton and William Joyce. Group urges physical attacks upon Jews in East London, which become common in the next seven years.
Feb. 1932	Disarmament conference begins.
1932	**Wyndham Lewis, *Doom of Youth.***
1932	**Graham Greene, *Stamboul Train.***
1933	Hitler becomes chancellor of Germany; sets up the Nazi regime, welcomed by conservatives in Britain, who regard communism as greater threat.
1933–39	House parties of "Cliveden Set" support Hitler. "Visits to Hitler" arranged for English fans, who find him reasonable.
Oct. 1933	Germany withdraws from disarmament conference, leaves League of Nations.
1933	In Germany, Jews are excluded from civil service, schools, legal professions.
1933	League of Nations "High Commission for Refugees Coming from Germany" set up. Lacked funds, support from governments.
1933	Representatives of Anglo-Jewish community agree Jewish community will bear all expenses for accommodation or maintenance of refugees from Germany without ultimate charge to the state. Fifty thousand to seventy-five thousand Jewish refugees arrive before 1939, with the help of the Academic Assistance Council, Movement for the Care of Children from Germany, and many private citizens. British Medical Association, home secretary, daily press protest against emigration. Jewish immigration to Palestine increases 80 percent.
Mar. 1933	English Jews support worldwide campaign to boycott German goods, though Board of Deputies holds back until 1934, and government and foreign ministry condemn boycott.
1933	**George Orwell, *Down and Out in Paris and London.***
1933	**Charles Williams, *Shadows of Ecstasy.***
1933	**Daphne Du Maurier, *Progress of Julius.***
1934	First meeting of the January Club, a discussion group for those interested in fascism.
1934	National Committee for Rescue from Nazi Terror set up.

June 1934	Olympia rally of BUF in which Blackshirts violently attack leftist counterdemonstrators.
1934	**Publication of T. S. Eliot's *After Strange Gods*: "Reasons of race and religion combine to make any large number of free-thinking Jews undesirable."**
1934	**Graham Greene, ed., *The Old School.***
1935	Nuremberg laws in Germany prohibit intermarriage between Jew and Gentile, establish categories of non-Aryans, deprive Jews of citizenship and other rights. Books are burned in an effort to purge Germany of Jewish culture. Laws extended to Austria in 1938.
1935	The British Legion and various Anglo-German link groups arrange for schoolbook propaganda, school visits to Germany on invitation of Goebbels.
1935	Mussolini conquers Abyssinia without opposition.
1935	British Non-Sectarian Anti-Nazi Council to Champion Human Rights reorganizes itself under Churchill's leadership as Focus for the Defense of Freedom and Peace. Aims: to convince government of immorality of Hitler regime and to lobby against appeasement.
1935	**Christopher Isherwood, *Mr. Norris Changes Trains.***
1935	**Sapper, *Bulldog Drummond at Bay.***
1935	**Leonard Woolf, *Quack! Quack!***
Mar. 1936	Left Book Club begins publication and educational activities.
Mar. 1936	Hitler occupies Rhineland, again without opposition.
Mar. 1936	Security Council of League of Nations meets in London. Only Soviet representative, Litvinov, proposes sanctions against Germany.
Apr. 1936	Arab general strike and revolt; Mufti of Jerusalem calls for an end to all Jewish immigration, ban on sale of land to Jews, government by Arabs.
July 1936	In opposition to the Board of Deputies, Jewish Labour Council organizes conference to defend against anti-Semitic agitation by fascists. Board of Deputies condemns JLC.
1936	**Wyndham Lewis, *Left Wings over Europe.***
1936	**Graham Greene, *A Gun for Sale and Journey without Maps.***
1936	**E. M. Forster, *Abinger Harvest.***
July 1936	Spanish Civil War begins. Fascist Italy and Germany send military aid to Franco; Soviet Russia sends some aid to republic. Important cause for British leftists, many of whom enlist on republican side.
Aug. 1936	Olympics are held in Germany with great British attendance and enthusiasm.

Oct. 1936	Battle of Cable Street, in which antifascists prevent BUF from marching into East End.
1936	Reannexation of Rhineland.
Jan. 1937	Public Order Act, prohibiting quasi-military organizations, uniforms, disruptions at public meetings; a reaction to increased attacks on Jews in London by fascists.
Apr. 1937	NCCL (National Council for Civil Liberties) hosts conference on fascism and anti- Semitism with the JPC (Jewish People's Council) and mounts successful campaign exposing and discrediting ILF, BUF.
July 1937	Peel Commission recommends the partition of Palestine into sovereign Arab and Jewish states. Greeted by Zionist acceptance, Arab violent rejection. Forty percent of British field force is stationed there to keep the peace.
1937	**Wyndham Lewis, *Count Your Dead: They Are Alive!* and *Blasting and Bombardiering.***
1938	Jewish Board of Deputies forms its own defense committee; engages mainly in antidefamation, self-improvement.
July 1938	International conference at Evian seeking coordinated international solution to refugee problem, sets up Intergovernmental Committee on Refugees, but takes no other action. Cabinet informed of M.I.5 report warning "the Germans were anxious to inundate this country with Jews, with a view to creating a Jewish problem in the United Kingdom."
Mar. 1938	Hitler annexes Austria.
Mar. 1938	Lord Allen of Hurtwood, archbishop of York, and others write a letter to the *Times* drawing attention to the concentration camps: "That we should continue to work for understanding with Germany and yet keep silent on this matter seems to us no longer tolerable."
Sept. 1938	The Munich Agreement. Czechoslovakia is now part of the Third Reich. In his broadcast, Chamberlain announces that there will be no war "[b]ecause of a quarrel in a faraway country between people of whom we know nothing.... Peace with honour, peace in our time."
Nov. 1938	In Germany, Kristallnacht pogrom. Ninety-one Jews killed; 20,000 arrested and sent to camps.
Nov. 1938	50,000 refugees from Reich now in Britain.
Nov. 1938	Auden, Isherwood leave for U.S.A.
Nov. 1938	*Times* correspondent reports from Germany: "The condition of most Jews here is one of misery, terror, and despair."
1938	**Graham Greene, *Brighton Rock.***
1938	**William Gerhardi, *My Wife's the Least of It.***
1938	**Christopher Isherwood, *Lions and Shadows.***

Jan. 1939	Hitler announces his intention to bring about "the end of the Jews in Europe." Speech largely ignored in England.
Aug. 1939	Nazi-Soviet pact: Molotov and Ribbentrop sign a pact of "neutrality and non-aggression" between the two countries.
Sept. 1939	Germany attacks Poland.
3 Sept. 1939	British ultimatum to Germany. Declaration of war. In Britain, "phoney war" begins. Position of Jews in German-dominated areas of Europe worsens. Ghettos created in Poland. Germany encourages Jewish emigration, sending official message to British government, which rejects offer.
17 Sept. 1939	Russian invasion from East.
Mar. 1939	After Colonial Secretary Malcolm MacDonald emphasizes need to maintain good relations with the Far East, new white paper published reversing Balfour Declaration. Paper declares that Palestine should not become a Jewish state after all, divides country into three zones, and almost completely eliminates Jewish immigration to Palestine. Establishes nonelective government run by Colonial Office until 1945. Chaim Weizman, Zionist leader, responds: "It is the darkest hour of Jewish history that the British government proposes to deprive the Jews of their last hope and to close the road back to the homeland."
1939	**Wyndham Lewis, *The Jews, Are They Human?***
1939	**Christopher Isherwood, *Goodbye to Berlin.***
1939	**Graham Greene, *The Lawless Roads.***
1939	**Montagu Modder, *The Jew in the Literature of England.***
1939	The Link, an organization for friendship with Germany and against organized Jewry, has a membership of over 4,300.
Apr. 1940	Germany invades Norway and Denmark.
May 1940	Germany attacks Holland, Belgium, and France.
1939–46	Three guiding principles of British policy toward Jewish refugees during the war firmly established: no admission of refugees from Nazi Europe to Britain; no entry to British Empire or to Palestine despite German policy of exclusion; invitations to other countries to accept Jews from Reich.
1940	Britain seals ports of Palestine, returning ships full of Jewish refugees from the Reich back to internment camps or death at sea.
1940	Reports of "Fifth Column Menace" cause waves of hysterical antialien feeling, mass internments in Britain, deportation of 8,000 mostly Jewish aliens to Canada and Australia. Many are killed at sea in sinking of the *Arandora Star*. This deportation policy is later gradually reversed.

1940	Leaflets appear all over London with the inscription: "JEWS/ they plan it/ make it/ finance it/ and you fight it/ WAR." Notices proclaiming, "Perish Judah," "Kill the Jews, End the War" posted.
1940	Winston Churchill replaces Neville Chamberlain as prime minister. "I have nothing to offer but blood, toil, tears and sweat. . . . What is our policy? It is to wage war against a monstrous tyranny, never surpassed in the dark, lamentable, catalogue of human crime."
June 1940	Germans conquer France. British troops evacuated at Dunkirk.
July 1940	Battle of Britain.
Sept. 1940	Blitz (night bombing of Britain) begins; ends May 1941.
Oct. 1941	Himmler issues order prohibiting all further emigration of Jews from German-occupied lands.
Oct. 1941	Mass deportations of Jews from Germany begins, followed by deportation of Jews from Poland, Netherlands, occupied France. Polish ghettos liquidated.
Dec. 1941	The *Struma*, filled with Roumanian Jews, is refused admittance to Palestine; after two months afloat, it sinks in Black Sea.
Dec. 1941	Chelmno, first extermination camp, begins operating.
1940–41	Britain continues to refuse to accept any more refugees; refuses Jews of Luxemburg and France, who are sent to Poland and perish in camps.
late 1941	News of extermination camps begins to reach Britain from Polish ambassador, Netherlands minister, countless Jewish sources. Veracity of reports questioned; no action taken.
June 1941	Hitler attacks Soviet Union.
Dec. 1941	Japan attacks Pearl Harbor, Germany and Italy declare war against U.S.A.; Britain against Japan; U.S.A. against Germany, Japan, Italy. War is now World War.
1941	**Charles Williams, *Witchcraft.***
Jan. 1942	Wannsee conference: official plans for German "final solution" are worked out.
Aug. 1942	Geneva representative of World Jewish Congress, Dr. Gerhart Riegner, reports plan to exterminate all Jews in Nazi Europe. Reports ignored.
Dec. 1942	Polish ambassador, Count Raczynscki, reports liquidation of Warsaw ghetto, extermination of Polish Jews.
Dec. 1942	In House of Commons, Anthony Eden joins declaration from Allies of condemnation of extermination, promises retribution for crimes against Jews, but makes no suggestion offering refuge or relief to them. Vatican refuses to condemn exterminations.
1942	**Virginia Woolf, "Thoughts on Peace in an Air Raid" (written Sept. 1940) published in *The Death of the Moth.***
1942	**Evelyn Waugh, *Put Out More Flags.***

Apr. 1943	Anglo-American Bermuda conference meets, decides not to approach Hitler to intercede for Jews. Determines to refuse all offers to exchange lorries, soap, tea, etc., for Jewish lives, as Eichmann has requested. Determines to send no food relief to Jews of Europe, but offers other refugee groups asylum.
Apr. 1943	Last of Jews in Warsaw ghetto perish, sending out the message, "The world of freedom and justice is silent and does nothing ... responsibility for the murder of the innocent also falls on the democracies."
1941–43	In Britain, Jewish immigrants are accused of blackmarketeering and of causing panic of March 1943 in Bethnal Green tube station, in which 173 died.
1941–44	The flow of illegal immigrants dries up as German policy switches from extrusion to extermination.
1943	Beveridge Report provides for universal social security in England.
1943	**Charles Williams, *The Figure of Beatrice.***
May 1943	Bundist deputy to Polish National Council, Shmuel Zygielbojm, commits suicide in London: "Let my death be an energetic cry of protest against the indifference of the world which witnesses the extermination of the Jewish people without taking any steps to prevent it."
1943–44	British and Americans do not bomb concentration camps or railways leading to them, although they obliterate German cities and kill thousands of civilians in massive indiscriminate bombing.
1944	British Education Act guarantees compulsory free education for everyone up to fifteen.
June 1944	D Day: invasion of France by British, American, and Canadian forces.
July 1944	Battle of London: flying bombs kill 6,184 civilians.
Nov. 1944	As German armies are driven to retreat, gas chambers at Auschwitz are dismantled. Surviving inmates of Auschwitz and other camps are transferred to camps inside Germany.
Nov. 1944	As Weizmann negotiates with Churchill on new Palestine policy on partition, Lord Moyne, anti-Jewish minister to Middle East, is assassinated by *Lehi*, a Zionist terrorist organization.
1944	**Charles Williams, *Region of the Summer Stars.***
1945	**Charles Williams, *All Hallows' Eve.***
1945	**George Orwell, "Notes on Nationalism" and "Antisemitism in Britain."**
Jan. 1945	Red Army captures Auschwitz; under 3,000 inmates still alive.
Feb. 1945	Home Office advocates compulsory renationalization of surviving German or Austrian Jews.
Feb. 1945	Bombing of Dresden.

Feb. 1945	Yalta Conference, dividing Germany into zones.
Apr. 1945	Allied forces cross Rhine. Hitler shoots himself; Mussolini captured and shot.
Apr. 1945	British delegation visits Buchenwald, liberated by Americans ten days earlier. British public consciousness is awakened for the first time to what has happened to European Jewry.
7 May 1945	German surrender.
Apr.–June	United Nations set up.
July 1945	General election in Britain. Labor government formed under Atlee.
July–Aug. 1945	Potsdam conference: Allies agree on reparations. Cold War begins.
6, 9 Aug. 1945	Bombing of Hiroshima and Nagasaki. Japanese surrender.
Aug. 1945	Nuremberg trials.
Oct. 1946	Ten Nazi war criminals executed. Hitler, Goebbels, Himmler already dead by suicide; Goering kills himself in cell.
1946	**Jean-Paul Sartre, *Réflexions sur la Question Juive.***
Aug. 1947	Anti-Jewish riots in nearly every large English city, following the hanging of two British sergeants by Zionists in Palestine.
1947	**George Orwell, "Such, Such, Were the Joys" probably written.**
1947	Britain gives up mandate for Palestine.
1948	**Ezra Pound's "Pisan Cantos" appear; awarded Bollingen Prize.**
1949	**George Orwell, *1984.***

Notes

Introduction

1. Wyndham Lewis, *The Art of Being Ruled* (1926; New York: Haskell, 1972), 286.
2. Leslie Fiedler, "Some Notes on the Jewish Novel in English; or, Looking Backwards From Exile," in *To the Gentiles* (New York: Stein, 1972), 157.
3. For a semiautobiographical exploration of these themes in my own life, see *The Worry Girl* (Ithaca: Firebrand, 1992).
4. Leslie Fiedler, "What Can We Do About Fagin? The Jew-Villain in Western Tradition," *Commentary* 7 (May 1949); "Negro and Jew in America," *No! In Thunder* (Boston: Beacon, 1960); *The Stranger in Shakespeare* (New York: Stein, 1972); Christopher Ricks, *T. S. Eliot and Prejudice* (London: Faber, 1988).
5. Chinua Achebe, *Hopes and Impediments: Selected Essays* (London: Heinemann, 1989); David Dabydeen, ed., *The Black Presence in English Literature* (Manchester: Manchester University Press, 1985).
6. Some of the books I refer to are Henry Louis Gates, Jr., *"Race," Writing, and Difference* (Chicago and London: University of Chicago Press, 1986); Edward W. Said, *Orientalism: Western Concepts of the Orient* (London: Penguin, 1978); Sander L. Gilman, *Jewish Self-Hatred* (Baltimore: Johns Hopkins Press, 1986) and *Difference and Pathology: Stereotypes of Sexuality, Race, and Madness* (Ithaca: Cornell University Press, 1985). For an introduction to this theory I relied heavily on Terry Eagleton, *Literary Theory* (Minneapolis: University of Minnesota Press, 1983).
7. Leslie Fiedler (see above) and Edgar Rosenberg, *From Shylock to Svengali: Jewish Stereotypes in English Fiction* (Stanford: Stanford Univesity Press, 1960).
8. See Eagleton, *Literary Theory*, 59, on the banning of biographical criticism in the phenomenological approach.
9. See Roland Barthes, "The Death of the Author," in *Image-Music-Text*, trans. S. Heath (New York: Hill, 1977).

10. Patricia Ann Alden, *Social Mobility in the English Bildungsroman: Gissing, Hardy, Bennett, and Lawrence* (Ann Arbor: Research, 1986), 14.
11. W. K. Wimsatt and Monroe C. Beardsley, "The Intentional Fallacy," in Hazard Adams, ed., *Critical Theory Since Plato* (New York: Harcourt, 1971).
12. Klaus Theweleit, *Male Fantasies*. vol. 1. *Women, Floods, Bodies, History*, trans. Stephen Conway (Minneapolis: University of Minnesota Press, 1987); vol. 2. *Male Bodies: Psychoanalyzing the White Terror*, trans. Erica Carter and Chris Turner (Minneapolis: University of Minnesota Press, 1989).
13. The "good Jew," a post warden who was "one of the bravest men I have known and the most unaware of his own courage," can be found in Graham Greene, *A Sort of Life* (New York: Simon, 1983), 87. The three books Greene altered are *Stamboul Train* (Heinemann, 1932; Penguin, 1963), *A Gun for Sale* (Heinemann, 1936; Penguin, 1963), and *Brighton Rock* (Heinemann, 1938; Penguin, 1943). Unless specifically stated otherwise, my references are always to the original Heinemann version of these three books.
14. T. W. Adorno, *The Authoritarian Personality* (New York: Harper, 1958); Gordon Allport, *The Nature of Prejudice* (Cambridge, Mass.: Addison-Wesley, 1954); Joel Kovel, *White Racism: A Psychohistory* (New York: Pantheon, 1970); Jean-Paul Sartre, *Anti-Semite and Jew*, 1946, trans. George J. Becker (New York: Schocken, 1965).
15. Sophie Freud, "Social Constructivism and Research," unpublished paper, 1989.
16. Stephen Pepper, *World Hypothesis* (Berkeley: University of California Press, 1966), 91; quoted by Gilman, *Difference and Pathology*, 22.

1. The Jews of Britain

1. For a more consecutive account of some of the dates, events, and publications discussed in this study, please see the appended "Timeline."
2. Harold Fisch, *The Dual Image: The Figure of the Jew in English and American Literature* (New York: Ktav, 1971), 14
3. For the information in the Timeline and in this chapter on preexpulsion British Jewish history, I relied on the following sources: "Great Britain," *Encyclopedia Judaica* (Jerusalem: Keter, 1971); Solomon Grayzel, *A History of the Jews: From the Babylonian Exile to the Present* (New York: New American Library, 1968); Fisch, *The Dual Image*; Solomon Grayzel, *A History of the Contemporary Jews from 1900 to the Present* (New York: Atheneum, 1972). V. D. Lipman, ed., *Three Centuries of Anglo-Jewish History* (Cambridge: Jewish Historical Society of England, 1961); Cecil Roth, *The History of the Jews in England*, 3d ed. (Oxford: Clarendon, 1964); Modder, *The Jew in the Literature of England.*
4. For general information on British Jewish history from the expulsion to the twentieth century, I consulted the sources in n. 3 above and Colin Holmes,

Anti-Semitism in British Society: 1876–1939 (London: Arnold, 1979); Tony Kushner, *The Persistence of Prejudice: Antisemitism in British Society during the Second World War* (Manchester and New York: 1989); Tony Kushner and Kenneth Lunn, *Traditions of Intolerance: Historical Perspectives on Fascism and Race Discourse in Britain* (Manchester: Manchester University Press, 1989; Gisela Lebzelter, *Political Anti-Semitism in England 1919–1939* (New York: Holmes and Meier, 1978).

5. W. Williams, "The Anti-Semitism of Tolerance: Middle-Class Manchester and the Jew 1870–1900," in A. J. Kidd and K. W. Roberts, eds., *City, Class, and Culture: Studies of Social Policy and Cultural Production in Victorian Manchester* (Manchester, 1985), 94; quoted by Bryan Cheyette in "Jewish Stereotyping and English Literature 1875–1920: Towards a Political Analysis," in Tony Kushner and Kenneth Lunn, eds., *Traditions of Intolerance* (Manchester: Manchester University Press, 1989), 13.
6. Ira B. Nadell, *Joyce and the Jews* (Iowa City: University of Iowa Press, 1989), 58.
7. Disraeli's own texts included the novels *David Alroy* (1832), *Coningsby* (1844), and *Tancred* (1847), and a biography, *The Life of Lord Bentinck* (1852). To name an example from each side of the spectrum, a positive image of Disraeli can be seen in Ford Maddox Ford's *Mr. Fleight* (1913), a negative one in Trollope's *Prime Minister*. In "Jewish Stereotyping and English Literature," Cheyette notes "the ambivalence of this discourse": "It was the popular identification of the baptised Disraeli with a racial Jewishness that can be said to be the beginnings of modern antisemitism in Britain paralleling its European counterparts" (15–16).
8. For this idea and a discussion of Wells's changing position, see Bryan Cheyette, "H. G. Wells and the Jews: Antisemitism, Socialism and English Culture," *Patterns of Prejudice* 22.3 (1988): 22–33. A more current version of this essay may be found in Cheyette's "Beyond Rationality: H. G. Wells and the Jewish Question," *Wellsian* 14 (Summer 1991): 41–64.
9. Ira B. Nadell points out that "the August 1985 publication of a new edition of *The Protocols* in French in Beirut attests to its undying racist popularity" (251, n. 36).
10. Beaverbrook to Lord Gannet, 9 December 1938, quoted in A. J. P. Taylor, *Beaverbrook* (London: 1972), 387; cited in Lebzelter, 43.
11. *Morning Post* editorial, 6 November 1922, quoted in David Cesarani, "Anti-Zionist Politics and Political Antisemitism in Britain, 1920–1924," *Patterns of Prejudice* 23.1 (1989): 31.
12. Leonard Stein, *The Balfour Declaration* (London: Vallentine-Mitchell, 1961); quoted in Wasserstein, *Britain and the Jews of Europe: 1939–1945* (Oxford: Oxford University Press, 1988), 33.
13. H. H. Beamish, "Mr. Beamish Answers a Jew," *Hidden Hand* 2.9 (1921): 5; quoted in Lebzelter, 61.
14. *Times*, leading article, 8 February 1922; quoted in Cesarini, 32.

15. *Daily Express*, W. E. B. Whittaker dispatch, 6 January 1923; quoted in Cesarini, 37.
16. Elaine Smith, "Jewish Responses to Political Antisemitism and Fascism in the East End of London, 1920–1939," in Kushner and Lunn, eds., *Traditions of Intolerance*, 53–71.
17. Tony Kushner, "The British and the Shoah," in *Patterns of Prejudice* 23.3 (1989): 5; hereafter, Kushner, "Shoah."
18. Richard Griffiths, *Fellow Travellers of the Right: British Enthusiasts for Nazi Germany: 1933–1939* (London: Constable, 1980). I refer also to Richard Thurlow, *Fascism in Britain: A History, 1918–1985* (Oxford: Blackwell, 1987) and Lebzelter, *Political Anti-Semitism in England*.
19. Lionel Trilling, in response to a letter from T. S. Eliot in *The Home Nation*, of 15 January 1944; quoted in Ricks, 26–27.
20. George Watson, *Politics and Literature in Modern Britain* (Totowa, N.J.: Rowman and Littlefield, 1977), 125–26.
21. Gertrude Himmelfarb, *Victorian Minds* (New York: Knopf, 1968), 261; quoted in Ricks, 65.
22. Watson, 122–23; attributed, rather vaguely, to "a friend of Eliot's."
23. George Orwell, *Collected Essays, Journalism, and Letters*, ed. Sonia Orwell and Ian Angus, 4 vols. (London: Secker and Warburg, 1968–70), 4: 509.
24. Nesta Webster, *World Revolution: The Plot Against Civilization* (London, 1922), 307; quoted in Griffiths, 63.
25. John Wolf, *Nazi Germany* (London: 1934), 26–28; quoted in Griffiths, 68–69.
26. Tony Kushner, "The Paradox of Prejudice: The Impact of Organized Antisemitism in Britain during an Anti-Nazi War," in Kushner and Lunn, eds., *Traditions of Intolerance*, 86–87.
27. Hilaire Belloc in *G. K's Weekly*, Aug. 1936; quoted in Watson, 76.
28. W. S. Churchill to D. Lloyd George, 26 December 1918; quoted in M. Gilbert, *Winston S. Churchill*, vol. 4, *1917–1922* (London, 1975), 176–77; quoted in Lebzelter, 9.
29. Lord Londonderry, *Ourselves and Germany* (London: Hale, 1938), 97 (21 February 1936); quoted in Martin Gilbert and Richard Gott, *The Appeasers* (Boston: Houghton, 1963), 11–12.
30. The results of these polls are discussed by Kushner in "Shoah."
31. An excellent summary of Jewish resistance against fascism at home and abroad can be found in Elaine Smith, "Jewish Responses to Political Antisemitism and Fascism in the East End of London," in Kushner and Lunn, eds., *Traditions of Intolerance*, 53–71. Smith describes the Board of Deputies' outrage at the JPC's stand against fascism and the response of the president of its board, Neville Laski: "I am not concerned with Fascism as such, but with Defamation of the Community from whatever quarter it may come."
32. Bernard Wasserstein, "The British Government and the German Immigration 1933–1945," in Gerhard Hirschfeld, ed., *Exile in Great Britain: Refugees from Hitler's Germany* (Leamington Spa: Berg, 1984), 68.

33. For information about the literary scene of the thirties and forties, see Cunningham, *British Writers of the Thirties*; Watson, *Politics and Literature in Modern Britain*; David Daiches, *The Present Age in British Literature* (Bloomington: Indiana University Press, 1958); Krishnan Kumar, "Social and Cultural Setting," in *The New Pelican Guide to English Literature* (Harmondsworth: Penguin, 1983); John Lewis, *The Left Book Club: An Historical Review* (London: Gollancz, 1970); David Lodge, *Novelist at the Crossroads* (Ithaca: Cornell University Press, 1971); Andrew Davies, *Where Did the Forties Go: A Popular History* (London: Pluto, 1984); W. W. Robson, *Modern English Literature* (Oxford: Oxford University Press, 1970); Stephen Spender, *The Thirties and After: Poetry, Politics, People, 1933–1975* (London: Macmillan, 1978); Charles Moore and Christopher Hawtree, *1936 as Recorded by the Spectator* (London: Michael Joseph, 1986).
34. Maude Royden, "Bid Me Discourse," unpublished MS, chapter 8; quoted in Oldfield, 64.
35. Cecil Day Lewis, in "The Dedicatory Stanzas to Stephen Spender" from the preface of his translation of Virgil's *Georgics* (1940); quoted in Watson, 59 (not annotated).
36. For the Chesterbellocs, see Lodge, *Novelist at the Crossroads*; D. J. Conlon, ed., *G. K. Chesterton: The Critical Judgement*, part 1, *1900–1937* (Antwerp: Antwerp Studies in English Literature, 1976); Jay Corrin, *G. K. Chesterton and Hilaire Belloc: The Battle against Modernity* (Athens: Ohio University Press, 1943); A. K. Chesterton, *Oswald Mosley: Portrait of a Leader* (London: Action, 1937).
37. See Judith Ruderman, *D. H. Lawrence and the Devouring Mother* (Durham, N.C.: Duke University Press, 1984).
38. Aldous Huxley to Jacob Zeitlin, 19 November 1938, in Grover Smith, ed., *Letters of Aldous Huxley* (New York and Evanston: Harper, 1970), 439.
39. George Orwell, "Notes on Nationalism," in *Such, Such Were the Joys* (New York: Harcourt, 1945), 92; hereafter, Orwell, "Nationalism."
40. A. J. P. Taylor, *English History 1914–1945* (New York and Oxford: Oxford University Press, 1965), 420.
41. Spender, *The Thirties and After*, 96.
42. George Bolitho, *The Other Germany* (London, 1943); quoted in Griffiths, 72.
43. Minutes dated 1 September 1944, Public Record Office, Foreign Office, 371/42817/16; quoted in Wasserstein, 351.
44. For evidence concerning the British attitude toward the plight of the Jews, see Wasserstein, *Britain and The Jews* ; Walter Laqueur, *The Terrible Secret: Suppression of the Truth about Hitler's Final Solution* (Boston: Little Brown, 1980); and Monty Noam Penkower, *The Jews Were Expendable: Free World Diplomacy and the Holocaust* (Urbana and Chicago: University of Illinois Press, 1983). Each of these books gives much the same picture and uses the same information; I have relied here most extensively on Wasserstein, because his book concentrates solely on Great Britain, has the most up-to-date in-

formation, and is the most thoroughly documented. See also George Morse, *While Six Million Died: A Chronicle of American Apathy* (New York: Hart, 1967), and Gilbert and Gott, *The Appeasers*.

45. Minutes by F. K. Roberts, 14 August 1942, Public Record Office, Foreign Office 371/30917; quoted in Wasserstein, *Britain and the Jews*, 168.
46. Minutes by Cadogan, 16 September 1939, Public Record Office, Foreign Office 71/23105/3; quoted in Wasserstein, *Britain and the Jews*, 164.
47. Minutes, 21 April 1940, Public Record Office, Foreign Office 371/26515; quoted in Wasserstein, *Britain and the Jews*, 167.
48. Minutes by I. L. Henderson, 11 January 1945, Public Record Office, Foreign Office 371/51134; quoted in Wasserstein, *Britain and the Jews*, 178.
49. *Catholic Herald*, 24 December 1942; quoted in Kushner, "Shoah," 10.
50. Public Record Office, Foreign Office 371/23105 C16788; quoted in Kushner, "Shoah," 9.
51. Bradley F. Smith, *The Road to Nuremburg* (New York, 1981), 94; quoted in Penkower, 215.
52. Harold Nicolson, *Diaries and Letters, 1930–1939* (London, 1966), 327; quoted in Lebzelter, 34.
53. James Margach, *The Abuse of Power: The War between Downing Street and the Media from Lloyd George to Callaghan* (London: Allen, 1978), 53.
54. Robert Bruce Lockhart, *Diary*, vol. 1, 13 July 1933; quoted in Griffiths, 78.
55. Minutes by E. M. Rose, 20 January 1941, Public Record Office, Foreign Office 371/30000; quoted in Wasserstein, *Britain and the Jews*, 47 and 346.
56. Minutes by T. M. Snow, 17 December 1940, Public Record Office, Foreign Office 371/25241/38/48; quoted in Wasserstein, *Britain and the Jews*, 77.
57. Memorandum dated 17 January 1940, Public Record Office, Foreign Office 371/25238/274ff.; quoted in Wasserstein, *Britain and the Jews*, 49.
58. Minutes by Latham, 24 December 1940, Public Record Office, Foreign Office 371/255254/487; quoted in Wasserstein, *Britain and the Jews*, 109.
59. Minutes by J. S. Bennett, 18 April 1941, Public Record Office, Colonial Office 733/445/ Part II 76021/308; quoted in Wasserstein, *Britain and the Jews*, 50.
60. Minutes by Shuckburgh, 27 April 1940, Public Record Office, Colonial Office 733/426/75872/16; quoted in Wasserstein, *Britain and the Jews*, 50.
61. Recorded by Jan Karski in "Messenger from Poland," Channel 4 Television (England), 25 May 1987, produced by Martin Smith; quoted in Cheyette, "Wells," 31.
62. It should be noted here that few of the comments above apply to the British government alone. The Americans, until the very end of the war, were equally and sometimes more culpable.

2. *A Survey of the Surveys*

1. Raman Seldon, *A Reader's Guide to Contemporary Literary Theory* (Brighton: Harvester, 1095), 1.
2. Wayne Booth, *The Company We Keep: An Ethics of Fiction* (London and Berkeley: University of California Press, 1988), 232.
3. The critics cited in the first part of this chapter were Jews, with the exception of Christopher Ricks, Bernard Grebanier, Graham St. John Stott, and Charlotte Lea Klein, who was born Jewish and became a Catholic nun, a mixed identity I have mentioned in my discussion of her. Of the others, several were rabbis; all were scholars of Jewish culture.
4. Milton Hindus, "F. Scott Fitzgerald and Literary Anti-Semitism: A Footnote on the Mind of the 20s," *Commentary* 3 (1947): 516.
5. David Philipson, *The Jew in English Fiction* (New York: Publishers Printing Company, 1901), 30.
6. For this "anti- Semitism of tolerance" see chapter 1, notes 5 and 17.
7. Edward N. Calisch, *The Jew in English Literature as Author and Subject* (1909; Port Washington, N.Y.: Kennikat, 1969), 27.
8. M. J. Landa, *The Jew in Drama* (Port Washington, N.Y.: Kennikat, 1926), 10.
9. Montagu Modder, *The Jew in the Literature of England* (Philadelphia: Jewish Publication Society of America, 1939), vii.
10. Charles Dickens, letter to Mrs. Eliza Davis, 10 July 1863, in Modder, 220.
11. T. S. Eliot, quoted in William Turner Levy and Victor Scherle, *Affectionately, T. S. Eliot* (Philadelphia: Lippincott, 1968), 81; in Christopher Ricks, *T. S. Eliot and Prejudice* (London and Boston: Faber, 1988), 61.
12. Sander L. Gilman's *Jewish Self-Hatred: Anti-Semitism and the Hidden Language of the Jews* (Baltimore: Johns Hopkins University Press, 1986) provides a thoughtful and inclusive historical and literary examination of that internalized shame.
13. Hermann Sinsheimer, *Shylock: The History of a Character* (New York: Benjamin Bloom, 1968), 19.
14. Bernard Grebanier, *The Truth About Shylock* (New York: Random, 1962).
15. Two books published recently, Esther Panitz, *The Alien in Their Midst* (London and Toronto: Associated University Presses, 1981) and Anne Aresty Naman, *The Jew in the Victorian Novel* (New York: AMS, 1980), are worth a note here, as despite their dates of publication, they are theoretically much closer to Modder and Calisch than to Trachtenberg or to the more sophisticated studies which followed his. Panitz, writing forty-two years after Modder, shares with him the belief that literature directly mirrors contemporary reality. Like Modder, she consequently needs to refute the charges of usury, ritual murder, and lack of family-feeling made against the Jews, explaining these as lies. Also like Modder, she disputes the portrait of Shylock because "there is no evidence . . . that Shakespeare knew anything of Jewish

family life" (51). Panitz, who shares Landa's pessimistic theory of progression, attempts to show that the Jew has remained an alien and an outsider in both British literature and British society, regardless of deceptive signs of social progress. In *The Jew in the Victorian Novel*, Anne Arresty Naman illustrates the way Victorian novels mirrored the shift in the late nineteenth century from religion-based to race-based anti- Semitism. She finds the prevalent twentieth-century belief in the Jewish world conspiracy is rooted in this nineteenth-century racism and links both these beliefs to the mass immigration of Jews to England in the 1880s and 1890s. In her discussion of these immigrants, Naman falls into the old distinction between the wrong and the right kinds of Jew. In his portrait of Fagin, Naman agrees, Dickens was only faithfully mirroring the Jews he saw around him; a truthfulness only the grossly oversensitive could blame him for.

16. Joshua Trachtenberg, *The Devil and the Jews: The Medieval Conception of Jews and Its Relation to Modern Antisemitism* (New Haven: Yale University Press, 1943), vii.
17. Edgar Rosenberg, *From Shylock to Svengali: Jewish Stereotypes in English Fiction* (Stanford: Stanford University Press, 1960), 13.
18. For a summary of this theory and an excellent introduction to "reader-response" criticism, see Susan Suleiman's introduction to the anthology edited by her and Inge Crossman, *The Reader in the Text: Essays on Audience and Interpretation* (Princeton: Princeton University Press, 1980).
19. As Bryan Cheyette pointed out during my dissertation examination, Melmotte is not indubitably a Jew, although his wife is. On repeated readings, I, like Rosenberg, had always assumed Melmotte was a Jew. However, Trollope quite deliberately leaves us in suspense as to his character's actual origins, and I agree that such noteworthy ambiguity may be as important an authorial statement as the deliberate hints.
20. Harold Fisch, *The Dual Image* (London: World Jewish Library, 1971), 12.
21. In 1992 Fisch's statement no longer resonates for me as it did in 1971: in modern Israel it seems to me that Jews have proven themselves as willing as other peoples to kill for religious, racial, or national reasons.
22. Otto Kernberg, *Borderline Conditions and Pathological Narcissism* (New York: Jason Aronson, 1975), 233.
23. Two shorter studies have recently appeared, which, while well researched and inclusive, add little to the existing body of knowledge. Graham St. John Stott's doctoral thesis, "A Consideration of the Roles Assigned to Jewish Characters in Nineteenth-Century English Fiction" (University of Southampton, April 1973), is for the most part a dualistic classification. Rejecting even George Eliot, Stott finds the only redeeming Jewish characters among the nineteenth-century novelists in William Hale White's *Clara Hopgood* (1896), a void which he feels was not filled until Joyce's *Ulysses* in 1922. Stott, like Fisch, argues convincingly that the negative images of Jews are projections of the self, embodying the authors' own fears and failures. In "Type and Anti-Type: A Study of the Figure of the Jew in Popular Literature

of the First Half of the Nineteenth Century" (M.A. diss., Kent University, 1963), Janet E. M. Killeen corroborates Fisch's and Rosenberg's theory of the two contradictory types of Jew, agreeing that "whether saint or devil... a sense of humanity and normality are denied him." Killeen does take an interesting look at sexuality, pointing out the asexual nature of both types of Jewish male characters. She finds the first sexual portrait of a Jew in Scott's Rebecca, whom she feels "embodies a forbidden sexuality,which is continually at risk." Later on, in such characters as Svengali, the male Jew also becomes "a quasi-sexual figure, carrying connotations of sadism and castration" (viii).

24. Charlotte Lea Klein, "The Portrait of the Jew in English and German Fiction and Drama, 1830–1933" (Ph.D. diss., University College London, 1967), 13; hereafter Klein, "Portrait."
25. Daphne Du Maurier, *The Progress of Julius* (London: Heinemann, 1933), 190; quoted in Charlotte Lea Klein, "The Changing Image of the Jew in Modern English Literature," in *Patterns of Prejudice* 5.2 (March–April 1972): 28 (hereafter, Klein, "Image"). Klein's discussions of this threat in Du Maurier's *Trilby* (1894), Arnold Bennett's *Grand Babylon Hotel* (1902), Wells's *Marriage* (1912), John Buchan's *Thirty-Nine Steps* (1915), Sheila Kaye Smith's *End of the House of Alard* (1923), Hilaire Belloc's *Post Master General* (1932), Daphne Du Maurier's *Progress of Julius* (1933), and numerous other novels, is both illuminating and inclusive.
26. Her employment of the word "Zionism" refers specifically to the desire and planning on the part of British Jews for a designated Jewish state.
27. Bryan Cheyette, "Superman and Jew: Semitic Representations in the Work of Bernard Shaw," *Shaw: The Annual of Bernard Shaw Studies* 12 (1992): 249–68.
28. Gina Mitchell, "Caricature of the Bulldog Spirit: When Peace Seems Dull," *Patterns of Prejudice* 8.5 (1974): 30.
29. Vera Ebels Dolanova, "On 'The Rich Jew' of Fassbinder: An Essay on Literary Antisemitism," *Patterns of Prejudice* 23.4 (1989).
30. Leslie Fiedler, "Negro and Jew: Encounter in America," in *No! In Thunder* (Boston: Beacon, 1960), 239–40; hereafter, Fiedler, "Negro."
31. This dialectic seems often to arise in discourse based on strategies for resisting oppression. See the historical disagreement between Booker T. Washington and W. E. B. Dubois on the causes of and solutions for African-American oppression. See also the ongoing argument between liberal and conservative factions of the gay and lesbian community as to the best tactic against oppression: to prove that we are essentially "just like" the average bourgeois American, or to proclaim and endorse our differences.
32. Leslie Fiedler, "What Can We Do About Fagin? The Jew-Villain in Western Tradition," *Commentary* 7 (May 1949): 418; hereafter, Fiedler, "Fagin."
33. Leslie Fiedler, *The Stranger in Shakespeare* (New York: Stein, 1972), 99; hereafter, Fiedler, *Stranger*.
34. I disagree with Fiedler as to the source of the shame and fear. As a Jewish

child in this situation, I remember these feelings, but they were not caused by the play itself, which I relished, but rather by the uneasy reaction of the teacher toward me and the one other Jewish child in the class during its reading.

35. Joel Kovel, *White Racism: A Psychohistory* (New York: Pantheon, 1970).
36. John A. Garrard, "Now and 70 Years Ago," *Patterns of Prejudice* 1.4 (July–August 1967): 24–28.
37. Harry Levin, "The Jewish Writer and the English Literary Tradition," *Commentary* 8 (1949): 364.
38. Harold Rosenberg, "The Jewish Writer and the English Literary Tradition," *Commentary* 8 (1949): 218.
39. Stephen Spender, "The Jewish Writer and the English Literary Tradition," *Commentary* 8 (1949): 216–17.
40. For an example of this controversy, see "Eliot's Uglier Touches," *Times Literary Supplement*, 4 November 1988; Correspondence, *TLS*, 30 December 1988; *New York Times*, 9 August 1988, sec. 3, p. 20, col. 3; *New York Review of Books*, 6 November 1986, 18 December 1986.
41. Virgina Woolf, "Thoughts on Peace in an Air Raid," in *The Death of the Moth* (New York: Harcourt, 1942), 245.
42. T. S. Eliot in *Time and Tide*, 19 January 1935; quoted by Ricks, 93.
43. Ricks explains the method of "profound insinuation" in his discussion of the line from "The Lovesong of J. Alfred Prufrock": "In the room the women come and go/ Talking of Michelangelo." While we may, as many critics have done, conjure up an image of petty women chattering insignificantly about a great male artist, these implications are in fact in our own minds, not in Eliot's lines; and part of Eliot's purpose, according to Ricks, is to trigger them off.
44. "The rhetoric of power" is used by Christopher Norris, *Deconstruction: Theory and Practice* (London: Methuen, 1982). "Discourse and Power" is used by Raman Seldon in *A Reader's Guide to Contemporary Literary Theory*.
45. The works of Michel Foucault, including *The History of Sexuality* (New York: Vintage, 1980), show the rise and fall of various theories of "knowledge" about sexuality, crime, psychiatry, and medicine, conclusively challenging the idea that there is such a thing as "scientific truth" in this or other fields. I refer to Edward Said's *Orientalism* (London: Penguin, 1978). See also Edward Said, "The World, the Text, and the Critic," in Josue V. Harari, ed., *Textual Strategies: Perspectives in Post-Structuralist Criticism* (London: Methuen, 1979).
46. Seldon, 40, quoting Louis Althusser, *A Letter on Art* (no page reference given).
47. Seldon, 99, quoting Foucault's *History of Sexuality*.
48. Henry Louis Gates, Jr., *"Race," Writing, and Difference* (Chicago: University of Chicago Press, 1985), 2. See in particular the essays by Mary Louise Pratt, Patrick Bantlinger, Gayatri Chakravorti Spivak, and Sander Gilman.

49. Edward W. Said, "An Ideology of Difference," in Gates, 53.
50. Houston A. Baker, Jr., "Caliban's Triple Play," in Gates, 388–89.
51. I refer here to Matthew 14:6 and Mark 6:22 and to the apocryphal Book of Judith.
52. Tzvetan Todorov, " 'Race,' Writing and Culture," in Gates, 377.

3. In Search of a Psychoanalytic Theory

1. Sybil Oldfield, *Women Against the Iron Fist: Alternatives to Militarism 1900–1989* (Oxford: Blackwell, 1989), 119. For my discussion of Woolf, I am indebted to Oldfield's book, in particular to chapter 5.
2. Virginia Woolf, *Three Guineas* (1938; New York: Harcourt, 1966), 53.
3. For a modern version of this theory which asserts that mental conditioning becomes integrated into the body through physical and anatomical changes, see Oliver Sacks, "Neurology and the Soul," *New York Review of Books*, December 1990.
4. In his *Idea of the State*, von Treitschke wrote: "It is war which turns a people into a nation. . . . The features of history are virile, unsuited to sentimental or feminine natures. . . . To Aryan races . . . the foolish preaching of everlasting peace has always been in vain" (Heinrich von Treitschke, *Politics*, vol. 1, *The Idea of the State*, translated and published in London in 1916 as British anti-German war propaganda); quoted in Oldfield, 8.
5. Kate Millett, *Sexual Politics* (1969; New York: Avon, 1971), 53.
6. Gottfried Feder, in a letter of 4 April 1942, that appears in "Die Deutsche Frau im Dritten Reich," *Reichstagkorrespondenz der Bayrischen Volkspartei*; quoted in Millett, 223.
7. Adolf Hitler, quoted in N. S. *Frauenbuch* (Munich: Lehmann, 1934), 10–11; quoted in Millett, 223.
8. Hannah S. Decker, *Freud, Dora, and Vienna 1900* (New York: Free Press, 1991), 39.
9. Robert G. L. Waite, *Vanguard of Nazism: The Free Corps Movement in Postwar Germany, 1918–1923* (New York: Norton, 1952), 42; quoted by Barbara Ehrenreich in her foreword to Klaus Theweleit, *Male Fantasies* vol. 1. *Women, Floods, Bodies, History*, trans. Stephen Conway (Minneapolis: University of Minnesota Press, 1987); hereafter Theweleit, 1.
10. Jessica Benjamin and Anson Rabinach, Foreword to Klaus Theweleit, *Male Fantasies* vol. 2. *Male Bodies: Psychoanalyzing the White Terror*, trans. Erica Carter and Chris Turner (Minneapolis: University of Minnesota Press, 1989), xii; hereafter Theweleit, 2.
11. Ernst Salomon, *Die Geaechteten* [The Outlaws] (Berlin, 1930), 10–11; quoted in Theweleit, 2: 12.
12. Barbara Ehrenreich, Foreword, Theweleit, 1: xiii.
13. Nancy Chodorow, *Feminism and Psychoanalytic Theory* (New Haven: Yale

University Press, 1989), 11. Chodorow is here discussing Hand Loewald's essay "The Waning of the Oedipus Complex," *Papers on Psychoanalysis* (1979): 394, 401–3.

14. The work of these theorists can be found in Chodorow, and in Jessica Benjamin, *The Bonds of Love: Psychoanalysis, Feminism, and the Problem of Domination* (New York: Pantheon, 1988), 25–31; Beatrice Beebe and Daniel Stern, "Engagement-Disengagement and Early Object Experiences," in N. Freedman and S. Frand, eds., *Communicative Structures and Psychic Structures* (New York: Plenum, 1977).
15. Alice Miller, *For Your Own Good: Hidden Cruelty in Child-Rearing and the Roots of Violence*, trans. Hildegarde and Hunter Hannum (1980; New York: Noonday Press, 1983).
16. William G. Niederland, *The Schreber Case: Psychoanalytic Profile of a Paranoid Personality* (New York: Quadrangle, 1974).
17. Leon Salzman, *The Obsessive Personality: Origins, Dynamics, and Therapy* (New York: Science, 1968), 30.
18. David Shapiro, *Autonomy and Rigid Character* (New York: Basic, 1981), 71–73; hereafter, Shapiro, *Autonomy.*
19. David Shapiro, *Neurotic Styles* (New York: Basic, 1965), 41; hereafter Shapiro, *Neurotic Styles.*
20. Otto Kernberg, *Borderline Conditions and Pathological Narcissism* (New York: Jason Aronson, 1975), 237 (referred to hereafter as Kernberg).
21. Otto Kernberg, *Severe Personality Disorders: Psychotherapeutic Strategies* (New Haven and London: Yale University Press, 1984), 23.

    An alternative viewpoint is offered by Judith Herman, in *Trauma and Recovery* (New York: Basic, 1992). Herman challenges the traditional view of the borderline personality as defined by Kernberg, suggesting that characteristics which clinicians have labeled under the rubric "borderline" are often reactions to childhood sexual abuse. In this light the "distorting and frightening versions of the primal scene" which Kernberg documents can be seen as realistic rather than distorted, while the "distrust of mutual love offered by others" becomes a logical reaction, based on experience. I regret that I found Herman's work too late to influence my unquestioning acceptance of Kernberg's terminology throughout this book.
22. Miriam Johnson and Jean Stockard, *Sex Roles* (Englewood Cliffs, N.J.: Prentice- Hall, 1980), 22.
23. Melanie Klein, "Notes on Some Schizoid Mechanisms," in *Envy and Gratitude and Other Works, 1946–1963* (1975; New York: Free Press, 1984), 8.
24. Karen Horney, "The Dread of Women," *International Journal of Psychoanlysis* 13 (1932): 356.
25. Dorothy Dinnerstein, *The Mermaid and the Minotaur: Sexual Arrangements and Human Malaise* (New York: Harper, 1976), 36–37.
26. Margaret Mead, *Male and Female* (New York: William Morrow, 1949), 303; quoted in Chodorow, 40.
27. Roger V. Burton and John W. M. Whiting, "The Absent Father and Cross-

Sex Identity," *Merrill- Palmer Quarterly of Behavior and Development* 7 (1961): 91; quoted in Chodorow, 39.

28. Ellen Bass and Laura Davis, *The Courage to Heal: A Guide For Women Survivors of Sexual Abuse* (New York: Harper, 1988), 34.
29. Mike Lew, *Victims No Longer: Men Recovering from Incest and Other Sexual Abuse* (New York: Nevraumont, 1988), 63.
30. Lenore Terr, *Too Scared to Cry: Psychic Trauma in Childhood* (New York, Harper, 1990), 209.
31. Cyril Connolly, "A Georgian Boyhood," in *Enemies of Promise* (New York: Macmillan, 1948), 253.
32. Christopher Isherwood, *Down There on a Visit* (London: Signet, 1962), 48.
33. W. H. Auden, "Gresham's School, Holt," in Graham Greene, ed., *The Old School: Essays by Divers Hands* (London: Cape, 1934), 17.
34. My conclusions here are based on Greene's *Old School*; John Reed, *Old School Ties: The Public Schools in British Literature* (Syracuse: Syracuse University Press, 1964); Jonathan Gathorne-Hardy, *The Old School Tie* (New York: Viking, 1977); and selected "schoolboy" novels and memoirs by Cyril Connolly, Graham Greene, Rudyard Kipling, George Orwell, Simon Raven, Hugh Walpole, and Evelyn Waugh.
35. George Orwell, title essay in *Such, Such Were the Joys* (New York: Harcourt, 1945), 36; hereafter, Orwell, *Such.*
36. Hugh Walpole, Preface, *Jeremy at Crale* (London: Macmillan, 1934); quoted in Reed, 39.
37. Although girls have also written of traumatic experiences at boarding school, many fewer girls were sent away to school, and those who were tended to be sent at a later age. Moreover, reports on the schools for girls indicate that they were usually less brutalizing than those for boys.
38. Graham Greene, *A Sort of Life* (New York: Simon, 1971), 128.
39. Connolly, "A Georgian Boyhood," 159, 179, 181.
40. George Orwell, in "Some Letters of George Orwell," *Encounter* 18.1 (Jan. 1962): 60; quoted in Reed, 63.
41. Because Orwell did not date this essay, which was found among his papers after his death, it is impossible to determine just how many years later than his letter to Connolly Orwell himself wrote his essay. Valentine Cunningham in *British Writers of the Thirties* dates the essay from May 1947, and I have adopted his date.
42. Stephen Spender, "University College School," in Greene, ed., *The Old School*, 189.
43. E. M. Forster, *Abinger Harvest* (London: Arnold, 1936), 13.
44. Dr. Arnold, headmaster of Rugby in 1828, changed the course of the English public school, establishing the prefectorial or monitorial system and the liberal curriculum. See Reed, 5–6.
45. Rudyard Kipling, *Stalky and Co.* (1897; Garden City: Doubleday, 1920), 176.
46. In *Lions and Shadows*, Christopher Isherwood describes his childhood en-

joyment of the homoerotic and sadomasochistic content of this book, an experience shared by several of my gay male friends.

47. Hugh Walpole, *Jeremy at Crale: His Friends, His Ambitions, and His One Great Enemy* (New York: Doran, 1927), 147–48.
48. Simon Raven's Jews are greedy as well as appallingly ugly: "Must you looks so *Jewy*? some of us would say to a shambling, dirty, scrofulous Jewish clown, who had a way of wolfing down all the (rationed) potatoes at lunch when no one else was looking" (*The Old School* [London: Hamish Hamilton, 1986], 16).
49. Alec Waugh, *The Loom of Youth* (London: Grant Richards, 1917), 285.
50. Daphne Patai, *The Orwell Mystique: A Study in Male Ideology* (Amherst, Mass.: University of Massachusetts Press, 1984). In her brilliant book, Patai links Orwell's misogyny to his early anti-Semitism and effectively demolishes the Orwell his admirers cherish.
51. Bernard Crick, *George Orwell: A Life* (Boston: Little Brown, 1980), xxviii.
52. Christopher Isherwood, *Lions and Shadows* (London: Hogarth, 1938), 75–79.
53. E. M. Forster, "Jew Consciousness," in *Two Cheers for Democracy* (London: Arnold, 1951), 25.

4. Wyndham Lewis

In citing works by Lewis in the notes, short titles have been used. After their initial citation, works frequently cited have been identified by the following abbreviations:

Left Wings Over Europe	*Left*
Doom of Youth	*Youth*
Count Your Dead: They Are Alive!	*Count*
Hitler	*Hitler*
The Hitler Cult	*Cult*
The Jews, Are They Human?	*Jews*
"Cantleman's Spring Mate"	"Cantleman"
Tarr	*Tarr*
Apes of God	*Apes*
Blasting and Bombardiering	*Blasting*
Self Condemned	*Self*
Rude Assignment	*Rude*
The Letters of Wyndham Lewis	*Letters*

The citation "Meyers" refers to Jeffrey Meyers, *The Enemy* (London: Routledge, 1980). Other works by Meyers are clearly identified by title.

1. Fredric Jameson, *Fables of Aggression* (Berkeley: University of California Press, 1979), 4. Jameson states that these attitudes on the part of Lewis will be "abundantly documented" in his book; unfortunately, Jameson's rather impenetrable and dense approach, which he calls the "libidinal apparatus model," makes a great part of his own book inaccessible to all but the most determined contemporary readers.
2. Jeffrey Meyers, *The Enemy* (London: Routledge, 1980), 110.
3. *DSM-III* (Washington: American Psychiatric Association, 1987), 35. While the *DSM- III*, a reference book used for diagnosis, expresses it most succinctly, this same "diagnosis" of Lewis is confirmed by reference to all of the other clinicians I cite in the previous chapter, in particular David Shapiro.
4. Julian Symons, ed., *The Essential Wyndham Lewis: An Introduction to His Work* (London: Deutsch, 1989), 2.
5. Wyndham Lewis, *Rude Assignment: An Intellectual Biography* (1950; Santa Barbara: Black Sparrow, 1984), 126. In this and subsequent citations of Lewis's work, I have of course reproduced his rather idiosyncratic system of spelling, punctuation, capitalization, and italics: all irregularities reflect the original text.
6. Wyndham Lewis, *Tarr* (1918; London: Methuen, 1951), 9.
7. Jeffrey Meyers, "The Quest for Wyndham Lewis," *Biography* 4.1 (Winter 1981): 71–81 and 89–91.
8. Jeffrey Meyers, "Quest for Wyndham Lewis," 70–71. Meyers's account of the plot to prevent publication of his books ("All my books seem cursed") has a decidedly Lewis-like tone!
9. Wyndham Lewis, *Blasting and Bombardiering* (1937; Berkeley and Los Angeles: University of California Press, 1967), 9.
10. In fact, Woolf's "misunderstanding" presaged Jeffrey Masson and others who have denounced Freud's assumption that female reports of molestation by the father or other older men were based on the female version of the Oedipus complex; that is, that the girl's desire to make love to her father led to "wish- fulfilling" fantasies of being sexually approached. As later evidence has shown, these women were reporting not fantasy but devastating experience.
11. Wyndham Lewis, *The Art of Being Ruled* (1926; New York: Haskell, 1972), 286.
12. Wyndham Lewis, *Paleface* (New York: Haskell, 1929), 208.
13. W. K. Rose, ed., *The Letters of Wyndham Lewis* (Norfolk, Conn.: New Directions, 1963), 14.
14. Wyndham Lewis, "The Do-Nothing Mode," *Agenda* 7–8 (Autumn–Winter 1969–70): 217.
15. *Rude*, 249; from an early, previously unpublished draft of chapter 21, "How One Begins," which is included in the Appendix to the Black Sparrow edition.
16. As Daphne Patai has demonstrated, Orwell's stance as rescuer of the oppressed did not apply to his dominating and exploitative relationships with

women. In his texts, as in Lewis's, women and despised effeminate men receive the full force of his fear and loathing.

17. *Rude*, Appendix, 250. This note on the effects of public school was again expurgated from the final version.
18. Robert Chapman, "Letters and Autobiographies," in Jeffrey Meyers, ed., *Wyndham Lewis: A Revaluation. New Essays* (London: Athlone, 1980).
19. For this pattern, see Valerie Parker, "Lewis, Art, and Women," 211–25, in Meyers, ed., *Wyndham Lewis: A Revaluation*. This interesting article is marred by its lack of any kind of notes or documentation.
20. See Timothy Materer, "Lewis and the Patriarchs: Augustus John, W. B. Yeats, T. Sturge Moore," in Meyers, ed., *Wyndham Lewis: A Revaluation*, 47–63. Materer suggests that "Lewis, a virtually fatherless child, searched all his life for a father figure," and then rejects this theory as "too Freud-infected" and something Lewis would not have approved of. Materer's article itself nevertheless effectively supports this thesis.
21. T. S. Eliot had been especially supportive of Lewis's work, and, knowing his financial need, had guaranteed him a lead article in every issue of the *Criterion* when Eliot edited that magazine. When Eliot told Lewis that a certain piece was too long for the *Criterion*, Lewis responded with a series of typical letters suggesting that "either you or some person or persons who are able to influence you . . . appear for some time before Christmas to have decided to treat me in such a way as to make my estrangement a foregone conclusion" and threatening, "If . . . you do not reply to this letter in a reasonable time, or arrange a meeting with me, then I shall conclude that the devil has you by the heel, and there will be no necessity for me to tell you where to go for you will be there already" (Lewis, *Letters*, 152, 154). Eliot's reply, included in Lewis's collected letters, demonstrates his perception of Lewis's paranoia: "I cannot work with you as long as you consider me either the tool or the operator of machinations against you" (Lewis, *Letters*, 120). Lewis treated Ezra Pound, his friend, staunch supporter, and collaborator on "Blast," in the same way, calling him an "intellectual eunuch" in *Time and Western Man* of 1927.
22. In *Blasting and Bombardiering*, Lewis gives his own explanation of why his sitters did not pay up: "Sitters are apt to be very nice up to the final sitting. They are hoping that at the last minute something will happen to the picture which will transform an extremely interesting- looking young woman into a raving society beauty. . . . When this doesn't happen, the storm breaks. The cheque that is to pay your studio-rent (which is already overdue) is not forthcoming" (*Blasting*, 216).
23. It is difficult to judge whether he used his friends' Jewishness in his accusatory letters to them, as many letters to correspondents who were living in 1963, at the time the letters were published, were left out of this collection.
24. For example, he calls Marx "a german-jewish economist," as part of a larger attack on him, and talks about Marx's Jewishness and his "*cash*" in a letter

to Herbert Read in 1934 (*Letters*, 227). In a letter to David Kahma in 1948, he calls Kenneth Burke "little, pinched, partly Jewish" and declares, "I should never be interested in anything Burke wrote" (440).

25. C. H. Sisson, "The Politics of Wyndham Lewis," *Agenda* 7.3, 8.1 (Autumn and Winter 1969–70, Wyndham Lewis Special Issue): 115.
26. Martin Seymour-Smith in *Agenda* 7.3, 8.1 (Autumn and Winter, 1969–1970), 10.
27. William Chace, "On Lewis's Politics: The Polemics Polemically Answered," in Meyers, ed., *Wyndham Lewis: A Revaluation*, 150.
28. W. A. Thorpe, "On The Art of Being Ruled," *Criterion* 5 (1926): 758.
29. Edgell Rickword, "The Art of Being Ruled," *Calendar* 3 (1926–27): 247.
30. "On Paleface: The Philosophy of the Melting Pot," *Times Literary Supplement*, 30 May 1929, 432.
31. In his 1931 poem "The Georgiad," Lewis's friend Roy Campbell praised his "toreadoring skill" in attacking D. H. Lawrence. Ernest Hemingway wrote to Lewis praising "the purgative effect" of *Paleface* and saying, "I . . . thought you destroyed the Red and Black enthusiasm very finely in *Paleface*" (Meyers, 143–45).
32. Rebecca West, "On Making Due Allowances for Distortion," *Time and Tide* 24 May 1929: 624; also quoted in *Rude*, 217.
33. "Hitler and his Movement," *Times Literary Supplement* 16 April 1931, 296.
34. The *Spectator* reviewer objected to Lewis's gullibility and narcissism: "Lewis has evidently believed almost everything which his Hitlerite informant told him" ("Mr. Lewis among the Nazis," *Spectator*, 18 April 1931, 296). Clennell Wilkinson criticized Lewis's vague and unsubstantiated acceptance of the Nazi case ("Wyndham Lewis on Hitler," *Everyman*, 2 April 1931, 303). Reginald Berkeley complained that Lewis was, as usual, tangential and wrote more about himself than his topic ("The Dictators," *Saturday Review*, 11 April 1931, 535).
35. Wyndham Lewis, *Hitler* (London: Chatto, 1930), 14.
36. See chapter 3 for similar examples of this reasoning on the part of the Freikorpsmen, as demonstrated by Theweleit.
37. Wyndham Lewis, *Doom of Youth* (1932; New York: Haskell, 1973), 62.
38. Wyndham Lewis, *Left Wings over Europe* (London: Cape, 1936), 37.
39. "Left Wings over Europe," *Times Literary Supplement*, 20 June 1936, 508.
40. L. M Horton, "The Flights of Wyndham Lewis," *London Mercury* 37 (1936): 277.
41. E. H. Carr, review of *Left Wings over Europe*, in Charles Moore and Christopher Hawtree, eds., *1936 as Recorded by the Spectator* (London: Michael Joseph, 1986), 233–34.

42. Wyndham Lewis, *Count Your Dead: They Are Alive! or, A New War in the Making* (London: Lovat Dickson, 1937), 98.
43. T. S. Eliot, in Meyers, 120 and 354n. 30.
44. Wyndham Lewis, *The Jews, Are They Human?* (1939; New York: Gordon, 1972), 30.
45. "*The Jews, Are They Human?* by Wyndham Lewis," *Times Literary Supplement*, 25 March 1939.
46. Wyndham Lewis, *The Hitler Cult* (London: Dent, 1939), 15.
47. Wyndham Lewis, *Rude Assignment*, appendix 2, "Two Fragmentary Drafts of Chapters on the Hitler Writing of the Thirties," 255.
48. The story of the repression of "Cantleman" is from Meyers, 85. "Cantleman's Spring Mate" was later published in 1937 by Eyre and Spottiswood and is now available as part of *Blasting and Bombardiering*.
49. Repeated efforts to identify the word "epira" have yielded nothing. Lewis may have been referring to the female praying mantis, which devours the male after the act of mating.
50. T. S. Eliot, "Tarr," *Egoist* 5 (September 1918): 106.
51. Ezra Pound, "Wyndham Lewis" (1920), in *Literary Essays* (London, 1954), 424, 429.
52. Rebecca West, "Tarr," *Nation*, 17 August 1918, 176.
53. Meyers, 182, quoting T. S. Eliot, "Charles Whibley" (1931), in *Selected Essays* (New York, 1932), 409.
54. Wyndham Lewis, *Satire and Fiction* (London: Arthur, 1930). Lewis on the whole does not cite the publications in which specific reviews appeared, giving only the authors' names.
55. Here and elsewhere in this book, I have used the term "homosexual" as opposed to the more respectful and contemporary word "gay" when referring to Lewis's perspective and that of the other authors in this study. When referring to Lewis, I have sometimes also used his word "invert."
56. Wyndham Lewis, *The Apes of God* (1930; Santa Barbara: Black Sparrow, 1981), 44.
57. Leon Poliakov, *The History of Anti-Semitism*, trans. Richard Howard (New York: Vanguard, 1965), 1: 143; quoted in Gilman, *Difference and Pathology*, 151.
58. These women, though they may have enjoyed Lewis on a short-term basis, would probably have known better than to get saddled with him!
59. Paul Edwards, Afterword, *The Apes of God*, 635. Edwards identifies Rodker as "a poet, novelist, and publisher, the author of *Adolphe*, which Lewis parodies in Part V."
60. Ira B. Nadell, *Joyce and the Jews* (Iowa City: University of Iowa Press, 1989), 180.
61. "He himself sat, spider-like, in the center of an impressive commercial network. Other animal metaphors which described him were the hog, the

dog, the rat, the vulture, the weasel, the fox, the toad, the serpent, and the wasp" (Edgar Rosenberg, *From Shylock to Svengali*, 35).

5. *Charles Williams*

In citing works by Charles Williams in the notes, short titles have been used. After their initial citation, works frequently cited have been identified by the following abbreviations:

The Figure of Beatrice	*Beatrice*
Witchcraft	*Witchcraft*
The Region of the Summer Stars	*Stars*
Shadows of Ecstasy	*Shadows*
War in Heaven	*War*
All Hallows' Eve	*Hallows*
"The Jews" in *Image of the City*	"Jews"

In the case of the often-cited Lois Lang- Sims, *Letters to Lalage: The Letters of Charles Williams to Lois Lang-Sims* (Kent, Ohio, and London: Kent State University Press, 1989), which contains letters by Charles Williams and commentary by Lois Lang-Sims and Glen Cavaliero, I have abbreviated with the short title *Lalage*, followed, where necessary, by the name of one of the three authors. I have also referred to Anne Ridler's introduction to *Image of the City* by the name Ridler. I refer to T. S. Eliot's introduction to Williams's *All Hallows' Eve* by inserting the name Eliot after the short title *Hallows*.

1. Norman Cameron and Joseph F. Rychlak, *Personality Development and Psychopathology: A Dynamic Approach*, 2d ed. (Boston: Houghton, 1985), 206.
2. *Lalage*, Lang-Sims, 15.
3. This phrase is found in all the memoirs by Williams's devotees and appears often, in somewhat different forms, in his writing in various genres. For an example, see *Lalage*, Cavaliero, 8.
4. I make no claim to explicate Williams's complicated theological system in its own terms here. For a study which does just that and which explains, in addition to the few concepts in the Williams system which I elucidate, such concepts as the "Way of the Image" and the "Way of Affirmation," see Mary McDermott Shideler, *The Theology of Romantic Love: A Study in the Writings of Charles Williams* (Grand Rapids: Eerdmans, 1962).
5. Anne Ridler, quoting a memorial broadcast Eliot gave in 1946, in her introduction to Charles Williams, *The Image of the City* (London: Oxford University Press, 1958).
6. Glen Cavaliero, *Charles Williams: Poet of Theology* (Grand Rapids: Eerdmans, 1983), 4.

7. James Agee, *Letters to Father Flyn*, in Gunnar Urang, *Shadows of Heaven: Religion and Fantasy in the Writing of C. S. Lewis, Charles Williams and J. R. R Tolkien* (Philadelphia: Pilgrim, 1971), 84.
8. Agnes Sibley, Preface to *Charles Williams* (Boston: Twayne, 1982), unpaginated.
9. Isaac Rosenfeld, *An Age of Enormity: Life and Writing in the Forties and Fifties* (Cleveland, N.Y.: World, 1962).
10. For other examples of the defense of authorial intention, see the discussion of Dickens and Eliot in chapter 2, nn. 10 and 11.
11. Thomas Howard, *The Novels of Charles Williams* (London: Oxford University Press, 1983), 164–65.
12. Nancy-Lou Patterson, "The Jewels of Messias: Images of Judaism and Antisemitism in the Novels of Charles Williams," *Mythlore: A Journal of J. R. R. Tolkien, C. S. Lewis and Charles Williams Studies* 6.2 (Spring 1979): 31.
13. For example, Agnes Sibley describes his parentage in terms that suggest the birth of Christ: "If the unborn soul chooses its parents for Incarnation in this world, Charles must have chosen them" (1).
14. I will from now on refer to the Oxford University Press as OUP or "the Press."
15. T. S. Eliot, Introduction to Charles Williams, *All Hallows' Eve* (1945; Grand Rapids: Eerdmans, 1981), xiii and xi.
16. For childhood patterns remarkably like Williams's, see the case histories of obsessive-compulsive patients in Cameron and Rychlak, 203–30.
17. Alice Mary Hadfield, *Charles Williams: An Exploration of His Life and Work* (London: Oxford University Press, 1983), 6.
18. Hadfield is quoting here from an unpublished MS by Williams's sister, Edith Williams, "Memories of Early Days at Home" (Hadfield, 12).
19. Kathleen Spencer, *Charles Williams* (Mercer Island, Wash.: Starmont, 1986), 12.
20. For instance, Hadfield calls her chapter on Williams's life at the Press "Taliessin in Arthur's Logres" and refers to this system throughout the book.
21. Most critics refer to his membership in the "Order of the Golden Dawn" or a derivative. In 1989 Cavaliero and Lang-Sims identified the group as the Fellowship of the Rosy Cross (*Lalage*, Lang-Sims, 19).
22. Among the apologists are Gunnar Urang, Hadfield, and Sibley. Shideler does not mention Waite's movement at all. Hadfield claims: "Surely his outlook and philosophy were not generated or indeed much affected by it" (30).
23. Ridler mentions that when she knew Williams much later, in the thirties, he recommended that she read Waite's *The Secret Doctrine in Israel* (1913), which she calls "the study of a Jewish mystical work, the Zohar" (Ridler, xxv). Nancy-Lou Patterson points out that this book was based on the writing of Eliphas Zahed Levi, a Roman Catholic priest who took a Jewish name and "completely romanticized the whole magical and alchemical tradition, the interpretation of the tarot cards, and what little he knew of the Hebrew Qabalah" (28).

24. Hadfield quotes here from Williams's *Poems of Conformity* (Oxford, 1917) but does not cite a page (Hadfield, 25).
25. Charles Williams, *Witchcraft* (1941; Cleveland: Meridian, 1959), 54.
26. Charles Williams, *The Figure of Beatrice* (1941; Cleveland: Meridian, 1959), 36.
27. There are of course abundant instances of myths of engulfing and cannibalistic women in many mythological/religious systems. Time and space limitations prevent me from exploring these myths here.
28. Charles Williams, "The Jews" [1943], in *The Image of the City* (London: Oxford University Press, 1958), 161.
29. Charles Williams, *The Region of the Summer Stars* (London: Editions Poetry, 1944), 11.
30. Shapiro, *Autonomy*, 107. Many of Williams's devices, including transferral, exchange, and co-inherence, involve just such resistance to, and estrangement from, one's desires.
31. Sigmund Freud, "The Predisposition to Obsessional Neurosis" (1913) in *Collected Papers*, vol. 2 (London: Hogarth Press and Institute of Psycho-analysis, 1949), 122–32; quoted in Shapiro, *Autonomy*, 102.
32. Simone de Beauvoir, *The Marquis de Sade (Must We Burn Sade?)* (New York: Grove, 1953), 31–43; quoted in Shapiro, *Autonomy*, 129.
33. The novel which deviates from this plot is *Descent into Hell* (1937), which I will not discuss here. Even in this case, the deviation is slight.
34. Charles Williams, *Shadows of Ecstasy* (1933; Grand Rapids: Eerdmans, 1970), 41.
35. For example, Cavaliero calls it "a prelude," "the least of the novels," "a confused inchoate affair": "the novel is uneasy with itself, Sir Bernard's scepticism gets into the very fabric of the narrative . . . and is applicable to the book as well (*Charles Williams*, 63–66). Ridler claims, without narrative evidence, that Considine is defeated in the end, but adds, "[I]ts ideas are not its strength" (Ridler, 46). Shideler admits that "Williams does not indicate whether he [Considine] has damned himself eternally," but she feels that he "is perfectly clear that he who persists in attempting to make man ruler of the universe does end in hell" (135). In fact, a close reading of the book does not make this perfectly clear at all.
36. It is interesting to note that Williams's biographer, Alice Mary Hadfield, who was one of Williams's favorite female disciples, praises Isabel Ingram, along with Barbara Rackstraw in *War in Heaven*. She calls them "such wives as one would wish to be, loving, perceptive, practical, sustaining" (95).
37. Charles Williams, *War in Heaven* (1930; Grand Rapids: Eerdmans, 1985), 137–38.
38. This is based on my own observations of patients while working on an acute care in-patient unit at the Bay Cove Mental Health Center in Boston, Massachusetts. It is also noteworthy in this context that, like the anxiety of many paranoid patients, the obsessive-compulsive's fears have proven accurate: our atmosphere is indeed poisoning us.

39. Chocolates seem to represent decadence and evil to Williams: they were also associated with Rosamund's depravity in *Shadows of Ecstasy.*
40. See 2 Kings 21.
41. Charles Williams, *All Hallows' Eve* (1945; Grand Rapids: Eerdmans, 1981), 217–18.
42. T. S. Eliot, *The Waste Land*, in *Complete Poems and Plays: 1909–1950* (New York: Harcourt, 1971), 39.

6. Graham Greene

In citing novels and autobiographical works by Graham Greene in the notes, short titles have been used. After their initial discussion, works frequently cited have been identified by the following abbreviations:

Gun for Sale	*Gun*
Journey without Maps	*Journey*
The Lawless Roads	*Lawless*
The Man Within	*Man*
The Name of Action	*Name*
The Other Man (interviews with Marie-Françoise Allain)	*Other*
Orient Express (*Stamboul Train*)	*Orient*
A Sort of Life	*Sort*
Ways of Escape	*Ways*

1. Norman Sherry, *The Life of Graham Greene*, Vol. 1, *1904–1939* (New York and London: Penguin, 1989), 84. For references to his manic-depressive nature, see Greene's introduction to his plays: "My critics have so far, I think, failed to disinter the manic-depressive side of any talent I possess (in the future I feel sure that I will regret disclosing it to them)" (*Three Plays* [London: Heinemann, 1961], ix); quoted by David Pryce-Jones, *Graham Greene* (New York: Barnes, 1967), 13. See also: "a manic depressive—that would be the verdict on me today" (Graham Greene, *A Sort of Life* [New York: Simon, 1971], 128). In fact, as he does not experience true manic episodes, Greene would probably be diagnosed today as suffering from a depressive personality. My own diagnosis is that he suffered, in addition, from post traumatic stress disorder.
2. Greene himself objected to the terms "Greeneland" and "Greenian." He felt he was describing reality as it really was and that the terms were coined by those who were afraid to acknowledge reality's grimness. See Marie-Françoise Allain, *The Other Man: Conversations with Graham Greene* (1981; New York: Simon, 1983), 19.
3. Allain, *The Other Man*, 26.
4. From the poem "Germinal" by A. E.; quoted in Allain, *The Other Man*, 28.

5. Graham Greene, "The Burden of Childhood," in *Collected Essays* (New York: Viking, 1951), 126.
6. Greene, *Journey*, 31.
7. Greene, *Lawless*, 6. Sherry identifies this as a quotation from *Apologia pro Vita Sua* by Cardinal Newman (Sherry, 9).
8. Marion Greene's coldness provides a marked contrast with Wyndham Lewis's relationship with his doting mother: perhaps this has something to do with Greene's self-image in later life as a cracked bell and Lewis's self-image as a genius.
9. Graham Greene, ed., *The Old School* (London: Cape, 1934), 250.
10. Greene noted that his father always wore his long academic robes while at school, and numerous respondents remember him moving through the halls of the school like an avenger, the robes flying behind him . . . perhaps like bat wings?
11. For examples of three stories about such terrified and victimized male children who share Greene's phobias, see "Under the Garden," "The Basement Room," and "The End of the Party," in Graham Greene, *Collected Stories* (New York: Viking, 1973). I regret that considerations of space do not allow me to discuss these stories here.
12. For example: "The sense of inevitable betrayal. Being caught by two fires, I was ostracized, I found myself in the situation of a leper" (*Other*, 27); and "I was surrounded by the forces of the resistance, and yet I couldn't join them without betraying my father and my brother" (*Sort*, 74). See also Greene's often reiterated feeling of division, of being a kind of double agent or Quisling.
13. This diagnosis was "discovered" in the treatment of Vietnam war veterans. It is most commonly attributed to survivors of war or of some other devastating experience.
14. Greene's mother, Marion Greene, wrote to Vivien Greene that Graham was "a different person" after his treatment by Richmond, more confident and happier. Some of his contemporaries, on the other hand, did not approve of the change and were suspicious of the treatment which caused it. Graham's cousin, Ben Greene, blamed Graham's future morbidity on the treatment, suggesting that "if you are a perfectly ordinary diffident boy, you could be corrupted and twisted by a psychiatrist so that dangerous fantasies are put in your head" (Sherry, 109). Peter Stanier, a classmate, objected that after the treatment, "You couldn't just whisk him off and beat him or something of that kind if he was cheeky" (Sherry, 109–10).
15. Graham Greene, "Revolver in the Corner Cupboard," in *The Portable Graham Greene: The Lost Childhood and Other Essays*. Ed. Philip Stratford (New York: Viking, 1973), 11.
16. She was known as Vivienne at that time but later changed her name to Vivien, and prefers that spelling. I will refer to her here as Vivien unless quoting from a letter.

17. Sherry does not attribute this poem, which he quotes on p. 352; I assume it is Greene's own. If so, in it Greene anticipates one of Sylvia Plath's several poems on not forgiving one's parents, "The Disquieting Muses." In Plath's poem, the muses are female: "Mother, mother, what illbred aunt/ Or what disfigured and unsightly/ cousin did you so unwisely keep/ Unasked to my christening, that she/ Sent these ladies in her stead/ With heads like darning-eggs to nod/ And nod and nod at foot and head/ And at the left side of my crib?" Sylvia Plath, *The Colossus and Other Poems* (New York: Knopf, 1962). Both Greene and Plath are referring to the bad fairy who slipped into Sleeping Beauty's christening.
18. In *Stamboul Train*, "Jew" is frequently changed to "man" and "Jewish" occasionally substituted for "Jew." In *A Gun for Sale*, "those damned Jews," a phrase that is in fact appropriate to the thought process of the character, Raven, to which it is attributed, is omitted, and the unpleasant Jewish shopgirl becomes a mere shopgirl. In *Brighton Rock*, Colleoni, clearly labeled repeatedly as a Jew in the original version, becomes Italianate, while the "jewesses" become "bitches." I thank Bryan Cheyette for pointing out these changes, of which I had been previously ignorant, during the course of my thesis examination.
19. Kenneth Allott and Miriam Farris, *The Art of Graham Greene* (New York: Russel, 1963), 44. Other novels written during this period which did not include Jewish characters were *Rumour at Nightfall* (1931), *It's a Battlefield* (1934), and *England Made Me* (1935).
20. Martin Turnell, *Graham Greene: A Critical Essay* (Grand Rapids: Eerdmans, 1967), 20–21.
21. Graham Greene, *The Man Within* (1929; London: Heinemann, 1956), unpaginated author's note.
22. The boyish antiheroes of two other Greene books, Raven in *A Gun for Sale* (1936) and Pinkie in *Brighton Rock* (1938), experience similar longings for motherly redemption as they make their hunted progress through the world.
23. Greene, *Ways*, 20.
24. The *Bookman* called it "a guileless tale, the narrative hollow and factitious," while the *New Statesman* wrote, "[H]is story is half in Cloud-cuckoo land and half in Ruritania and fits ill with his style" (Sherry, 385).
25. Greene, *Name*, 14, 19.
26. *Stamboul Train* did sell very well, but Greene owed so much money to his publisher, Heinemann, from the low sales on two previous, unsuccessful books that this did not alter his dismal financial situation. The book almost had to be withdrawn when J. B. Priestley, who claimed that Greene had caricatured him in the character of the Cockney novelist Savory, instituted a lawsuit and was only put off by several last- minute changes in the text.
27. Grahame Smith, *The Achievement of Graham Greene* (Brighton: Harvester, 1986), 26–27.
28. Graham Greene, *Stamboul Train* (1932; London: Heinemann, 1961), 256.

29. It makes for an interesting and not irrelevant digression here to note some of Greene's assumptions or myths about virginity, assumptions he probably shared with the majority of his readers. While Greene, unlike most of his contemporaries, often chooses chorus girls rather than well-bred ladies as his exemplars of virtue, they are always virgins, as if the sexual act outside of marriage automatically destroys female goodness. Just as a Jew's identity will out, despite the Bible in the lavatory, so will a virgin's. Thus, Coral's cry of pain is a proof of her virtue and a badge of her virginity. The possibility that sex in an uncomfortable train compartment with an uncaring stranger might be painful even for a nonvirgin (and especially for a woman about to die of heart disease!) is simply not a consideration. Greene's own mythology here is based on larger established myths of "virgin," "whore," and "Jew"—myths he accepts as universal verities.
30. I refer here to Groucho Marx's ironical statement to the effect that he wouldn't want to join any club that would have him for a member.
31. Sherry seems to question that Coral actually dies at the end of the book. He mentions that Greene wrote two versions of the book's ending and kept the one in which she lives! I believe that a close reading of this paragraph will prove him wrong.
32. Greene, *Gun* (1936), 13.
33. See Turnell; Allott and Farris.
34. The young guard shot in the back by the Jew Kapper in *The Name of Action* was in the act of petting a cat.
35. The phrase "the damned Jews" is omitted from the Penguin version.
36. Greene spoke of Eliot as one of "the two great figures of my young manhood" (*Ways*, 42). The other was Herbert Reade. For a thorough tracing of references to Eliot by various other authors, which I found useful for this chapter as well as for the last two, see Fred T. Crawford, *Mixing Memory and Desire: The Waste Land and British Novels* (University Park: Pennsylvania State University Press, 1982).
37. Graham Greene, *Brighton Rock* (London: Heinemann, 1938), 346.
38. This interesting and efficient method of revision bears some thinking about. What would happen if, for instance, a revisionist changed Nigger Jim in Huckleberry Finn to "Polack Jim" and changed the references to the institutions of slavery to references to indentured servitude? What would happen if Shylock became a Scotsman? Or if Othello became a Greek? What I am trying to point out through these examples is that systems of Otherness run deeply through a text, and while the unsuspecting reader may be thrown off target by surface changes, as I certainly was on my first readings of *Brighton Rock*, such cosmetic revision is no ready solution for an author who, in horror and dismay, perceives too late that he or she has set a text with such embedded stereotypes loose into the world. Having had such an experience with my portrayal of a Jewish character in my first novel, I have sympathy for such a solution, but cannot endorse it.

Bibliography

I have attempted to arrange my sources by category for easier reference. In cases where a source seemed to belong equally to two categories, I have cross-referenced. The first category, "General Critical Theory, Literary Criticism, Literary History," refers to critical works which either deal with more than one author or have a relevance beyond the one author they discuss.

General Critical Theory, Literary Criticism, Literary History

Achebe, Chinua. *Hopes and Impediments: Selected Essays*. London: Heinemann, 1989.

Birnbaum, Milton. *Aldous Huxley's Quest for Values*. Knoxville: University of Tennessee Press, 1971.

Booth, Wayne. *The Company We Keep: An Ethics of Fiction*. London and Berkeley: University of California Press, 1988.

Calisch, Edward N. *The Jew in English Literature as Author and Subject*. 1909. Port Washington, N.Y.: Kennikat, 1969.

Cheyette, Bryan. "H. G. Wells and the Jews: Antisemitism, Socialism and English Culture." *Patterns of Prejudice* 22.3 (1988): 22–36.

Dabydeen, David, ed. *The Black Presence in English Literature*. Manchester: Manchester University Press, 1985.

Daiches, David. *The Present Age in British Literature*. Bloomington: Indiana University Press, 1958.

Daraaganih, H. "Portrait of the Outsider in the Postwar English Novel." Ph.D. diss., University of Nottingham, 1969.

Davies, Andrew. *Where Did the Forties Go?: A Popular History*. London: Pluto, 1984.

DeKoven, Sidra Ezrahi. *By Words Alone*. Chicago: University of Chicago Press, 1980.

Eagleton, Terry. *Ideology: An Introduction*. London: Verso, 1991.

———. *Literary Theory*. Minneapolis: University of Minnesota Press, 1983.

———. "Towards a Science of the Text." Chapter 3 in *Criticism and Ideology: A Study in Marxist Literary Theory*. London: Verso, 1978.

Ebels Dolanova, Vera. "On 'The Rich Jew' of Fassbinder: An Essay in Literary Antisemitism." *Patterns of Prejudice* 23.4 (1989): 3–16.

Evans, B. Ifor. *English Literature between the Wars*. London: Methuen, 1948.

Fiedler, Leslie. "Negro and Jew: Encounter in America." *No! In Thunder*. Boston: Beacon, 1960, 239–40.

———. *The Stranger in Shakespeare*. New York: Stein, 1972.

———. *To the Gentiles*. New York: Stein, 1972.

———. "What Can We Do about Fagin? The Jew-Villain in Western Tradition." *Commentary* 7 (May 1949).

Fisch, Harold. *The Dual Image*. London: World Jewish Library, 1971.

Garner, Shirley Nelson, et al., eds. *The Mother Tongue: Essays in Feminist Psychoanalytic Interpretation*. Ithaca: Cornell University Press, 1985.

Gates, Henry Louis, Jr. *"Race," Writing, and Difference*. Chicago: University of Chicago Press, 1986.

Gellar, Mark. "Pedagogical Guidelines for Literary Antisemitism." *Patterns of Prejudice* 20.1 (1986): 35–44.

Gilman, Sander L. *Difference and Pathology: Stereotypes of Sexuality, Race and Madness*. Ithaca: Cornell University Press, 1985.

———. *Jewish Self-Hatred: Anti-Semitism and the Hidden Language of the Jews*. Baltimore: Johns Hopkins University Press, 1986.

Grebanier, Bernard. *The Truth about Shylock*. New York: Random, 1962.

Hindus, Milton. "F. Scott Fitzgerald and Literary Anti-Semitism: A Footnote on the Mind of the 20s." *Commentary* 3 (1947).

Johnson, Edgar. "Dickens, Fagin, and Mr Riah." *Commentary* 9 (1950).

Killeen, Janet E. M. "Type and Anti-Type: A Study of the Contemporary Jew in English and German Fiction and Drama from 1830–1880." M.A. diss., Kent University, 1963.

Klein, Charlotte Lea. "The Changing Image of the Jew in Modern English Literature." *Patterns of Prejudice* 5.2 (1972): 23–31.

———. "English Antisemitism in the 1920s." *Patterns of Prejudice* 6.2 (1972): 23–28.

———. "The Portrait of the Jew in English and German Fiction and Drama, 1830–1933." Ph.D. diss., University College, London, 1967.

Kumar, Krishnan. "Social and Cultural Setting." Boris Ford, ed., *The New Pelican Guide to English Literature*. Harmondsworth: Penguin, 1983.

Landa, M. J. *The Jew in Drama*. New York: Kennikat, 1926.

Lane, Lauriat, Jr. "Dickens' Archetypal Jews." *PMLA* 73 (1958): 94–100.

Langer, Lawrence. *The Holocaust and the Literary Imagination*. New Haven: Yale University Press, 1975.

Leavis, F. R. *The Great Tradition*. New York: Stewart, 1948.

Levin, Harry. "The Jewish Writer and the English Literary Tradition." *Commentary* 8 (1949).

Lodge, David. *Novelist at the Crossroads*. Ithaca: Cornell University Press, 1971.

Mitchell, Gina. "Caricature of the Bulldog Spirit: When Peace Seems Dull." *Patterns of Prejudice* 8.5 (1974): 25–33.

Modder, Montagu. *The Jew in the Literature of England: To the End of the 19th Century*. Philadelphia: Jewish Publication Society of America, 1939.

Nadel, Ira B. *Joyce and the Jews: Culture and Texts*. Iowa City: University of Iowa Press, 1989.

Naman, Anne Arresty. *The Jew In the Victorian Novel*. New York: AMS, 1980.

Norris, Christopher. *Deconstruction: Theory and Practice*. London: Methuen, 1982.

Oldfield, Sybil. *Women Against the Iron Fist: Alternatives to Militarism 1900–1989*. Oxford: Blackwell, 1989.

Panitz, Esther. *The Alien in Their Midst: Images of Jews in English Literature*. London and Toronto: Associated University Presses, 1981.

Philipson, David. *The Jew in English Fiction*. New York: Publishers Printing Company, 1901.

Quenell, Peter. *A History of English Literature*. Springfield, Mass.: Merriam, 1973.

Reed, John. *Old School Ties: The Public Schools in British Literature*. Syracuse: Syracuse University Press, 1964.

Ricks, Christopher. *T. S. Eliot and Prejudice*. London and Boston: Faber, 1988.

Robson, W. W. *Modern English Literature*. Oxford: Oxford University Press, 1970.

Rosenberg, Edgar. *From Shylock to Svengali: Jewish Stereotypes in English Fiction*. Stanford: Stanford University Press, 1960.

Rosenberg, Harold. "The Jewish Writer and The English Literary Tradition." *Commentary* 8 (1949).

Rosenfeld, Isaac. *An Age of Enormity: Life and Writing in the Forties and Fifties*. Cleveland, N.Y.: World, 1962.

Said, Edward W. *Orientalism*. London: Penguin, 1991.

Seldon, Raman. *A Reader's Guide to Contemporary Literary Theory*. Brighton: Harvester, 1985.

Sicher, Efraim. *Beyond Marginality: Anglo-Jewish Literature after the Holocaust*. Albany: State University of New York Press, 1985.

Sinsheimer, Hermann. *Shylock: The History of a Character*. 1947. New York: Benjamin Bloom, 1968.

Spender, Stephen. "The Jewish Writer and the English Literary Tradition." *Commentary* 8 (1949).

———. *The Thirties and After: Poetry, Politics, People, 1933–75*. London: Macmillan, 1978.

———. "University College School." Greene, ed., *The Old School*.

Stott, Graham St. John. "A Consideration of the Roles Assigned to Jewish Characters in Nineteenth Century English Fiction." M.Phil. diss., University of Southampton, April 1973.

Suleiman, Susan, and Inge Crosman, eds. *The Reader in the Text*. Princeton: Princeton University Press, 1980.

Tennenhouse, Leonard, ed. *The Practice of Psychoanalytic Criticism*. Detroit: Wayne State University Press, 1976.

Theweleit, Klaus. *Male Fantasies*. Vol. 1. *Women, Floods, Bodies, History*. Trans. Stephen Conway. Minneapolis: University of Minnesota Press, 1987. Vol. 2. *Male Bodies: Psychoanalyzing the White Terror*. Trans. Erica Carter and Chris Turner. Minneapolis: University of Minnesota Press, 1989.

Trachtenberg, Joshua. *The Devil and the Jews: The Medieval Conception of Jews and Its Relation to Modern Antisemitism*. New Haven: Yale University Press, 1943.

Trilling, Lionel. *Beyond Culture*. New York: Harcourt, 1965.

Watson, George. *Politics and Literature in Modern Britain*. Totowa, N.J.: Rowman and Littlefield, 1977.

Wilk, Melvin. *The Jewish Presence in T. S. Eliot and Franz Kafka*. Atlanta: Scholar's, 1986.

Wood, Michael. "Bleistein and Mr Eliot." Review of *T. S. Eliot and Prejudice* by Christopher Ricks. *New York Review of Books*, Feb. 1990, 32–35.

Woolf, Leonard. *Quack, Quack!* New York: Harcourt, 1935.

Woolf, Virginia. "Thoughts on Peace in An Air Raid." *The Death of the Moth*. New York: Harcourt, 1942.

———. *Three Guineas*. 1938. New York: Harcourt, 1966.

Worpole, Kenneth. *Dockers and Detectives: Popular Reading, Popular Writing*. London: Verso, 1983.

Psychology, Sociology, Feminist Theory

Adorno, T. W., ed. *The Authoritarian Personality*. New York: Harper, 1958.

Allport, Gordon. *The Nature of Prejudice*. Cambridge, Mass.: Addison-Wesley, 1954.

American Psychiatric Association. *DSM*-III. Washington: APA, 1987.

Arendt, Hannah. *The Jew as Pariah*. New York: Grove, 1978.

Bass, Ellen, and Laura Davis. *The Courage to Heal: A Guide for Women Survivors of Sexual Abuse*. New York: Harper, 1988.

Benjamin, Jessica. *The Bonds of Love: Psychoanalysis, Feminism, and the Problem of Domination*. New York: Pantheon, 1988.

Berman, Jeffrey. *Narcissism and the Novel*. New York: New York University Press, 1990.

Cameron, Norman, and Joseph F. Rychlak. *Personality Development and Psychopathology: A Dynamic Approach*. 2d ed. Boston: Houghton, 1985.

Chodorow, Nancy. *Feminism and Psychoanalytic Theory*. New Haven and London: Yale University Press, 1989.

Decker, Hannah S. *Freud, Dora, and Vienna 1900*. New York: Free Press, 1991.

Dinnerstein, Dorothy. *The Mermaid and the Minotaur: Sexual Arrangements and Human Malaise*. New York: Harper, 1976.

DSM-III. (*Diagnostic and Statistical Manual of Mental Disorders*. 3d ed.) Spitzer, et al. Washington, D.C.: American Psychiatric Association, 1987.

Erlich, Howard J. *The Social Psychology of Prejudice*. London: John Wiley, 1973.

Garrard, John. "Now and 70 Years Ago." *Patterns of Prejudice* 1.4 (1967): 24–28.

Gathorne-Hardy, Jonathan. *The Old School Tie*. New York: Viking, 1977.

Gellar, Mark. "Pedagogical Guidelines for Literary Antisemitism." *Patterns of Prejudice* 20.1 (1986): 35–44.

Gilman, Sander L. *Difference and Pathology: Stereotypes of Sexuality, Race and Madness*. Ithaca: Cornell University Press, 1985.

———. *Jewish Self-Hatred*. Baltimore: Johns Hopkins University Press, 1986.

Horney, Karen. "The Dread of Women." *International Journal of Psychoanalysis* 13 (1932).

Johnson, Miriam, and Jean Stockard. *Sex Roles*. Englewood Cliffs: Prentice-Hall, 1980.

Kernberg, Otto. *Borderline Conditions and Pathological Narcissism*. New York: Jason Aronson, 1975.

Klein, Melanie. *Envy and Gratitude: A Study of Unconscious Sources*. New York: Basic, 1957.

Kovel, Joel. *White Racism: A Psychohistory*. New York: Pantheon, 1970.

Lew, Mike. *Victims No Longer: Men Recovering from Incest and Other Sexual Abuse*. New York: Nevraumont, 1988.

Miller, Alice. *For Your Own Good: Hidden Cruelty in Child- Rearing and the Roots of Violence*. 1980. Trans. Hildegarde and Hunter Hannum. New York: Noonday, 1983.

Millett, Kate. *Sexual Politics*. 1969. New York: Avon, 1971.

Niederland, William G. *The Schreber Case: Psychoanalytic Profile of a Paranoid Personality*. New York: Quadrangle, 1974.

Oldfield, Sybil. *Women Against the Iron Fist: Alternatives to Militarism, 1900–1989*. Oxford: Blackwell, 1989.

Salzman, Leon. *The Obsessive Personality: Origins, Dynamics, and Therapy*. New York: Science, 1968.

Sartre, Jean-Paul. *Antisemite and Jew*. Trans. George J. Becker. New York: Schocken, 1965.

Segal, Hanna. *Introduction to the Work of Melanie Klein*. New York: Basic, 1964.

Shapiro, David. *Autonomy and Rigid Character*. New York: Basic, 1981.

———. *Neurotic Styles*. New York: Basic, 1965.

Theweleit, Klaus. *Male Fantasies*. Vol. 1: *Women, Floods, Bodies, History*. Trans. Stephen Conway. Minneapolis: University of Minnesota Press, 1987. Vol. 2: *Male Bodies: Psychoanalyzing the White Terror*. Trans. Erica Carter and Chris Turner. Minneapolis: University of Minnesota Press, 1989.

Jewish and Anglo-Jewish History

Arendt, Hannah. *The Jew as Pariah*. New York: Grove, 1978.

Bermant, Chaim. *The Cousinhood: The Anglo-Jewish Gentry*. London: Eyre and Spottiswoode, 1971.

———. *Troubled Eden: An Anatomy of British Jewry*. New York: Basic, 1970.

Billig, Michael. "Anti-Jewish Themes and the British Far Left—II." *Patterns of Prejudice* 18.2 (1984): 28–34.

Cesarini, David. "Anti-Zionist Politics and Political Antisemitism in Britain, 1920–1924." *Patterns of Prejudice* 23.1 (1989): 28–54.

Cheyette, Bryan. "H. G. Wells and the Jews: Antisemitism, Socialism and English Culture." *Patterns of Prejudice* 22.3 (1988): 22–35.

Davidowicz, Lucy. *The War against the Jews*. Harmondsworth: Penguin, 1975.

DeKoven, Sidra Ezrahi. *By Words Alone*. Chicago: University of Chicago Press, 1980.

Gilbert, Martin, and Richard Gott. *The Appeasers*. Boston: Houghton, 1963.

Grayzel, Solomon. *A History of the Contemporary Jews from 1900 to the Present*. New York: Atheneum, 1972.

———. *A History of the Jews: From the Babylonian Exile to the Present*. 1947. New York: New American Library, 1968.

"Great Britain." *Encyclopedia Judaica*. Jerusalem: Keter, 1971.

Hirschfeld, Gerhard, ed. *Exile in Great Britain: Refugees from Hitler's Germany*. Leamington Spa: Berg, 1984.

Holmes, Colin. *Anti-Semitism in British Society: 1876–1939*. London: Arnold, 1979.

Jarman, T. L. *A Short History of 20th Century England: 1868–1962*. New York: Mentor, 1963.

Kushner, Tony. "The British and the Shoah." *Patterns of Prejudice* 23.3 (1989): 3–16.

———. *The Persistence of Prejudice: Antisemitism in British Society during the Second World War*. Manchester: Manchester University Press, 1989.

Kushner, Tony, and Kenneth Lunn, eds. *Traditions of Intolerance*. Manchester: Manchester University Press, 1989.

Laqueur, Walter. *The Terrible Secret: Suppression of the Truth about Hitler's Final Solution*. Boston: Little Brown, 1980.

Lebzelter, Gisela. *Political Anti-Semitism in England, 1919–1939*. New York: Holmes and Meier, 1978.

Levin, Harry. "The Jewish Writer and the English Literary Tradition." *Commentary* 8 (1949).

Lipman, V. D., ed. *Three Centuries of Anglo-Jewish History*. Cambridge: Jewish Historical Society of England, 1961.

Modder, Montagu. *The Jew in the Literature of England*. Philadelphia: Jewish Publication Society of America, 1939.

Morse, George. *While Six Million Died: A Chronicle of American Apathy*. New York: Hart, 1967.

Penkower, Monty Noam. *The Jews Were Expendable: Free World Diplomacy and the Holocaust*. Urbana and Chicago: University of Illinois Press, 1983.

Poliakov, Leon. *The History of Anti-Semitism*. Vol. 3. Trans. Miriam Kochen. London: Routledge, 1975.

Rosenberg, Edgar. *From Shylock to Svengali: Jewish Stereotypes in English Fiction*. Stanford: Stanford University Press, 1960.

Rosenberg, Harold. "The Jewish Writer and The English Literary Tradition." *Commentary* 8 (1949).

Roth, Cecil. *The History of the Jews in England*. Oxford: Clarendon, 1964.

Sicher, Efraim. *Beyond Marginality: Anglo-Jewish Literature after the Holocaust*. Albany: State University of New York Press, 1985.

Sinsheimer, Hermann. *Shylock: The History of a Character*. New York: Benjamin Bloom, 1968.

Thurlow, Richard. *Fascism in Britain: A History, 1918–1985*. Oxford: Blackwell, 1987.

Trachtenberg, Joshua. *The Devil and the Jews: The Medieval Conception of Jews and Its Relation to Modern Antisemitism*. New Haven: Yale University Press, 1943.

Wasserstein, Bernard. *Britain and the Jews of Europe: 1939–1945*. Oxford: Oxford University Press, 1988.

———. "The British Government and the German Immigration, 1933–1945." Hirschfeld, *Exile in Great Britain*.

The Thirties: History and Culture

Allen, Walter. *Tradition and Dream*. Harmondsworth: Penguin, 1960.

Appleyard, Brian. *The Pleasures of Peace: Art and Imagination in Post-War Britain*. London: Faber, 1989.

Auden, W. H. "Gresham's School, Holt." Graham Greene, ed., *The Old School*.

Cockburn, Claud. *Bestseller*. London: Sidgwick and Jackson, 1972.

Connolly, Cyril. "A Georgian Boyhood." *Enemies of Promise*. New York: Macmillan, 1948.

Cunningham, Valentine. *British Writers of the Thirties*. Oxford: Oxford University Press, 1989.

Daiches, David. *The Present Age in British Literature*. Bloomington: Indiana University Press, 1958.

Davies, Andrew. *Where Did the Forties Go?: A Popular History*. London: Pluto, 1984.

Evans, B. Ifor. *English Literature between the Wars*. London: Methuen, 1948.

Griffiths, Richard. *Fellow Travellers of the Right: British Enthusiasts for Nazi Germany: 1933–1939*. London: Constable, 1980.

Hewison, Robert. *Under Siege: Literature and Life in London, 1934–1945*. Oxford: Oxford University Press, 1977.

Jarman, T. L. *A Short History of 20th Century England: 1868–1962*. New York: Mentor, 1963.

Kumar, Krishnan. "Social and Cultural Setting." Boris Ford, ed., *The New Pelican Guide to English Literature*. Harmondsworth: Penguin, 1983.

Lewis, John. *The Left Book Club: An Historical Review*. London: Gollancz, 1970.

Margach, James. *The Abuse of Power: The War between Downing Street and the Media From Lloyd George to Callaghan*. London: Allen, 1978.

Moore, Charles, and Christopher Hawtree. *1936 as Recorded By the Spectator*. London: Michael Joseph, 1986.

Raven, Simon. *The Old School*. London: Hamish Hamilton, 1986.

Reed, John. *Old School Ties: The Public Schools in British Literature*. Syracuse: Syracuse University Press, 1964.

Robson, W. W. *Modern English Literature*. Oxford: Oxford University Press, 1970.

Rosenfeld, Isaac. *An Age of Enormity: Life and Writing in the Forties and Fifties*. Cleveland, N.Y.: World, 1962.

Spender, Stephen. *The Thirties and After: Poetry, Politics, People, 1933–75*. London: Macmillan, 1978.

———. "University College School." Greene, ed., *The Old School*.

Taylor, A. J. P. *English History 1914–1945*. New York and Oxford: Oxford University Press, 1965.

Thurlow, Richard. *Fascism in Britain: A History, 1918–1985*. Oxford: Blackwell, 1987.

Wasserstein, Bernard. *Britain and the Jews of Europe: 1939–1945*. Oxford: Oxford University Press, 1988.

Watson, George. *Politics and Literature in Modern Britain*. Totowa, N.J.: Rowman and Littlefield, 1977.

Other Relevant Literature and Criticism

Auden, W. H. *Collected Poems*. Ed. Edward Mendelson. New York: Random, 1976.

———. "Gresham's School, Holt." Graham Greene, ed., *The Old School*.

Bedford, Sybille. *Aldous Huxley*. New York: Knopf, 1974.

Belloc, Hilaire. *The Jews*. London, 1922.

Birnbaum, Milton. *Aldous Huxley's Quest for Values*. Knoxville: University of Tennessee Press, 1971.

Bowen, Elizabeth. *The House in Paris*. 1935. New York: Vintage, 1957.

Chaucer, Geoffrey. "The Prioress's Tale." *The Canterbury Tales*. London: Arnold, 1980.

Chesterton, A. K. *Oswald Mosley: Portrait of a Leader*. London: Action, 1937.

Cheyette, Bryan. "H. G. Wells and the Jews: Antisemitism, Socialism, and English Culture." *Patterns of Prejudice* 22.3 (1988): 22–35.
Conlon, D. J., ed. *G. K. Chesterton: The Critical Judgement.* Part 1, *1900–1937.* Antwerp: Antwerp Studies in English Literature, 1976.
Corrin, Jay. *G. K. Chesterton and Hilaire Belloc: The Battle against Modernity.* Athens: Ohio University Press, 1943.
Cox, C. B., and P. Hinchliffe, eds., *T. S. Eliot, The Waste Land: A Casebook.* London: Macmillan, 1968.
Crawford, Fred T. *Mixing Memory and Desire: The Waste Land and British Novels.* University Park: Pennsylvania State University Press, 1982.
Crick, Bernard. *George Orwell: A Life.* Boston: Little Brown, 1980.
Cumberland, Richard. *The Jew: A Comedy.* 1794. London: J. Mawman, 1801.
Davis, B. *William Gerhardie: A Biography.* Oxford: Oxford University Press, 1990.
Dickens, Charles. *Oliver Twist.* London: Oxford University Press, 1838.
Disraeli, Benjamin. *Coningsby.* 1844. London: Penguin, 1983.
Du Maurier, Daphne. *The Progress of Julius.* London: Heinemann, 1933.
Du Maurier, George. *Trilby.* 1894. New York: Harper, 1949.
Edgeworth, Maria. *Harrington.* 1817. Vol. 8, *The Works of Maria Edgeworth.* Boston: S. H. Parker, 1822–26.
Eliot, George. *Daniel Deronda.* 1876. Oxford: Oxford University Press, 1984.
Eliot, Thomas Stearns. *After Strange Gods.* London: Faber, 1934.
———. *Complete Poems and Plays: 1909–1950.* New York: Harcourt, 1971.
Fitzgerald, F. Scott. *The Great Gatsby.* 1925. New York: Scribner's, 1968.
Forest, Antonia. *End of Term.* Harmondsworth: Puffin, 1978.
Forster, E. M. *Abinger Harvest.* London: Arnold, 1936.
———. *Aspects of the Novel.* 1927. New York: Harvest, 1954.
———. "Jew Consciousness." 1939. *Two Cheers for Democracy.* London: Arnold, 1951.
Gerhardi, William. *Memoirs of a Polyglot.* London: Macdonald, 1931.
———. *My Wife's the Least of It.* London: Faber, 1938.
Hindus, Milton. "F. Scott Fitzgerald and Literary Anti-Semitism: A Footnote on the Mind of the 20s." *Commentary* 3 (1947).
Hughes, Thomas. *Tom Brown's Schooldays.* 1857. London: Dent, 1951.
Huxley, Aldous. *Antic Hay.* 1923. New York: Bantam, 1951.
———. *Brave New World.* New York: Harper, 1932.
———. *Brave New World Revisited.* New York: Harper, 1965.
———. *Crome Yellow.* 1921. Harmondsworth: Penguin, 1955.
———. *Do What You Will: Twelve Essays.* London: Chatto, 1956.
———. *Island.* 1962. Harmondsworth: Penguin, 1964.
———. *Letters of Aldous Huxley.* Ed. Grover Smith. New York: Harper, 1970.
———. *Point Counter Point.* 1928. New York: Harper, 1965.
Isherwood, Christopher. *All the Conspirators.* 1928. London: Methuen, 1984.
———. *Down There on a Visit.* London: Signet, 1962.
———. *Goodbye to Berlin.* 1939. Harmondsworth: Penguin, 1945.

———. *Lions and Shadows*. London: Hogarth, 1938.
———. *The Memorial: Portrait of a Family*. 1946. New York: Avon, 1977.
———. *Prater Violet*. 1946. London: Methuen, 1984.
———. *The World in the Evening*. New York: Avon, 1978.
Joly, Maurice. *Protocols of the Elders of Zion*. 1903. Herman Bernstein, *The Truth about the Protocols of Zion*. New York: Ktav, 1971, 295–359.
Kaye-Smith, Sheila. *The End of the House of Alard*. London: Cassel, 1923.
Kipling, Rudyard. *Stalky and Co.* 1897. Garden City: Doubleday, 1920.
Lane, Lauriat, Jr. "Dickens' Archetypal Jews." *PMLA* 73 (1958): 94–100.
Marlowe, Christopher. *The Jew of Malta*. 1592. Manchester: Manchester University Press, 1978.
Massingham, Hugh. *The Harp and the Oak*. London: Faber, 1945.
O'Connor, William Van, and Edward Stone, eds. *A Casebook on Ezra Pound*. New York: Crowell, 1959.
Orwell, George. *Animal Farm*. 1945. Harmondsworth: Penguin, 1952.
———. *Burmese Days*. 1934. New York: Time, 1962.
———. *A Clergyman's Daughter*. 1935. New York: Harcourt, 1960.
———. *Collected Essays, Journalism, and Letters*. Ed. Sonia Orwell and Ian Angus. 4 vols. London: Secker and Warburg, 1968.
———. *Coming Up for Air*. 1939. New York: Harcourt, n.d.
———. *Down and Out in Paris and London*. 1933. New York: Harcourt, 1950.
———. *Homage to Catalonia*. 1938. Harmondsworth: Penguin, 1962.
———. *Keep the Aspidistra Flying*. 1936. London: Secker and Warburg, 1954.
———. *1984*. 1949. New York: New American Library, 1961.
———. "Notes on Nationalism." *Such, Such Were the Joys*. New York: Harcourt, 1945.
———. *The Road to Wigan Pier*. 1937. Harmondsworth: Penguin, 1966.
———. *Such, Such Were the Joys*. New York: Harcourt, 1954.
Patai, Daphne. *The Orwell Mystique: A Study in Male Ideology*. Amherst: University of Massachusetts Press, 1984.
Pound, Ezra. *The Cantos of Ezra Pound*. New York: New Directions, 1948.
Protocols of the Elders of Zion. *See* Joly, Maurice.
Rutherford, Mark [William Hale White]. *Clara Hopgood*. 1896. New York: Doran, n.d.
Scott, Sir Walter. *Ivanhoe*. 1819. New York: A. L. Burt, n.d.
Shavi, Alice, ed. *Daniel Deronda: A Centenary Symposium*. Jerusalem: Academy, 1976.
Snow, C. P. *The Conscience of the Rich*. New York: Scribner's, 1958.
Stannard, Martin. *Evelyn Waugh: The Early Years, 1903–1939*. London: Dent, 1986.
Sterne, Lawrence. *The Life and Opinions of Tristram Shandy*. 1769. New York: Odyssey, 1940.
Sykes, Christopher. *Evelyn Waugh: A Biography*. Boston: Little Brown, 1975.
Trollope, Anthony. *The Eustace Diamonds*. 1872. London: Oxford University Press, 1930.

———. *Nina Balatka*. 1867. London: Oxford University Press, 1951.
———. *The Way We Live Now*. 1875. New York: Knopf, 1950.
Walpole, Hugh. *Jeremy at Crale: His Friends, His Ambitions, and His One Great Enemy*. New York: Doran, 1927.
Waugh, Alec. *The Loom of Youth*. London: Grant Richards, 1917.
Waugh, Evelyn. *Diaries of Evelyn Waugh*. Boston: Little Brown, 1976.
———. *Letters of Evelyn Waugh*. Ed. Mark Amory. New Haven and New York: Ticknor and Fields, 1980.
———. *Officers and Gentlemen*. 1955. Harmondsworth: Penguin, 1970.
———. *Put Out More Flags*. Harmondsworth: Penguin, 1943.
Wells, H. G. *Marriage*. 1912. New York: Scribner's, 1926.
———. *Tono Bungay*. 1909. New York: Duffield, 1919.

Wyndham Lewis

Campbell, Sueellen. "The Enemy Attacks: Wyndham Lewis Versus Ezra Pound." *Journal of Modern Literature* 10.2 (June 1983): 247–56.
Carr, E. H. Review of *Left Wings over Europe*. Charles Moore and Christopher Hawtree, *1936 as Recorded by the Spectator*. London: Michael Joseph, 1986.
Chace, William. "On Lewis's Politics: The Polemics Polemically Answered." Jeffrey Meyers, ed., *Wyndham Lewis: A Revaluation*.
———. "Tarr." *Egoist* 5 (September 1918): 106.
Horton, L. M. "The Flights of Wyndham Lewis." *London Mercury* 37 (1936).
Jameson, Fredric. *Fables of Aggression*. Berkeley: University of California Press, 1979.
Lewis, Percy Wyndham. *The Apes of God*. 1930. Santa Barbara: Black Sparrow, 1981.
———. *The Art of Being Ruled*. 1926. New York: Haskell, 1972.
———. *Blasting and Bombardiering*. 1937. Berkeley and Los Angeles: University of California Press, 1967.
———. "Cantleman's Spring Mate." *Blasting and Bombardiering*. Berkeley and Los Angeles: University of California Press, 1967.
———. *Count Your Dead: They Are Alive! or, A New War in the Making*. London: Lovat Dickson, 1937.
———. "The Do-Nothing Mode." *Agenda* 7.3, 8.1 (Autumn–Winter 1969–70).
———. *Doom of Youth*. 1932. New York: Haskell, 1973.
———. *Hitler*. London: Chatto, 1931.
———. *The Hitler Cult*. London: Dent, 1939.
———. *The Jews, Are They Human?* 1939. New York: Gordon, 1972.
———. *Left Wings over Europe*. London: Cape, 1936.
———. *Letters*. Norfolk, Conn.: New Directions, 1963.
———. *Paleface*. 1929. New York: Haskell, 1969.
———. *Rude Assignment: An Intellectual Biography*. 1950. Santa Barbara: Black Sparrow, 1984.

———. *Satire and Fiction*. London: Arthur, 1930.
———. *Self Condemned*. London: Methuen, 1954.
———. *Tarr*. 1918. London: Methuen, 1951.
———, ed. *Blast*, no. 1 (June 1914); no. 2 (July 1915). Santa Barbara: Black Sparrow, 1981.
Materer, Timothy. "Lewis and the Patriarchs: Augustus John, W. B. Yeats, T. Sturge Moore." Jeffrey Meyers, ed., *Wyndham Lewis: A Revaluation*, 47–63.
———, ed. *The Letters of Ezra Pound and Wyndham Lewis*. New York: New Directions, 1985.
Meyers, Jeffrey. *The Enemy*. London: Routledge, 1980.
———. "The Quest for Wyndham Lewis." *Biography* 4.1 (Winter 1981): 71–81.
———, ed. *Wyndham Lewis: A Revaluation. New Essays*. London: Athlone, 1980.
Parker, Valerie. "Lewis, Art, and Women." Jeffrey Meyers, ed., *Wyndham Lewis: A Revaluation*, 211–25.
Porteus, Hugh Gordon. *Wyndham Lewis: A Discursive Exposition*. London: Desmond Harmsworth, 1933.
Pound, Ezra. "Wyndham Lewis." *Literary Essays*. 1920. London, 1954.
Rickword, Edgell. "The Art of Being Ruled." *Calendar* 3 (1926–27).
Rose, W. K., ed. *The Letters of Wyndham Lewis*. Norfolk, Conn.: New Directions, 1963.
Sisson, C. H. "The Politics of Wyndham Lewis." *Agenda* 7.3, 8.1 (Autumn and Winter 1969–70, Wyndham Lewis Special Issue).
Symons, Julian, ed. *The Essential Wyndham Lewis: An Introduction to His Work*. London: Deutsch, 1989.
Thorpe, W. A. "On The Art of Being Ruled." *Criterion* 5 (1926).
West, Rebecca. "On Making Due Allowances for Distortion." *Time and Tide* 10 (24 May 1929), 624.
———. "Tarr." *Nation* 107 (17 August 1918), 176.

Charles Williams

Cavaliero, Glen. *Charles Williams: Poet of Theology*. Grand Rapids: Eerdmans, 1983.
———. Introduction to *All Hallows' Eve* by Charles Williams. 1945. Grand Rapids: Eerdmans, 1981.
Hadfield, Alice Mary. *Charles Williams: An Exploration of His Life and Work*. London: Oxford University Press, 1983.
Howard, Thomas. *The Novels of Charles Williams*. London: Oxford University Press, 1983.
Lang-Sims, Lois. *Letters to Lalage: The Letters of Charles Williams to Lois Lang-*

Sims. Ed. Glen Cavaliero. Kent, Ohio, and London: Kent State University Press, 1989.
Patterson, Nancy-Lou. "The Jewels of Messias: Images of Judaism and Anti-semitism in the Novels of Charles Williams." *Mythlore: A Journal of J. R. R. Tolkien, C. S. Lewis and Charles Williams Studies* 6.2 (Spring 1979): 27–31.
Shideler, Mary McDermott. *The Theology of Romantic Love: A Study in the Writings of Charles Williams*. Grand Rapids: Eerdmans, 1962.
Sibley, Agnes. *Charles Williams*. Boston: Twayne, 1982.
Spencer, Kathleen. *Charles Williams*. Starmont Reader's Guide No. 25. Mercer Island, Wash.: Starmont, 1986.
Urang, Gunnar. *Shadows of Heaven: Religion and Fantasy in the Writing of C. S. Lewis, Charles Williams and J. R. R. Tolkien*. Philadelphia: Pilgrim, 1971.
Williams, Charles. *All Hallows' Eve*. 1945. Grand Rapids: Eerdmans, 1981.
———. *The Figure of Beatrice*. 1943. Cleveland: Meridian, 1959.
———. *The Image of the City*. London: Oxford University Press, 1958.
———. *The Region of the Summer Stars*. London: Editions Poetry, 1944.
———. *Shadows of Ecstasy*. 1933. Grand Rapids: Eerdmans, 1970.
———. *War in Heaven*. 1930. Grand Rapids: Eerdmans, 1985.
———. *Witchcraft*. 1941. Cleveland: Meridian, 1959.

Graham Greene

Allain, Marie-Françoise. *The Other Man: Conversations with Graham Greene*. New York: Simon, 1983.
Allott, Kenneth, and Miriam Farris. *The Art of Graham Greene*. New York: Russel, 1963.
Greene, Graham. *Brighton Rock*. New York: Viking Press, 1938. Harmondsworth: Penguin, 1970.
———. *Collected Essays*. New York: Viking, 1951.
———. *Collected Stories*. New York: Viking, 1973.
———. *The End of the Affair*. New York: Pocket Books, 1975.
———. *A Gun for Sale*. London: Heinemann, 1936.
———. *A Gun for Sale*. 1936. Harmondsworth: Penguin, 1973.
———. *The Heart of the Matter*. 1948. Harmondsworth: Penguin, 1962.
———. *It's a Battlefield*. 1934. New York: Viking, 1962.
———. *Journey without Maps*. London: Heinemann, 1936.
———. *The Lawless Roads*. London: Heinemann, 1939.
———. *The Lost Childhood and Other Essays*. *The Portable Graham Greene*. Ed. and intro. Philip Stratford. New York: Viking, 1973.
———. *The Man Within*. 1929. London: Heinemann, 1956.
———. *The Name of Action*. London: Heinemann, 1930.
———. *Orient Express*. 1933. New York: Pocket Books, 1961.

———. *The Power and the Glory*. Harmondsworth: Penguin, 1962.

———. *A Sort of Life*. New York: Simon, 1971.

———. *Stamboul Train*. London: Heinemann, 1932.

———. *The Third Man*. New York: Pocket Books, 1974.

———. *Three Plays*. London: Heinemann, 1961.

———. *Ways of Escape*. New York: Simon, 1980.

———, ed. *The Old School*. London: Cape, 1934.

Pryce-Jones, David. *Graham Greene*. New York: Barnes, 1967.

Sherry, Norman. *The Life of Graham Greene*. Vol. 1, *1904–1939*. New York and London: Penguin, 1989.

Smith, Grahame. *The Achievement of Graham Greene*. Brighton: Harvester, 1986.

Turnell, Martin. *Graham Greene: A Critical Essay*. Grand Rapids: Eerdmans, 1967.

Index